THE STUDY OF MAN

THE CENTURY SOCIAL SCIENCE SERIES

The Study of Man

AN INTRODUCTION

BY RALPH LINTON, Ph.D.

Professor of Anthropology
Columbia University

Student's Edition

D. APPLETON–CENTURY COMPANY

Incorporated

NEW YORK   LONDON

PRINTED IN THE UNITED STATES OF AMERICA

To

THE NEXT CIVILIZATION

PREFACE

This book has been largely inspired by the difficulties which the author has encountered in his search for some work which was broad enough in its scope to provide beginners with a grounding in the essentials of Anthropology. The literature of the science is vast but, for the most part, highly specialized. Even the best and most complete account of a particular culture remains only a collection of curious facts as long as the reader is unable to relate these facts to culture in general. Moreover, many of the works which attempt to establish such relationships reveal a strong bias both in their evaluation of the importance of particular aspects of culture relative to the total configuration and in their preference for particular lines of approach to cultural problems. While such works are valuable to the specialist, they provide the beginner with only an incomplete or warped picture of the actual conditions.

Anthropology, like all young sciences, is still somewhat unsure of its objectives and of the ways in which its materials should be handled. This has resulted in the development of a number of different schools, all of which have made valuable contributions to the development of the science but all of which have also put forward somewhat extravagant claims. This condition of multiple schools has been characteristic of the first phase in the development of all sciences, and as any science matures such conflicting schools tend to fuse and disappear. The author feels that Anthropology now includes a sufficient body of established fact to make possible the first steps toward a synthesis of this sort. He has presented the conclusions which appear to him to be valid without reference to the particular school which happens to be responsible for them. He is willing to go part way with any one of these competing schools but not all the way with any one.

This book has a further purpose. It is wise for any science to pause from time to time and sum up what it has already accomplished, the problems which are perceived but still unsolved, and the inadequacies of its current techniques. The author has attempted to provide such a summary. It is also wise for any science to test the basic premises upon which it has developed the theories which it expects to use as guides to further research. If these premises are false, the theories can only lead investigators astray. There will be a loss of time and energy even if there are no more serious consequences. Since the nature of its material makes it impossible for cultural Anthropology to carry on such tests in the laboratory, workers in this field should be doubly careful to check their premises by logic and observation. In the present volume the premises upon which certain schools of Anthropology have built their systems have been tested in this way.

The author's acknowledgments should extend to all those who have contributed toward his education in the science. These would include not only his teachers and fellow anthropologists but also those native friends, Fiu, Hapuani, Ralambo, Randrianomanana, Herman Asanap, and Naya, who helped him toward an understanding of their respective cultures. In the actual preparation of this book he has been aided by the constructive criticism of his colleagues in the Department of Sociology and Anthropology, notably Dr. E. A. Ross, Dr. Charlotte Gower, and Dr. Kimball Young.

RALPH LINTON.

Madison,
Wisconsin.

CONTENTS

THE STUDY OF MAN

INTRODUCTION

This book has been written in a time of confusion and uncertainty. It is still too soon to tell whether the Western World will recover from the self-inflicted wounds of the World War or whether, as seems more probable, partial recovery will only be a signal for a second and presumably successful attempt at suicide. There have been dark ages before, and there is no reason to suppose that they cannot recur. No one can doubt that there is urgent need for action looking to the reorganization of our society and culture on a sounder basis, and many readers may be disappointed to find that I have offered no plan for action or even tried to evaluate the plans now current. However, they should remember that effective planning requires a thorough and comprehensive knowledge of both situations and materials. In the struggle with disease therapeutic measures may have to wait on systematic research into the nature and behavior of the organisms involved. The bacteriologist, working in the quiet of his laboratory, makes as great a contribution in the long run as the doctor working in the hospital ward. In the struggle with current confusion and maladjustment, the work of the reformer must similarly be backed by that of the social scientist. The more objectively this scientist can approach the phenomena with which he deals, the more accurate and, therefore, the more valuable his results will be. Here, as in all other sciences, real understanding calls for an impersonal approach to problems and an open mind. These cannot be achieved so long as the investigator is seeking for evidence to bolster up some pet theory or to provide rationalizations for some plan of reform. It is too easy for even a thoroughly conscientious individual to ignore or minimize the importance of evidence at variance with his preconceived ideas.

No science dealing with human beings can ever attain the

degree of objectivity possible to the physical and biological sciences. No one can study living people as impersonally as he studies white rats or fossils: he has too much in common with his subjects. There will always be some emotional involvement, and this will be strongest when he is studying the phenomena of his own society and culture. Even the most superficial investigation of current conditions reveals so much that needs to be done that he can hardly avoid formulating plans for doing it and then trying to justify them. Moreover, his very closeness to these phenomena makes it extremely difficult for him to see them in their proper perspective or to appreciate all the factors involved.

Anthropology is commonly defined as the study of man and his works. This definition would include certain of the natural and all the social sciences, but, by a sort of tacit agreement, anthropologists have taken as their primary fields the study of human origins, the classification of human varieties, and investigation of the life of the so-called "primitive" peoples. The study of human origins and varieties has little bearing on our current problems. It might have if human varieties differed markedly in intelligence or ability, but all the evidence which we now have seems to indicate that they do not. The study of "primitive" peoples, on the other hand, may hold the key to the understanding of many of our problems. It is a far cry from a Kaffir *kral* to a modern city, and it is sometimes hard to convince the sociologist or economist that anything learned from the first will help him to understand the second. However, the two have a common denominator, since both depend upon the qualities which pertain to human beings living in organized societies. Until we understand these qualities it is obvious that we cannot really understand the phenomena for which they are responsible.

If anthropology has succeeded in proving any one thing, it is that peoples and races are fundamentally very much the same. If we wish to understand the nature of society and culture in the abstract, any society and any culture will help to throw light on the problem. There are even marked advantages in beginning the study with non-European peoples. The student can approach them with less emotional involvement, and the very differences between their culture and his own serve to throw the details of both into relief. Moreover, these alien groups offer a partial substitute for the laboratory techniques which are of such value to the natural and physical sciences. The social scientist will never be able to study societies or cultures under predetermined test conditions, but he can observe them under a great variety of conditions. He can deduce the common denominators for society and also for what we vaguely term "human nature" from such observations much more readily than he can deduce them from studies carried on within the frame of a single society. In particular, such comparative studies provide some measure of the degree to which individuals can be shaped by their social environment.

This last is vital to all forms of social planning. The reformer, like any other planner, must take into account the properties of his materials. Before he can hope to change the habits and attitudes of human beings he must know what has been done, and what therefore presumably can be done, with them. It is the ultimate aim of anthropology to discover the limits within which men can be conditioned, and what patterns of social life seem to impose fewest strains upon the individual. The problems must be stated in this negative form, since even our present knowledge shows that the range of possible adaptation in each of these respects is very wide.

Anthropology is one of the youngest of the sciences and has only made a beginning toward the solution of these problems. Its work is still hampered by a lack of adequate techniques and even by some confusion as to its objectives. It is the purpose of the present book to show the results which have already been obtained and to point out certain of the more important questions which still remain unanswered.

CHAPTER I

HUMAN ORIGINS

Man's origin is still unknown. That the human body was evolved from some lower form of life is no longer doubted by any one who is familiar with the evidence. Structurally man has so much in common with the other mammals, especially those of the primate order, that no other theory seems tenable. That the human mind was similarly evolved from animal mentality is less clearly demonstrable, but there can be no doubt that the human brain and nervous system, its instruments, were so evolved. The problems of the existence and origin of the human soul do not fall within the scope of this book. However, granting the existence of the soul, there is no basic inconsistency between this and a belief in the evolution of man's body. Divine grace was certainly capable of awarding man a soul at any stage in his physical development.

The recently revived conflict between religion and science on the question of evolution seems to be based on misconceptions on both sides. A belief in evolution and in the existence of a Creative Intelligence are in in no way incompatible. The study of evolution is merely a study of the mechanics of creation with a recognition of the continuity of the creative process. The evolutionist can determine the steps by which new forms of life have come into being, but he remains ignorant of the *force* responsible for these changes and for their direction. He can prove that life, whose source itself is unknown, has assumed more and more complex forms with the passage of time, but he cannot tell us why it has done so. He cannot even forecast, with any degree of accuracy, what forms evolving life will assume. His researches to date make the existence of a Creative Intelligence more rather than less probable. If religion condemns the study of evolution it

7

must also, in common logic, condemn all other studies of the nature of the world in which we live and all attempts to understand it. The Old Testament statements on the nature of the universe are quite as definite as its statements on the origin of man, both being somewhat vague and conflicting, yet the Church no longer condemns men for believing that the world is round or that it moves about the sun. Neither does it condemn them for studying the behavior of bacteria and using the knowledge thus gained to combat disease or for those studies of materials which have made possible the suspension bridge and skyscraper. It is to be hoped that the enemies of evolutionary studies will sometime realize that there is no conflict between the recorded teachings of Christ, on which they claim to base their creeds and the attempt to understand nature. Christ came to show men how to live in the world, not to tell them what the universe was like. His message is as vital to the inhabitants of a spherical earth as of a flat one, to a race which evolved from some lower form of life as to one created instantaneously from the slime of the earth.

Most readers will already be familiar with the principles of evolution and the proofs that it has taken place. We will only concern ourselves with the place of man in zoölogical classifications, his probable line of descent, and the time at which he appeared on earth. The structure of the human body at once places man as a vertebrate, as a mammal, and lastly as a member of a particular order of mammals, the primates. This order includes not only man but also all the apes and monkeys. Some of these, such as the South American monkeys, are very different from man in their structure, while others, like the anthropoid apes, are very much like him. The important point is that in every element of his structure man is more like one or another of these sub-human forms than certain of these forms are like each other. By every anatomical test all the primates, from the marmoset to the chimpanzee, are his more or less remote cousins.

Man's closest relatives among the primates are the big tailless apes called anthropoids. There are four genera of these: the chimpanzee, gorilla, orang-utan, and gibbon. Of these the chimpanzee and gorilla are the most manlike. Chimpanzees are now fairly common in zoölogical collections and will be familiar to most readers. No one who has watched them will question their similarity to man, even though he may not be enthusiastic about admitting the resemblance. Actually, this resemblance is even closer than appears on the surface. Their structure parallels that of man bone for bone and organ for organ. Even their brains, although proportionately much smaller in size, are surprisingly manlike. Their senses of sight, hearing, smell, etc., seem to be almost exactly like those of men while their mental processes, in so far as these can be tested, seem to be nearly identical with those of human children three to four years old. The resemblance does not even end here. Recent years have seen the development of extremely delicate tests for distinguishing between the blood of animals of different genera and even species. These tests are unable to distinguish between the blood of an anthropoid and that of a man, although they can distinguish between the blood of either and that of a monkey.

Unless all scientific techniques are at fault, the anthropoids are not only our relatives but our rather close relatives. However, they are not our ancestors. With the possible exception of the gibbon, which seems to be a primitive form, it is unlikely that any of the genera of anthropoids are older than man himself. They are not living fossils but the end products of divergent lines of evolution. While man has specialized and developed along certain lines, the apes have gone on developing along others. Men and apes no doubt have a common ancestor somewhere in the remote past, but this ancestor is long since extinct.

Since fossil evidence for man's ancestry is fragmentary and unsatisfactory, we can only try to deduce the form from which he evolved by studying what he is. Most of the living primates are tree-dwellers, and there can be little doubt that our own ancestors were so at one time. The structure of the human arm and shoulder bears mute witness to a long-lost habit of swinging from branch to branch. So do the flexible human hand and the five toes of the human foot, once a grasping organ. Even the adaptation of our bodies to a vertical posture probably goes back to the days when our ancestors hung by their arms much more than they stood on their legs. It seems almost certain that, somewhere in our line of ancestry, there was an arboreal form not very different from some of the existing Old World monkeys. He did not swing by his tail, since only the New World monkeys developed that refinement, but we may be sure that he was educated in the higher branches.

There can be little doubt that both man and the anthropoids evolved from the same small tree-dwelling form, but the point at which the developing human line split off from the anthropoid line is still vigorously disputed. Certain writers date the separation from the beginnings of the primate order. The main inspiration for this theory seems to be a desire to place a large and comfortable distance between man and his sub-human relatives. Actually, the structural and especially the blood similarities between man and anthropoids are so close that it is hard to conceive of them as results of independent parallel evolution. It seems much more likely that the human and anthropoid lines have been the same for most of their length. Before we take up the questions of where they separated it will be necessary to inject a little geology.

Geologists divide the past of the earth into eras and then subdivide the eras into periods. Each of the eras is characterized by the dominance of certain forms of life. At the beginning of the last or Cenozoic era mammals came to the fore. They had existed in the preceding era but had been of very minor importance. The Cenozoic era is subdivided into the Eocene, Oligocene, Miocene, Pliocene, Pleistocene, and Recent periods, in the last of which we live. The primate order emerged in the Eocene, and by the beginning of the Oligocene it had already differentiated into several families. A fossil ape from the Lower Oligocene, *Propliopithecus,* has characteristics which suggest that it may be the ancestor of both man and the anthropoids. It was a small, tree-dwelling form. We do not know what was happening to *Propliopithecus'* descendants during the Upper Oligocene and Lower Miocene, but we have an extensive series of fossils from the Middle Miocene. These prove that by this time anthropoids were numerous, in fact much more numerous than they are to-day, and that they had already developed the large size which is still one of their outstanding characteristics.

All the earliest primates which are known to us and most of the existing species are little animals. The members of the order began as tree-dwellers, and light weight is a distinct advantage in arboreal life. Any adult who has tried to follow a boy to the end of a limb will understand why. However, the ancestral anthropoid-human stock evidently developed a tendency toward giantism. This evolutionary trend seems to culminate in the modern gorilla, adult males of which genus may weigh 600 pounds. Such huge beasts are quite unsuited to arboreal life. Even an animal of one-third the weight has difficulty in finding branches strong enough to support it. As the members of the ancestral stock grew larger they must have spent more and more of their time on the ground and developed increasing structural adaptations to traveling on the ground. Their legs became longer, with more rigid attachment at the hip joint, and the foot, released from its task of grasping branches, drew together and adapted itself to the new task of supporting the weight of the body. This evolutionary trend can also be observed in the gorilla. The mountain gorilla, which reaches the largest size and is most completely ground-living, has a more manlike foot than any other sub-human primate.

It seems highly probable that the first of our manlike ancestors came down out of the trees because he had gotten too heavy for arboreal life. Changing food habits may have been a contributory factor. Although the remote ancestors of the primates seem to have been insect-eaters, most of the primates are vegetarians. None of them is above sucking eggs or devouring an occasional small bird or lizard, but they live mainly on fruits, young shoots, and other growing things. Man is the only really carnivorous primate, yet his large size makes him poorly adapted to chasing agile prey through the branches. If we assume that his ancestors acquired their taste for meat at a time when they had already grown fairly large and were dividing their time between the trees and the ground, there would have been an extra stimulus to ground living. The hunting there was better for big animals.

The Miocene was evidently a time of great evolutionary activity among the anthropoids, and even the small group of fossils which have survived from this period show a number of starts in the human direction. Although none of the known species seem to be in our direct line of ancestry, certain of them are more human in particular respects than any living anthropoid. Apparently nature was experimenting with the human idea at this period, and there probably were a great number of genera and species which were more apelike than any known humans but more manlike than any existing apes. It seems probable that the split between the anthropoid and hominoid, i.e., human, lines of evolution occurred at this period and that the direct ancestor of man was a large Miocene anthropoid with tendencies toward terrestrial life and a carnivorous diet.

Although it is disappointing that we have so little fossil evidence of man's ancestry, it is not surprising. All the living species of anthropoids have a rather small geographic range, and the same may very well have held for our remote ancestors. It is quite possible that no search for fossils has so far been made in the territory in which they lived. Both the anthropoids and the human groups which live by simple food-gathering form sparse populations even in the regions which they occupy, so it seems probable that our ancestors were rare animals even in their home territory. Moreover, the chances of their skeletons being preserved were slight. Fossilization requires special conditions. The remains must be protected from predatory animals and the effects of weather and at the same time impregnated with mineral matter. Even our Miocene ancestors were probably intelligent enough to avoid bogs and quicksands, to wait for rivers in flood to go down, and to keep out of wet caves. At the same time they probably were not advanced enough to bury their dead. The chances of their remains being fossilized were therefore slight, and the chances of such fossils being found are still smaller. To deliberately set out to find man's ancestors is a much harder task than the proverbial hunt for a needle in a haystack. Most of the pre-human and early human fossils known to us have been found by accident and owe their preservation to the chance of some one interested in such material being on the spot when the find was made. Outside Europe there are very few persons with such interests, and until the last century there have been none at all in Africa and southern Asia, the most promising hunting grounds for our ancestors.

The only Miocene fossil belonging to the hominoid stock which has so far come to light is the Java man, *Pithecanthropus erectus*. This fossil was actually found in deposits of Upper Pliocene date but Sir Arthur Keith, the greatest authority on these matters, thinks that it may be a late Miocene type which had survived into the next geological period. The remains consist of a thigh-bone, a skull-cap, and a few teeth. The thigh-bone is intermediate in its characteristics between men and anthropoids but leans somewhat to the human side. Its form indicates that the species had already assumed fully erect posture and hence was probably ground-dwelling. The skull-cap is long and narrow, with massive bony ridges over the eyes and a very low vault. The brain capacity was apparently about 900 cubic centimeters, larger than that of any known ape but smaller than that of the smallest normal men. Aside from its capacity the skull is so apelike that certain investigators have concluded that it is that of a gigantic gibbon. The teeth are, however, on the human side, and their wear indicates that the species chewed with a rotary bite, like modern man. This would have been impossible if the canines had projected beyond the line of the other teeth, as they do in apes. This fossil certainly lies in the line of evolution of the hominoid stock, although it may not be directly ancestral to our own species.

With this single questionable exception there is a complete break in the fossil record from the middle Miocene to the close of the Pliocene. From the late Pliocene or early Pleistocene we have two more manlike fossils, but both of these seem to lie further from our own line of ancestry than does Java man. The more remote of the two is the Taungs species, based on a single skull from Northern Rhodesia in Africa. This skull is, unfortunately, that of an infant, and some of its manlike characteristics may be due to this fact. The skulls of young anthropoids are, in general, more manlike than those of adults of the same species. The Taungs fossil is that of an anthropoid somewhat similar to a modern chimpanzee except for its very large brain capacity. The deposit in which it was found had apparently been laid down in a small cave which had later been completely filled with lime-stone. Although this deposit contained no implements, it con-tained many animal bones, including the skulls of a number of baboons of an extinct species. Several of these skulls show a peculiar type of depressed fracture which looks as though they had been killed with a club. Although it cannot be proved, it seems quite possible that the Taungs species was a big-brained ape of carnivorous habits and that it had advanced to the point of living in caves and using weapons of some sort in hunting. The fossil history of South Africa is still too imperfectly known for us to be able to date these finds with accuracy, but they are probably early or middle Pleistocene. By this time more manlike forms were certainly present in Africa.

The most puzzling of the semi-human fossils is that known as Piltdown man or *Eoanthropus*. It was found in Sussex, Eng-land, and apparently belongs to the close of the Pliocene. A few very crude stone tools were obtained from the same deposit. The remains consist of most of a skull and a half-jaw. Unfortunately, the fragments of the skull do not join the two sides of the brain-case, and this has led to lively disputes as to the size of the brain. The most probable estimate puts this at 1,400 cubic centimeters, well within the range of variation in normal members of our own species. At the same time the structure of the brain, as revealed by the contours of the inside of the skull, seems to have been con-siderably simpler and more apelike than that of any living race. Externally the skull is thoroughly human. Even the bony ridges over the eyes, which are heavily developed in *Pithecanthropus* and the earliest human fossils, fall within the range of variation for modern man. The startling features of this species are the jaw and teeth. The jaw is very much like that of a young chimpanzee and is so out of harmony with the skull that the first investigators doubted whether the two belonged together. The teeth are also intermediate in their form between anthropoid and human, and the canines project in anthropoid fashion. Apparently we have here a form which had almost reached the level of modern man in its brain and upper face while retaining a large number of ape characteristics in its lower face.

Although only one of the three species just discussed can conceivably be ancestral to our own, they may indicate the evolutionary trends which were at work from the Miocene on. All of them are disharmonic in certain respects, suggesting that each of the evolving semi-human species was progressive in certain respects and conservative in others. All of them show an increase in brain size considerably beyond the level of the present anthropoids. *Eoanthropus* and *Pithecanthropus* had attained completely erect posture and were probably constant ground-dwellers, while for the Taungs species the evidence on this point is not negative but lacking. Moreover, the presence of these forms in regions as far apart as Java, England, and South Africa indicates that by the beginning of the Pliocene Nature's experiments in the human direction had already spread over the major part of the Old World.

It may be well to mention here that there are no indications that any of these semi-human forms ever reached America or that any starts in the human direction were made on this continent. The American primates became separated from their Old World relatives at a very early time and followed their own divergent lines of evolution. These did not lead toward either large size or big and complex brains. When man finally appeared in America he was a fully evolved form and already familiar with the use of tools and fire. Apparently he entered the new continent from northeastern Asia in not very remote times.

From the first third of the Pleistocene we have still another semi-human species but one which is much nearer to our own genus than any of those hitherto described. This is the Peking man, found near the city of that name in China. At the time of this writing fragments of a number of individuals have been found, but the study of the remains is still under way and final conclusions have not been published. Apparently this species is related to Java man but shows a marked advance in the human direction. The skull retains the heavy brow ridges but has a much higher vault and considerably larger brain capacity. The jaw is much more apelike than that of modern man, but the teeth are rather on the human side. The canines were short, as in man. A peculiar feature is the great enlargement of the pulp cavities in the teeth. This characteristic is lacking in both modern men and anthropoids but is found in two extinct human species, Heidelberg and Neanderthal. A single foot-bone seems to indicate that the foot structure of this species was markedly different from that of modern man. That this species was already human in some of its habits is proved by the presence of crude stone implements in association with the remains. We will discuss its possible relations to our own genus later, when we have described some of the ancient species of true men.

The oldest fossil assigned to our own genus is the Heidelberg jaw, found in a sand-pit near the village of Mauer in Germany. It was recovered from undisturbed deposits nearly eighty feet below the surface and is certainly of early Pleistocene date. The jaw is extraordinarily massive and lacks a chin, but its form is essentially human and the teeth are thoroughly so. They differ from those of modern man only in the feature of an enlarged pulp cavity. No other remains of this species have been found, and until we know more about it it may be wise to reserve judgment on its exact generic position. Although it is classed with Genus *Homo*, we must not forget that if *Eoanthropus* could combine an apelike jaw with a human skull some other species may have combined a manlike jaw with an apelike skull.

The earliest unquestionably human remains are those of Neanderthal man, a race or species which seems to have occupied most of Europe during the middle and later part of the Pleistocene. Many individuals of this group have been found, and this is the earliest point in human history at which we stand on really firm ground with complete skeletons on which to base our conclusions. Although Neanderthal was more apelike than any living race, there can be no doubt that he was a fully developed man. He was a short, stocky individual, barrel-chested and strongly muscled. Both his arms and his legs were short, and the proportions of the upper and lower bones in each were, curiously enough, less anthropoid than those of our own species. He seems to have been unable to straighten his knees completely and must have had a rather slow and shambling gait. His head was tilted back, due to a high attachment of the neck muscles on the skull, so that he must have shown a single unbroken curve from the crown of his head to the small of his back. His head was large, with a very heavy face, broad and probably flat nose, and a massive chinless jaw. The eyes were protected by projecting brow ridges even heavier than those of a modern Australian black. His forehead was low and his skull long and rather flat on top, with the bulk of its capacity toward the rear. His brain was, proportionately to his size, quite as large as that of modern men, but it was organized somewhat differently and he was probably distinctly inferior in mental ability. He differed from modern man most markedly in his tooth structure, which showed a constant development of large pulp cavities and a tendency toward plug-rooted molars instead of fang-rooted ones of modern type. He seems to have known the use of tools and fire from the earliest period in which we find him and before his extinction had evolved a considerable series of specialized tools. In fact he was little inferior in this respect to our own ancestors at the time that they replaced him on the European continent.

There is one other species of our genus which deserves only a passing mention. This is Rhodesian man, based upon a single skull found in Rhodesia in Africa. This skull is very large, with an extraordinarily low forehead and huge face. The lower jaw is missing, but the teeth are thoroughly human. Long bones from the same deposits are modern in all respects. This form is a puzzle, but the associated fossils indicate such a late date for it that it must have been a contemporary of our own species and thus has no bearing on our possible ancestry.

In attempting to draw this material together and to give some coherent picture of even the last phases of human evolution, the investigator at once lays himself open to attack. Every one of the semi-human and ancient human species has been enthusiastically fought over by experts, and even now the divergences of opinion are more numerous than the agreements. However, this much seems certain: *Pithecanthropus, Sinanthropus* (Pekin man), and Neanderthal are closely related and together form a consistent evolutionary series which would be accepted without question if we were studying the past of any animal other than man. The Heidelberg fossil, although more primitive than any known jaw of the Neanderthal species, is very much as we would expect the jaw of an ancestral and less highly evolved Neanderthal to be. It should probably be assigned to the same evolutionary line at a point a little below the Neanderthal end. The Rhodesian species certainly does not lie in the direct line, but it has so much in common with Neanderthal that it seems just to interpret it as an offshoot from the same stem and one whose separation probably was not very ancient. The Taungs and Piltdown species, on the other hand, show no close relations with this line of hominoid evolution. Their lines must have diverged even before *Pithecanthropus*.

It remains to establish the relation of our own species, *Homo sapiens,* to this *Pithecanthropus*-Neanderthal line. It seems fairly certain that we did not evolve from Neanderthal, for this species was actually less apelike than our own in certain respects, and the evolutionary process very rarely retraces its steps. At the same time, our species and Neanderthal have so many features in common that it seems incredible that their similarities should be a result of parallel evolution. The most probable explanation of these similarities would seem to be that the two species have a common ancestry up to some point well beyond *Sinanthropus*. Recent finds in Palestine indicate the presence there during the upper half of the Pleistocene of a species of man with about equally divided similarities to Neanderthal and our own species. Very little information on these finds has so far been published, but it seems possible that this species lies at the parting of the ways and is ancestral to both.

From these Palestinian finds it is a short step to the most primitive representatives of our own species who have so far been discovered. This is the Wadjak race, represented by two skulls from Pleistocene deposits in Java. These skulls are much like those of the modern Australian aborigines. They are long, with very heavy brow ridges, retreating foreheads, and massive faces. The most striking feature is their unusual brain capacity, which is well above the average for modern Europeans. It seems probable that the Australians are the somewhat degenerate descendants of this race. Aside from numerous similarities in the living natives, the oldest Australian fossil, the Talgai skull, seems to be an authentic link between the two. The Wadjak race may also be ancestral to certain primitive groups in southern India. Whether it lies in the evolutionary line of any of the other races is uncertain. At least it represented a primitive, generalized form with potentialities for evolving toward any one of several modern types.

In spite of their primitive characteristics, the Wadjak skulls are not very ancient. A number of still older finds of members of our own species have been claimed, but unfortunately the exact geological age of all these finds is in doubt. Moreover, the structure of these individuals is, in every case, less primitive and generalized than that of the Wadjak race. Some of these finds are probably authentic, and if so the Wadjak man must be considered as an archaic survival, an ancient form which had lingered on in Java, as did *Pithecanthropus*, long after higher forms had been evolved elsewhere.

Even the most conservative students of human evolution will be ready to admit that at least 100,000 years ago our species had assumed its full modern characteristics, although all its present varieties probably were not in existence by this date. It is also probable that by this time the generalized ancestors of modern man had spread over most of the tropical and temperate regions of the Old World. If even the semi-human forms were able to do this, there is no reason to suppose that our own ancestors, who were more intelligent and better equipped to cope with a variety of environments, could not have followed their example. It is one of the tenets of evolution that the struggle for existence is always sharpest between closely related species which utilize much the same natural resources of any region. In their spread our own ancestors probably "mopped up" all the other human or semi-human species which had survived to come into competition with them.

The last campaign in this long war for world sovereignty seems to have been fought in Europe. Here the Pleistocene was an age of ice with alternate glacial advances and retreats. *Homo sapiens* was a tropical or at most temperate species, hairless and susceptible to cold. Neanderthal, on the other hand, seems to have been a sub-arctic species. He was able to live in Europe under conditions as severe as those which confront the modern Eskimo and with a vastly less adequate equipment. We know that he has left no tools suitable for sewing skins together, and it is doubtful whether he had clothing at all. Perhaps he had retained the furry coat of his anthropoid ancestors. It was only when the ice moved north for the last time that our ancestors entered the continent and began to contest Neanderthal's supremacy. These first immigrants were of fully modern type and their descendants are still present in the European population. They seem to have carried on a war of extermination with the Neanderthal species, and there are no indications that they ever interbred with them. This is so much at variance with the usual practices of wife-stealing and race mixture that it suggests the presence of some great difference between the two groups. It is hardly conceivable that the physical differences of the two species made breeding impossible. It is more likely that there was some superficial characteristic of Neanderthal, perhaps a furry coat, which placed him completely outside the human family. Whatever the reason, Neanderthal was wiped out without leaving a trace and our own species emerged as the sole representatives of the *Hominidæ*.

It was toward the close of the Pleistocene also that members of our own species reached the American continent. Whether they came by the bleak Bering Strait route or by some now sunken bridge farther to the south is still uncertain. However, we know that man was only one of a series of Asiatic mammals which penetrated to America at this time and at least one of these, the bison, has never been an arctic form. In the new continent men found a rich although somewhat archaic fauna and no anthropoid or hominoid forms which might challenge their supremacy. They increased rapidly and spread widely, but they lost time in pioneering and did not begin to lay the foundations of civilization until some 3,000 or 4,000 years after their Old World relatives had taken the first steps in the same direction.

Anyone who writes on the origin of man must make a liberal use of "probably" and "perhaps." There are long gaps in the record, and some of these may never be filled. At the same time, evidence is accumulating so rapidly that any book on the subject becomes antiquated within five years. In the light of our present knowledge the history of our species can be summarized as follows: Our most remote primate ancestor was some small tree-dwelling form ancestral to men and apes alike. For a long time the human and ape lines of evolution were the same, the individuals becoming steadily larger and also developing disproportionately large brains. During the Miocene period some of the members of this line became too large to live in trees and began to adapt themselves to existence on the ground. One or more species of these big ground-dwellers developed carnivorous habits and branched off from the ancestral stem, increasing the size of its brain and adopting completely erect posture. This was the beginning of the hominoid stem, which put forth many branches during the late Miocene and Pliocene. One of these branches reached the human level, probably during the later half of the Pliocene, and gave rise to a number of species one of which finally evolved into modern man. This species spread far and wide, exterminated its competitors, and began in turn to differentiate into various races, species in the making. It is with these varieties of modern man that we will deal in the next chapter.

CHAPTER II

RACE

It is natural that man should be intensely interested in the physical characteristics of his own species, but the very strength of this interest is likely to lead to a certain loss of perspective. The study of human varieties, i.e., races, is really a branch of zoölogy. Man is subject to exactly the same biological laws as other mammals and owes his present variations to the same evolutionary processes. If we are to understand the origins of race and evaluate the importance of racial differences correctly, we must try to forget that we are dealing with men and study our own species as objectively as we would study any other. That so many students of physical anthropology have failed to do this seems to be due mainly to historic causes. This science seems to have had more difficulty in breaking with its past than has any other of the natural sciences.

Physical anthropology took shape as a distinct science during the later eighteenth and early nineteenth centuries. It grew out of a combination of anatomy and the systematic zoölogy of the period, and its early efforts were directed entirely toward the establishment of classifications of human varieties and the development of techniques of observation which would make more accurate classifications possible. In its inception it was a purely descriptive science only incidentally interested in the problem of racial origins and the dynamics of human variation. Although these problems could not be completely ignored, it disposed of them in summary fashion. Unfortunately, the early guesses on these points became dogmas which still have a strong influence on the thought of many workers in this field.

The first physical anthropologists were handicapped by a scarcity of material from outside Europe and by ignorance of the principles of heredity and a lack of any adequate techniques for distinguishing between pure and mixed strains. The material which they did have indicated the existence of a great number of human varieties, and these varieties offered such irregular combinations of physical traits that it was extremely difficult to find any satisfactory classification for them. A classification based on any one trait, such as head form, would be totally out of agreement with one based on some other trait such as skin color or hair texture. At this time the principles of evolution were just beginning to be enunciated but were not yet generally accepted. The first physical anthropologists still believed that every species and variety was the result of a separate act of creation and was therefore fixed and unchangeable. However, it strained even their credulity to believe that all the human varieties they were forced to recognize had been created separately. The phenomenon of race mixture, which could be observed wherever different human varieties came into even casual contact, offered a convenient way out. They were able to solve their problems of origin and classification simultaneously by setting up a small series of ideal types, each characterized by a particular combination of physical traits, and assuming that all varieties which did not conform to these ideal types were a result of hybridization.

Each of these ideal types corresponded to an actual variety of man, but the selection of a particular variety as constituting a basic type depended entirely upon the judgment of the observer. However, this fact was conveniently forgotten as soon as the type hypothesis had come to be accepted. Although there has never been the slightest proof that any one of these ideal types was actually ancestral to any other human variety, it has become heresy to question the idea. To do so strikes at the very foundation of those classifications in which the science is still primarily interested. Even when the idea of separate creations had to be abandoned, the concept of primary types survived. It was assumed that these types had been evolved from different subhuman species or, at the very least, had become differentiated at the very dawn of our species development.

It is plain that the whole problem of racial origins and relationships needs to be reviewed in the light of modern biological knowledge. In attempting to do this we can ignore the question of classification for the present. Although classifications have a profound effect upon our thinking, they are always imposed from without and have no functional relationship to the material which they arrange. In the first place, all existing human varieties are members of a single species by the most elementary of biological tests. They all produce fertile hybrids on crossing. Moreover, these hybrids appear to be, if anything, more fertile than the parent strains and at least equally vigorous. The results of crossing human varieties appear to be identical with those obtained from crossing strains within any plant or animal species after these strains have become fixed by inbreeding. In view of this, it seems highly improbable that any of the human varieties derive from different sub-human species.

Even without the hybridization test, the evidence that all human beings belong to a single species is overwhelming. The physical differences between various human varieties look large to us because we are so close to them, just as the physical differences between individuals whom we know seem much more marked than the differences between strangers. Actually, the differences between even the most diverse human varieties are not very great, and all of them lie in secondary characteristics. Man has his color phases, as have many other mammalian species, his large and small varieties, and a wide range of minor variations in such matters as hair texture, shape of the skull, and limb proportions. However, his skeletal structure, organs, and musculature are practically the same in all varieties, and the differences which do exist are so slight that they can be detected only by experts. An equally intensive study of any other mammalian species of fairly wide range would reveal almost as much variation and in many cases a good deal more. Thus the widest range of variation in our species is much less than that in the black bears and only about one-half that in a single species of South American spider monkeys. When we come to domestic animals, the range is several times as great. There are no differences between human varieties which even remotely approach those between a pug and a grey-

hound or even between a Hereford and an old-style Texas long-
horn. Since man is a domestic animal and has the widest range
of any mammalian species, the striking thing about him is not
that he has developed different varieties but that these varieties
are not more widely different than they are.

How the present human varieties have come into existence is
a problem which is by no means solved, but our present knowledge
of evolutionary process makes it possible to guess with a fair
degree of probability. In the previous chapter we spoke of the way
in which even the semi-human primates seem to have spread
over the world and suggested that our own species, when it
appeared, must also have been capable of a very rapid spread.
Even our first ancestors were probably equipped with tools and
fire, making it possible for them to exist in many different environments, while they certainly had no non-portable property
which might tie them to a single locality. Every species has a
tendency to breed up to the available food supply, which, for
gregarious animals, is fixed by the territory which the herd,
moving as a whole, can cover. It seems highly probable that the
first men, like all modern men, were gregarious. When the
human band became too large for its territory, it split in two and
one part moved into new territory. This process, which can still
be observed among peoples at the hunting stage, is described in
detail in a later chapter. As long as there was plenty of unexploited territory available this process of population increase
and band fission must have gone on rapidly, and it is not impossible that our species had occupied most of the habitable portions
of the Old World within a few thousand years of its emergence.

The social horizon of uncivilized groups is always very limited. They know only the members of their own band and possibly
those of the bands whose territory immediately adjoins theirs.
They are often on hostile terms even with these close neighbors.
The result of this is fairly close and continuous inbreeding. Although all tribes forbid marriage between relatives in certain
degrees, all the members of a small tribe marrying within itself
will come in a few generations to have very much the same
heredity. Thus in such a group as the Cape York Eskimo,

who probably never numbered more than 500 individuals and who had been completely inbred for at least 300 years, the whole tribe had become a single family line. From the genetic point of view it would make little difference whether a man married his first cousin or the least-related individual whom he could find. Such a condition is especially favorable to the fixation of muta-tions. A physical variation of any sort, if hereditary, will soon become a part of the heredity of every individual in the group and have a double chance of appearing in the offspring of any marriage. The whole tribe is really one large family, genetically speaking, and all its members soon come to show a family re-semblance.

If we are correct in our belief that all existing men belong to a single species, early man must have been a generalized form with potentialities for evolving into all the varieties which we know at present. It further seems probable that this generalized form spread widely and rapidly and that within a few thousand years of its appearance small bands of individuals of this type were scattered over most of the Old World. These bands would find themselves in many different environments, and the physical peculiarities which were advantageous in one of these might be of no importance or actually deleterious in another. Moreover, due to the relative isolation of these bands and their habit of inbreeding, any mutation which was favorable or at least not injurious under the particular circumstances would have the best possible chance of spreading to all the members of the group. It seems quite possible to account for all the known variations in our species on this basis without invoking the theory of a small number of originally distinct varieties.

We know that environment has a selective effect on physical variations after they appear. It ensures to individuals who vary in certain directions a better chance of survival and therefore of passing on such variations to later generations, while it de-creases the chances of survival for those who vary in other direc-tions. This is the well-known principle of natural selection. Whether environment also has a positive effect in producing variations or even encouraging variation in a particular direction remains to be proved. It seems quite possible that it does, although the mechanics involved are still completely unknown. Thus a study of plants shows that certain species show a great increase in the number of mutants produced when they are introduced into a new environment, this tendency decreasing with the length of residence. We also know that even in man settlement in a new environment may result in changes in physical type which are not arrived at by the selective process. Thus Dr. Boas's studies of emigrants in America have shown that even in the first generation there is a slight change in head form which certainly cannot be accounted for on the selective theory. Children of long-headed groups are, on the average, shorter-headed than their own parents, and the tendency increases in direct ratio to the length of time the parents had been in America when the children were born. Conversely, the children of short-headed groups tend to be longer-headed than their parents, with the same ratio between degree of change and length of residence. It certainly looks as though the American environment was working in some non-selective fashion toward the production of an intermediate head form, but we cannot even conjecture the how or why of this.

While we cannot exclude the possibility that the settlement of the ancestral, generalized human type in various environments may have stimulated variation and even directed it in certain lines, we know so little of the processes involved that it is safest to leave this out of the discussion. The processes of natural selection are much better understood, but it must be remembered that the influence of environment is, in this case, negative. It cuts off certain variations from among the wide range of those brought to it by the processes of mutation, but there are many others which are neither advantageous nor disadvantageous. Thus it is hard to see how curly hair gives its possessor either a better or a worse chance for survival than straight hair, unless there happen to be certain social factors present in the situation. The establishment of such variations of neutral value must be due to genetic factors of dominance and recession. Even with these, it is difficult to see how such neutral traits could ever be completely bred out of a strain.

It is a curious fact that of all the variations which have become fixed in particular human groups only those connected with skin color seem to have any significance with regard to natural environment. It has been recognized since classical times that in the Old World dark-skinned people occupy tropical regions and light-skinned ones temperate to cold regions. The possible explanation for this has only recently been discovered. It seems to lie in differences not of heat but of light intensity. The actinic rays of the sun are beneficial to man's system in small quantities, harmful in large ones. Skin pigment seems to act as a ray filter, its efficiency in this respect being correlated with its depth of color.

Let us suppose that two divisions of the same strain settled one in Somaliland and the other beside the Baltic and that both had, in the beginning, medium brown skin color. The Somaliland group would be exposed to intense sunlight. Individuals who varied toward lighter pigmentation would get more actinic rays than were good for them. Like modern Europeans living in the tropics they would be subject to nervous disorders, and females of this type would show a higher percentage of disorders of the reproductive system than females of darker skin color. Although by no means all of these lighter individuals would die young, those who survived would be at a certain disadvantage and less likely to perpetuate their type than individuals who varied toward the dark end of the scale. In the course of time the norm for skin color for the group would move over toward the dark end and might, with the aid of favorable mutations, become very dark indeed.

The group which settled beside the Baltic would be faced by a totally different light situation. This region lies far north to begin with, and the amount of light is further decreased by a great deal of fog and cloudy weather. Individuals whose skin color varied in the direction of heavy pigment would not get enough actinic rays into their systems. Unless they ate raw fish, like the Eskimo, and thus obtained the vitamin which these rays help to produce, they would be very likely to suffer from rickets. Even individuals of a medium shade would have the same difficulty, but those who were lightest, especially partial albinos, would have little or none of it. The absence of pigmentation would make it possible for their systems to get the full benefit of the scanty sun. Rickets is rarely a fatal disease, but it deforms the bones, and women who have suffered from it in childhood frequently have malformations of the pelvis which make child-bearing difficult or impossible. In due course of time the norm for pigmentation for the group would shift toward the light end of the scale and might, with the aid of occasional semi-albino mutations, become as light as that of the modern Nordic.

It is easy to see how a human group living in a particular environment might, in course of time, reach the optimum condition with regard to skin color, but this is only one of many variable traits which have assumed fairly constant form in particular human strains. We cannot say positively that such traits are unconnected with biological survival, since they may reflect some deep-seated condition which is favorable to the survival of the particular group. Thus to cite a purely hypothetical case, the kinky hair of the Negro does not in itself give its possessors any advantage for life in the tropics, but it may be one of several things all of which result from a particular balance of endocrine secretions. Some of the invisible results of this condition might be highly important to survival. It might, for example, give the individuals who had it a high degree of immunity to malaria. If so, those who had this condition, outwardly manifested in kinky hair, would have a better chance of reproducing themselves than those who lacked it, and, in time, kinky hair would become the normal form for the group. The example just cited is purely imaginary, and we have no proof that any linkages of this sort actually exist, but at least the matter would repay study. It seems certain that there is some connection between physical type and the ductless glands. To cite only one example, failure of thyroid secretions will produce many Mongoloid characteristics in persons of pure European stock. These glands, in turn, have a profound influence on the life processes of the individual and even on his personality. It is quite possible that a hormone balance which would be favorable in one environment might be unfavorable in another.

We have then, as possible causes for the present diversity of human types, the tendency toward variation which is common to all mammalian species, the operation of natural selection in each of the varying environments in which human groups live, and the favorable conditions for the fixation of variations present in small, continually inbreeding groups. However, there is another factor in the situation the importance of which must not be overlooked. This is the matter of social selection arising from the group's preference for a particular physical type. This type of selection sometimes assumes a direct and vigorous form. Thus among the Tanala, in Madagascar, there are two groups which differ markedly in skin color although they seem to be much alike in their other physical characteristics and are nearly identical in culture and language. These groups are known by terms which may be translated as the Red clan and the Black clan. Normal members of the Red clan are a very light brown, the pigmentation being slight enough to show a blush. Normal members of the Black clan are a deep brown, as dark as the average American Negro. If one may judge from superficial observations, these two groups represent the limits of the range of skin color present for the tribe as a whole, although the average for the tribe would be nearer the dark end of the scale. If a dark child of unquestioned clan parentage is born into the Red clan it is believed that it will grow up to be either a sorcerer, a thief, a person guilty of incest, or a leper. It is therefore put to death. The Black clan holds exactly the same belief with regard to light children and disposes of them in the same summary fashion. Since nearly all marriages are still made within the clan, this type of social selection could hardly fail to affect the physical type of the group. Variants in the socially undesired direction would be eliminated generation after generation, while even if they were allowed to grow up they would find themselves at a disadvantage and have less opportunity to reproduce their type.

It has often been urged by those who question the importance of social selection as a mechanism for fixing a particular physical type that all members of a primitive community normally marry and beget children. This is perfectly true, but they do not all marry the same people. Quite as among ourselves, the ablest or richest men take what are, by tribal standards, the prettiest girls. There may be some exceptions to this in societies which give their members no choice in matings, but such societies are rare. In general, ugly women have to content themselves with inferior men. Even at the simplest hunting level the children of a good hunter have more and better food and therewith a better chance of survival than those of poor hunters. Conversely, the handsome man has a better chance of perpetuating his type than the ugly one. Even if he lacks the qualities which make for a desirable husband, he will be in demand as a lover. Social selection of this sort works more slowly than the direct elimination practised by the Tanala clans, but its cumulative effects must be considerable.

Of course the direction taken by social selection will depend upon cultural factors. Standards of beauty vary profoundly from one group to another and even, in sophisticated societies, from one period to another. Many persons still in middle age have witnessed the full bloom of feminine curves, their attempted elimination, and their gradual return to favor. Such short-time changes can have no permanent effect on the physical type of a group, but admiration for the black that shines or for ample hips or for heavy whiskers, if maintained for a thousand years, might very well shift the norm for the entire group toward the goal of physical perfection which it has set for itself.

Hitherto our discussion has dealt only with the factors affecting the evolution of divergent varieties from older and more generalized ones. However, there is another aspect of the problem. Human varieties have an incurable tendency to mix wherever and whenever they are brought into contact with each other. Whether new varieties may arise as a result of such hybridization is still an open question. First-generation hybrids between two pure-bred human varieties tend to be fairly uniform in type, but when these hybrids are interbred the offspring appear to be highly variable with throwbacks to both the pure ancestral types and all sorts of intermediate forms. It seems quite possible that, through a combination of natural and social selection, such inbred hybrid groups might in time develop a new stable type, since animal-breeders are able to attain the same end by careful selection and line breeding. However, the process must be a slow one, and the actual production of a new human variety from a hybrid group has never been observed. Herskovitz finds evidence that something of the sort is occurring among the American Negroes, who represent a very complex mixture of various Negro, European, and American Indian breeds, but the process of fixation of the new type is still incomplete.

Throughout the history of our species two forces have constantly been at work. On the one hand the combined factors of variation, selection, and fixation of traits by inbreeding have worked steadily toward the production of a greater and greater number of human varieties. On the other hand, the ease with which human strains can and do cross has worked to blur the outlines of these varieties and to produce multitudes of individuals of mixed heredity and variable physical type. The first of these forces was dominant during the early period of man's existence. The second became increasingly important as time passed and has risen to a crescendo with the elimination of space and the breakdown of old local groupings which are characteristic of modern civilization.

The early history of our species probably witnessed its fairly rapid dispersal over the Old World and the development of a large number of local varieties. Some of these varieties were no doubt more vigorous and more intelligent than others, which made it possible for them to increase and to occupy additional territory at the expense of their less able neighbors. However, if we admit that the processes of variation and of fixation of new types have gone on continuously, as the study of all other mammalian species seems to indicate, no single human variety could have established itself over a very wide area without undergoing local modifications. As soon as a group of individuals of any given variety established themselves in an environment markedly different from that in which this variety had been developed, the evolution of a new variety would begin. The possible forms which this new variety might assume would be limited not only by the new environment but also by the potentialities for variation inherent in the parent variety. Thus members of a pure-bred blond strain could hardly develop into a new brunette variety. Pigmentation is a genetically dominant factor in heredity and, once eliminated from a strain, apparently cannot be reassumed. However, such an original blond strain might retain potentialities for variation in other physical characteristics such as head form and might give rise, in different environments, to both round-headed blond varieties and long-headed blond varieties. In other words, the spread of certain able varieties and the elimination of less able ones would not, in the long run, lead to the establishment of a uniform physical type over a wide area. It would simply lead to the development of a series of new varieties.

To complicate the situation still more, any movement of members of a particular variety into territory which had previously been occupied by another variety accelerated the process of hybridization. Even in the lowest stages of culture wars between groups rarely end in the complete extermination or expulsion of the vanquished. The more attractive women are taken as concubines by the victors, and through them some of the heredity of the vanquished passes into the conquering group. In the higher stages of culture, when agriculture, manufactures, and trade have been developed, it becomes more profitable to settle among and exploit the vanquished than to exterminate them. This results in close and continuous contact between conquerors and conquered and a rapid and extensive mixture of the two strains. Although hybrids produced under these conditions may be at a social disadvantage, they have at least as good a chance of survival as pure-bred members of the conquered group and by interbreeding with them spread the blood of the conquerors downward in ever-widening circles.

Even the conquerors cannot maintain their purity of blood

under these conditions. Although history affords numerous examples of conscious attempts to do this, all of these attempts have failed. The conquerors may be able to guard their women successfully, limiting crosses to those arising from relations between their men and conquered women, but as soon as any crossing begins the purity of their type is doomed. Certain of the offspring of the hybrids will throw back toward the type of their aristocratic relatives, and such individuals can usually worm their way into the aristocratic group. The "passing" of Negroes in our own society would be a case in point. Such individuals carry the heredity of both groups, and through their intermarriage with the aristocrats more and more of the heredity of the conquered is introduced into the ruling group, until finally the physical distinction between the two types disappears.

It has been said that the only group which would have any chance of maintaining absolute purity of blood would be one all of whose women were too hideous to attract the men of any other tribe and all of whose men were too cowardly to steal the women of any other tribe. To this might be added inhabitants of islands never visited after the original settlement. However, primitive groups, with their narrow geographic ranges and limited contacts, have a much better chance of retaining relative purity of blood than have civilized ones. Any conditions which bring individuals of different varieties into more frequent contact will increase the number of hybrids. Every civilized group of which we have record has been a hybrid group, a fact which disposes effectively of the theory that hybrid peoples are inferior to pure-bred ones.

Attitudes toward hybridization have varied profoundly in different societies and at different periods, but there seems to be no biological justification for any strong feeling either for or against it. It is true that the purest human strains now extant are to be found among culturally backward groups and that all civilized peoples are predominantly of hybrid composition, but this does not indicate that hybrids are intrinsically superior. The same contacts which stimulate the development of civilization stimulate the production of hybrids, so that both conditions owe their presence to a common cause. Conversely, the fact that hybrid populations are quite capable of perpetuating and adding to the cultural equipment which they have received from their pure-bred ancestors shows that they are at least equal to these in ability. The social connotations of hybridization may be important in particular situations, but the biological and cultural connotations appear to be negligible. In the long run it causes more grief to the students who are trying to classify human varieties than to any one else.

It seems slightly ludicrous that the main exponents of the theory of the superiority of pure strains should be inhabitants of Europe, one of the most thoroughly hybridized regions in the world. It is improbable that there is a single European alive to-day who does not have at least one hybrid among his ancestors, while most Europeans are the result of a long series of crossings. Tribes have marched and countermarched across the face of this continent since before the dawn of history, and the ancestry of most of the present population is not even pure white. The Huns, a yellow tribe from far eastern Asia, raided almost to the Atlantic and, after their defeat, dissolved into the European population. Other Asiatic tribes such as the Avars and Magyars settled large areas in eastern Europe, interbreeding with the earlier inhabitants until they disappeared as a distinct physical type. The Romans brought in Negro slaves while, in later times, the Mohammedan conquerors of Spain and Sicily had more than a tinge of black blood. Lastly, there have been several varieties of whites in Europe since before the close of the Old Stone Age. Although numerous books have been written on the origins, characteristics, and interrelations of these varieties, hardly two eminent authorities will agree exactly as to what these have been, and there is even some disagreement as to number of varieties which can be recognized. It seems that the only thing we can be perfectly sure of is that every variety wandered, underwent local modifications, and crossed with other varieties whenever the opportunity arose. The result of all this has been an extreme mixture of heredity in Europe and a perfect hodgepodge of varying physical types.

Even when the characteristics of one of the original white

varieties can be determined with a fair degree of probability, it by no means follows that individuals who show these characteristics will breed true. Members of mixed groups have a strong tendency to throw back toward the original varieties which have gone into the mixture. In spite of their physical type, such throwbacks carry and transmit a mixed heredity. To resurrect any of the original European varieties in pure form would require several generations of careful selective breeding with the elimination in each generation of all individuals who did not conform to the desired type. This presents practical difficulties insurmountable even by a totalitarian state.

European physical types have been studied more intensively than those of any other region, but it seems certain that similar conditions of extreme mixture exist in all regions of dense population and advanced culture. The situation which confronts physical anthropologists in their attempts to determine original human varieties and to classify them is therefore extremely complex. Their work has also been hampered by a lack of agreement on terminology and by the very loose usage of certain terms, particularly *race*. This has been applied indiscriminately to classificatory units ranging all the way from small and presumably closely inbred groups whose members show a very high degree of physical uniformity to huge divisions of mankind within which the differences are actually more numerous than the similarities.

It must be clearly understood at the outset of any attempt to classify human varieties that such classifications rest entirely upon observable physical characteristics. Although similarities in the characteristics of various human groups may imply genetic relationships and more or less remote common origins, these relationships cannot be proved. All classifications rest upon the presence of a number of characteristics, and the greater part of these are, unfortunately, of a sort which cannot be ascertained from skeletal material alone. Skeletons provide no clue to their former owners' skin color, hair texture, or eye, nose, and lip form, all of these being items currently used as a basis for racial classifications. There is no human group whose ancestry is known for even five generations in the exact terms necessary for racial determinations. In fact, there is not even a family line for which we have satisfactory information over this brief period. Most genealogies are simply lists of names, and even the family portrait gallery fails to yield information on many important points. All that we can do is to classify human varieties as we find them to-day. Any conclusions as to their relationships which may be based on these classifications are merely conjectures with varying degrees of probability.

The term *race* has been used so loosely that it seems wisest to substitute for it a series of three terms: *breed, race,* and *stock*. Even this terminology is too limited for a really accurate classification, but one that was exact enough to meet all conditions would be so complex that it would lose much of its utility. Under this terminology, a *breed* is a group of individuals all of whom vary about a particular norm with respect to each of their physical characteristics. This usage corresponds exactly to the usage of the same term when applied to domestic animals, say Scotch terriers.

It is almost impossible to find any human group which constitutes a pure breed, but the condition is approached in certain primitive tribes living in relative isolation. It seems fairly certain that such breeds are established by long-continued inbreeding with the elimination of extreme variants, although absolute proof of this is lacking. Even in the most isolated human groups there are some individuals who fall outside the normal range of variation for the group as a whole with regard to certain of their characteristics. This may be due either to remote crosses with other breeds or to individual mutations. In either case such atypical persons can be eliminated from the study by statistical methods. If there are a number of them all of whom vary from the norm in very much the same way, this is usually considered an indication of an earlier crossing with some other breed.

After such individuals have been eliminated, the investigator proceeds to establish the norms for the group with regard to each of a series of physical characteristics. Those most commonly employed are head form, including the face; color of the skin, hair, and eyes; form of the features; hair texture; amount of body hair and beard; and stature. Any number of additional characteristics can be taken into consideration, but those just named are the most easily ascertainable, and most of them can be recorded in exact terms. If we take the adult males or females of the group, we will find that although no two of them are identical with respect to any one of these characteristics, say stature, the bulk of them will cluster about a particular point in the total range of variation. Thus the whole series of adult males may range in height from five feet six inches to six feet, but there will be few individuals at the two extremes and more as we move toward the center, with the largest number falling around five feet nine inches. Five feet nine inches would then be considered the norm with regard to this particular trait. A combination of the norms for all the traits observed will give the ideal physical type for the breed. This bears somewhat the same relation to the members of the breed as a whole that the ideal type for the Scotch terrier at a dog-show bears to the dogs actually exhibited. No individual, whether animal or human, is ever a perfect example of the ideal type for his breed, but this type represents what the completely average individual would be.

By the use of statistical methods applied to large series of individuals it is possible to distinguish such breeds even in fairly mixed populations and from this to deduce, with a fair degree of probability, what were the original pure strains which went to their making. The same methods make it possible to determine whether a group which appears to be intermediate between two known breeds is a distinct, pure-bred strain or a hybrid one. Of course this does not eliminate the possibility that such an intermediate breed may have come into existence through an ancient hybridization with the subsequent development and fixation of a new physical type, but this does not lessen the value of the method for classificatory purposes.

Only a small part of the world's population has been studied by this method, but the results indicate that there are, or have been, hundreds of human breeds scattered over the earth. It also seems probable that these units are in a constant state of

flux, new breeds coming into existence wherever a small group
of individuals settle in relative isolation and intermarry among
themselves for several generations. Conversely old breeds are
constantly being eliminated through mixture or failure in the
struggle for survival. A classification of mankind by breeds would
thus represent the situation only at a particular point in human
history. It would be invalid even ten generations before this
point or after it.

The next larger classificatory unit in our system is the *race*.
This consists of a number of breeds whose ideal types have a
series of characteristics in common. In establishing such races it
is impossible to use the same exact methods applied to the establishment of breeds. In the study of breeds the group of individuals to be considered is clearly outlined, while the racial
groupings have no such well-defined boundaries. If we take any
one physical characteristic and study its variations throughout
the whole range of human breeds, we will find that certain of
these breeds are closely similar with regard to it, others somewhat similar, and still others markedly different. However, the
relative position of any breed with regard to one trait will be
different from its relative position with regard to another. Thus
a classification of breeds which is based on head form may be
quite at variance with one based on some other trait, such as
skin color. Two breeds which have much the same head form
may have markedly different pigmentation or vice versa.

Racial classifications are, therefore, based upon the presence
of similarities with respect to a selected series of physical traits.
The content of any group within the classification depends both
upon the traits selected and upon the degree of similarity which
the investigator considers significant. Although there are certain
breeds whose resemblances are so close and numerous that their
assignment to a single racial grouping is never questioned, there
are many others which lie on the border lines of such groupings
with their resemblances rather equally divided. Where such
breeds will be placed in the racial classification depends, in the
last analysis, on the judgment of the investigator. To cite a
single example, there is in eastern Europe a breed of large but

stockily built blonds with medium to round heads and broad faces. In pigmentation this breed resembles the characteristics used to determine membership in the Nordic racial group, in head and face form it resembles the Alpine group, while in bodily build and stature it is intermediate between the two, leaning a little toward the Nordic side. Whether this breed is to be classed with the Nordic or with the Alpine race depends upon which of these resemblances are judged to be more significant.

The real point of all this is that, while breeds are genuine biological entities, races, as we have chosen to use the term, are creations of the investigator and creations with regard to which all the creators are by no means in agreement. The same thing holds in even greater degree for the third and largest division of our classification, the stocks. *Stocks* are groups of races, the content of any stock being established by the same techniques as those used for establishing racial classifications. The only difference is that a still smaller series of traits are taken into consideration and the limits of the group are correspondingly extended. The difficulties encountered in arranging races into stocks are much the same as those connected with the assignment of breeds to races. Here again, there are races which lie on the border line between stocks and whose assignment to one or another stock will always be open to question. Thus in northeast Africa there is a race which is like the Negro stock in its skin color and, to a lesser degree, in its hair form, but which lies closer to whites than it does to Negroes with respect to its head form and especially its features. Where it shall be placed in the classification depends, in the last analysis, on the judgment of the investigator.

The difficulty of classifying the varieties of mankind resulted in a tendency to increase the number of races and stocks until the system became so complex and unwieldy that it broke down of its own weight. At the present time the tendency is to classify the whole of mankind under three stocks, with a recognition that there are certain races and breeds which it is impossible to place. These stocks are the Caucasic, or white, the Negroid, or black, and the Mongoloid, or yellow. The Caucasic stock as a whole is characterized **by high,** thin noses, medium lips, slight prognathism (i.e., projection of the face), straight eyes, wavy to curly hair, and considerable body hair and beard. In all other respects it is variable, including tall and short, long- and round-headed, and both blond and very dark-skinned groups. Although we are accustomed to think of Caucasians as white, some of the breeds in this stock are darker than the average American Negro.

Within the Caucasic stock at least five races are commonly distinguished. The much advertised Nordic race, which centers in northern Europe, has the general characteristics of the stock plus long heads, tall stature, and blond pigmentation. The Alpine race, strongest in central Europe, has the general characteristics plus round heads, medium to short stature with a strong, stocky build, and medium pigmentation with brown hair and eyes. The Mediterranean race, centering in southern Europe, has the general characteristics plus long heads, medium to short stature with a light build, and rather dark pigmentation with dark brown to black hair and eyes and a tendency toward quite curly hair. In southeastern Europe and the Near East there is another race, the Armenoid, which is characterized by dark pigmentation, short, high heads, and a curious facial type. The nose is large and forms a continuous line with the somewhat sloping forehead. An idealization of this type may be seen in Greek statues. Lastly, in India, the Hindi race combines most of the characteristics of the Mediterraneans with taller stature and a much deeper skin color which becomes almost black in certain breeds.

The Negroid stock as a whole is characterized by flat noses, thick lips, considerable prognathism, straight eyes, kinky hair, very dark pigmentation, and a tendency toward long-headedness, although it includes a few medium- to short-headed breeds. It is more variable than any other stock with regard to stature, including both the tallest and the shortest of the human breeds. Its racial composition has never been adequately worked out, but at least five races can be distinguished tentatively. The Nilotic Negroes are distinguished by extremely tall, thin build and a relative absence of body hair and beard. The Forest Negroes are shorter and more powerfully built, with a fairly heavy development of body hair and beard and exaggeratedly negroid fea-

tures. It was from this group that the ancestors of most of the
American Negroes were drawn. In the dense forests of Central
Africa there is a third racial group, the Pigmies. These are much
like the Forest Negroes except for their extremely short stature,
which rarely reaches five feet even in adult males, and their
somewhat shorter heads.

There are two other races which are usually classed with the
Negroid stock although their habitat lies far from the rest. The
Negritoes or black dwarfs have a broken distribution throughout far southeastern Asia and the neighboring islands. They are
almost as short as the African pigmies but have a much lighter
build and a tendency toward round-headedness, with little or no
body hair and beard. The Oceanic Negroes are found in New
Guinea and the neighboring islands. They present the stock
characteristics, but it is extremely difficult to characterize them
as a race. The region is one of numerous highly localized breeds
and of extensive mixture with other stocks.

In South Africa there is still another race, the Bushmen-
Hottentots, which defies assignment to any of the stocks. These
people are short, lightly built, with Negroid noses and lips and
extremely kinky hair, but they have light yellow skins and slant
eyes. Largely because of their geographical position they are
frequently classed as an extreme variant of the Negro stock.
Some of the breeds within this race have the further peculiarity
of steatopygia, the storing-up of masses of fat in the buttocks,
but this is not characteristic of the race as a whole.

The Mongoloid stock is the most difficult of all to define,
since it has not only been very incompletely studied but has also
been used as a catch-all for races and stocks which clearly were
not Negroid but which the Caucasian scholars were unwilling to
admit to their own select company. In general, this stock is
characterized by medium dark skin color, ranging from the
copper-brown of the American Indian to the light yellow of the
North Chinese, straight, lank hair, and sparse body hair and
beard. Its members are variable in all other respects. Even the
slant eye, frequently mentioned as characteristic of this stock, is
of only sporadic occurrence among American Indians. The stock

really falls into two divisions, the Old World Mongoloids and the New World ones, i.e., the Indians. The Old World division includes at least two well-marked races and probably a much greater number. The North Chinese race is tall, round-headed, with light yellow skins, small, straight noses, thin lips, and slant eyes. The Malay race, which centers in southeastern Asia, is short, with rather variable head form and features and with medium brown skin color. In northeastern Asia there is still another race or group of races which resembles the American Indian.

The American Indians might almost be classified as constituting a distinct stock. They have developed into many different breeds, most of which have the common factors of copper-brown skin color and straight hair while showing extreme variation in other respects. Thus the shortest and longest undeformed skulls known to us come from different Indian breeds. Even skin color and hair texture are somewhat variable. There are certain light, yellowish breeds in South America, and wavy to moderately curly hair occurs sporadically in both continents. No satisfactory racial classification for these various breeds has so far been developed.

In northern Japan and the neighboring island of Sakhalin there is a small racial group, the Ainu, who are of doubtful status. These people are short, stocky, with medium heads, brown hair, and gray or green eyes, somewhat wavy hair texture and abundant body hair and beard, and dusky white skins with a slightly brownish cast. Their eyes are usually straight, but the general cast of their features is more Mongoloid than European. They appear to be one of those border-line groups who show relationships with two stocks in about equal measure, but they have been very tentatively classed with the Caucasians. Throughout the farther islands of the Pacific we have still another race, the Polynesian, which is of even more doubtful status. This race shows a fairly equal proportion of Caucasic and Mongoloid traits with a few not very pronounced Negroid characteristics. This region is one of numerous and widely scattered islands, particularly well adapted to the development of a multiplicity of breeds, and some of these breeds apparently differ as much from each other as they do from particular breeds assigned to the Caucasic or Mongoloid stocks.

There is one other race which defies classification under the standard three-fold grouping and which is, at the same time, of especial interest to anthropologists. This is the Australians. The ancestors of this group seem to have entered their continent in very ancient times and to have had little contact with the outside world afterward. The present members of this race seem to have more in common with certain extinct breeds of man than with any existing breed, and it seems possible that they are only slightly modified descendants of the ancient generalized human type from which all the later breeds and races were evolved. The Australians are characterized by long heads with retreating foreheads, very massive ridges over the eyes, short, wide noses, moderately full lips, very marked prognathism, abundant body hair and beard, wavy hair texture, and medium to dark brown pigmentation. They show vague resemblances to all the stocks in one respect or another, but all these are outweighed by their primitive characteristics.

While the classification which has just been given is a convenient tool for the arrangement of descriptive material, the only units within it which are functionally significant are the breeds. These are genuine biological entities, groups characterized by close physical resemblances and common heredity. Races and stocks, on the other hand, are abstractions. This becomes much clearer when we study the distribution of breeds and their resemblances to each other. Except in regions where there have been extensive recent movements of population, it will usually be found that each breed resembles its immediate neighbors in most respects and more remote breeds in a decreasing number of respects. Even the most markedly different breeds are connected by a graded series of other and intermediate ones. Breeds seem to grade into each other very much as environments grade into each other, both showing gradual but cumulative changes as we move out from any given point. This is exactly the situation which we would expect to find in a species which had spread widely and then differentiated into a series of local varieties. At the same time, it is extremely difficult to account for it on the theory of a small series of originally distinct types unless we assume that the bulk of all existing breeds are a result of hybridization.

The difficulties of the hybridization theory have already been pointed out. If new breeds can be produced in this way, at least it requires a long and drastic process of selection. For the present this theory can neither be proved nor disproved, and until the matter has been settled we must reserve judgment on the assumption that all human varieties have been derived from a few widely different ancestral types. In particular, we must be cautious of all historic reconstructions which are based on the assumption that all the breeds assigned to any one stock have a common ancestry other than that presumably common to all members of our species. To cite one example, it has been generally assumed that the Oceanic Negroes and the Negritoes must share a common origin with the Africa Negroes, and various migration theories have been advanced to account for their presence so far from the other members of the stock. Actually, the environment in which we find them is much like that of tropical Africa, and it seems quite possible that the same ancient generalized human type, if it established itself in both localities, might undergo a parallel evolution. Again, the Caucasic traits which we find in Ainu and Polynesians do not necessarily indicate that these groups have had any historic connection with our own ancestors. The Ainu environment, in particular, was much like that of some parts of Europe. It is safer, for the present, to consider all racial and stock classifications as tools for descriptive study and to avoid building theories of any sort upon them.

CHAPTER III

THE SIGNIFICANCE OF RACIAL DIFFERENCES

The last hundred and fifty years have witnessed the growth of an extensive literature on race and the promulgation of numerous theories regarding the relative status of the various races. While this can be accounted for partly by our increasing interest in all branches of science, it derives still more from a particular set of social and historic factors. Prior to the sixteenth century the world was not race-conscious and there was no incentive for it to become so. The ancient world was a small world and, because of the gradual transition in physical types which is to be found in all continuous geographic areas, the physical differences between the classical and barbarian peoples were not very marked. Thus although the Romans commented on the fact that the Gauls were, in general, taller and more blond than themselves, any Roman could find tall, blond individuals among his own neighbors while, conversely, there were plenty of short, dark types in Gaul. Even when the existence of such physical differences was recognized, they had no immediate social connotations. The hordes of slaves on which the classical economy was based were all drawn from near-by regions, in the case of the Greeks often from neighboring cities, and physical type offered no valid basis for distinguishing slave from master. Even in the widespread Roman Empire most of the subject peoples presented a mixture of breeds so much like that of their conquerors that they could only be distinguished by their dress, language, and customs. Actually, the classical peoples only knew one group whose physical type was markedly different from their own. These were the Nilotic Negroes, whose territory lay at too great a distance to make them important either as enemies or as a source of slaves. The classical attitude toward these people was, therefore, neutral. In fact the Greek poets showed a tendency to idealize them more than they idealized nearer-lying barbarians whom they knew better and commonly spoke of them as "the happy Ethiopians."

This same condition persisted through the Middle Ages. Even the Crusades failed to make Europe race-conscious, since it would have been difficult to tell many South European crusaders from their Saracen enemies when both were stripped of their trappings. It was only with the discovery of the New World and the sea routes to Asia that race assumed a social significance. From the sixteenth century on Europeans were everywhere conquering native peoples and setting themselves up as ruling aristocracies. Although members of the subject groups could readily adopt the language and customs of their rulers, they could not change their own physical type, and for the first time in history race became an infallible criterion for the determination of social status. Since any white man was a member of the ruling group and any brown or black one a member of the subject group, both sides became increasingly conscious of their physical differences. This consciousness was still further stimulated by the rise of the African slave-trade and the importation into both Europe and America of large numbers of Negroes who soon came to constitute a distinct caste at the bottom of the social scale.

Europeans have not been content merely to accept their present social and political dominance as an established fact. Almost from the first they have attempted to rationalize the situation and to prove to themselves that their subjugation of other racial groups was natural and inevitable. Perhaps they have been stimulated to this by an unconfessed realization that anything which has been won by the sword can be lost by the sword. If the European world domination were merely the result of a historic accident, another accident might bring it to an end.

The earliest attempts to rationalize European dominance were based on supernatural sanctions. Since the Europeans were Christians and most of the subject peoples were not, it was natural that the all-powerful God of the Christians should reward His own. The owners of Negro slaves could even justify the practice by a specific passage in the Old Testament where the sons of

Ham were condemned to be hewers of wood and drawers of water. However, these supernatural sanctions soon began to lose their force and the whites cast about for naturalistic rationalizations. The theory of evolution and of the survival of the fittest was a tool ready to their hand. The rapidity with which this purely biological concept came to dominate all fields of European thought is a proof of how badly something of the sort was needed. Under this theory European domination became its own justification. Since the whites had been more successful than the other races, they must be, *per se,* superior to the other races. The fact that this dominance is of very recent date was glossed over by the average European's lack of any world perspective and by elaborate attempts to prove that other races actually stood lower in the scale of physical evolution.

The idea of evolutionary inequalities between races is generally accepted in lay circles, but it has little justification in fact. There is only one human group, the Australian aborigines, who appear to be less highly evolved, in the sense of more primitive and generalized, than the rest. All human breeds which are extant to-day have an equally long evolutionary history, and in all of them evolution has been disharmonic. Each human breed has remained primitive in certain physical traits while it has advanced far beyond the original human condition in others. Thus the whites are the most primitive of any existing group except the Australians with respect to their massive brow ridges and abundant body hair, the least primitive with respect to their high, thin noses and light pigmentation. The Negroes are the most primitive with respect to their flat noses, but the least so in their hair texture and lip form. All existing anthropoids are straight-haired and thin-lipped. Even the very heavy pigmentation of certain Negro breeds is probably a result of divergent evolution and thus no more primitive than the blondness of the North European. The Mongoloid peoples are more primitive than whites with respect to their hair and lip form, less so in the matter of body hair and brow ridges and much less so with regard to their slant eyes. A plotting of racial characteristics on the basis of their degrees of evolutionary advance shows such an even balance between the various races and breeds that we are forced to conclude that all of them stand at about equal distances from their common ancestor.

White dominance, therefore, can hardly be accounted for on the basis of more advanced physical evolution. If it can be explained at all on purely physical grounds, it must rest upon some superior qualities of toughness, strength, and physical adaptability. This "best man" theory has become a favorite in certain circles, but it also seems to have little justification in fact. Superiority of this sort is always a relative matter, depending upon the setting in which it is expected to manifest itself. In West Africa, for example, the white man cannot be considered the physical superior of the native by any stretch of the imagination. This region used to be known as the white man's graveyard, and even with the modern improvements in tropical medicine no white man who settles there is a good insurance risk. The heat, the humidity, and especially the fever sap the white man's strength, while the local Negro, living under much less favorable conditions of food and housing, works hard and thrives. The very region which is fatal to most whites supports a native population which is as dense, in many areas, as that of Belgium. Again, our own Oriental exclusion acts are mute evidence that the white man cannot compete successfully with the Chinaman. If the yellow man could not work harder on less food and under worse living conditions, there would be no danger of his lowering the standards of white labor.

If, as appears probable, each human breed has developed its distinctive characteristics in response to a particular set of environmental conditions, we should expect each breed to be superior in the environment to which it has adapted itself. Actually, this appears to be the case. The West African, at the cost of hundreds of thousands of deaths through hundreds of generations, has developed a strain which is immune to the local malaria and able to work hard under conditions of extreme heat and humidity. Every West African carries in his blood-stream malarial parasites which would be fatal to a white man within a week, yet if he manifests the disease at all he will only have a light childhood attack, not much more serious than chicken-pox among ourselves.

The Chinaman, subjected for at least 2,000 years to conditions of crowding, bad sanitation, and underfeeding, has developed an amazing resistance to them and can thrive under our worst slum conditions. The real test of the white man's physical superiority lies not in his ability to conquer and rule but in his ability to do more work and breed more freely in any environment than the natives of that environment. Actually, the only places in the world where he has been able to establish himself as anything but a member of a ruling caste whose ranks were constantly recruited from Europe have been those in which the natural environment was much like that in which his type was evolved. He has never really gotten a foothold in the tropics or even among Asiatics who were already adapted to city life.

There remains the problem of whether the white man may not be innately superior in determination and fighting ability, the qualities most necessary to a ruling group. There can be no question that he has shown himself superior in these respects to most of the races whom he has encountered, but whether this has been due to innate qualities is at least open to question. White expansion is a very recent historic phenomenon, and if the white man's success as a conqueror arises from innate qualities these qualities in turn must be the result of a mutation which took place not earlier than the fifteenth century. Throughout its entire history prior to this date the inhabitants of Europe were on the defensive against the hordes of Asiatics who came sweeping into the continent from the east. The Huns raided almost to the Atlantic, and in 1242 A.D. the Mongol hordes overran eastern Europe, annihilating every army which came against them and retiring only because they were recalled at the death of the Khan Ogotai. As recently as 1529 the Turks, originally a group of Asiatic nomads, were besieging the walls of Vienna. If the white man was a superior fighter at this period, at least history gives no indication of the fact.

It may also be mentioned that the superior ability of Europeans for discipline and organization entirely failed to manifest itself during this long period. Prior to the rise of modern states Europe produced only one disciplined nation, the Romans, and even they failed lamentably in their efforts to establish a stable empire. In so far as they succeeded at all they did so mainly by imitating Asiatic models. Byzantium, the only really enduring descendant of the Roman empire, traced its organization much more from Persia, by way of the Hellenistic empires, than from the Roman city-state. Even military discipline in Europe passed with the fall of Rome, and European armies degenerated into more mobs of individual fighters. These had no more chance against the disciplined, thoroughly drilled Mongol forces than any mob of brave men would have against professional soldiers. Until the seventeenth century Europe produced no state which was as well organized as China and no army which was as well drilled as the followers of the Mongol khans.

Of course the innate qualities of human groups do not change with such startling swiftness. The potentialities of the present-day inhabitants of Europe are much the same as those of their ancestors during the last 2,000 or 3,000 years. The thing that has changed is European culture. The real reasons for European domination have been summed up in a single verse:

> What ever happens, we have got
> The Maxim gun and they have not.

It remains to be seen whether the Europeans have peculiarities which have made it possible for them to produce the Maxim gun and apply it where it would do the most good and whether the members of other races lack these qualities; in short, whether Europeans are, on the whole, more intelligent than other human groups.

This problem of the relative intelligence of different races and stocks is the crux of the whole question of racial differences. Upon it depends whether all varieties of mankind will eventually be able to take over the modern complex civilization, with its use of machines and applied science. If all races have very much the same innate abilities, it is safe to assume that modern civilization will spread to all parts of the world. It is improbable that this would ever result in a dead uniformity of culture. For example, the housing, clothing, and food which were suited to tropical life would not be suited to life in northern Europe. However, it would mean a universal familiarity with modern techniques of production and a leveling of most of the present economic differences. This, in turn, would remove the main incentives for conquest and political domination. If colonies did not provide markets for the surplus manufactures of their owners, they would not repay the cost of administration. The various races of mankind would thus be put in a position of practical equality out of which social equality could easily develop. If, on the other hand, there are certain races which are innately incapable of accepting modern civilization, such races are doomed to extinction or to endless economic servitude and social inferiority.

The most direct approach to this problem of relative racial intelligence would seem to be that of scientific testing of groups of individuals. A number of such tests have already been invented and appear to give valid results when they are applied to persons who have much the same background. Thus a test of this sort can distinguish exact grades of intelligence within a group of professors' children. The same test can distinguish similar grades in a group of farm children, but it fails when one tries to use it as a basis for comparing the two groups. The intelligence of the individual can only be ascertained indirectly through the medium of information, technical skills, and the like, and this equipment is determined much more by culture than by innate ability. Any country child of six can tell which end of a horse gets up first, while most city-bred adults would be uncertain on the point. Conversely, the city boy of ten may be much more expert in the handling of machines than many country adults. Although refinements of testing technique may reduce the importance of this source of error, it is hard to see how they can ever eliminate it.

Cultural factors are least influential in those tests which deal with various forms of perception, such as sight, hearing, and time required for response to stimuli. It seems significant that no tests of this type have so far revealed any important racial differences. In fact they have rendered untenable certain conclusions based on superficial observations. Thus the fact that certain tribes use a single term for *green* and *blue* had been considered an indication that they could not distinguish visually between the two. Actual tests showed that they could distinguish even varying shades of each with as much accuracy as Europeans. The lack of special terms was apparently due to the fact that these colors had no cultural importance. There was no more need to distinguish between them in ordinary speech than there is for the average American to distinguish between various shades of pink.

When it comes to intelligence tests of the familiar academic variety, cultural factors are so important that they rob the results of all validity. Let us suppose that a Chinaman taking one of these tests is confronted with the simple problem of copying a figure within a given time. The paper on which he works will be familiar to him, but the pencil will be quite unfamiliar. He will not know how hard he has to bear down to make a mark, and the technique for turning corners will be quite different from that of his accustomed brush drawing. Also, the design may be totally different from anything with which he is familiar, requiring preliminary study and a conscious decision where to start. He is thus handicapped at all points, and his score will be no index of his real ability. Perhaps the situation will be brought home to us if we think of having to copy a simple row of Chinese characters with Chinese writing materials while a Chinese psychologist held a stop-watch on us.

It seems certain that any set of tests devised with reference to a particular cultural background will show persons with a different background to have a gratifyingly lower I. Q. Since practically all the tests used to date have been made by Europeans, the Europeans have uniformly emerged triumphant. It seems improbable that it would have been so if Arabs or Hindus or Chinese had been the first to get the idea. Until the cultural factor can be eliminated, the only verdict which we can base upon such formal tests is one of not proven. It becomes necessary, therefore, to turn to the results of less formal observations. Although these can never be expressed in statistical terms, they have considerable value. A trained European observer who has lived with a native group for some time, speaks their language, and has come to know a number of individuals on intimate, personal terms is in a position to draw valid conclusions with regard to their average mental ability and normal personality types. In particular, he can discount many of the cultural factors in the situation and understand the logic underlying many seemingly illogical acts.

One rarely encounters an ethnological field worker who believes that the native group which he knows best is inferior in intelligence to Europeans. Although many of these workers believe that there are racial differences in intelligence, they prefer to ascribe inferiority to groups with whom they have never worked or whom they know only slightly. Although such judgments may be tempered by sentiment, they suggest that the actual differences in intelligence between various groups cannot be very great. At most, certain groups may have a somewhat larger percentage of brilliant individuals than others. This condition might contribute to the elaboration of culture but would have little effect on its acceptance or perpetuation. The average individual in all societies appears to be a rather passive carrier of culture, receiving it from his predecessors and passing it on to his descendants without any particular modifications. The bulk of the individuals in all races are probably intelligent enough to acquire modern mechanized civilization and transmit it without any important additions or losses just as does the bulk of the modern white population. That this can be done even by individuals of a rather low I. Q. is proved by the results of our own intelligence tests and still more by certain current tabloids and movies.

This conclusion as to the essential mental equality of all racial groups seems to be borne out by historical evidence. The growth and spread of civilization has gone on with a serene indifference to racial lines. All groups who have had an opportunity to acquire civilization have not only acquired it but also added to its content. Conversely, no group has been able to develop a rich or complex culture when it was isolated from outside contacts. There is abundant evidence that all the historic civilizations of the Old World had a remote common origin and that the basic elements of this ancestral culture were transferred to various racial groups and underwent divergent development in each case. However, in no case were they allowed to remain at the level at which they had been received. Each group built its own structure of civilization upon them, and first one group and then another took the lead in the general upward trend. Inventions were constantly passed from one center of civilization to another, and the culture of Europe, as it exists to-day, is a complex blend of elements from many sources. If asked to name the elements which are mainly responsible for the present white supremacy most of us would cite gunpowder, which gave the European a military advantage over most native groups, and paper and printing, which have made possible a wide dissemination of education and the pooling of information on which modern scientific progress depends. Both of these were invented by the Chinese.

It has been urged in certain quarters that the physiological differences between races can hardly fail to be correlated with psychological differences. The logic of this position is an excellent one, since intelligence is a function of the brain and nervous system and variations in these would presumably tend to become fixed in any inbred group just as would any other physical characteristics. The weakness of this position derives from a loose usage of the term *race*. We have seen in the preceding chapter that races and stocks are more or less artificial divisions and that the only genuine biological entities are the human breeds. It seems highly probable that the average intelligence for various human breeds does differ just as it does between different breeds of dogs or other domestic animals. However, breeds represent relatively small units of population and appear to be in a constant state of flux with old breeds dropping out of the picture and new ones developing. The competition between such breeds is stiff enough to ensure the elimination of any breed in which a really low order of intelligence might become hereditary. The only exceptions would be in the case of extremely isolated groups where absence of competition might allow survival in spite of mental degeneration. Since every racial group is composed of a number of breeds which have been more or less arbitrarily assigned to it for classificatory purposes, the existence of breed

differences in intelligence does not necessarily imply racial differences in this respect. After all, intelligence has never been used
as a racial criterion. Any breed within a given racial group may
be superior to certain breeds within another racial group and
inferior to others, the result being that all racial groups, as such,
would stand very much on the same level. The ease with which
civilization has been transmitted from one racial group to another seems to afford good evidence that such is the case. In short,
while breeds probably do differ in intelligence, races probably do
not, or at most differ very little.

Human psychology has other aspects than those of pure intelligence. Individuals show marked differences in personality,
and these differences are of considerable importance in connection
with their ability to adapt to various conditions. All of us are
familiar with really brilliant persons who are nevertheless social
misfits, unhappy and inefficient in the environment in which they
find themselves. The field of personality is only beginning to be
explored, and the techniques for measuring it are even less satisfactory than those for the measurement of intelligence. No valid
conclusions can, therefore, be drawn regarding the possible linkage of certain breeds with psychological types. However, it seems
not improbable that there may be some connection. If so, it would
have an important influence on the ability of certain breeds to
assume particular types of culture.

I believe that all investigators who have a first-hand knowledge of non-European groups will agree that the total range of
psychological types in such groups is very much the same as
among ourselves. After the investigator has succeeded in getting
behind the screen of culture, he will be able to pick out from
among any group of natives a series of individuals whose personalities correspond almost exactly to those of various Europeans whom he knows. He can recognize not only a series of
extreme types such as paranoids and megalomaniacs but also the
various mixed types which make up the bulk of any European
community. At the same time, it seems certain that there are
well-marked differences in the percentages of the various psychological types in different native groups. Thus the members of

one group may be predominantly paranoids, those of another group predominantly megalomaniac, etc.

These group differences in psychological norms can be partially explained on cultural grounds. Every society approves of certain psychological types and disapproves of others, favoring or handicapping their possessors accordingly. It is natural that persons with no very marked predispositions toward any particular type should unconsciously assume the one approved by their society. However, the presence of the same total range of types in all groups is hard to explain unless factors other than the cultural ones are at work. While the rôle of individual experience, especially of early personal-social relations, in shaping the personality may account for some of these differences, it seems probable that there is also some physiological basis. Thus our own society seems to afford good evidence that the balance between the secretions of an individual's glands gives him a predisposition toward the development of a particular psychological type. Other things being equal, a hyperthyroid will develop a different sort of personality from a hypopituitary.

If such physiological conditions are hereditary, as they appear to be, it is quite possible that certain human breeds do have definite predispositions toward particular psychological types. Between these predispositions and the socially approved personalities for any group belonging to the breed there would be a constant interaction. In the first place, the socially approved personalities would tend to be in agreement with the group's predispositions. Any other course would entail too much strain on too many individuals. Thus it is hard to imagine a breed whose members were predominantly hypopituitary maintaining as an ideal personality one which called for emotional instability and a high degree of nervous energy. Conversely, the social approval of a particular psychological type would give those who had hereditary tendencies toward it an advantage in the struggle for existence. Social selection would operate here just as it operates with respect to certain physical characteristics and would, in the long run, shift the hereditary norm for the group in the desired direction. All this is pure conjecture. I am merely trying to point out that the possibility that certain breeds have a hereditary tendency to produce a high percentage of a particular psychological type cannot be ignored.

That such inherent psychological differences, if they exist, would have considerable influence on the ability of particular breeds to acquire particular types of culture can hardly be doubted. In fact, they would be more important in this respect than possible differences in absolute intelligence. It is easy to conceive of a group with mental powers far above the average which would, at the same time, have such personality characteristics that the modern machine civilization would be abhorrent to it. Such a group might produce an over-sufficiency of artists and inventors but lack individuals who could work happily and effectively under the régime of the time-clock. In contact with white civilization a group of this sort would be likely to fight acculturation to the last ditch and to prefer race suicide to regimentation.

The existence of breed differences in personality need not imply any far-reaching racial differences. Just as in the case of intelligence, the variation between breeds within a single race might very well be greater than the difference between selected breeds in different races. The modern machine civilization constitutes a new environment, and those breeds which are unable to adapt to it for reasons of either intelligence or personality will be eliminated as surely as were, in the past, those breeds which were unable to adapt to changes in their physical surroundings. Breeds come and go, but the races and stocks remain and there is no probability that any of these will be eliminated within the next few centuries. So long as differences in physical type are made the basis for social discrimination, the present potentialities for trouble between races will also remain. The only real solution of what we call racial problems lies in a change in the white man's attitude toward members of other groups. His contempt is vastly more galling to the non-white races than his economic exploitation, which can only be transitory. The diffusion of civilization which is now in progress will eventually remove the latter, but the former requires some conscious effort on his part. If he fails to accord equality to other racial groups he will certainly receive a rude awakening. The present generation has witnessed the rise of one Asiatic group to world power, and there can be little doubt that others will follow. The white man is increasingly finding himself in a position where it is the part of wisdom to yield gracefully.

CHAPTER IV

THE BACKGROUND OF HUMAN MENTALITY

In the chapters on human origins and on race we have treated man as an animal and have attempted to show that he is simply another and not very divergent product of vertebrate evolution. The only thing about him which appears to be distinctive is his extraordinary behavior, and we will turn now to a discussion of this.

Human behavior is vastly different from the behavior of the other mammals, even that of our cousins the apes. Nevertheless, just as the physical differences between men and apes diminish in importance and cease to be a bar to relationship when they are studied against the background of mammalian variation, the differences in behavior diminish in importance when they are seen in their proper perspective. There is a gap to be sure, and this gap will never be bridged by fossil evidence of the sort which is gradually bringing the structure of men and apes into a continuous evolutionary series. Behavior does not fossilize, and the actual links disappeared when the half-men of the late Pliocene and early Pleistocene became extinct. However, human and animal behavior can be shown to have so much in common that the gap ceases to be of great importance.

The outstanding quality of living as opposed to dead matter is that living matter responds to stimuli in ways which increase its chances of survival. The living being apprehends its environment and acts to adapt itself to it. This irritability of protoplasm, its capacity to receive and transmit stimuli and to react to them purposefully, is the foundation of behavior. It is equally characteristic of the amœba, that speck of jelly which lies at the root of the animal family tree, and of man. who has perched himself on its highest branch.

In unicellular organisms such as the amœba all parts of the individual are sensitive to all sorts of stimuli and the whole individual responds to them. In slightly more complex organisms, where a number of cells have banded together for their mutual advantage, there is a specialization in function. The surface cells receive and transmit stimuli while the interior cells respond to bring about the changes necessary for the survival of the organism. In still more complex organisms, including our own, there is a further specialization in function. All such organisms begin as mere aggregations of cells which become differentiated into a surface layer, highly sensitive to stimuli, and a less sensitive interior. As the individual develops, part of this surface layer remains on the outside and develops into the skin and the various sense organs. Another part is folded in and buried among the less sensitive cells. This becomes the nervous system. The buried part of the original sensitive surface layer specializes in the transmission of stimuli just as the exposed part specializes in their reception.

In animals organized on the radial principle, such as jellyfish and allied forms, the nerves form a continuous net. In those organized along axial lines, which includes all long, bilaterally symmetrical beings from worms to men, there is an axial nervous system. This means that there is a main trunk of nerves running down the center line of the animal with branches leading off from it to the various organs. From our point of view, these organs may be divided into two classes, the receptors, such as eyes, nose, and ears, which are in touch with the outside world and receive stimuli from it, and the effectors, such as the muscles, which act to bring about changes adapting the individual to his immediate surroundings. The function of the nerves is to carry stimuli from the receptors to the effectors much as a telephone line carries messages from one person to another.

The link-up of receptor, conductor, and effector is known as the *reflex arc* and is the mechanical basis of behavior in all organisms advanced enough to have nervous systems. In those which have axial nervous systems, the structure of the conductor part of this circuit is highly complicated. The nerves which link receptor and effector are composed of a series of specialized cells, *neurons,* whose ends approach but do not actually join each other. The gaps between the neurons are called *synapses* and play a vital part in all the more complicated forms of behavior. Neurons are so organized that they will carry impulses in only one direction. The impulse started by a stimulus impinging on one of the receptors passes along the connecting neuron at the rate of about 400 feet a second until it comes to a synapse, which it jumps, passing on into another neuron, and so on until it reaches the effector. At the synapses there is a resistance of some sort which affects the impulse. It may be slowed down or even blocked at the point. It may also be deflected to any one of several neurons, if their ends lie close enough, or split so that it continues to travel down several of them simultaneously to different effectors. However, the resistance to impulses offered by the synapses diminishes with use. The oftener a synapse has been jumped, the easier it is for the next impulse to jump it. This wearing of paths through the synapses is the neurological basis of learning and habit formation.

In the more complex organisms, such as our own, there is a constant reception of varied and often conflicting stimuli. The impulses arising from these stimuli have to be sorted out and directed to ensure the sort of reaction which will be most profitable to the whole body. The conductors of the various reflex arcs are therefore routed through various *reflex centers,* which serve somewhat the functions of a telephone central. In these centers the ends of many neurons are brought close together so that the incoming impulses can be sorted out, switched from one line to another or distributed. Just how the reflex centers distinguish between impulses, inhibit some, and direct others is still a profound secret, but they do this in frogs and philosophers alike. The mechanics of the reflex arcs and reflex centers are the same in all animals having axial nervous systems.

The main trunk of an axial nervous system (in vertebrates, the spinal cord) is itself a reflex center. All impulses are routed through it on their way from receptor to effector. However, within this trunk there are specialized areas which have superior powers of discrimination. These might be compared to district, as opposed to local, telephone centrals. In axially organized animals one of these superior reflex centers is always located at the forward end of the main nerve trunk, in the head, where it is in close touch with the specialized sense organs also located there. In vertebrates this forward reflex center, the brain, dominates the other reflex centers. To continue the telephone simile, the brain is a sort of super-central which leaves routine business to the district centrals in the spinal cord and elsewhere but which has forwarded to it all calls which are of uncertain significance or which seem to require special action.

The dominance of the brain over the other reflex centers was much less marked in the early vertebrates than in the later ones. In some of the dinosaurs, for example, the brain was actually smaller than the reflex center at the rear end of the body. One of the most important features of vertebrate evolution has been the increase in brain size relative both to the size of the body and to the size of the other reflex centers. Coupled with this there has been a steady increase in complexity of brain structure and in specialization of function within the brain.

In the lower vertebrates the brain functions mainly in the direct reception of stimuli from the sense organs and in making automatic adjustments to these stimuli. At the amphibian level a new division of the brain appears, the *cerebrum*. This specializes in more complex and selective reactions. As we come up the evolutionary scale, the cerebrum increases in size in relation to the other parts of the brain and more and more takes over the function of directing the individual. In primates and especially in man it quite overshadows the rest of the brain and takes care of the organism's activities, with the exception of a few simple necessary ones such as breathing, swallowing, and changing the size of the pupil of the eye.

The cerebrum is made up of an enormous number of neurons set in a bed of connective tissue. There are at least 10,000,000,000 of these in the brain of a normal human being. Each neuron is separated from its neighbors by synapses. The paths of impulses through this maze of neurons and synapses are not organized at birth but are established by the process of path-wearing already described. Every time an impulse passes through the cerebrum on its way from receptor to effector a large number of neurons and synapses are involved and there is a change of some sort in the cerebral structure. These changes are the structural basis of memory and habit in the individual. The cerebrum is a specialized organ for learning and also for those higher forms of selection and integration of stimuli which we call thought.

The nervous system is the foundation of behavior, and, as far as we can determine by any means now at our disposal, there is nothing distinctive in the human nervous system. In this just as in every other part of their physical structure men fit squarely into the general mammalian patterns. Even the human brain is almost identical with the anthropoid brain. We must grant that the structural and mechanical elements underlying behavior are the same in men and in animals. Let us see whether the uses to which this equipment is put differ in the two cases.

All behavior consists of *reflexes*, combinations of stimulus and reaction made possible by the structural and mechanical features just described. Reflexes are of two types, *unconditioned* and *conditioned*. In *unconditioned reflexes* the path of the impulse from receptor to effector is already established when the individual is hatched or born. The link-up of the elements within the reflex arc is hereditary, like any other part of the individual's physical structure. In *conditioned reflexes* the path of the impulse from receptor to effector is not determined at birth. The link-up of the elements within the reflex arc comes as a result of selection and routing of impulses within the reflex centers coupled with the gradual wearing of paths through the synapses. The unconditioned reflex is the foundation of automatic or instinctive behavior, the conditioned reflex the foundation of learned behavior. All animals with nervous systems have reflexes of both types, but the relation which the reflexes of each type bear to the total behavior of the individual varies tremendously with the kind of animal. For example, insects owe most of their behavior to unconditioned reflexes, while men owe most of theirs to conditioned reflexes.

It used to be believed that animal behavior was controlled by instinct, human behavior by a mysterious and purely human quality called thought. No psychologist holds this view to-day. What we call thought is really an integral part of behavior, for there can be no mental activity without muscular activity of some sort. The muscular activity may be reduced to the point where it can be detected only by the most delicate instruments, but it is there just the same. Thinking is as much a matter of reflex arcs as is the winking of the eye. It is based on a combination of unconditioned and conditioned reflexes and on the selection and routing of stimuli.

In a comparative study of the mental activities of men and animals, the investigator is handicapped at the outset by the fact that with animals there can be no recourse to the introspective method. If any student could be a white rat or a chimpanzee for half an hour he could give us a clearer picture of what goes on inside animals' minds than we are likely to get in twenty years of experimental work. As it is, we can only deduce the mental processes of animals from their behavior. If we approach the human mental processes from the same angle, the results are almost identical.

Let us take first of all the matter of learning, i.e., of establishing conditioned reflexes. In experiments at the University of Wisconsin the ability for learning mazes in white rats and in sophomores was tested and compared. The results revealed no important differences in the learning processes of the two groups, while in speed of learning the rats had somewhat the best of it. Of course maze-learning presents a problem of a very simple sort, with a solution dependent on trial and error and the establishment of habits through repetition. There is no need to establish complicated reactions.

Perhaps the most interesting experiments in animal learning which have been made to date are those being carried on at the time of this writing by Dr. Wolfe at the Institute of Human Relations at Yale University. Dr. Wolfe has been experimenting with young chimpanzees, using slot-machines which have been dubbed "chimpomats." By the insertion of poker chips, the chimpanzees get food. The chimpanzees have learned not only to insert chips, but to distinguish between chips of different sizes and colors, using each type of chip in the proper machine and inserting two chips where two were required. They learned the process first by imitating their human instructor and then by imitating one another. They have established associations between the chips and food which are so strong that they will work as hard to get the chips as to get the food itself. When chips are scattered among them in their living quarters, where there are no "chimpomats," they will select those which are of value and keep them until they are taken to the room where the "chimpomats" are. The stronger will also take chips from the weaker in very human fashion.

It is safe to say that if there are differences in the learning processes of men and animals these differences are quantitative rather than qualitative. Men may learn more or learn more readily, but they learn in the same way. It is in the solving of problems, where the individual has had no opportunity for learning, that the mental superiority of human beings is most evident, so let us see whether there are any fundamental differences in the human and animal thinking processes.

It has been held that the superior performance of men in solving new problems is due to their having imagination and reason, qualities which animals lack. Recent experiments make this appear improbable. Imagination is the ability to picture in the mind situations which are not present. Reason is the ability to solve problems without going through a physical process of trial and error. Reason would be impossible without imagination, for in reasoning the situation has to be comprehended and the results of certain actions have to be foreseen. The trials are made and the errors eliminated *in the mind*. If we study human and animal behavior from the same objective standpoint, it seems certain that if we allow these qualities to men we must allow them to animals as well.

When the young chimpanzees pick up the chips scattered in a room where there are no "chimpomats," selecting those which are usable in the machines and discarding those which are not, they show imagination. They must have some sort of mental image of the machines and of the use to which the chips can be put. Moreover, from their behavior in the face of situations new to them, we must allow them at least the rudiments of reasoning power. One of the best-known experiments used to determine this consists in putting a banana in the middle of a pipe, where the ape cannot reach it from either end. After trying direct methods and convincing himself that they are useless, the ape will take a stick and push the banana along the pipe, then go around to the other end and get it. Between the first direct attempts and the use of the stick there will usually be a period of physical quiescence during which the animal is mentally sizing up the situation. During this period mental images of the banana in various non-existent positions must be formed and various methods of getting it into one of these positions pictured, tested against past experience, and discarded, for when the ape begins operations once more he usually seems to have a clear idea of what he is going to do. Moreover, once the problem has been solved, the solution is remembered and the same thing will be done immediately when he is again confronted by the same situation. Apes can even go a step further and fit two sticks together to get a poking tool of the necessary length. In one instance a female chimpanzee confronted by the pipe-and-banana problem and given a pair of sticks which could be fitted together tried them singly and then gave up and began to play with them. When they fitted together by accident, she showed signs of considerable excitement, took them apart and fitted them once more, then used them to get the banana. Even after getting it, her interest in the sticks continued, and she kept joining and separating them until she had mastered the principle. It is difficult to see how the mental processes underlying such behavior differ from those of a man who makes a discovery and realizes its possible application. Apes will also coöperate in projects for getting food, showing by their actions that they are able to comprehend both the basic situation and what the other apes who are working with them are trying to do.

In all fields where exact tests can be applied, chimpanzees seem to have the same mental powers as human children three to four years of age. There is a strong presumption, therefore, that the differences in animal and human mentality are purely quantitative. The ape stops at a certain point in the development of the mind, while the human goes on. However, as the ape cannot tell us what is going on inside his head, the best that we can do at present is to render the Scottish verdict of "not proven." Even if there are qualitative differences in human and ape thinking, so many of the thought processes appear to be the same that no scientist would doubt that human thinking is a direct outgrowth of animal thinking. Human intelligence, like the brain which produces it, is the result of certain recognizable tendencies in mammalian evolution.

No one can deny that there are profound quantitative differences in human and ape thinking. The facts are too obvious to require exposition. At the same time, even the quantitative differences must not be overestimated. The complexity of normal human activities as compared with those of animals does not give us a just basis for measurement. In both men and animals most behavior is a matter of habit. Having learned to do a thing, we can thenceforth do it without having to think about it. Our thinking ability is only brought into play when we are confronted by new situations. The civilized man can do more things than the savage because he has had an opportunity to learn to do more things. All the tests which have been applied to the two to date seem to show that their innate mental ability is approximately the same. In the same way, men have better opportunities for learning than apes and this puts them far ahead. The superior mental equipment of men is responsible for the existence of this wealth of things to be learned, but the wealth has been produced by many brains working over many generations. It could not have been created by any one mind. The son of a civilized man, if he grew up in complete isolation, would be nearer to an ape in his behavior than to his own father.

CHAPTER V

THE BACKGROUND OF CULTURE

Human beings owe their present preëminence partly to their superior mental equipment but even more to the ideas, habits, and techniques which have come down to them from their ancestors. The child who is born into any society finds that most of the problems with which he is confronted in the course of his life have already been met and solved by those who have lived before. He has only to learn the solutions. If he does this successfully, he will need very little intelligence. This accumulation and passing-on of ideas and habits is often put forward as a purely human attribute, but here, as in all other phases of human existence, it is possible to show at least the beginnings of the thing at the animal level.

In the preceding chapter I described the mechanisms underlying unconditioned and conditioned reflexes and said that, while both are present in all animals having nervous systems, the part which each plays in the total behavior of the individual varies enormously with the kind of animal. Insects and vertebrates are the classic examples of this. These two forms represent the highest types of life so far evolved, and the members of both of these orders are capable of extremely complex behavior, but the insects have achieved this by the development of the unconditioned reflexes, i.e., instinctive behavior, while the younger vertebrates have achieved it by the development of conditioned reflexes, i.e., learned behavior.

There is no standard against which the relative values of instinctive and learned behavior can be measured. Each proves itself superior under a particular set of circumstances. Insects have very limited learning ability, yet certain species have achieved an adaptation to their environment better than that of most of the vertebrates. There seems to be no limit to the complexity of the behavior patterns which can be transmitted in the germ plasm. A mud wasp is hatched with instincts which enable her to build a nest, hunt spiders of a particular sort, sting the spiders in the exact spot which will paralyze them without killing them, store them in the nest, lay an egg with them, and seal up the nest. By the time the young wasp emerges the mother will be dead, yet the new wasp will repeat the process detail for detail. Some of the ants and bees have still more complex forms of automatic behavior and have developed upon these a communal life which functions more smoothly and efficiently than anything which men have produced so far. There is an old saying that the proof of the pudding is the eating of it, and that instinctive behavior suffices to meet the insects' needs is shown by their success in the struggle for existence. Insects are the only form of life which can compete with men on anything like equal terms. With all the resources which science has placed at our disposal, they cause us more loss and inconvenience than all other animals put together and we are barely able to hold them in check.

Insects have amplified their instincts and vertebrates their learning ability because in each case this was the line of development which was most satisfactory under the particular conditions. The possible size to which insects can grow is limited by the fact that their skeleton is external and by their peculiar breathing apparatus. The largest insects alive to-day are not much bigger than mice. This means that a given area can support many more insects than vertebrates and that the number of individuals in a species can be correspondingly greater. Moreover, insects are relatively short-lived and are produced in enormous numbers with only short intervals between generations. A single house-fly, if all its descendants lived and bred, would be the ancestor of 2,000,000 flies at the end of one summer. Under the circumstances, the individual insect counts for little in the continuation of the species. The need for adaptation in behavior can be met successfully by the ordinary mechanisms of free biological mutation and selection. Environmental changes which might threaten the existence of a species are spread over many generations. Individuals who respond to certain stimuli in a way favorable to their survival, doing this as a result of some mutation in the organization of their reflex arcs, pass this peculiarity on to their offspring. The species is so prolific that thousands of deleterious mutations can appear and be eliminated without threatening its existence.

Vertebrates have been confronted by a quite different situation. Their structure makes possible the development of large forms. The larger the form, the greater its food consumption and the fewer individuals a given area can support. Vertebrates are relatively long-lived. Moreover, although some of the water-living vertebrates are nearly as prolific as insects, the land-living forms breed slowly and in small numbers. The breeding rate of certain reptiles is at the upper limit for land vertebrates, yet it hardly overlaps with the lower limit of insect breeding. This slowing-down of the breeding rate of vertebrates on land is linked with the fact that the order began its evolution in the sea and, as a corollary, its members still have to pass the early stages of their development in a fluid medium. The earliest land-living vertebrates solved the problem by returning to the water to breed, like the modern frogs and salamanders. Later the difficulty was met by enclosing the embryo and the fluid necessary to it in a water-tight container, i.e., by producing eggs or by allowing the embryo to develop to an advanced stage within the body of the parent. In either case, the drain on the parent's vitality was considerable, and the number of offspring which a given individual could produce was correspondingly lessened. The same factors operated to lengthen the time between generations, especially in those forms which brought forth their young alive. As a result of all this, it has come about that while the average insect species is composed of a great number of short-lived, highly prolific individuals with short intervals between generations, the average species of land-living vertebrates is composed of a relatively small number of long-lived, slow-breeding individuals.

Under the conditions which confronted land-living vertebrates, adaptations in behavior could not be left to chance mutation and selection. The average species was not numerous enough to survive the huge wastage of individuals which this process entailed. The need was met by the development of ability for rapid change in the behavior of individuals, that is, by increasing the ability to learn.

The shift from instincts to learning as the main motivation of behavior must have been a long and gradual process. It was correlated with a gradual change in the relations between parents and offspring. Most reptiles consider that their parental duties have been completed when they have laid their eggs in a safe place. A few species guard their nests, and a still smaller number are said to protect their young for a short time after hatching, but no reptiles feed or tend their offspring. Birds, with very few exceptions, incubate their eggs and tend their young. Mammals bring forth their young alive, feed them from their own bodies, and tend them until they are well grown. In general, the higher the mammal in the scale of evolution, the longer the period of parental care.

Given the ability to learn, instincts are most useful to the individual at the beginning of his existence, before he has had an opportunity to learn. They tide him over the difficult initial period of adjustment to his environment. After this they become a liability rather than an asset, for they limit the possible range of adaptation in behavior. The more carefully and completely individuals are cared for during infancy, the fewer instincts they need. As the length and thoroughness of parental care increase, more and more behavior can be left to be developed through learning. In such long-tended forms as men and apes we find that instinctive behavior has been reduced to a minimum. In men, it seems to be limited to such things as breathing, swallowing, and grasping, which are necessary from the moment of birth, and to a few simple fear reactions.

In its inception, learned behavior seems to have been little more than an adjunct to instinctive behavior. For the first land-living vertebrates it was probably a stop-gap, a means by which the increasingly important individual could be preserved, thus saving the species from extinction and giving it a breathing space in which to develop new instincts. If so, it defeated its own ends.

The ability to learn, and hence to adapt individually, must have lessened the rigors of natural selection and thus slowed down the process of fixing any new favorable forms of automatic behavior that might arise. Learning in itself contributed nothing to the fundamental adaptation of the species to its environment, for the habits acquired in this way could not be transmitted through the germ plasm. If the land vertebrates had stopped at this point, they would probably have been outdistanced in the struggle for existence. Their ultimate triumph was due to their development of methods of transmitting learned behavior from generation to generation outside the germ plasm. They became able to learn not only from experience but from one another as well.

We do not know the exact point in vertebrate evolution at which the ability to transfer learned behavior from one individual to another first appeared, but it certainly did not become important until the development of warm-blooded forms which cared for their young. It was the long association between parents and offspring during the period when the latter were acquiring habits most readily that made possible the transmission of learned behavior on a large scale. As this association became increasingly close and prolonged, more and more of the parents' habits could be and were passed on to the offspring.

A necessary accompaniment to the transmission of behavior outside the line of biological heredity was the development of some method of communication between individuals. No matter how great an individual's capacity for imitating others of the same species, there had to be some way in which the individual who knew what to do could convey to the one who did not a sense of the situation and of the desirability of action. There can be no doubt that mammals and even birds do communicate with each other by means of movements and sounds. The apes in particular make a variety of vocal noises expressive of emotional states. Other apes within hearing will respond to these noises by showing similar emotions. The response is especially marked in the case of cries of rage or fear, which suggest danger of come sort. These sounds with their emotional responses play a considerable part in the transmission of behavior. The individual who is familiar with a situation transfers his emotion in regard to it to another individual who, if he has not already developed a pattern of behavior to fit that emotion, will imitate the actions of the first. The vocal sounds of the apes are made in the same way and with the same apparatus as human speech. At the same time, they can do little more than express and transfer emotional states. By a special cry the ape can convey a general idea of danger or food, but it cannot convey an idea of the form which either one takes or of the proper line of behavior. Its various sounds might be compared to such ejaculations as "Look out!" or "Ouch!" At present, the gap between men and animals in this matter of communication is wider than that in any other field of thought or behavior, and the evidence which might have enabled us to trace the evolution of language is lost beyond recall. Only the faintest foreshadowings of language exist at the animal level.

Unfortunately, the processes by which animals learn from each other are very imperfectly understood. Deliberate instruction even of the young by their parents seems to be rare, although any one who has watched a family of kittens or puppies brought up under their parents' tutelage can cite examples of what looks like teaching. Most of the transfers of behavior seem to be the result of imitation, the animal imitated being indifferent. The ability to imitate apparently varies tremendously with the species, the age of the individual and even with the individuals themselves. On the whole, adult animals appear to imitate less readily than young animals, and in some species they will not imitate at all. Thus adult cats make the same score in solving problems when they have seen other cats solve them and when they have not. Apes, on the other hand, readily imitate each other. If a chimpanzee is confined and allowed to see another chimpanzee going through a process and obtaining a reward, he will take deep interest in the proceeding and will even imitate some of the free ape's movements. When he is given an opportunity to attempt the same thing, he will make a better score than a chimpanzee which has not witnessed the procedure. Moreover, an ape will learn more readily from another ape than he will from a human being. In the "chimpomat" experiments already mentioned, the technique was learned nearly three times as quickly when the student watched another ape as when he watched a man.

Neither the processes of learning nor the extent to which adult animals can learn from each other are of great importance to this study, for the vital thing in the transmission of learned behavior has been the ability of each generation to take over the habits of the one preceding it. That young animals can learn very complicated patterns of behavior from older ones is proved by a great mass of evidence. There are dozens of recorded instances of this among domestic animals, and the behavior transmitted in this way is sometimes so peculiar that no other explanation of its appearance in the younger animals is at all tenable. One of the writer's friends had a setter dog which had learned to ring the door-bell when she wanted to come in, and two of her puppies, brought up with her, developed the same habit. Other puppies of hers, brought up away from her, never developed it.

In all mammals the total behavior of the individual is composed of three elements, instinctive behavior, behavior which is the result of individual experience, and behavior which has been learned from other individuals. It has been widely assumed that while human behavior owes most of its content to the last of these, animal behavior is built up mainly on the first two. We have little information on the real proportion of each element in animal behavior, but the results of Dr. Zing Yang Kuo's experiments on cats and rats [1] are highly suggestive. While these deal with a single item of behavior, the killing of small animals, this is so necessary to the survival of cats under wild conditions that we would expect instinct and learning from independent experience to play as large a part in it as in anything. Dr. Kuo reared some kittens with mothers who killed rats in their presence, others with no contact with rats until they were some months old, and still others with rats as companions. In the first group, 85 per cent killed rats before they were four months old. In the second group only 45 per cent became rat-killers. In the

[1] "Genesis of Cat's Responses to Rats," *Journal of Comparative Psychology*, Vol. XI, 1931.

third group no cat killed any of its companion rats or any strange rat of the same variety, although 16 per cent killed rats of other varieties. The importance of very early contacts between parents and offspring in establishing patterns of behavior in the latter was shown by the fact that kittens whose mothers killed rats in their presence before they were eight days old showed a higher percentage of rat-killers than those which had not had this experience. It is clear from the foregoing that cats have a hereditary tendency to kill small animals, but it is also evident that this tendency can be developed, directed, or almost completely inhibited by early conditioning. In this conditioning, the behavior of the parent in the presence of the offspring plays a very large part. There is a transfer of behavior patterns from one to the other, and the figures, 85 per cent of rat-killing with this transfer and 45 per cent without, seem to indicate that, in the final behavior of the individual, the transferred patterns play nearly as large a part as instinct and individual learning combined.

The ability to transmit learned behavior from generation to generation gave the mammals an overwhelming advantage in the struggle for existence. It became possible for them to develop and transmit a series of behavior patterns which were as definite as those provided by instincts but which were capable of much more rapid modification. The individual profited by his ancestors' experience without losing his own flexibility. Under such an arrangement not only could the individual vary his behavior to meet emergencies, but the transmitted patterns could themselves be changed easily and rapidly to meet changing conditions in the environment.

It has already been said that the main line in the transmission of learned behavior between individuals is that from parents to offspring. The members of each generation take over their parents' habits and pass these on to their own young with such additions or changes as may result from their own experiences. In every mammalian strain there is, therefore, a double line of inheritance. The physical structure of the individual and his instinctive behavior, which is directly dependent upon this, are inherited biologically. A large part of his learned behavior, on the other hand, is inherited socially. During the evolution of the higher mammals this social heredity has become increasingly important. In men it has assumed a dominant rôle in shaping the conduct of the individual.

As the importance of social heredity has increased, certain habits have come to be characteristic of groups of animals. This has been brought about by a process comparable to that which leads to the fixation of an instinct within a species. The propagation of learned behavior from one individual to others, unless it is speeded up by adults learning from each other, proceeds along much the same lines as the propagation of a biological mutation. The new habit arises in some one individual and is transmitted to the offspring. Its survival and final assimilation into the social heritage of the group is dependent on the environment. If the change in behavior which it represents is one favorable to survival, those who learn it will have more success in the struggle for existence. Conversely, if the habit is unfavorable, those who learn it will be at a disadvantage and will either relinquish it or be eliminated. Even if the transmission of habits among animals were strictly limited to a transfer from parents to offspring, a new and favorable habit would, theoretically, spread to more and more individuals in each generation until it became part of the social heritage of the entire species. Its dissemination would be more rapid than that of a biological mutation, for it would be transmitted by the parent to all the offspring, not simply to a mathematically fixed portion of them.

Actually, only a few particularly favorable habits are likely to become part of the social heritage of an entire mammalian species. Such species usually have a rather wide range, so that the individuals composing them are subject to a number of varied environments. A habit which would be desirable in one of these settings might very well be undesirable in another. Accordingly, we find that, within a given species the social heredity is not uniform but consists of a series of strains each of which is characteristic of one locality. The animals living in this locality and sharing in this social heritage will have certain habits differing from those of animals living in another locality and sharing in another line of social heritage. Examples of this are familiar to most naturalists. The local differences come out most prominently in accounts of the habits of game animals, perhaps because these have been more carefully studied. A single example will suffice here. All African lions belong to a single species. Throughout most of Africa lions hunt alone or at most in pairs accompanied by their partly grown offspring. In Kenya colony, however, they have taken to hunting in packs with a regular division of function. The pack spreads out in a surround and closes in, roaring, thus driving the game within the circle to a point where one lion lies quietly in ambush. Old hunters say that this is a recent development and that, within the memory of persons still living, the Kenya lions hunted in the ordinary way. They suggest that the change in the lions' methods may be due to a diminishing supply of game. Whether this is the real reason or not, it is plain that we have here a new pattern of behavior which has become established in a group of animals in a time so short that it cannot possibly be correlated with any change in their instinctive endowment.

Homo sapiens has the widest range of any mammalian species and the greatest ability for making rapid changes in both individual and group behavior. It is not surprising, therefore, that the social heredity of this species is broken up into a bewildering array of local strains, some of the habits running in each of these strains differing from those found in any of the rest.

No special term has so far been coined for the social heredity of animals. In human beings the social heredity is called *culture*. The term is used in a double sense. As a general term, *culture* means the total social heredity of mankind, while as a specific term *a culture* means a particular strain of social heredity. Thus *culture,* as a whole, is composed of a vast number of *cultures* each of which is characteristic of a certain group of individuals.

The ability of human beings to learn, to communicate with each other, and to transmit learned behavior from generation to generation outside the germ plasm, as one element; and their possession of a social as well as a biological heredity and the differentiation of this social heredity into a multiplicity of local strains, as a second element, are features which link man to the other mammals instead of distinguishing him from them. The diferences between men and animals in all these respects are enormous, but they seem to be differences in quantity rather than in quality. Men learn more readily, communicate more easily and completely, transmit more learned behavior from parent to offspring and have a greater variety of strains of social heredity, yet in none of these respects, with the possible exception of their ability to communicate abstract ideas, can we detect any intrinsic differences. In each of these things, the human condition is such as might logically be expected to result from the orderly working-out of tendencies already present at the sub-human level. At the same time, we must not fail to recognize that these human abilities, each of which can be traced back to the animal level, have by their interaction produced something new and unique. Every part of the modern automobile can be shown to be a modification or amplification of some appliance which was in use before the automobile was developed, yet the automobile itself is a new and distinct entity. In the same way, human culture, although it has developed from an animal background, is unlike anything to be found among animals. It has been produced by one of the mammalian species, but it, in turn, has made that species human. Without the presence of culture, conserving past gains and shaping each succeeding generation to its patterns, *homo sapiens* would be nothing more than a terrestrial anthropoid ape, slightly divergent in structure and slightly superior in intelligence, but a brother to the chimpanzee and gorilla.

CHAPTER VI

THE DISTINCTIVE ASPECTS OF CULTURE

In the preceding chapter I have attempted to show that the culture (i.e., social heredity) of human beings is an outgrowth of certain tendencies which are evident in vertebrate and especially mammalian evolution. It is unnecessary to invoke anything supernatural to account for it. At the same time it differs profoundly from anything present at the sub-human level. It would be foolish to attempt to list all the things which men have and animals have not, for their number would run into millions. We can content ourselves by saying that the social heredity of man differs from that of animals in its incomparably richer content and in its tendency toward progressive enrichment. Our studies of man's past show that, in spite of occasional periods of quiescence or even retrogression for certain societies, his social heredity has constantly increased in quantity and probably will go on increasing as long as he retains his present mental equipment. This does not seem to be the case with the social heredity of other mammalian species. Let us see what factors present in men but lacking in other mammals have been responsible for this condition.

One of the most important factors in advancing culture to its present condition has been *the use of language*. That human speech was evolved from animal cries can hardly be doubted, but we do not know when or how our own ancestors made the great forward step involved in symbolizing ideas by aggregations of sounds. Animals of many different species can be taught to establish an association between words and acts or things, as when horses or dogs learn to obey commands, but animals do not seem to make any use of this ability among themselves. Even the anthropoids, who have much the same physiological equipment for speech as man, cannot be taught to talk. They may learn the meaning of a fairly large number of words, but they never attempt to reproduce them.

Unfortunately, it is quite impossible to tell either the point in human evolution at which language first appeared or to trace the route by which it has been developed to its present efficiency for conveying ideas. We cannot deduce anything in regard to its beginnings from a study of sub-human or early human fossils, for the section of the brain which controls speech in men is present even in the anthropoids. However, language is so necessary to the existence of human life as we know it that it seems probable that it developed at the same time, if not before, such first steps in the human direction as the use of tools and fire. This would carry it back at least a million years. It is even more difficult to conjecture what the first languages may have been like. We have no knowledge of any language prior to about 4000 B.C., when writing was first invented. These earliest recorded languages were comparable in every way to those now in use, and we could hardly expect them to be otherwise. In comparison to the million or more years of human development, 6,000 years is only five minutes in the human day. By the time man learned how to write, the evolution of language had already been completed.

The languages of so-called "primitive" peoples also fail to throw any light on the problem of origins. There appears to be no correlation between the complexity of the language spoken by any particular group of human beings and the complexity of any other aspect of their behavior. English, in spite of its enormous vocabulary, has a very simple structure, while Chinese is still simpler. On the other hand, the languages spoken by many uncivilized peoples are very elaborate in structure, with a wealth of grammatical forms. Although we may be able to trace the changes and developments within a single group of languages, such as the Indo-European, over a period of 3,000 or 4,000 years, this throws no light on the evolution of language as a whole. The earliest Indo-European languages were as adequate vehicles for the transmission of ideas as any of their later derivatives.

The origin and evolution of language will always remain a free field for speculation. Shrewd guesses will be made, but it will never be possible to check them against facts. The functions of language are more readily ascertainable. It is an instrument for both thought and communication.

The functions of language as an aid to thought lie beyond the scope of this book and require only a brief mention. Apparently there can be no thought without muscular activity of some sort, and the associations between certain ideas and certain movements of the speech organs must be a tremendous aid in thinking. We do most of our thinking in words, or it might be more correct to say in sentences, and such thinking is accompanied by impulses sent out to the speech organs. In most of us these impulses are weakened and inhibited to the point where there are no audible results, but they are there just the same. Other forms of muscular activity may be substituted for speech in the thinking process, as in the case of deaf-mutes, but none of these offer the same facilities for dealing with abstractions.

It is as an instrument of communication that language has played its most important rôle in the building-up of human social heredity. Without the easy and accurate transmission of ideas which it makes possible, culture as we know it could never have come into being. Among animals, the lack of speech imposes narrow limits upon the possible content of the social heredity. An animal can show her young how to act in the face of a situation which has arisen. For example, by her terror and haste to hide or run when she and her offspring encounter a man with a gun she can impress upon her young a similar attitude of fear and similar forms of behavior. However, she cannot tell her young about men or guns in the abstract, and if the situation does not arise while she is with them she cannot transmit that particular item of her behavior to them. This means that everything that a parent has learned can very rarely be passed on to the offspring. Ways of meeting usual situations are transmitted from generation to generation, but, unless there is a lucky accident, each individual must learn to meet the unusual ones for himself. The fact that parents or other members of the group have been confronted by the same situation and have met it successfully helps him not at all unless one of these experienced individuals happens to be present.

Men, thanks to the possession of language, can convey to one another a clear idea of situations which are not present and of the behavior appropriate to such situations. This makes possible an enormous increase in the content of the human social heredity. The growing individual can profit by the total experience of the preceding generation and be prepared for unusual as well as usual events. Thus, though I have never been bitten by a poisonous snake or even seen any one else bitten, I know that such accidents occur and have a fairly clear idea of what to do in such a situation. With language the transmission of learned behavior ceases to be subject to chance. The knowledge possessed by each generation can be transmitted to the succeeding one as a whole.

To appreciate the importance of language in the transmission of culture it is only necessary to consider the condition of deaf-mutes who have not been taught any substitute for speech. The cleverest of them may acquire a certain amount of manual dexterity and learn, through imitating what they see, to carry on the occupational activities of their group, but great areas of culture, the whole field of religion for example, are permanently closed to them. Before methods of teaching them substitutes for vocal speech were developed, most congenital mutes were believed to be half-witted.

While human culture is indebted to language for the rich content which distinguishes it from the social heredity of animals, language itself is an integral part of culture. Speech is made possible by the structure of the human brain and speech organs, but the attachment of symbolic values to certain combinations of sounds and the ability to make these sounds do not constitute language. Language only comes into existence when two or more individuals have learned to attach the same values to the same sound combinations and to use these sound combinations for communicating ideas. The associations between sounds and ideas are purely arbitrary. The same sound combination may carry totally different meanings in different languages or a number of meanings in a single language, as in the case of our own *bare* and *bear*. Language is thus a form of transmitted learned behavior, and the individual must acquire it in the same way that he acquires any other item in the culture to which he has fallen heir. However, it is always one of the first items to be learned, and, once acquired, it becomes a key which opens to him the rest of the culture.

With language, it is possible for one individual to transmit practically the whole of his experience to another individual. However, this in itself would never have made possible the incredible richness of the human heritage. There are limits to the learning ability of any one person. Cultures can attain their wealth of content because they are carried by groups of individuals, i.e., societies. It has been said that Aristotle was the last man to be familiar with the sum total of the human knowledge of his time. After him, the accumulation became too great. Such a statement is absurd on its face, for by the time of Aristotle there were already thousands of cultures extant, and the existence, let alone the content, of most of these was unknown to him. He certainly did not know how to throw a boomerang or how to call a moose. Even if we take the total of human knowledge to mean simply the total knowledge embodied and transmitted in his own particular line of social heredity, the Greek, it is still impossible. Aristotle may have known all about Greek philosophy, literature, and art, but he probably did not know how to forge and temper a sword, or set a wolf-trap, or where mullet were thickest. The knowledge of these things was as much a part of Greek culture as were the plays of Euripides or the speculations of Plato, yet each of them was known, in complete and usable detail, to only a small part of the population which shared that culture. Society, then as now, was made up of groups of specialists, each group using and transmitting certain elements of the culture and leaving other elements to other groups.

It is doubtful whether there has ever been any one man who possessed a complete knowledge of the culture of the society in which he lived, and there is no necessity for any individual to try to acquire such comprehensive knowledge. The shoemaker can have the advantage of iron tools without learning the smith's trade, and the author can have his writings put into permanent form without troubling his head about the processes of type-casting, paper-making, and the like which are a preliminary to publication. Each member of a society need only acquaint himself with as much of its total culture as he needs to fit himself to fill a particular place in the life of the community. This means that the only limit to the possible content of a culture is the combined learning abilities of the individuals who together compose the society which bears it. Actually, this limit has never even been approached. No matter how rich or complex a culture may be, there is always room for new elements.

Language and organized social life have given man instruments for the transmission and passive preservation of cultures of any conceivable complexity. Social life has also worked to necessitate a much richer social heredity for men than for animals. Human societies are maintained by the training of successive generations of individuals and are thus in themselves a product of culture. It is doubtful whether men have even a generalized instinct toward gregarious life. At least, the need for company felt by all normal human beings can be adequately explained on the basis of the conditioning to companionship which all individuals receive during childhood. Individuals certainly are not born with any instincts for the special activities which are their contribution to the life of the group or for the formalized patterns of behavior necessary to the continuation of social life. All these things must be learned, and society is too delicate a mechanism for this learning to be left to chance and individual experience.

The social heredity—i.e., culture—of human beings has thus come to have a double function. It serves to adapt the individual to his place in society as well as to his natural environment. The social heredity of animals is only concerned with the second of these. Even in gregarious species the organization of the herd or pack is so loose that the individual can be left to find his place in it through experience and innate ability. The transmission of those items of behavior which are advantageous to the animal in its struggle for existence can also be left to chance. Actually, the social heredity of animals seems to be passed on mainly by imitation. The young animal sees its parent achieve some end which it wishes to achieve and copies the parent's actions. Whether the young animal will imitate the parent or not is optional with it.

In human life the society rather than the individual has become the primary unit in the struggle for existence. Men confront nature not as isolated units but as members of organized coöperative groups. The incorporation of the individual into the group and his training in one or another of the specialized activities necessary to the group's well-being has thus become the primary function of man's social heredity. As a result, every culture must and does include a series of techniques for group living and for the training of young individuals to such life. The minimum required content for culture is thus vastly greater than that required for the social heredity of any animal group.

This fundamental difference between the social heredity of man and that of animals can be illustrated with the aid of a pitcher of milk, a table, a kitten, and a boy. Given the milk on the table, the kitten may learn from its mother to jump on a chair and from there to the table-top, to knock over the milk pitcher, and to make a quick exit when it hears any one coming. The mother will not encourage it to learn any of these things. She may even hiss at it or strike it if it comes up while she is drinking. If the boy wants the milk, he must learn to go to his mother, wait quietly until he can attract her attention, ask for the milk politely, being sure to say "please," and, in case she refuses, conceal his disappointment. The kitten's training leaves her an individualist with improved techniques for a lone-hand struggle for food. The boy's training finds him an individualist and, if successful, leaves him a coöperative member of society. Of course such training never is completely successful. There are always a few points at which the individual fails to assume the culture of his group, and this fact has important repercussions on human life.

The complexity of the conditions under which men must live

as members of society is not enough to account for the rich content of even the simplest culture. Still less can it account for the seemingly universal human tendency to amplify culture and constantly enrich its content. Why men have gone on amplifying culture generation after generation is still an unsolved problem. We can only say that it is a result of what we may call, rather vaguely, the restless energy of the human mind. At all times and in all societies there have been individuals who were not content to let well enough alone and who have tried to find new solutions for problems which have already been met passably well. This is a very different matter from the search for solutions to problems which are new and pressing. Here there is the active spur of necessity, but there is abundant proof that the process of invention goes on even when this spur is not present. In fact, it seems to operate a little more successfully when the need for finding a solution is not too pressing.

If culture, like the social heredity of animals, were simply a means of ensuring survival for the species, its progressive enrichment might be expected to slow down and ultimately cease. All the problems connected with the continued existence of societies could ultimately be solved and techniques of maximum possible efficiency developed. However, this has not been the line of culture evolution. Every society has developed techniques for meeting all the problems with which it was confronted passably well, but it has not gone on from there to the development of better and better techniques along all lines. Instead, each society has been content to allow certain phases of its culture to remain at what we might call the necessity level, while it has developed others far beyond this point. No society has been content to leave the whole of its culture at the necessity level, and no society has elaborated all phases of its culture equally.

There is always a point beyond which further elaboration of behavior does not yield returns in increased efficiency which are commensurate with the labor involved. However, existing cultures show that such limits bear little relation to culture growth. All societies have elaborated their responses to certain situations to a point beyond that of maximum relative utility. Even in the case of tools and utensils, where the disadvantages of such a course would seem most obvious, we have plenty of examples of quite unnecessary expenditure of labor and materials. Hundreds of tribes ground and polished their stone axes completely, although such instruments cut no better than those ground only at the bit and are actually more difficult to haft. The Imerina of Madagascar make their spade-handles of fine cabinet woods, palisandre, spotted ebony, and the like. Such handles are neither more nor less efficient in use than those of ordinary wood, and the trees from which they are made do not grow in the tribe's territory. A good spade-handle will cost a laborer in the rice fields a week's wages and its purchase will entail short rations for several weeks. To come closer home, no one would suggest that the formal silver services which we use at banquets are more efficient for the business of eating than the simple knife, fork, and spoon from which they have been developed.

It is true that such refinements may have an esthetic value or may serve to give the owner social prestige, but this does not answer the problem of why they have been developed. They satisfy esthetic needs or give prestige because of the values which the society has attached to them rather than through any inherent qualities. The Indian or the archæologist may derive an esthetic pleasure from a fully polished stone axe, but it has no such effect on the farmer who finds it and throws it into his fence corner. To a group trained to eat with carefully washed hands, the banquet service would appear unclean and its exhibition on the table an act of vulgar ostentation, lowering rather than raising the owner in their estimation.

Similar tendencies toward unnecessary elaboration can be observed in all other phases of culture. Some societies have developed an extreme elaboration and formalization of the rules governing the behavior of their members toward each other. Such elaborations contribute somewhat to the ease of social intercourse, but they impose a real burden upon the individual both in the labor of learning them and in the constant attention and frequent thwarting of personal inclinations which they call for. Even if they make for greater ease of existence within the society, they do not seem to give the society as a whole any noticeable advantage over other societies in which the regulations are less elaborate and formal. The Comanche, for example, had a social organization of extreme simplicity with a minimum of formal, clearly defined social behavior patterns. Most of the tribes with which they were in contact had much more elaborate social systems and a much greater body of etiquette, yet the Comanche were able to defeat them and drive them out. Comanche culture was low in content but high in efficiency.

In the field of religion this tendency toward needless elaboration is even more marked. The variety of religious beliefs and practices is almost infinite, yet the system developed by each society appears to meet all its members' needs. Some groups have developed elaborate creeds and philosophies, while others have barely attempted to rationalize the rites which they perform, yet the satisfaction to the worshiper seems to be the same in both cases. It would be hard to find a greater contrast than that between the simple creed of early Islam and the contemporary Hindu philosophy, yet each served its purpose and the Mohammedans conquered the Hindus.

In rare cases the elaboration of certain phases of culture is even carried to the point where it becomes actively injurious and endangers the existence of the society. The Jews of the classical period increased their strictures on Sabbath activity until they were unwilling even to defend themselves on that day. This contributed considerably to their subjugation, since the Romans were quick to take advantage of it. The medieval Japanese sacrificed strategy to courtesy in their warfare. When armies met, champions came out from either side, introduced themselves and gave a brief résumé of their ancestry and previous exploits. The champion's antagonist heard him out politely but was allowed to interrupt if the champion made a misstatement; in fact to catch him in an error and thus embarrass him was considered an excellent start for the combat. Only when both men had had their say was battle joined, and as long as neither one was getting the worst of it no other warriors interfered. When the Japanese encountered the less sportsmanlike but more practical Mongols.

they lost heavily in champions cut to pieces before they were ready to fight.

The examples just given represent cases in which over-elaborations of culture put societies at a disadvantage in competition with outsiders. However, a few cases have been recorded of elaboration carried to the point of actual injury when there was no outside interference. Many Eskimo tribes prohibit the hunting of seals in summer. Although this means little under ordinary circumstances, there are times when it is highly injurious. It is said that if land game fails a tribe will often starve when there are plenty of seals in sight. This taboo even extends to bringing the flesh or skins of land and sea animals into contact and is thus a constant source of inconvenience. A still more curious example of such over-elaboration is reported from Australia. The natives in some parts of that continent appear to be obsessed with social organization and prohibit marriage between many different classes of relatives. It is said that in one tribe these regulations were worked out to the point where no one in the tribe could properly marry any one else. The situation was finally met by an informal recognition of improper matings if these were accompanied by elopement and absence from the tribe until a child had been born.

This tendency toward unnecessary and in some cases even injurious elaboration of culture is one of the most significant phenomena of human life. It proves that the development of culture has become an end in itself. Man may be a rational being, but he certainly is not a utilitarian one. The constant revision and expansion of his social heredity is a result of some inner drive, not of outer necessity. It seems that man enjoys playing with both his mind and his muscles. The skilled craftsman is not content with endless repetitions. He takes delight in setting and solving for himself new problems of creation. The thinker derives pleasure from speculating about all sorts of things which are of no practical importance, while the individuals who lack the ability to create with either hand or mind are alert to learn new things. It seems probable that the human capacity for being bored, rather than man's social or natural needs, lies at the root of man's cultural advance.

CHAPTER VII

SOCIETY

The phenomena of social life have been studied from many different angles, and society has been defined in many different ways. According to the dictionary a definition is a brief description or explanation, and all definitions of society are of necessity descriptive. Since all objects or phenomena have multiple qualities, no descriptive definition can ever be complete, and the test of a good definition is whether it selects for emphasis those qualities which are pertinent to the work in hand. Thus a particular cobble-stone may be quite truthfully described as a smooth, heavy object, a piece of quartzite, or a relic of glacial action. The first description is pertinent from the point of view of the farmer who is looking for something with which to block a door, the second from that of a mineralogist, and the third from that of a geologist. Similarly, society may be correctly defined in a number of different ways, but for our present purposes a simple, colloquial definition will suffice. A *society* is any group of people who have lived and worked together long enough to get themselves organized and to think of themselves as a social unit with well-defined limits.

The life of thoroughly organized, stabilized societies is so complex that it is difficult to determine which of the many elements present are really vital to the society's existence. It is better to begin our analysis by watching the development of societies. We can thus ascertain their starting points and the elements which are added as the development goes on. The process can be observed wherever individuals who have been brought together more or less casually and accidentally continue to live and work together. Army units, ship forecastles, and lumber gangs are cases in point. Such groups fall short of ideal conditions in two respects. They normally include individuals of only one sex, while ordinary societies include both sexes. Also, their organization is more or less influenced by patterns for such groupings which already exist in our culture. However, the transformation of such aggregates into societies throws into sharp relief the minimum conditions necessary to the existence of a society.

The foundation of every society is an aggregate of individuals. This provides the raw material from which the society, as such, may be developed. Equally basic to the existence of the society is the persistence of this aggregate in time. Unless the association between the aggregate's component individuals endures for a considerable period, the integrative forces which will ultimately transform the aggregate into a society will have no opportunity to act. Thus a crowd brought together for a football game constitutes an aggregate, but it does not constitute a society. Its members are closely related in space and are temporarily united by a common interest. They even have a small series of responses to particular stimuli in common and will all react to certain happenings, say a long end-run, in much the same way. However, any organization or sense of unity which they may have is of a fleeting and superficial sort. As soon as the game is over, the aggregate dissolves. The crowd's persistence in time is too short to permit of its metamorphosis into a society. The same crowd, if marooned for six months on an unpeopled island, would transform itself into a society as its members developed a series of common ideas and interests, of habitual attitudes toward each other, and of techniques for living and working together.

Any one who has observed the transformation of chance-determined aggregates into societies will testify that there are two fundamental processes involved: (1) the adaptation and organization of the behavior of the component individuals and (2) the development of a group consciousness, a feeling of unity which, for lack of a better term, we will call *esprit de corps*. The transformation normally begins with a division of the activities necessary to the immediate well-being of the group and their assignment to particular individuals. This process is often unconscious and often proceeds on a trial-and-error basis until the various members of the aggregate have found the work which is most congenial to them or which they can do best. As the division of activities is worked out and stabilized, there is a corresponding increase in the mutual dependence of the group's members and a development of habitual attitudes and patterns of behavior between individuals. Their conduct toward one another becomes increasingly predictable and their coöperation increasingly complete and effective.

This mutual adaptation in individual behavior and attitudes transforms the aggregate into a functional whole and enables it to do most of the work of a society. However, the creation of a society as a self-conscious entity requires something more than the training of its component members to work together. Any officer who has the task of transforming a group of recruits into an army unit knows that he can get them perfect in drill and formal coöperation long before it is safe to lead them into battle. Under stress the company cannot be trusted to behave as a unit until its members have developed a certain psychological unity, a community of ideas and values as well as habits. It is this psychological and emotional unity, the *esprit de corps,* which ensures common emotional reactions and makes the individual willing to sacrifice his own interests to those of the whole and to do the things which need to be done even when there is no one watching him. Since life in any society requires a good many sacrifices of personal inclination and considerable voluntary coöperation, no society can run smoothly or function with real efficiency unless its members have developed *esprit de corps.*

The contagion of emotions and their heightening through group participation are familiar to all of us through personal experience, although the mechanisms responsible for them are very imperfectly understood. Emotions will run through crowds, being heightened in the various individuals by the fact that they are part of the crowd, and making these individuals behave as they would not behave if isolated. This induction of emotions, in less violent and obvious form, is constantly at work among the members of a society. Ideas and emotions are reinforced in each individual by his contacts with other individuals who share them. The more completely such things are shared by every one in the group, the surer each member becomes that they are right. The dictum that "fifty million Frenchmen can't be wrong," given by one of them, is a slightly naïve expression of this condition. It is the sharing of a mass of ideas and emotional responses by the members of a society which gives the society its *esprit de corps* and with it unity of will and capacity for voluntary united action.

When any aggregate has reduced its members' coöperation to habitual, voluntary patterns and has developed *esprit de corps* it must be classed as a society. However, this transformation leaves its members entirely unaffected on the physical level. There is no test known to the physical sciences by which the army company can be distinguished from the original aggregate of raw recruits. This fact at once invalidates all attempts to arrive at an understanding of the nature of society or of social processes by reasoning from organic analogies. Societies and living organisms do present certain superficial similarities, but the two owe their existence to totally different types of adjustment in their component elements. Organisms come into existence through the development of specialization and interdependence in aggregates of cells. There is a physical adaptation of the component individuals which is so complete that the cell cannot exist without its organism. In societies the component individuals remain physically unaffected. Their specialization and interdependence are achieved through psychological adaptation. A society, as distinct from the aggregate which is its physical foundation, is an organization of mutually adapted personalities. Its integration takes place at the psychological level.

The integration which can be achieved through psychological adaptation of the component individuals is much less complete than that which is achieved in the organism through physical adaptations. This becomes apparent when we observe the different ways in which societies and organisms react to external stimuli. The members of any normal society have a stock of associations in common, and hence certain stimuli may elicit the same basic emotional response, say fear, in all of them. However, the expression of this emotion in behavior will differ from individual to individual. These overt expressions may be altered and coördinated through training, but there is no automatic coördination. Unless the situation has been foreseen and trained for, the members of the society will behave as individuals. Note the conduct of the members of the ordinary family when they discover the house is on fire.

If we turn from simple emotional reactions to more complex forms of response, we find that societies have still less capacity to react as wholes. Although the entire society may be made acutely uncomfortable by some situation for which it is not prepared, the problem of how to meet this situation is left to the minds of the component individuals. The interchange of ideas which language and close contact make possible may hasten the finding of a solution, but no society as a whole ever produced an idea. When a new idea does not spring from a single mind it is, at most, the product of a small group of minds which have temporarily pooled their efforts. Even in the acceptance of ideas societies never show an immediate and total response. There is always some one individual or a very small group of individuals who are the first to accept or definitely reject the new thing, and their reaction is followed by a gradual transmission of their attitudes to the rest of the society. Certain die-hard individuals may hold out against the new thing for years. Lastly, learning remains from first to last an individual matter. In short, the processes of specialization and integration in societies never progress to the point where they provide the society with anything corresponding to a mind.

No matter how thoroughly the persons who compose a society may have been trained, they remain individuals, distinct physical and psychological entities. They may have a store of associations and emotional responses in common and reduce most of their complementary activities to matters of unconscious habit, yet they retain the capacity for independent thought, feeling, and action. Although the individual is dominated and shaped by his social environment he is not obliterated by it. Under favorable conditions he can even change and mold it. Thus the personality of an outstanding individual, such as a successful religious leader, may leave a mark upon his society which will endure for generations.

It will be evident from the foregoing that the integrative forces which produce society operate at the emotional and behavioral levels, rational activities remaining in the hands of the component individuals. Although both *esprit de corps* and mutual adaptations in the behavior of the society's members are necessary to its successful functioning, it seems that the behavioral adaptations are of more fundamental importance. We have already seen that these adaptations take precedence in the transformation of aggregates into societies. That they are the real foundation of societies as functional entities comes out very clearly if we observe what has happened when conscious attempts have been made to change social systems or to establish new ones. Such attempts are a recent development in human history, linked with the rise of a realization that there are such things as social systems. Plato and Confucius were probably the first to try to draw up plans for ideal societies, although there have been many attempts since. Nearly all social planners have begun by constructing a skeleton system of ideas and values, designed to give the new society *esprit de corps* and a united will, and have trusted to the individuals who accepted these for the working-out of the minutiæ of behavior which would be compatible with the system. Wherever this method has been tested in practice it has become painfully evident that the average individual is incapable of doing this. People live mainly by habit, acting as they have been taught to act without stopping to think first.

The greatest difficulty which confronts a leader who seeks to develop a new society is that he has to start with persons who have already been trained to life in some other society. This training begins at birth, and by the time the individual is even half grown he has acquired a mass of unconscious habits adapted to the society in which he has been reared. These habits can be changed, as when an individual comes to live with a new society and is gradually incorporated into it, but it is almost impossible to change them unless the new society offers patterns of behavior which the newcomer can learn directly and objectively. When the new society lacks such patterns, each individual must stop and think each time before he acts. Moreover, what one individual decides is proper with relation to the basic ideas and values of the new society may not agree with what another individual thinks is proper. The result is endless confusion and involuntary interference, and the people who are attempting to develop the new society soon fall back into their old habits. This tendency can be observed again and again in the history of religious sects. Such sects usually have a well-defined group of ideas and values in common and a strong *esprit de corps*. Lacking patterns for the expression of these in concrete, predictable behavior, they nearly always end by reverting to the behavior patterns of the society from which the bulk of the converts have been drawn. These patterns may be reinterpreted and rationalized in terms of the new beliefs, but the patterns themselves undergo only minor changes in the process.

The only cases in which new forms of society have been established successfully have been those in which the plan for the new society has included a large body of concrete rules for behavior. Sects in which the founder and his immediate successors exercise autocratic control will acquire such a body of rules. Situations can be brought to the prophet as they arise, and the behavior which he prescribes in each case becomes a precedent for action in similar cases. Eventually the precedents become numerous enough to provide for the ordinary exigencies of group living, and converts can learn the new ways objectively and substitute them for the old. It is significant that the most successful of social reformers, Confucius, laid great emphasis on the behavior of individuals toward each other and included in his system a great body of specific rules for it. He was not content to develop a skeleton system of ideas and values but went on to work out the actual behavior which would be congruous with such a system. As a result, he has influenced Chinese society profoundly for over 2,000 years.

It is only under unusual conditions that the transformation of aggregates into societies can be observed. Most societies are continuums persisting for hundreds or thousands of years. Their beginnings are lost in the past, and their ends come only when the individuals who compose them are killed or scattered. The perpetuation of the aggregate which constitutes the society at the biological level is ensured by biological means. The society's members marry and beget children. The perpetuation of the society as a functional entity is ensured by the transmission from generation to generation of the common stock of ideas and values which give the group its *esprit de corps* and of the mutual adaptations in behavior which make it possible for the members of the group to live and work together. Under such circumstances the perpetuation of *esprit de corps* is easy. The association of the society's members endures from birth to death, and the individual acquires his society's ideas and values as a part of his general development. They are usually taken so much for granted by both the individual and the society that individual and society are hardly conscious of their existence. Such a concept as that of the inferiority of women will be tacitly accepted by both sexes, and if they think about it at all some superficial rationalization will suffice. Again, the Polynesian, when he feeds any one who happens to come to the house at mealtime, is quite unconscious that he is reflecting values of generosity and courtesy which are deep-seated in his culture. He is merely behaving as it seems to him any normal individual would behave, and feeding a stranger gives him no feeling of conscious virtue. To this unconscious community of ideas and values there are added a consciousness of common interest and a wealth of personal associations which bind the group together still more firmly and give it unity of will.

The perpetuation of the mutual adaptations in behavior which make it possible for the members of a society to live and work together presents a more difficult problem. To understand the situation let us look at that in less complexly organized aggregates such as football teams. A particular team may survive for many years with a number of complete turnovers in its membership. It is perpetuated by a series of replacements, new men being brought in as old ones drop out. If it is to play successful football, these replacements must be trained not only in the general rules of play but also for the particular positions which they are to fill when they make the team. They must be sorted out while they are still scrubs and some trained to play in the line, others as half-backs, etc. Similarly, the perpetuation of societies as functional units requires the constant training of new individuals for particular positions in the society. The new members must be divided into various categories, and those of each category taught to do different things. The society must also develop more or less conscious patterns of what the behavior of individuals in certain positions should be so that it will have guides to the training of these individuals.

This matter of positions in society and the activities which go with them will be discussed in a later chapter. For the present we will confine ourselves to an attempt to understand the nature and significance of the patterns which are used as guides to training. That such patterns originate in remembered and rationalized behavior can hardly be doubted. Moreover, even after they have become established they can be modified as a result of changes in behavior. Thus our own patterns for the permitted activities of women have undergone marked changes in the last fifty years, and we can trace these changes step by step. Our society did not suddenly decide that respectable women could work in offices and begin training women to that end. Instead certain women, as individuals, decided that they wanted to work in offices and did so in spite of the fact that they were violating the accepted patterns for ladylike behavior. As women working in offices became an established fact, the patterns for ladylike behavior were extended to include this activity. Fifty years ago the average middle-class woman expected to be a wife and housekeeper and regarded having to make her own living as a calamity. In accordance with this she was trained for marriage and nothing else. To-day women of the same class normally look forward to holding a position of some sort in the interval between college and marriage and receive at least some training to this end.

If the ideal patterns upon which every society depends for the specialized training of its members were not subject to modifications of this sort, they would soon fail of their essential purpose. Every society is a continuum, and the environment in which it must function is never exactly the same at any two points in time. Behavior, if it is to be effective, must be adapted to the environment. Since the members of the society, in spite of their training, remain individuals with capacity for independent, unlearned response, such behavioral adaptations are fairly easy. When the behavior which the ideal patterns enjoin departs too far from that which is advantageous under the actual conditions, the patterns themselves change. If they failed to do so they would become a liability to the society rather than an asset, since individuals trained according to them would be in a worse position for meeting actual conditions than those not trained at all. Actually, we find in all cultures that the patterns are normally in process of change. They follow the trends of changing behavior but usually lag somewhat behind them.

In spite of their origin in behavior and their susceptibility to modification through changing behavior, ideal patterns are something quite distinct from behavior. As systems of ideas they become a part of the culture of the group and are transmitted from generation to generation by conscious instruction as well as imitation. While they guide society in its attempts to shape the individual, they are also guides to the individual in situations for which he has not been specifically trained. The fact that such patterns are conscious makes it possible for them to survive the interruption of their expression in overt behavior for a considerable period. Thus an Indian tribe may preserve the patterns for correct behavior between the leader of a war party and his followers for generations after all warfare has ceased. The old men tell them to the young men so that the latter will have them ready to hand if they do go to war. This consciousness of patterns as something distinct from the overt behavior for which they serve as models also plays a part in retarding the development of new patterns. The pattern itself gathers emotional associations and assumes value in the eyes of the society. While the expediency of forms of behavior which are not in accordance with it may be recognized and their practice tacitly permitted, the group is loath to discard any part of the old pattern or to give the new forms of behavior the stamp of its approval. The society prefers to regard the new forms as temporary departures from proper behavior and to insist that they will return to proper behavior as soon as the conditions are propitious.

This distinction between the patterns and the overt behavior for which they serve as models is made still clearer by the fact that the patterns rarely if ever achieve complete expression in behavior. In all social relationships there is an irreducible element of variation due to differences in the individuals involved in different cases. If the ideal patterns for such relationships are to find complete and repeated expression, the personalities of the individuals participating in these patterns must be cut exactly to measure. This is impossible. The infants from whom society must renew its membership arrive on the scene with inherent differences in physique, in intelligence, and probably in temperament. During their formative period they are subject to shaping not only by culture and by a limited range of personal contacts with other members of the society but also by a series of individual experiences which are often quite atypical. All these factors are reflected in their adult personalities, with the result that the combination of personalities brought within the scope of a particular pattern is never twice the same. Further complications are introduced by the fact that the actual relations of individuals who find themselves in any formal relationship will vary at different periods during the duration of the relationship. Thus the actual relations between a chief and his people will not remain the same even throughout the lifetime of one incumbent. It will vary with the chief's age, his physical condition, and the composition of the group which he rules. Similarly, the actual relations between a husband and wife will vary at different periods in their marriage. The wife may expect great things from her husband in the beginning and live to realize that he is a fraud or a failure.

Since the ideal patterns are built upon a presumption of constant conditions in the relationships to which they refer, while the actual conditions are almost infinitely variable, the chance of a pattern finding complete expression is extremely small. It can only achieve this through a happy combination of circumstances which will recur very infrequently. Nevertheless, the behavior in all relationships is strongly influenced by the ideal patterns. These patterns are constantly held up to the individual as models and serve to shape developing relationships into at least approximations of the ideal form. The variations in behavior which differences in the actual situation make expedient are oriented upon the ideal pattern and represent a compromise between it and the circumstances. Thus the whole society, including the chief, believes that he should lead his followers and look after their welfare and that his people should follow and obey him. If he is unable to perform his duties with entire success some temporary arrangement will be developed, approximating the ideal pattern where possible. Again, although no two marriages are ever alike, every society has a clear pattern of how spouses should act and feel toward each other. The spouses try to conform to this pattern, at least in public, and if they depart from it in private they take pains not to let the neighbors know.

Although the ideal patterns are carried in the minds of individuals and can find overt expression only through the medium of individuals, the fact that they are shared by many members of the society gives them a super-individual character. They persist, while those who share them come and go. The death of a particular person may interrupt the exercise of a pattern, but if this exercise is at all necessary to the well-being of the group the interruption will be only temporary. The pattern will still be known to many persons, and a new individual will soon step forward to occupy the place which has been left vacant and to express the pattern in overt behavior. An interesting expression of this continuity of patterns, as distinct from the individuals which express them, is found in English law. The English courts have ruled that the king is technically a corporation. The instant that a reigning sovereign dies the heir apparent becomes reigning sovereign, so that the exercise of the patterns for the ruler-subject relationship is never interrupted.

All this indicates that the ideal patterns by which the behavior of a society's members is organized are genuine entities.

The exact kind of reality which they possess can be left to the philosophers to determine. It must be of much the same quality as the reality of an often told story. The important thing for us is that the patterns behave like entities, influencing individuals and being in turn influenced by them and persisting while individuals come and go. They even possess a considerable degree of internal organization and are susceptible to objective study and analysis.

Every culture includes a series of patterns for what the behavior between individuals or classes of individuals should be. The essence of such patterns is reciprocity. This comes out very clearly if we take a pattern of the simplest type, say that governing the mutual behavior of brothers. A does certain things for B and holds certain attitudes toward him, but B also holds certain attitudes toward A and does certain things for him. Thus if A and B are an older and a younger brother, the behavior and attitudes prescribed to each by the pattern will be different but complementary. The pattern may prescribe that A shall protect B from larger boys, but it will simultaneously prescribe that B shall run errands for A. The expression of the pattern in terms of behavior requires action by both participants. A simple pattern of this sort is really a circuit of reciprocal behavior in which A and B constitute the opposite poles. There is a flow of benefits from each to each, and the failure of either party to exercise his rights and duties under the pattern breaks the circuit and prevents the expression of the pattern in this particular case. The pattern just cited is of the simplest type. Such patterns may be extended to include whole series of individuals and much more extensive circuits of reciprocal behavior. Thus under the pattern A may do certain things for B, who makes no direct return but does certain things for C, who consequently does certain things for A.

It is more difficult to trace this reciprocity in the patterns which govern the behavior of individuals or particular categories of individuals with relation to their society as a whole. Societies are so constituted that they can only act or be acted upon through the individuals who compose them. Thus any woman normally makes contributions toward the perpetuation and well-being of her society, but she can only do this by bearing children and helping other individuals. Her services to the society as a whole can be expressed only in individual terms. At the same time, the society makes certain returns to her simply as a woman, not as a particular individual. It sets up and enforces patterns of conduct toward women in general, as in our own rule of "women and children first" when the ship is sinking. The reciprocal behavior of the society must again express itself in individual terms. Everything that is done for the woman because she is a woman is actually done by some person or other. It is a particular man who surrenders his place in the life-boat to her. If he expresses the pattern, he will surrender his place even if he has never seen her before. In doing this he is acting as society's agent, submerging his own volition in that of his society as a whole.

Whole categories of individuals may occupy the same polar position in one of these reciprocal patterns. Thus we can discuss the behavior of nobles toward serfs and vice versa, since there is a basic pattern of how any noble should behave toward any serf in the particular society. This pattern is not nullified by the fact that a noble will behave differently toward a serf from his own estate and toward a strange serf. The patterns for master-serf behavior are simply superimposed upon those for the general noble-serf behavior. Conversely, every individual participates in the expression of a long series of reciprocal patterns. Thus in our own society a man may participate in one pattern as a doctor and in another as a taxpayer, both of these involving relations to the society as a whole. He will participate in still another pattern controlling his behavior toward women in general, in another toward children, in another toward his wife, and in still another toward his own children. Each of these patterns ascribes to him a series of rights and duties. As a doctor he is expected to render service to any one who is sick, while at the same time society recognizes his right to payment for his services and provides legal means by which he can collect. As a taxpayer he gives money to society but receives in return certain services, such as police and fire protection. Simply because he is a man he is expected to behave in certain ways toward all women, even strangers, while they are expected to behave in certain ways toward him. As an adult he is under obligation to help children in general and expects a certain amount of respect and obedience in return. As a husband he supports his wife while she keeps house for him, while as a father he supports and helps to train his children with the expectation that they will obey him while young and help him when he is old.

The sum total of the ideal patterns which control the reciprocal behavior between individuals and between the individual and society constitute the social system under which the particular society lives. Certain things must be done if the society is to survive, and they can only be done by individuals. Consequently, the patterns which control the activities of individuals must be adjusted in such a way that these activities can be carried on without mutual interference. There can be plenty of duplication in the activities assigned to individuals under the various patterns, but there can be no direct and constant conflicts or the society will be unable to function. A particular pattern must not enjoin conflicting duties upon the same person. Thus the ideal pattern for family life cannot prescribe that the wife shall be in constant attendance upon her husband wherever he is and at the same time that she shall stay at home and look after the children. It would be physically impossible for one individual to do both. Similarly, since every individual participates in a number of patterns, these patterns as wholes must also be adjusted to each other in such a way that they will not make conflicting demands upon the same person. Thus no social system could simultaneously prescribe that all male members of the society must spend one month a year in a monastery and that no husband should leave his wife alone for more than twenty-four hours. Actually, all social systems show a fairly close adjustment both in the forms of behavior prescribed by single patterns and between their various patterns as wholes. It is these mutual adjustments which make it proper to speak of the totality of the patterns controlling the life of any society as constituting a system.

Social systems are rarely if ever the result of conscious

planning. The average individual is not even conscious that the mutually adapted patterns which serve as models for his behavior constitute a system. We have already seen how patterns are derived from behavior and may be modified by it. If a new social situation develops, say the introduction of the employer-employee relationship into a society which previously lacked anything of the sort, the behavior between individuals standing in the new relationship will at first be unpatterned. However, the possible behavior of both employers and employees will be limited and circumscribed by the preëxisting patterns of the system. In time those standing in the new relationship will develop forms of behavior which are simultaneously effective in the new relationship and compatible with the preëxisting patterns. Such new forms of behavior are usually developed by the trial-and-error method, those which are ineffective or which produce conflicts being gradually eliminated. Finally, these new developments in behavior will be reduced to a pattern and incorporated into the social system.

The adjustments between the patterns which constitute a social system must be fairly close or the society will be unable to function. At the same time it is doubtful whether these adjustments are ever so perfect that no individual ever finds himself in a conflict situation. The best that any system can do is to make such conflicts rare. When they do occur, society regards them in a quite different light from conflicts between the inclinations or interests of the individual and the prescriptions of a pattern. In these the individual receives little sympathy from society, since his duty is plain and evasion of duty is always frowned upon. In pattern conflicts, on the other hand, the individual's duty is not plain. The whole group can comprehend the issues and participate in the emotions of the victim, and they sympathize with him accordingly. Legends based upon pattern conflicts thus have a universal appeal, and the *motif* is a frequent one in literature. The Greeks had their story of the House of Œdipus, conflicts of this type run like a thread through the whole of the Nibelungen-lied, and the Scotch have their legend, claimed by several clans, of the man who finds himself host to his clan's hereditary enemy.

In the preceding discussion we have tried to make it clear that societies owe their existence to a combination of three distinct elements: an aggregate of individuals, an organized system of patterns by which the interrelations and activities of these individuals are controlled, and the *esprit de corps* which provides motive power for the expression of these patterns. The aggregate exists at the physical level and the system at the psychological level. The system can find expression in the physical world only through the medium of the individuals who compose the aggregate, while without the system the aggregate would remain simply a group of individuals incapable of functioning as a whole. A social system is really a plan for society, and its relation to the society as a functioning entity is roughly comparable to that of the specifications for a machine to the actual machine built according to them. The specifications serve as a guide for the shaping of metal into a series of different but mutually adapted parts and for assembling these parts into a whole with certain potentialities for work. The specifications are something quite distinct from either the materials used in the machine or the power which sets it in motion, although if the machine is to work properly they must take both into account. Similarly, social systems serve as a guide to the shaping of individuals and to their arrangement in certain relations to each other, this combination of shaping and arrangement making it possible for the mutually adjusted individuals to function together as a society. The system is quite distinct from either the raw materials for society, the individuals whom it shapes and arranges, or the forces which set societies in motion. The former are provided by the normal biological processes of reproduction. The latter are provided by the volition of the component individuals reinforced by their association. The point at which the machine simile breaks down is, of course, that the part of the raw material, i.e., individuals, which is shaped according to the system is not their physical bodies but their personalities. However, as in the case of the machine, the system must take into account both the innate qualities of the materials which are to be shaped according to it and the forces which will set the completed whole in motion.

In the case of the machine the specifications are reduced to visible, tangible form through the medium of blue-prints. In the case of societies this step is omitted, although the individual's consciousness of the social patterns serves somewhat the same purpose. These conscious patterns serve as a guide both to the shaping of his own behavior and to his coöperation in the shaping of new individuals, such as children, who may come directly under his influence .It is through a combination of verbal transmission and the shaping of individuals to the patterns by other individuals that the social system is perpetuated. At the same time, no one person ever comprehends the total system of his society. As a rule he is familiar only with that sector of it which concerns him directly. We know that every society has a complete set of specifications, for we can observe their results and gather them from various individuals piece by piece, but these specifications are nowhere presented as a whole.

Societies owe their existence to a combination of physical and psychological factors and as such represent a distinct order of phenomena which cannot be correctly understood by reasoning from either physical or psychological analogies. They depend for their ability to function upon a long series of interactions between factors of both types, and most of these interactions are reciprocal, the factors which influence being simultaneously influenced. The conditions of social life are extremely complex, as are all situations connected with man and his culture, and their analysis is correspondingly difficult and uncertain. However, this in itself is no justification for assuming a mystic attitude toward society or positing such absurdities as a group mind or a group soul. A society is a group of biologically distinct and self-contained individuals whose psychological and behavioral adaptations have made them necessary to each other without obliterating their individuality. All life in society is a compromise between the needs of the individual and the needs of the group, and it has the indefiniteness and instability of all compromise situations. The development of social systems represents an attempt to fix and perpetuate these compromises, an attempt which is always doomed to ultimate failure. If societies existed *in vacuo* it might succeed, but it cannot do so in the face of ever-changing external conditions which throw their weight now on the side of the individual, now on that of the group.

It remains to say a few words regarding the phenomena of social conflict which preëmpt so much of the attention of the sociologist. These conflicts fall at once into two groups: conflicts between the individual and society and conflicts between segments of the society, i.e., class conflicts. All societies are witnesses to the former, and all cultures include a series of techniques for dealing with individuals who refuse to abide by the patterns. These techniques range all the way from collective ridicule, noncoöperation, or ostracism to elaborate methods of legal procedure with fixed and foreknowable penalties for every anti-social act. The important point is that these techniques rarely have to be brought into play. In all societies the average individual is successfully conditioned to the patterns he is expected to conform to and carries them out without any consciousness of external compulsion. It is the unusual which attracts attention, and for this reason the occasional thief or murderer is likely to loom larger in our thinking than the hundreds of honest men who never kill or steal.

Of course another element which contributes to this disproportionate interest is that the anti-social individual does present a problem, especially in our own culture. Due to certain of our culture values, the direct and obvious method of dealing with socially troublesome persons, that of eliminating them, sets up emotional conflicts and stresses in the group. In societies which do not attach the same emotional value to human life in the abstract, the career of criminals is likely to be brief. Thus among the Sakalava of Madagascar a first theft was followed by a careful investigation. If it could be shown that the offender had been driven to stealing by necessity, he was given land by the chief and allowed a chance to reform. If he stole a second time, he was speared, not in a spirit of revenge but because he had shown himself a social liability and the tribe did not wish to be bothered with him. The harassed modern taxpayer may even feel a touch of sympathy for such methods.

The culture of a modern society contains so many alien elements introduced from hither and yon that it is not one-piece and self-consistent. Look at the contradictory attitudes of outstanding thinkers regarding suicide, birth control, gambling, monopoly, and blood revenge. A simple society with a culture all its own and with no disturbing contacts with the outside, enjoys a success in conditioning its members no modern society can expect.

To turn now to the matter of class conflicts, such conflicts do not seem to be of profound significance to the study of societies in general. The class struggle is a special phenomenon which has developed in only a few societies and then as a result of a complex series of factors the most important of which has been a contemporary state of rapid cultural change. Most of the world's societies have not been even class-organized, and in those which were so prior to the sudden rise of machine industry the classes had, in nearly every case, reached a condition of satisfactory adjustment. This does not mean that there was an equal distribution of wealth or power or opportunity. It merely means that the bulk of the individuals within each class were contented with the *status quo* and that the classes did not come into active opposition to one another and were not antagonistic. Each of the classes really constituted a society in itself, the whole collection of societies living together in a state of symbiotic interdependence. The Indian caste system with its patterns of extreme economic interdependence coupled with amiable avoidance between its various social units is an extreme example of this condition.

Classes can scarcely be said to exist within any society until the individuals who exist at different social or economic levels have become conscious of their common interests and organized themselves. Our own much advertised social classes are much more real to those on the outside than to those on the inside. The agitators who lament the lack of class consciousness in the proletariat are prone to overlook the fact that this lack is equally characteristic of all our groupings based on economic status. Not one of these groups has developed any internal organization or any real feeling of solidarity. They are still mere aggregates

composed of individuals whose only common interests are those
arising from their common economic status. These individuals
come from different backgrounds and have different ideas and
habits. Even the content of these groups is shifting and uncertain,
and because of their members' lack of common cultural standards
it is almost impossible for the group to act as a unit.

It is obvious that the fewer the individuals in a particular
economic group the easier it will be, other things being equal, to
organize them, give them common cultural standards, and eventually transform them into a self-conscious class. The small group
of individuals who control big business and banking in this country are probably more conscious of their common interests than
the members of any of the other so-called classes, yet there have
been very few occasions on which they have been able to present
a united front. As individuals they disagree on many points of
policy, and when they do unite on any issue the union is rendered
precarious by their mutual jealousies and well-founded suspicions
of each other.

The lack of a definite aristocratic culture which might provide
the members of this ruling group with common ideals and standards of behavior and thus integrate them into a conscious society
is perhaps the most distinctive aspect of the modern condition.
Exploiters and exploited have existed since the dawn of written
history, but the only parallel to the modern situation is that of
Rome in the days of the late Republic. Here also power came to
be vested in the hands of a group of self-made men who had no
common standards and no feeling of responsibility to each other
or to the state.

Most of the world's aristocracies have arisen through conquest. In a surprising number of cases the conquerors have been
less numerous and less culturally advanced than the people they
conquered. Such invaders brought with them the integrated culture and conscious solidarity of the uncivilized tribe. They rarely
made any attempt to change the culture of the conquered, being
content to rule and exploit them. In the states formed in this way
the aristocrats formed one society and the commoners another,
each with its distinctive culture. The class struggle was thus really

a struggle between different peoples, the open fighting of the original conquest settling down to something like trench warfare in a quiet sector. As the two groups lived together they inevitably adapted themselves to each other by a series of compromises. The attitudes and forms of behavior which these compromises entailed became a part of the cultures of the two groups and simplified their relations. In certain situations the aristocrat could be counted on to behave in certain ways because he was an aristocrat and the serf to behave in a different but equally definite way because he was a serf. The aristocrat who broke the tacit agreement between his own class and the ruled by behaving out of character laid himself open to the same sort of disapproval from his own society as would have followed any other breach of its culture patterns. In their dealings with each other the members of the two classes could both feel that they stood on firm ground, and this made for mutual trust and effective coöperation if rarely for affection.

CHAPTER VIII

STATUS AND RÔLE

In the preceding chapter we discussed the nature of society and pointed out that the functioning of societies depends upon the presence of patterns for reciprocal behavior between individuals or groups of individuals. The polar positions in such patterns of reciprocal behavior are technically known as *statuses.* The term *status,* like the term *culture,* has come to be used with a double significance. *A status,* in the abstract, is a position in a particular pattern. It is thus quite correct to speak of each individual as having many statuses, since each individual participates in the expression of a number of patterns. However, unless the term is qualified in some way, *the status* of any individual means the sum total of all the statuses which he occupies. It represents his position with relation to the total society. Thus the status of Mr. Jones as a member of his community derives from a combination of all the statuses which he holds as a citizen, as an attorney, as a Mason, as a Methodist, as Mrs. Jones's husband, and so on.

A status, as distinct from the individual who may occupy it, is simply a collection of rights and duties. Since these rights and duties can find expression only through the medium of individuals, it is extremely hard for us to maintain a distinction in our thinking between statuses and the people who hold them and exercise the rights and duties which constitute them. The relation between any individual and any status he holds is somewhat like that between the driver of an automobile and the driver's place in the machine. The driver's seat with its steering wheel, accelerator, and other controls is a constant with ever-present potentialities for action and control, while the driver may be any member of the family and may exercise these potentialities very well or very badly.

A *rôle* represents the dynamic aspect of a status. The individual is socially assigned to a status and occupies it with relation to other statuses. When he puts the rights and duties which constitute the status into effect, he is performing a rôle. Rôle and status are quite inseparable, and the distinction between them is of only academic interest. There are no rôles without statuses or statuses without rôles. Just as in the case of *status*, the term *rôle* is used with a double significance. Every individual has a series of rôles deriving from the various patterns in which he participates and at the same time *a rôle*, general, which represents the sum total of these rôles and determines what he does for his society and what he can expect from it.

Although all statuses and rôles derive from social patterns and are integral parts of patterns, they have an independent function with relation to the individuals who occupy particular statuses and exercise their rôles. To such individuals the combined status and rôle represent the minimum of attitudes and behavior which he must assume if he is to participate in the overt expression of the pattern. Status and rôle serve to reduce the ideal patterns for social life to individual terms. They become models for organizing the attitudes and behavior of the individual so that these will be congruous with those of the other individuals participating in the expression of the pattern. Thus if we are studying football teams in the abstract, the position of quarter-back is meaningless except in relation to the other positions. From the point of view of the quarter-back himself it is a distinct and important entity. It determines where he shall take his place in the line-up and what he shall do in various plays. His assignment to this position at once limits and defines his activities and establishes a minimum of things which he must learn. Similarly, in a social pattern such as that for the employer-employee relationship the statuses of employer and employee define what each has to know and do to put the pattern into operation. The employer does not need to know the techniques involved in the employee's labor, and the employee does not need to know the techniques for marketing or accounting.

It is obvious that, as long as there is no interference from external sources, the more perfectly the members of any society are adjusted to their statuses and rôles the more smoothly the society will function. In its attempts to bring about such adjustments every society finds itself caught on the horns of a dilemma. The individual's formation of habits and attitudes begins at birth, and, other things being equal, the earlier his training for a status can begin the more successful it is likely to be. At the same time, no two individuals are alike, and a status which will be congenial to one may be quite uncongenial to another. Also, there are in all social systems certain rôles which require more than training for their successful performance. Perfect technique does not make a great violinist, nor a thorough book knowledge of tactics an efficient general. The utilization of the special gifts of individuals may be highly important to society, as in the case of the general, yet these gifts usually show themselves rather late, and to wait upon their manifestation for the assignment of statuses would be to forfeit the advantages to be derived from commencing training early.

Fortunately, human beings are so mutable that almost any normal individual can be trained to the adequate performance of almost any rôle. Most of the business of living can be conducted on a basis of habit, with little need for intelligence and none for special gifts. Societies have met the dilemma by developing two types of statuses, the *ascribed* and the *achieved*. *Ascribed* statuses are those which are assigned to individuals without reference to their innate differences or abilities. They can be predicted and trained for from the moment of birth. The *achieved* statuses are, as a minimum, those requiring special qualities, although they are not necessarily limited to these. They are not assigned to individuals from birth but are left open to be filled through competition and individual effort. The majority of the statuses in all social systems are of the ascribed type and those which take care of the ordinary day-to-day business of living are practically always of this type.

In all societies certain things are selected as reference points for the ascription of status. The things chosen for this purpose are always of such a nature that they are ascertainable at birth, making it possible to begin the training of the individual for his potential statuses and rôles at once. The simplest and most universally used of these reference points is sex. Age is used with nearly equal frequency, since all individuals pass through the same cycle of growth, maturity, and decline, and the statuses whose occupation will be determined by age can be forecast and trained for with accuracy. Family relationships, the simplest and most obvious being that of the child to its mother, are also used in all societies as reference points for the establishment of a whole series of statuses. Lastly, there is the matter of birth into a particular socially established group, such as a class or caste. The use of this type of reference is common but not universal. In all societies the actual ascription of statuses to the individual is controlled by a series of these reference points which together serve to delimit the field of his future participation in the life of the group.

The division and ascription of statuses with relation to sex seems to be basic in all social systems. All societies prescribe different attitudes and activities to men and to women. Most of them try to rationalize these prescriptions in terms of the physiological differences between the sexes or their different rôles in reproduction. However, a comparative study of the statuses ascribed to women and men in different cultures seems to show that while such factors may have served as a starting point for the development of a division the actual ascriptions are almost entirely determined by culture. Even the psychological characteristics ascribed to men and women in different societies vary so much that they can have little physiological basis. Our own idea of women as ministering angels contrasts sharply with the ingenuity of women as torturers among the Iroquois and the sadistic delight they took in the process. Even the last two generations have seen a sharp change in the psychological patterns for women in our own society. The delicate, fainting lady of the middle eighteen-hundreds is as extinct as the dodo.

When it comes to the ascription of occupations, which is after all an integral part of status, we find the differences in various societies even more marked. Arapesh women regularly carry heavier loads than men "because their heads are so much harder and stronger." In some societies women do most of the manual labor; in others, as in the Marquesas, even cooking, housekeeping, and baby-tending are proper male occupations, and women spend most of their time primping. Even the general rule that women's handicap through pregnancy and nursing indicates the more active occupations as male and the less active ones as female has many exceptions. Thus among the Tasmanians seal-hunting was women's work. They swam out to the seal rocks, stalked the animals, and clubbed them. Tasmanian women also hunted opossums, which required the climbing of large trees.

Although the actual ascription of occupations along sex lines is highly variable, the pattern of sex division is constant. There are very few societies in which every important activity has not been definitely assigned to men or to women. Even when the two sexes coöperate in a particular occupation, the field of each is usually clearly delimited. Thus in Madagascar rice culture the men make the seed beds and terraces and prepare the fields for transplanting. The women do the work of transplanting, which is hard and back-breaking. The women weed the crop, but the men harvest it. The women then carry it to the threshing floors, where the men thresh it while the women winnow it. Lastly, the women pound the grain in mortars and cook it.

When a society takes over a new industry, there is often a period of uncertainty during which the work may be done by either sex, but it soon falls into the province of one or the other. In Madagascar, pottery is made by men in some tribes and by women in others. The only tribe in which it is made by both men and women is one into which the art has been introduced within the last sixty years. I was told that during the fifteen years preceding my visit there had been a marked decrease in the number of male potters, many men who had once practised the art having given it up. The factor of lowered wages, usually advanced as the reason for men leaving one of our own occupations when women enter it in force, certainly was not operative here. The field was not overcrowded, and the prices for men's and women's products were the same. Most of the men who had given up the trade were vague as to their reasons, but a few said frankly that they did not like to compete with women. Apparently the entry of women into the occupation had robbed it of a certain amount of prestige. It was no longer quite the thing for a man to be a potter, even though he was a very good one.

The use of age as a reference point for establishing status is as universal as the use of sex. All societies recognize three age groupings as a minimum: child, adult, and old. Certain societies have emphasized age as a basis for assigning status and have greatly amplified the divisions. Thus in certain African tribes the whole male population is divided into units composed of those born in the same years or within two- or three-year intervals. However, such extreme attention to age is unusual, and we need not discuss it here.

The physical differences between child and adult are easily recognizable, and the passage from childhood to maturity is marked by physiological events which make it possible to date it exactly for girls and within a few weeks or months for boys. However, the physical passage from childhood to maturity does not necessarily coincide with the social transfer of the individual from one category to the other. Thus in our own society both men and women remain legally children until long after they are physically adult. In most societies this difference between the physical and social transfer is more clearly marked than in our own. The child becomes a man not when he is physically mature but when he is formally recognized as a man by his society. This recognition is almost always given ceremonial expression in what are technically known as puberty rites. The most important element in these rites is not the determination of physical maturity but that of social maturity. Whether a boy is able to breed is less vital to his society than whether he is able to do a man's work and has a man's knowledge. Actually, most puberty ceremonies include tests of the boy's learning and fortitude, and if the aspirants are unable to pass these they are left in the child status until they can. For those who pass the tests, the ceremonies usually culminate in the transfer to them of certain secrets which the men guard from women and children.

The passage of individuals from adult to aged is harder to perceive. There is no clear physiological line for men, while even women may retain their full physical vigor and their ability to carry on all the activities of the adult status for several years after the menopause. The social transfer of men from the adult to the aged group is given ceremonial recognition in a few cultures, as when a father formally surrenders his official position and titles to his son, but such recognition is rare. As for women, there appears to be no society in which the menopause is given ceremonial recognition, although there are a few societies in which it does alter the individual's status. Thus Comanche women, after the menopause, were released from their disabilities with regard to the supernatural. They could handle sacred objects, obtain power through dreams and practise as shamans, all things forbidden to women of bearing age.

The general tendency for societies to emphasize the individual's first change in age status and largely ignore the second is no doubt due in part to the difficulty of determining the onset of old age. However, there are also psychological factors involved. The boy or girl is usually anxious to grow up, and this eagerness is heightened by the exclusion of children from certain activities and knowledge. Also, society welcomes new additions to the most active division of the group, that which contributes most to its perpetuation and well-being. Conversely, the individual who enjoys the thought of growing old is atypical in all societies. Even when age brings respect and a new measure of influence, it means the relinquishment of much that is pleasant. We can see among ourselves that the aging usually refuse to recognize the change until long after it has happened.

In the case of age, as in that of sex, the biological factors involved appear to be secondary to the cultural ones in determining the content of status. There are certain activities which cannot be ascribed to children because children either lack the necessary strength or have not had time to acquire the necessary technical skills. However, the attitudes between parent and child and the importance given to the child in the family structure vary enormously from one culture to another. The status of the child among our Puritan ancestors, where he was seen and not heard and ate at the second table, represents one extreme. At the other might be placed the status of the eldest son of a Polynesian chief. All the *mana* (supernatural power) of the royal line converged upon such a child. He was socially superior to his own father and mother, and any attempt to discipline him would have been little short of sacrilege. I once visited the hereditary chief of a Marquesan tribe and found the whole family camping uncomfortably in their own front yard, although they had a good house built on European lines. Their eldest son, aged nine, had had a dispute with his father a few days before and had tabooed the house by naming it after his head. The family had thus been compelled to move out and could not use it again until he relented and lifted the taboo. As he could use the house himself and eat anywhere in the village, he was getting along quite well and seemed to enjoy the situation thoroughly.

The statuses ascribed to the old in various societies vary even more than those ascribed to children. In some cases they are relieved of all heavy labor and can settle back comfortably to live off their children. In others they perform most of the hard and monotonous tasks which do not require great physical strength, such as the gathering of firewood. In many societies the old women, in particular, take over most of the care of the younger children, leaving the younger women free to enjoy themselves. In some places the old are treated with consideration and respect; in others they are considered a useless incumbrance and removed as soon as they are incapable of heavy labor. In most societies their advice is sought even when little attention is paid to their wishes. This custom has a sound practical basis, for the individual who contrives to live to old age in an uncivilized group has usually been a person of ability and his memory constitutes a sort of reference library to which one can turn for help under all sorts of circumstances.

In certain societies the change from the adult to the old status is made more difficult for the individual by the fact that the patterns for these statuses ascribe different types of personality to each. This was the case among the Comanche, as it seems to have been among most of the Plains tribes. The adult male was a warrior, vigorous, self-reliant, and pushing. Most of his social relationships were phrased in terms of competition. He took what he could get and held what he had without regard to any abstract rights of those weaker than himself. Any willingness to arbitrate differences or to ignore slights was a sign of weakness resulting in loss of prestige. The old man, on the other hand, was expected to be wise and gentle, willing to overlook slights and, if need be, to endure abuse. It was his task to work for the welfare of the tribe, giving sound advice, settling feuds between the warriors, and even preventing his tribe from making new enemies. Young men strove for war and honor, old men strove for peace and tranquillity. There is abundant evidence that among the Comanche the transition was often a difficult one for the individual. Warriors did not prepare for old age, thinking it a better fate to be killed in action. When waning physical powers forced them to assume the new rôle, many of them did so grudgingly, and those who had strong magic would go on trying to enforce the rights which belonged to the younger status. Such bad old men were a peril to young ones beginning their careers, for they were jealous of them simply because they were young and strong and admired by the women. The medicine power of these young men was still weak, and the old men could and did kill them by malevolent magic. It is significant that although benevolent medicine men might be of any age in Comanche folklore, malevolent ones were always old.

Before passing on, it might be well to mention still another social status which is closely related to the foregoing. This is the status of the dead. We do not think of the dead as still members of the community, and many societies follow us in this, but there are others in which death is simply another transfer, comparable to that from child to adult. When a man dies, he does not leave his society; he merely surrenders one set of rights and duties and assumes another. Thus a Tanala clan has two sections which are equally real to its members, the living and the dead. In spite of rather half-hearted attempts by the living to explain to the dead that they are dead and to discourage their return, they remain an integral part of the clan. They must be informed of all important events, invited to all clan ceremonies, and remembered at every meal. In return they allow themselves to be consulted, take an active and helpful interest in the affairs of the community, and act as highly efficient guardians of the group's mores. They carry over into their new status the conservatism characteristic of the aged, and their invisible presence and constant watchfulness does more than anything else to ensure the good behavior of the living and to discourage innovations. In a neighboring tribe there are even individual statuses among the dead which are open to achievement. Old Betsileo men and women will often promise that, after their deaths, they will give the living specific forms of help in return for specified offerings. After the death of one of these individuals, a monument will be erected and people will come to pray and make offerings there. If the new ghost performs his functions successfully, his worship may grow into a cult and may even have a priest. If he fails in their performance, he is soon forgotten.

Biological relationships are used to determine some statuses in all societies. The mere fact of birth immediately brings the individual within the scope of a whole series of social patterns which relate him to his parents, either real or ascribed, his brothers and sisters, and his parents' relatives. The biological basis for the ascription of these family statuses is likely to blind us to the fact that the physiological factors which may influence their content are almost exactly the same as those affecting the content of sex and age statuses. While there is a special relationship between the young child and its mother, based on the child's dependence on nursing, even this is soon broken off. After the second year any adult woman can do anything for the child that its mother can do, while any adult male can assume the complete rôle of the father at any time after the child is conceived. Similarly, the physiological factors which might affect the statuses of uncle and nephew, uncle and niece, or brother and sister are identical with those affecting the relations of persons in different age or sex groupings. This lack of physiological determinants may be responsible in part for the extraordinarily wide range of variation in the contents of the statuses ascribed on the basis of biological relationships in various societies.

Actually, the statuses associated with even such a close biological relationship as that of brother and sister are surprisingly varied. In some societies the two are close intimates. In others they avoid each other carefully and cannot even speak to each other except in the presence of a third party who relays the questions and answers. In some systems the eldest child ranks the others regardless of sex and must be respected and obeyed by them. In others the question of dominance is left to be settled by the children themselves, while in still others the youngest child ranks all those who preceded him. Practically every possible arrangement is represented in one society or another, suggesting that we have here a free field for variation, one in which one arrangement will work quite as well as another. The same sort of wide variation is found in the content of all the other statuses based on blood relationship with the exception of those relating to mother and child, and even here there is a fair degree of variation. There are a number of societies in which there is a more or less conscious attempt to break up the child's habits of dependence upon the mother and to alienate the child from her in order to bring it into closer association with its father's relatives. The child is taught that its mother really is not a member of the family, and hostility between mother and child is encouraged.

Not only do the statuses assigned by different societies to persons standing in the same blood relationships vary markedly, but there is also a high degree of variation in the sorts of blood relationship which are recognized and used as reference points for the assignment of status. Some societies, like our own, tend to recognize only close relatives and to be vague as to the reciprocal rights and duties of any relationship more remote than first cousin. Others select the line of the mother or the father and utilize relationships in this line to remote degrees while ignoring all but the closest relationships in the other line. In a very few cases, relationship in both lines is recognized to remote degrees, with a consequent assignment of status. Where this is the case the statuses based on relationship may actually include a whole tribe and determine the mutual rights and duties of all its members. Thus in certain Australian groups recognized blood relationships are extended to include not only the whole tribe but numerous individuals in other tribes as well. It is said that when a stranger visits such a tribe the old men investigate his genealogy until they find some point in common with one of the genealogies within their own group. When such a point of contact has been established, they can determine the relationship of the newcomer to all the various members of their own group and assign him a series of statuses which immediately fit him into the social body. If they are unable to find such a common point of relationship, they usually kill the stranger simply because they do not know what else to do with him. They have no reference points other than blood relationships by which statuses might be assigned to him.

There is another type of biologically conditioned relationship which is recognized in practically all societies. This is the relationship arising from the more or less continuous sexual association of individuals, i.e., marriage. The real importance of such associations lies in their continuity, in social recognition, and in the new series of blood relationships to which they give rise through the offspring which they produce. Casual or temporary sexual associations usually receive only a negative recognition from society, being ignored when not actually reprehended. Patterns may be developed to govern the behavior of individuals in such casual associations, but these patterns are usually extremely limited in their scope. They only affect the individuals who are directly involved and do not establish new statuses for the members of the families to which the contracting parties belong. Marriage, on the other hand, always establishes a series of such statuses. Thus the parents of a man and his mistress do not become parties to any reciprocal pattern of rights and duties, while the parents of a man and his wife always do become parties to such a pattern.

While relationships arising from sexual association are intrinsically different from those deriving from blood relationships, the two types have become interrelated in all societies. Blood relationships are everywhere used as reference points for delimiting the group of individuals within which marriage relationships may be contracted. This regulation is usually of a negative sort, certain blood relatives being prohibited from marrying but at the same time permitted freedom of choice among individuals not standing in these relationships. However, there are a fair number of societies in which such regulations assume a positive aspect. In such societies a man is not only forbidden to marry certain female relatives, such as his mother or sister, but is also enjoined to marry within a particular group of female relatives, as his mother's brother's or father's sister's daughters. In some cases these prescriptions are so strong that a man may have no alternatives except to marry a particular woman or remain a bachelor.

The causes which underlie such limitations on marriage, technically known as incest regulations, are very imperfectly understood. Since these regulations are of universal occurrence, it seems safe to assume that their causes are everywhere present, but biological factors can be ruled out at once. Close inbreeding is not necessarily injurious. Even when hereditary defects in the strain may make it so, its deleterious results require a long time to manifest themselves. Moreover, the average uncivilized group is small and rarely marries with outsiders. Within a few generations the heredity of its members become so uniform that there is little if any biological difference between marriage with a first cousin and marriage with a fourth cousin. Neither are purely social explanations of incest regulations altogether satisfactory, since the forms which these regulations assume are extremely varied. The prohibition of marriage between mother and son is the only one universally present. Marriage between father and daughter is permitted in at least one society, the Azande, while several societies have recognized or even required marriage between brother and sister. This last seems to occur mainly in small ruling groups and seems to be designed to keep privilege and rank rigidly within the group. Thus in Hawaiian royal families brother and sister were required to marry and to cohabit until an heir had been born, although after this they might separate. It seems possible that there are certain psychological factors involved, but these can hardly be strong enough or constant enough to account for the institutionalization of incest regulations. This is proved by the fact that cases of incest between all the prohibited degrees do occur in all societies and that all societies have certain preventive regulations which would be unnecessary if the rules were self-enforcing. Incest regulations, once developed, are a valuable tool for preventing conflicts in the statuses held by individuals, but it is a little hard to imagine their invention for this purpose. They have probably originated from a combination of all these factors.

The bulk of the ascribed statuses in all social systems are parceled out to individuals on the basis of sex, age, and family relationships. However, there are many societies in which purely social factors are also used as a basis of ascription. There seems to be a general tendency for societies to divide their component individuals into a series of groups or categories and to ascribe to such categories differing degrees of social importance. Such divisions may originate in many different ways. They may grow out of individual differences in technical skill or other abilities, as in the case of craft groups or the aristocracies of certain Indian tribes, membership in which was determined by the individual's war record. They may also originate through the conscious formation of some social unit, such as the first college fraternity or the first business men's club, which is usually followed by the formation of a series of similar units organized upon nearly the same lines. Lastly, such divisions may originate through the subjugation of one society by another society, with the subsequent fusion of both into a single functional unit, as in the case of Old World aristocracies deriving from conquest. Even when the social divisions originate in individual differences of ability, there seems to be a strong tendency for such divisions to become hereditary. The members of a socially favored division try to transmit the advantages they have gained to their offspring and at the same time to prevent the entry into the division of individuals from lower divisions. In many cases these tendencies result in the organization of the society into a series of hereditary classes or castes. Such hereditary units are always used as reference points for the ascription of status.

The factor of social class or caste rarely if ever replaces the factors of sex, age, and biological relationship in the determination of status. Rather, it supplements these, defining the rôles of individuals still more clearly. Where the class system is strong, each class becomes almost a society in itself. It will have a series of sex, age, and relationship statuses which are peculiar to its members. These will differ from the statuses of other classes even when both are determined by the same biological factors. Not only is the commoner debarred from the occupation of aristocratic statuses, but the aristocrat is similarly debarred from the occupation of common statuses. It may be mentioned in passing that this arrangement is not always entirely to the advantage of the members of the upper class. During the nineteenth century the aristocratic prohibition against engaging in trade condemned many aristocrats to genteel poverty.

Feudal Europe offers an excellent example of the ascription of statuses on the basis of social class. A man born into the noble class could look forward to being a bachelor, in the technical sense of a boy beginning his training for knighthood, a squire, and lastly a knight and lord of a manor. The performance of the rôles connected with the final status required a long and arduous training both in the use of arms and in administration. The woman born into the same class could also look forward to being lady of a manor, a task which entailed special knowledge and administrative ability fully on a par with that of her husband. A man born into the peasant class could look forward only to becoming a tiller of the soil. He would pass through no statuses corresponding to those of bachelor or squire, and although he might be trained to the use of weapons, these would be different weapons from those used by the knight. The woman born in this class could only look forward to becoming a simple housewife, and her necessary training for this status was limited to a knowledge of housekeeping and baby-tending. The third class in medieval society, the burghers, also had its own series of statuses, the boy looking forward to becoming first an apprentice and then a master training apprentices in turn. All these divergent, class-determined statuses were mutually interdependent, and all contributed to the successful functioning of medieval society. The noble provided protection and direction, the peasant provided food, and the burgher took care of trade and manufactures.

Ascribed statuses, whether assigned according to biological or to social factors, compose the bulk of all social systems. However, all these systems also include a varying number of statuses which are open to individual achievement. It seems as though many statuses of this type were primarily designed to serve as baits for socially acceptable behavior or as escapes for the individual. All societies rely mainly on their ascribed statuses to take care of the ordinary business of living. Most of the statuses which are thrown open to achievement do not touch this business very deeply. The honored ones are extremely satisfying to the individuals who achieve them, but many of them are no more vital to the ordinary functioning of the society than are honorary degrees or inclusions in "Who's Who" among ourselves.

Most societies make only a grudging admission of the fact that a limited number of statuses do require special gifts for their successful performance. Since such gifts rarely manifest themselves in early childhood, these statuses are, of necessity, thrown open to competition. At the same time, the pattern of ascribing all vital statuses is so strong that all societies limit this competition with reference to sex, age, and social affiliations. Even in our own society, where the field open to individual achievement is theoretically unlimited, it is strictly limited in fact. No woman can become President of the United States. Neither could a Negro nor an Indian, although there is no formal rule on this point, while a Jew or even a Catholic entering the presidential race would be very seriously handicapped from the outset. Even with regard to achievable statuses which are of much less social importance and which, perhaps, require more specific gifts, the same sort of limited competition is evident. It would be nearly if not quite impossible for either a woman or a

Negro to become conductor of our best symphony orchestra, even
if better able to perform the duties involved than any one else
in America. At the same time, no man could become president of
the D. A. R., and it is doubtful whether any man, unless he
adopted a feminine *nom de plume*, could even conduct a syndi-
cated column on advice to the lovelorn, a field in which our
society assumes, *a priori*, that women have greater skill.

These limitations upon the competition for achieved statuses
no doubt entail a certain loss to society. Persons with special
talents appear to be mutants and as such are likely to appear in
either sex and in any social class. At the same time, the actual
loss to societies through this failure to use their members' gifts
to the full is probably a good deal less than persons reared in the
American tradition would like to believe. Individual talent is too
sporadic and too unpredictable to be allowed any important part
in the organization of society. Social systems have to be built
upon the potentialities of the average individual, the person who
has no special gifts or disabilities. Such individuals can be trained
to occupy almost any status and to perform the associated rôle
adequately if not brilliantly. The social ascription of a particular
status, with the intensive training that such ascription makes
possible, is a guarantee that the rôle will be performed even if
the performance is mediocre. If a society waited to have its
statuses filled by individuals with special gifts, certain statuses
might not be filled at all. The ascription of status sacrifices the
possibility of having certain rôles performed superlatively well
to the certainty of having them performed passably well.

When a social system has achieved a good adjustment to the
other sectors of the group's culture and, through these, to the
group's environment, it can get along very well without utilizing
special gifts. However, as soon as changes within the culture or
in the external environment produce maladjustments, it has to
recognize and utilize these gifts. The development of new social
patterns calls for the individual qualities of thought and initiative, and the freer the rein given to these the more quickly new
adjustments can be arrived at. For this reason, societies living

under new or changing conditions are usually characterized by a wealth of achievable statuses and by very broad delimitations of the competition for them. Our own now extinct frontier offered an excellent example of this. Here the class lines of the European societies from which the frontier population had been drawn were completely discarded and individuals were given an unprecedented opportunity to find their place in the new society by their own abilities.

As social systems achieve adjustment to their settings, the social value of individual thought and initiative decreases. Thorough training of the component individuals becomes more necessary to the survival and successful functioning of society than the free expression of their individual abilities. Even leadership, which calls for marked ability under conditions of change, becomes largely a matter of routine activities. To ensure successful training, more and more statuses are transferred from the achieved to the ascribed group, and the competition for those which remain is more and more rigidly delimited. To put the same thing in different terms, individual opportunities decrease. There is not an absolute correlation between the degree of adjustment of a social system to its setting and the limitation of individual opportunity. Thus if the group attaches a high value to individual initiative and individual rights, certain statuses may be left open to competition when their ascription would result in greater social efficiency. However, well-adjusted societies are, in general, characterized by a high preponderance of ascribed over achieved statuses, and increasing perfection of adjustment usually goes hand in hand with increasing rigidity of the social system.

Americans have been trained to attach such high values to individual initiative and achievement that they tend to look down upon societies which are rigidly organized and to pity the persons who live in them. However, the members of a society whose statuses are mainly prescribed are no less happy than ourselves and considerably more at peace. It would never occur to an orthodox Hindu that he was to be pitied because he could not change his caste. His whole life is arranged and oriented in terms of caste, and if he ever envies the members of other castes the emotion is on a par with our own envy of some animal's obvious comfort or satisfaction. His religion provides him with rationalizations of the whole system and with an explanation of his presence in the caste as a result of his soul's evolutionary status. It also holds out the hope of a better position in his next incarnation if his work in this is properly done. As a caste member his social and even emotional needs are amply provided for. There are even a small series of achievable statuses open to him if he is ambitious. He may become a member of the caste's governing body or the best goldsmith in a group of goldsmiths, admired by those whose admiration is based on a thorough knowledge of the work. In any struggle for advancement he knows exactly who his competitors are and what it is he wants to attain. He is much less likely to be disappointed than a man living under our own system, where every other man may be a rival and where the limits for ambition are not socially defined.

In India the idea of ceremonial pollution makes social intercourse between the castes difficult; but in societies which have strong class lines, without this idea, the presence of classes actually makes for ease of social intercourse. Here also, classes serve to delimit fields of competition. Where there can be no rivalry in vital matters and no social climbing, snubbing becomes unnecessary and indeed meaningless. Social status is something fixed and understood by both parties, so it can be ignored under circumstances where it has no direct bearing. Members of different classes can form friendships which are the stronger because their interests can never clash and they can evaluate each other as human beings with a clarity unclouded by fear of rivalry. Membership in a rigidly organized society may deprive the individual of opportunities to exercise his particular gifts, but it gives him an emotional security which is almost unknown among ourselves. Which of these is best or which makes for the greatest happiness to the greatest number the reader must decide for himself.

CHAPTER IX

THE RAW MATERIALS FOR SOCIETY

In the preceding chapters we have seen that societies owe their existence to the organization and mutual adjustment of the behavior and attitudes of their component individuals. This organization is achieved by the assignment to each individual of certain statuses and his training for the performance of the associated rôles. Although biological factors are largely used as reference points for the assignment of these statuses, it seems fairly certain that such factors play only a secondary part in determining their content. Even the statuses assigned to such physiologically distinct groups as men and women, children and the aged, vary so widely in different societies that we must assume that the determinants are mainly cultural. At the same time, there are certain constants which are present in all social situations and which must be allowed for in the development of patterns for social life. All human beings, simply as members of the primate species *Homo sapiens,* have certain inherent qualities which determine both their needs and their potentialities. Similarly, the types of aggregate in which members of this species normally live broadly delimit the ways in which such aggregates may be organized into societies. It is with these social constants and their effects that we propose to deal in the present chapter.

The most outstanding quality of *Homo sapiens* as a species is his extreme teachability. No other mammalian species learns so readily or relies so largely on learning in its attempt to deal with its environment. Human personalities, using this term in the broadest sense, can be shaped to an extraordinary degree by the cultures to which individuals are exposed during their formative period. The expression of almost any innate tendency can be inhibited or modified in such a way that the tendency will find indirect, socially acceptable expression. Actually, such training in inhibition and redirection is a vital part of the adaptation of individuals to life as members of any society. However, the training which inhibits or redirects such tendencies does not eradicate them. They remain as factors to be reckoned with, complicating all social situations and influencing the development of all social patterns. While they never indicate a single line as the only possible one in the evolution of social systems, they make certain lines of development easier than others and impose broad ultimate limits on the forms which societies may assume. All social systems which develop through the normal mechanisms of changing behavior and its final integration into a series of ideal patterns make allowance for them, and no individually developed theoretical system which fails to do so has any chance of becoming established in practice.

The influence of these innate qualities upon the establishment of social patterns may be made more comprehensible by a humble simile. In tramping across country one often encounters a barbed wire fence. There are a number of possible ways of getting to the other side. One may walk along it until he finds a gate, or roll under it, at the cost of some dirt and loss of dignity, or even step over it if the strands are slack enough, but whichever he chooses to do the presence of the fence definitely modifies his behavior at that point in his tramp. Similarly, the innate qualities of human beings can be directed or their immediate effects avoided in many different ways, but their presence influences the formation of all social systems. Even when the individual has been successfuly trained to inhibit some of these innate qualities, the inhibition is not pleasant for him and its social imposition entails the development within the culture of rewards and punishments to reinforce the effects of the training. Thus no society can rest content with teaching its members not to steal. It has to back up this teaching with punishments for stealing, even if the punishment is only ridicule. If it chooses to take more specific punitive measures, it must go on to develop methods for detecting the thief, making certain of his guilt, and applying the punishment.

We are so close to the innate qualities of human beings and take them so much for granted that it is often difficult for us to distinguish them. Thus it is hard for us to realize that the fact that man is an omnivorous primate has had a tremendous effect on the development of culture. His tolerance for all sorts of food made possible an almost complete exploitation of this feature of his environment and gave him an active interest in both plants and animals. It led, in time, to the development of both agriculture and domestication, a combination necessary to settled life throughout most of the world. A purely herbivorous species of equal intelligence might have developed the former, but they would hardly have developed the latter and in the absence of animal fertilizers soil exhaustion would have kept their villages moving at brief intervals. To cite only a few other effects of man's physiological characteristics, the fact that he is a biped is responsible for his use of stairs. A quadruped species would find ramps more convenient. The fact that he is hairless and thus singularly susceptible to cold and bad weather gave rise to both clothing and housing. If *Homo sapiens* had been provided with fur, it is unlikely that patterns of modesty or even of bathing would ever have been developed and still less likely that the Parthenon would have been built.

These general physiological characteristics of *Homo sapiens* have been so completely taken into account in the development of culture that it seems humorous even to mention them. At the same time they establish the physical needs of the individual, and the meeting of these needs is one of the main functions of any social system. Such systems must serve to coördinate the activities of the society's members in such a way that they are assured of food, shelter, and an opportunity to breed. If the system fails to do this, the society cannot survive for long, still less perpetuate itself. Let us turn to other innate qualities of *Homo sapiens* which have a more direct bearing on the relations between individuals and therefore a more immediate effect on the ideal patterns of social life.

The human male, like most if not all primates, is sexually active at all seasons. The female, although her interest is prob-ably more cyclic, is also capable of responding to his advances at any time. This is also characteristic of primates as an order, and it has been noted that among many of the lower primates the females, even at times of diminished sexual interest, use sexual advances as a means of placating the male. It is further char-acteristic of *Homo sapiens* as a species that the males are, on the average, larger and heavier than the females and able to domi-nate them physically. Whether the feminists like it or not, the average man can thrash the average woman. Continuity of sexual activity does not in itself make for permanence of mated rela-tionships. It ensures the active interest of the partners in each other, but it also leads each of them to have an active interest in all individuals of the opposite sex. However, the combination of continuous sexual activity and male dominance does make for the continuity of sexual partnerships. In such a species as the baboons, the males are jealous of each other and try to restrict the attentions of their female partners to themselves. At the same time, the males are actively interested in all females and try to collect and hold as many of them as possible. Whether the females object to this arrangement we do not know, but at least they are in no position to do anything about it. The double standard is probably as old as the primate order.

In man also the combination of continous sexual activity and male dominance makes for the continuity of sexual partnerships. Practically all societies have tacitly recognized the existence of these tendencies and capitalized them to a greater or less degree in their formal organization. Through the institution of marriage, sexual partnerships are given social recognition and made still more permanent, thus increasing their utility as a basis for the assignment of activities to individuals. In a very large number of societies marriage has become a means of assuring male assistance to the woman and her children.

The male tendency to accumulate and hold females, which springs from the same background, is much more difficult for society to capitalize. In fact it is a liability rather than an asset.

With a sex ratio balanced as it is by a normal birth-rate, the male's collecting tendencies can be exercised only at the expense of other males. Moreover, man's continuity of sexual interest is reflected in a jealousy which gives conflicts over women an unusually high emotional content. Machiavelli long ago noted that a ruler could do almost anything with his subjects as long as he did not interfere with their women or their religion, but that when he began to tamper with these his end was only a matter of time. All societies inhibit the male's tendency to collect females to some degree, setting limits to the competition for them and, through marriage, assuring the male of the possession of those which he has already gathered. Any society which failed to do this would be constantly disrupted by fights.

The direct expression of any one of the tendencies arising from continuous sexual activity and male dominance can be inhibited, and all of them are inhibited by one social system or another. At the same time, such inhibition requires the development of a series of compensating patterns, even if these do nothing more than to provide the individual with intensive inhibitory training. Thus among the Comanche sexual jealousy between brothers or even close friends was socially deprecated and rarely shown. Compensation for the individual was provided by another social pattern, that of wife exchange. In such exchanges the rights of the husband were fully recognized and he was compensated for restraining his jealousy partly by the social approval of his generosity, partly by his expectation of a return in kind. An older brother would loan his wife freely to his unmarried younger brother, but the latter would return the compliment after his marriage. If the younger brother did not live up to his obligation, the older brother would, in the words of an informant, "never feel the same about him again." Other societies encourage sexual jealousy and use it as an aid to the enforcement of faithfulness upon one or both partners to a marriage, but this pattern also entails inhibitions. The partners must restrain their roving tendencies, and society must aid them in this by providing special training and compensations.

Culture plays such an important part in both the inhibition

and encouragement of jealousy that it may very well be asked whether jealousy is one of the innate qualities of human beings. It is certainly present in the lower primates, and there seems to be a good deal of evidence that it is also characteristic of our own species. It appears sporadically even in those societies which reprehend it most severely. Thus in the Marquesas Islands both men and women enjoy an unusual degree of sexual freedom both before and after marriage. Both sexes begin to have intercourse at a very early age and are almost completely promiscuous until marriage, which is rather late. There is thus little opportunity for an early conditioning to the idea of exclusive sexual possession of any individual by another. Moreover, group marriage is, or rather was, the normal form, so that even after marriage there were few exclusive partnerships. The restrictions were further relaxed by frequent periods of license and by the regular practice of sexual hospitality. Any manifestation of sexual jealousy still exposes the individual to ridicule, and the natives rarely show any signs of it when sober. However, when they are drunk such jealousy promptly manifests itself and leads to numerous fights among both the men and the women. These are considered breaches of good manners, and the participants are ashamed of themselves when they become sober again.

The physical superiority of the human male has had a much greater effect on the development of social institutions than we usually realize. In combination with the differing rôles of the two sexes in reproduction and the early care of offspring, it has led to the delegation to men of the tasks of hunting and defense. Under uncivilized conditions both of these are of primary importance to the group's survival, and the social importance of males has been increased accordingly. In practically all societies the actual business of ruling is carried on by men. The official head of a society may be a woman, but the exercise of the powers which go with the position are nearly always delegated to some man or group of men. Similarly, male control of the family unit is nearly universal. There are certain societies in which women are officially recognized as dominant in the marriage relationship, but this is not incompatible with more inclusive patterns of male dominance. We are so accustomed to think of marriage as the core of the family that we are likely to jump to the conclusion that a social system under which a woman rules her husband and dismisses him at will is dominated by women. Actually, in most of these so-called matriarchies ultimate control is still vested in the males. A woman may dominate her husband, but she is normally dominated in turn by some male relative, usually her mother's brother or her own brother. Although a husband may have no control over his own wife and children, he will control some other woman and her children, thus evening the account.

It is questionable whether there is any society in existence which is actually dominated by women. Nevertheless, it is possible to imagine a situation in which this might come to be the case. Economic considerations are of great importance in the organization of all social systems. We all recognize that even in our own society the ultimate control of the family is vested in the partner who makes the greatest contribution to its support. The poor man who marries a rich wife is under his wife's thumb no matter what the theoretical relation of husband and wife may be in that particular society. When any group becomes mainly dependent for its subsistence on an occupation or series of occupations carried on exclusively by women, the social importance of women will be increased and their actual if not their theoretical position in the society correspondingly raised. If the inheritance of property necessary to the particular industry is involved, the position of women will be still further strengthened.

It is a general rule that property is inherited by the sex to whom it will be most useful. Thus in our own society if a man died leaving a son and a daughter, a dress-suit and a sewing-machine, and no will, there would be no question as to which child would get which. In a group in which agriculture is exclusively a woman's occupation, land will tend to pass from mother to daughter rather than from mother to son. If the group comes to depend mainly on agriculture, the women will be in the position of rich wives to poor husbands. They will own both the main natural resource of the group and the means of exploiting it. Given such a condition, women will have an actual dominance which may in time achieve social recognition. This was the case among the Iroquois, frequently cited as an example of strong matriarchal organization. However, in spite of the very important rôle of women in Iroquois society and their control of its economic basis, even here actual rule outside the family was carried on by men. Although men made little economic contribution they took care of defense, which was equally necessary to the survival of the group, and thus balanced their economic deficiencies. Actually, cases of extreme dependence upon women even in economic matters are rare. The activities assigned to the two sexes in any society are usually well balanced in their social importance, and this gives the physical superiority of the male a chance to assert itself.

In addition to the sexual differences in size and fighting ability, which are reflected in the general human pattern of male dominance, there are similar differences between the individuals of a single sex. However, most societies have a tendency to ignore these in their formal patterns for social life. Even when they recognize them and allow individuals to find their own level by competition, there are always patterns which rigidly circumscribe what the dominant person can do. It may be significant in this connection that among primates in general strength domination rarely extends beyond the family unit. The adult males in a baboon horde are not arranged in a graded series comparable to that in a herd of cattle or a flock of chickens. There are usuallly several males in the horde who are of nearly equal fighting ability, and these tend to ignore each other instead of fighting for absolute dominance. It is also significant that the only human societies in which strength dominance on the part of individuals is strongly emphasized are logging camps, boys' gangs, and similar groups composed of individuals of a single sex. Even in these the organization based on fighting ability lacks the regularity of a cattle "hook series." There will usually be a leader who can thrash any of the rest and one or two runners-up, but the bulk of the group will stand very much on a level.

It seems probable that the strongest bar to the utilization of pure strength domination as a basis for organizing societies is the tendency of strong and dominant males to take females from weaker ones. Almost any male who dominates a human group is likely to try this sooner or later, and it is usually his undoing. Injured husbands have long memories and are often reckless in seeking revenge. Moreover, the forcible seizure of one man's wife is a threat to all the other husbands in the community, since they realize that they may be next. Thanks to the general human ability for planning and coöperation, two or three episodes of the sort are usually enough to bring about concerted action by the other men and the elimination of the dominant party. Even when dominance in a society is formally ascribed on the basis of strength and fighting ability, as among the Comanche, actual dominance can be maintained only through a certain measure of self-restraint and respect for the rights of others. No individual can dominate a human society in the way that a bull dominates his herd. He cannot drive out the other males, since their activities are necessary to the group, and as long as there are other males his control really depends upon their good-will.

Sexual jealousy and male dominance both derive from easily recognizable physiological causes. However, when we turn to certain psychological qualities which seem to be present in all human beings the reasons for their existence are less clear. We find ourselves immediately confronted with the problem of instincts. This is a knotty question which will probably keep the psychologists occupied for years to come. At present, the weight of the evidence seems to be against the existence of any specific instincts in our species. Apparently man inherits a number of simple muscular reflexes and the capacity for certain emotions, but all save the most elementary items of his behavior are due to conditioning. Thus all children are born with the ability to feel fear, anger, and pleasure, but the stimuli which will evoke these emotions in later life depend almost entirely upon accidents of early experience. In spite of this, certain emotional reactions are so universal that, if they are not instinctive, they must be the result of conditions present during the formative period of all human beings. Such reactions, whether innate or not, are thus among the constants which affect the organization of societies.

One of the most important of these universal reactions is the individual's need for company and his desire for emotional response from other individuals. Gregarious life is so nearly universal among the primates that there may conceivably be an instinctive basis for it. However, the human reactions which encourage gregarious life can be explained equally well as a result of the early conditioning of the normal individual to the presence of a number of other individuals. The biological dependence of the human child lasts ten to twelve years as a minimum, while under natural conditions women seem to produce offspring at average intervals of eighteen months. The child thus becomes habituated to the presence not only of its parents but of a number of brothers and sisters. Since most human families live as members of larger localized aggregates, the child becomes so accustomed to having a number of people about him and to relying on their help in time of need that to be cut off from human associates in later life produces an emotional state bordering on panic.

The affectionate relations which the child establishes with his relatives during the formative period contribute toward the integration and continuation of family groupings, while his habituation to gregarious life gives society one of its strongest holds upon him. Persons who are cut off from human companionship suffer much more keenly from loneliness than from the economic disadvantages of living alone. They may be able to do very well for themselves, like Robinson Crusoe, but the continued solitude often leads to insanity. With this need for company there goes an equally acute need for response. Complete solitude is only one degree worse than life in a hostile community; in fact, the choice would be largely a matter of the individual's temperament. It is this need for response which makes it possible for certain societies to control their members without any formal machinery for doing so. The Eskimo say that if a man is a thief no one will do anything about it, but the people will laugh when his name is mentioned. This does not sound like a severe penalty, but it suffices to make theft almost unknown. Ridicule will bring almost any individual to terms, while the most stubborn rebel will bow before ostracism or the threat of expulsion from his group.

Another tendency which seems to be almost universal among human beings is the acquisitive one. At the present time there are certain circles in which this tendency is in disfavor, and some students even deny its existence. However, it is clearly recognizable at the sub-human primate level. Apes will fight for food, and the stronger will take it from the weaker. Their reactions differ from those of men in this respect mainly in that they have much less tendency to hoard. Apparently they lack the foresight necessary for this. Men, being able to look ahead, try to provide for the future. Their acquisitive tendencies are never completely lulled, and as a result we find that all societies have had to develop techniques for ensuring a share of the necessities of life to all their members. At the same time, there is no society in which there is a complete communal ownership of property. A man's trousers, or their local equivalent, always belong to him. It may be taken for granted by other members of the group that if a man has two pair of trousers he will pass over one of them to any one who happens to find himself trouserless, but this does not nullify the fact of ownership. The owner merely becomes a donor and is repaid in gratitude and social prestige.

Although all societies recognize the existence of individual property, all of them also place certain limits on its acquisition. The methods for doing this are highly variable, suggesting that the acquisitive tendencies of individuals are fairly easy to inhibit or direct as soon as physical needs have been provided for. Beyond this point prestige and the respect of other members of the group become more important to the individual than the knowledge that he has something laid aside for a rainy day. In fact, liberality becomes one of the surest forms of insurance against ill fortune, for where he has given he can legitimately expect a return. Many societies make free giving the highest virtue, and some of them have developed very curious rationalizations for it.

One of these rationalizations came under my own observation among the Comanche. In this tribe loot was the main source of wealth. The leader of a war party controlled the division of the spoils and, in theory, could keep as much as he wished for himself. Actually, such leaders rarely kept more than a small share for themselves and often gave all the loot away to their followers. Success in war, with its attendant spoils, was believed to be due to the leader's medicine, i.e., his supernatural powers. Such power came and went capriciously, and its presence was revealed to a man by a subjective reaction which he could immediately recognize. If the leader kept the bulk of the spoils, such an act was tantamount to a confession that he felt that his power was leaving him. He was keeping what he could because he knew that he might not be able to get more. The selfish leader would thus immediately lose prestige and would have difficulty in recruiting men for his next war party. If he gave freely, it showed that he knew that his medicine was strong and his prestige would rise accordingly. The practical aspects of the case were, in theory, largely ignored by both leader and followers. They no doubt had a good deal of influence on the actual recruiting, but members of the tribe were loath to admit it.

The social returns for generosity loom large in the lives of most uncivilized groups. There are many societies in which the rich normally pay more for the same things than the poor do. This represents more than an indifference to wealth or a reluctance to waste time in bargaining. The rich man seizes the making of a purchase as an opportunity to exhibit his wealth and reaffirm the social position which it gives him. There is abundant proof that even small-scale manufactures and trade can be carried on quite successfully in the absence of the profit motive, as we commonly use that term. Thus in the Marquesas trade was formerly carried on through the exchange of objects of exactly equivalent value. The advantage which each party derived from getting something he needed in return for part of his own surplus provided the practical incentive, while the transaction paid an equally important dividend in pleasant social intercourse. All trade was phrased in terms of gift exchange. The initiator of the deal visited the other party and made him a gift, with many expressions of respect and good-will. In the course of the subsequent conversation he would mention his own need as casually as possible. After a polite interval, perhaps a week, the recipient would make a return visit and present the other with the exact equivalent of the first gift. If he presented him with less he was deprecating the original gift, while if he presented him with more he was being guilty of vulgar ostentation. Either was a social error, a breach of etiquette which showed that the offender was not familiar with polite usage and which consequently laid him open to ridicule.

The pleasure to be derived from trade and the social contacts which it entails are also an important factor in ensuring exchanges. Even the Malagasy, who are shrewd traders by our own standards, count the amusement of bargaining as an integral part of the return on all commercial transactions. In the market at Tananarive I once bargained with a native merchant for a piece of raffia cloth and finally closed with him for a figure about one-fourth greater than he could have got from another native. I then offered to buy his entire stock, some nine or ten pieces, at the same figure. My offer was promptly refused. He explained that if he sold out he could sell no more cloths that day and would be left with nothing to do.

There are, of course, many uncivilized societies which do recognize the profit motive and in which the struggle to accumulate wealth is as keen as it is among ourselves. Such societies are a delight to the missionary, for their members have already learned the Christian virtues of frugality and industry. However, even in such societies the thing sought is not wealth for its own sake but wealth for the prestige it brings. Once his physical needs have been met, uncivilized man can use wealth only for prestige. There is no field for capital investment, and wealth cannot even contribute greatly to the creature comforts of its owner. Such things as food, housing, and clothing are controlled by custom, and the richest man lives very much like the poorest one. He may be able to wear more jewelry and clothes of finer material and to eat his rice from a carved bowl instead of a plain one, but his only real gain is the admiration such display excites. Actually, in most primitive communities which encourage wealth accumulation such hoarding is simply an intermediate stage between wealth creation and wealth distribution. The energetic man amasses wealth in order to give a great feast or join some society, thus returning most of his wealth to the group with a flourish and gaining prestige in return.

Behind the extraordinary variety of attitudes toward wealth and its proper employment which we find in uncivilized societies there lies one highly important factor. In nearly all of these societies private property is personal property. It consists of things which have been made or gathered, not of the sources of supply. The ownership of these sources is normally vested in some social unit, such as the clan or entire tribe. The wealth with which individuals play in their effort to gain prestige is created wealth, and any energetic individual can create more by his own efforts. Even when, as on the Northwest Coast of North America, wealth competitions and ostentatious waste are carried to almost incredible lengths, the sources of wealth are not interfered with. A man may give away or destroy everything he owns in an effort to surpass a rival, but he cannot touch the house or the fishing and hunting rights on which he depends for a livelihood. These are vested in his family or clan and must be passed on intact. This means that even the power which wealth gives in such communities is of a very different sort from that which it gives in our own. The rich man can always gain followers and hangers-on, but he can hold them only through generosity. They are not really dependent upon him, and any of them can make a decent living without him. The situation is somewhat comparable to that which existed in the United States as long as good land was available to any one who had the energy to clear and farm it. As long as access to the sources of wealth is guaranteed to all, the acquisitive tendencies of individuals are a real asset to the group They provide a stimulus to the creation of wealth and encourage the building-up of a surplus against the time of need. It is only when such access is cut off that they must be rigorously controlled and techniques developed for ensuring a share of the society's wealth to each of its members.

In the preceding discussions the human desire for prestige

has come up again and again. It is probably the most socially useful of all the innate qualities of man. The hope of gaining prestige or the fear of losing it does more than anything else to hold the average individual to the proper performance of his rôles. At the same time, the expressions of this need derive from the very rôles which it serves to enforce. They can be distinguished in practically every aspect of human activity from the extra polish that the good cabinet-maker puts upon his table to regularity in church attendance. The desire for prestige is universal, but the ways of obtaining it are determined by culture and are infinitely varied. In one society the road to prestige may lie through poverty and asceticism, in another through wealth accumulation and ostentatious waste. One group may accord it to the man who avoids competition, another to the one who is constantly trying to best his neighbors. No matter what the approved way may be, the results are equally satisfying to the normal individual.

In our discussion thus far we have been concerned with the current raw materials for society, the individuals through whom all societies have to perpetuate themselves. We have tried to show how the innate qualities of these individuals, simply as members of a particular mammalian species, influence the forms which social systems may assume. However, human society did not spring into being full-grown and without a past any more than did our particular species. Man was evolved from some sub-human form, and the structure and evolutionary potentialities of this form did more than anything else to determine what our species would be like. Similarly, it seems safe to conclude that the habits of this sub-human species served as a starting point for the development of human culture, of which social systems are an integral part. Before human societies could come into being there must have been aggregates of individuals, and the qualities of these immediately pre-human or earliest human aggregates would influence the forms which later societies might assume. Such aggregates were the raw materials from which societies have been developed.

Any statements as to the nature of the earliest human aggregates must remain pure speculations. The sub-human species from which our own was evolved long since passed out of existence, and a study of the social systems of the so-called primitive peoples can help us little if at all. It was once assumed that the differences between social systems were due to differences in their evolutionary status. Some groups had lagged in their social development and thus approximated past stages in the evolution of our own society. The further such systems diverged from our own, the lower in the scale they must be. Unfortunately, the more we learn of the actual history of societies the less tenable such an idea becomes. Societies have not followed a single consistent line of evolution, but a multitude of diverging lines. All of those now extant are separated from the beginnings of human existence by exactly the same time interval and have thus had an equal opportunity for developing individual peculiarities. Some of them no doubt approximate the original condition more closely than others, but there is no certain test by which this can be determined. There is not even any recognizable correlation between technological advance and social complexity. Thus the most intricate social systems known to us, those of certain Australian tribes, are associated with a very simple and genuinely primitive technology approximating that of Europe at the close of the Old Stone Age. Our own family organization, on the other hand, is so simple that it finds more parallels among the sub-human primates than in other human groups.

It is the conditions existing among sub-human primates which give us our most valuable clues to the nature of the earliest human aggregates. If we may judge from the present apes and monkeys, men have probably lived in fairly permanent family groupings ever since they became human. At least, such groupings are characteristic of all primate species which share with *Homo sapiens* the factors of male physical superiority and dominance and of long dependence of the offspring. The old concept of a promiscuous horde as the starting point for family development was required by the type of logic which made the Victorian family the last step in social evolution, but there is nothing else to support it. It is interesting to conjecture what the results might be in a primate species where the females, as a group, were larger and stronger than the males, but no such species has been reported. It also seems probable that the pattern of mating in these earliest human families was polygynous when any male was strong enough to take and keep several partners and monogamous when he was not.

The combination of rather short birth intervals and slow maturation, also characteristic of our species, would mean that the family group would be fairly large, including three or four immature individuals as a minimum. The attitude of the dominant male toward these individuals, again to judge from general primate conditions, was probably one of tolerant indifference. He would not interfere with them as long as they did not interfere with him. There is no point at which present-day man departs more widely from the general primate condition than in the male's assumption of responsibility for and care of his offspring. Even the anthropoids seem to leave the care of the young almost entirely to the females, although the males may exhibit good-natured curiosity or even play with them.

What happened in such families when the immature individuals became adult is a point on which one guess seems to be as good as another. We have almost no information on how such crises are handled among other primates, while whether the earliest human families were isolated or belonged to hordes would also have had an effect. The idea that the adult male drove out his grown sons and took his daughters into his harem may be correct, but the first part of this thesis might present practical difficulties. Human males mature so slowly that the "old man" would not be likely to retain full strength and fighting ability for many years after even his eldest son was fully grown. He could hardly take and keep females much below the age of fifteen, and by the time his first son reached the same age he would be thirty. Even to-day the man of thirty is definitely past his prime in many groups where living conditions are hard. If the son refused to leave of his own free will, the father might find it hard to drive him out. At the same time, the long period of paternal dominance would foster attitudes in both father and son which would tend to postpone a clash. The father would become accustomed to having the son about and would not think of him as a rival, while the son would become accustomed to paternal domination and would be loath to make the first move. Even after the physical maturity of the son the two might continue to live in the same group on a basis of mutual toleration very much like that existing between the males in a baboon horde. This tendency for the sons to remain with the family would be strengthened as soon as any coöperation in defense or hunting was developed, for the sons would then be too valuable to be driven out.

We have no satisfactory information as to whether males mate with their adult daughters among the sub-human primates. The situation would probably be considerably influenced by whether a species lived in isolated families or in hordes. In the first case the incentive to matings of this type would be stronger. In the second, the habituation of father and daughter to each other on an asexual basis, with the availability of other partners, would probably work against it. Much the same considerations would influence the mating of brother and sister. This would be much more likely to occur under an isolated family pattern than under a horde pattern, although even in the former it would be likely to arouse the jealousy of the father and lead to a clash. Here again, the factor of conditioning to companionship on an asexual basis would probably be a deterrent to mating, for it appears to be so in most mammalian species. Breeders recognize that it is often difficult to mate dogs which have been brought up together.

It seems reasonably certain that the family has existed since the beginning of human society. There is also a strong probability that the earliest men were accustomed to still larger aggregates, hordes composed of a number of families. The existence of such hordes does not derive directly from biological factors and hence cannot be assumed with as much certainty as in the case of the family. Primates as an order show a strong tendency toward gregarious life, but this tendency is less marked among our closest relatives, the anthropoids, than among the lower forms.

Only one of the four anthropoids, the gibbon, is regularly gregarious, although the chimpanzee may occasionally be so. At the
same time, this fact should not be given too much weight, since
the present anthropoids are frugivorous forest-dwelling forms,
while everything indicates that our own immediately pre-human
ancestors were adapted to rather open country and had fairly
well-developed carnivorous tendencies. Under such conditions
gregarious life would have had marked advantages, and if it was
not developed at the sub-human level it certainly developed very
early in human history.

Perhaps the life of a baboon horde may give us some idea
of what the earliest human hordes were like. The baboon horde
consists of a series of families, each with its dominant male and
one or more females with their immature young. There are no
unattached females, but there are a certain number of bachelors,
males who are not strong enough to take and keep females for
themselves. These bachelors attach themselves to family groups
and are tolerated by the dominant male as long as they do not
make advances to his females. We do not know whether these
bachelors are related in any way to the families they attend, a
point of considerable interest. They seem to be held by interest
in the females and will make advances to them as soon as the
dominant male is absent. The family heads are not arranged in
any definite series of dominance. Apparently any weak male will
lose his females, and those who can keep the family head status
are all strong enough and evenly enough matched so that they
hesitate to attack one another. Their policy is one of mutual
avoidance, and there is fighting only when one tries to take
another's mate. In spite of this potential hostility, all the family
groups live together amiably enough, and the horde travels and
forages as a unit. There is no one leader, and coöperation between
the members, if it exists at all, is of a very rudimentary sort.
This situation seems to be duplicated in practically all sub-
human species which are gregarious and at the same time have
male dominance.

It is highly probable that the first human beings lived in
male-dominated and frequently polygynous families. It is almost,

but not quite, as probable that several of such families lived and foraged together, forming a horde. There is no reason to suppose that the conditions within either of these types of aggregate were markedly different from those existing in the similar aggregates of the sub-human primates. If they were not markedly different, man at the beginning of his career had only faint foreshadowings of society as we know it. All the infinite ramifications of specialization, adaptation, and coöperation which go to make any existing society are man's own creation. At the same time, these initial aggregates made society possible by bringing groups of individuals together and holding them together. Without the continuity of association which they provided, patterns for the interrelations of individuals could never have been developed. In the family, continuity was ensured by a combination of biological factors: the sexual attraction between the mates and the dependence of the offspring. In the horde it was ensured by habit: the conditioning of the individual to the presence of a series of other individuals. As patterns of coöperation and interdependence developed, and with these the necessity for training individuals, the family offered the first reference point for the assignment of statuses and the first agency for providing such training. The horde set ultimate limits to the group of individuals who were to be trained and adjusted to each other. As societies developed, both of these original types of aggregate underwent certain modifications. It is with these and the possible causes for them that we will deal in the next few chapters.

CHAPTER X

THE FAMILY

It has been pointed out in an earlier chapter that the ideal patterns which direct and control social interactions never repeat themselves in identical form in any two social systems. It follows that the institutions which derive from combinations of such patterns will be dissimilar in their form and content. However, all known social systems include institutions which correspond in a general way to what we term the family.

All societies recognize the existence of certain close-knit, internally organized coöperative units intermediate between the individual and the total society of which he is a part. Theoretically, every person is assigned to one or another of these units on the basis of biological relationships established through mating or common ancestry. Actually, membership may also be ascribed on the basis of recognized substitutes for such relationships, such as presumptive paternity and adoption. Such units always have specific functions with relation both to their members and to the total society. Membership in the unit entails upon the individual specific rights and duties with regard to other members and also a series of rather clearly defined attitudes. The unit is expected to be the primary focus of its members' interests and loyalties. Those who belong to it are in duty bound to coöperate with and assist each other and to place each other's interests above those of outsiders. The interaction of the personalities within the unit is close and continuous, and their mutual adjustment is expected to be correspondingly complete. Ideally, the members of a family are bound together by ties of affection as well as by those of common interest, and quarrels between them are considered more reprehensible than quarrels between members and outsiders.

There can be little doubt that all such units are derivatives of the primitive, biologically determined grouping of mates and offspring. However, they are widely variable in both form and content. The most constant feature in connection with them seems to be the general attitudes enjoined upon their members. Both their personnel and their functions differ so much in various societies that we are forced to conclude that these features are now determined by cultural factors. In other words, the family, although it began as a biological phenomenon, a primate reproductive unit, has evolved into a social phenomenon, something more nearly comparable to such units as a monastic order or a craft guild than to its own remote ancestor. Although the biological factors which first brought the human family into being are still operative, their influence on families as social institutions appears to be about on a par with the influence of the innate qualities of members of particular sex or age categories upon the statuses and rôles actually assigned to members of such categories.

It is hard for Europeans to realize the sharp distinction which exists in many social systems between the reproductive unit composed of mates and their offspring and the authentic, institutional family. It happens that in our own society these two units coincide much more closely than in most. As a result, European students have shown a strong tendency to assume that any grouping composed of father, mother, and children must constitute the social equivalent of the family among ourselves. Actually, such groupings play an insignificant rôle in the lives of many societies. while at least one society refuses to give them any formal recognition. Never the less, all these societies which minimize the importance of the reproductive unit have other units which show a general correspondence in their social significance to the family among ourselves. These units agree with our own families in the attitudes enjoined upon their members and, less closely, in the functions ascribed to them. To the student of society and culture the functions of these units are vastly more important than their personnel. Their social significance lies in what they do for their members and the total group rather than in what they are. If we can get a fairly clear picture of these functions, we will be in a better position to understand why the membership of such units can be so variable.

Every society has assigned certain functions to its family units. In nearly all cases some of these derive from the biologically determined functions of the ancestral mating group, but such derived functions cannot be considered a part of the family pattern unless they are given social recognition and approval. Even the most intimate physiological aspects of the mate relationship are often controlled by culturally established patterns. Practically all societies have taboos on sexual intercourse between socially recognized spouses under certain circumstances. Thus most of the Madagascar tribes prohibit it for three months after the birth of a girl and for six months after the birth of a boy. Some societies also prescribe it at certain times. The modern Maya require it at the time of corn-planting to ensure the success of the crop. Thus even the oldest of all family functions, that of providing the spouses with satisfaction of their sexual needs, has been shaped and modified by cultural factors.

There is even one society which has completely excluded the satisfaction of sexual needs from the functions of its family units. These people, the Nayar, provide no place for husbands or fathers in their social system. Their women marry, in accordance with Hindu law, but the marriage is contracted with a stranger and is terminated at the end of three days by a formal divorce. The husband does not enter the picture again. The satisfaction of sexual needs and the perpetuation of the group are provided for by a series of informal love affairs which, although socially recognized, establish no permanent bond between the parties or between the man and his offspring. If the lovers are compatible the relationship may continue for years, but it can always be broken without notice. The woman is in complete control of the situation and can dismiss her lover by simply returning his last gift. She is free to have several lovers simultaneously, and no greater degree of faithfulness is required of the man. The real family unit in this society consists of a woman and her sons and daughters. The children continue their association after the mother's death, and the son regards his sister's house as home and takes much the same interest in her children that a father would take in his own children in our society. The rationalization which the Nayar give for this system is that since they are a warrior caste, making their living mainly as mercenaries, it is better for their men not to set up households or assume the duties of paternity. Freedom from such responsibilities makes it possible for them to take the field at a moment's notice and without regret.

Nayar society shows that it is possible to eliminate from the functions of the social family the very items which brought the biological family into existence. No better proof could be asked for the extreme mutability both of men and of their social institutions. At the same time there is another function which has its roots in the biological family which is still characteristic of all family units. This is the care and rearing of children. It seems that among the sub-human primates the care of the young is left almost entirely to the female. At the human level the assistance of some adult male is vitally necessary. This aid is of less importance on the economic side than it is on that of the proper training of children for participation in adult society. A woman can conceivably provide for the physical needs of her children without male assistance, but she cannot train her sons in the special male attitudes and activities necessary to their success as men. We recognize that even in our own society boys brought up by their mothers are at a serious disadvantage.

There is a tendency in nearly all societies for certain aspects of child training to be taken over by agencies outside the family, such as schools and initiation groups. However, the physical dependence of the young child on its mother sets an age limit below which these agencies cannot operate. Conditioning to social life begins so early that much of the groundwork of the personality is laid before such extra-family agencies can be brought into play. It has been said that it takes three generations of education to eliminate an error of grammar from a family line. It is conceivable that with further advances in scientific knowledge the mother may be rendered unnecessary from birth on and the child-rearing function may be completely divorced from the family, but this is still far in the future. The family unit still remains the most effective mechanism so far devised for the care and rearing of children, and these functions are still left to it in all societies.

In addition to these functions which derive directly from conditions present in the original biological family, each society has selected and ascribed to its family units a series of other functions. These are culturally determined and in no society do they exhaust the unit's potentialities for function. Thus in our own society the family is not used as a basis for a religious cult. In China it is utilized for this purpose, the family's worship of its ancestors taking precedence over all other forms of religious devotion. Again, our families do not, as units, assume responsibility for the conduct of their adult members. An American business man can transfer his assets to his wife and then, after an interval, "fail" with impunity. Many other societies do make the family responsible, thus assigning to the unit highly important functions in relation to social control.

Among these socially ascribed functions of the family unit the most important seem to be those connected with economic production. Our own culture is witnessing a rapid diminution in the importance of these, but our own situation is quite atypical for mankind as a whole. In all societies the family is normally the smallest organized unit for both production and consumption and tends to be self-sufficient as far as its members' ordinary needs are concerned. The labor involved in satisfying these needs is apportioned among its members in such a way that the activities of each individual supplement those of the rest and all share in the benefits. The male members do certain things and the female members other things, and the specialization is usually so complete that persons of each sex have only a vague general knowledge of the techniques employed by the opposite one. The difficulties of the average American husband when called upon to cook and look after the children in his wife's absence are familiar to most of us. This specialization and the organization which is its necessary accompaniment are of tremendous importance in ensuring the continuity of the family. Neither a man nor a woman can provide for all wants when alone, and when marriage is utilized as the core of the family unit realization of the discomforts inevitably resulting from separation make for tolerance of a partner's foibles. Similarly, when the unit rests on some other type of relationship the loss of a member means the disorganization of its coöperative system and will be prevented whenever possible.

The care of aged and infirm members is also an almost universal function of the family. There is no society in which the individual's connection with his family group is severed as soon as his usefulness to it is passed. Having given service, the old are entitled to receive service in return. There are certain societies which lighten the family's burden in this respect by killing the old, but such acts are usualy rationalized in terms of the best interests of the old themselves. It is said that in ancient Fiji it was the duty of a good son to watch his father and to kill him when he showed signs of approaching senility or extreme decrepitude. Since the condition of the soul in the next world corresponded to that of the individual at the time of his death, it would be cruel to do otherwise. In any case the family has an obligation to provide its aged members with good funerals and to look after their well-being in the next world.

Another universal function of the family is that of protecting its members' interests against outsiders. This function varies rather in degree than in kind. There are societies in which the individual can feel sure of his family's support no matter what the nature of his trouble with outsiders may be, where the fault lies, or what the cost to his relatives. In certain Madagascar tribes the possession of land was vitally necessary to the family's survival, yet it would be sold to ransom a relative who had been captured and enslaved. The family honor required that he be redeemed even though the act entailed hardship for generations to come. Again, in some tribes which have the pattern of vendetta a murderer's relatives must shield him at all costs and fight for him even when they know that to do so means almost certain destruction for the family. More commonly, there are socially defined limits to the demands which the individual may make upon his family. Thus a murderer's relatives may be forbidden to shield him from vengeance by force, which would lead to additional killings, but they are free to aid his escape, try to compound the murder, and contribute to payment of the damages. In some societies the pattern of mutual assistance between family members has been reduced to the point where it is almost meaningless. They are expected to have a certain feeling of solidarity, but the expressions of this feeling are left mainly to the judgment of the component individuals. For example, we ourselves have no patterns governing assistance to relatives as distant even as first cousins. There is a feeling that we should help them, but the kind and degree of assistance always depend upon personal factors.

In addition to these universal or nearly universal functions of the family group there is a wealth of special functions which have been assigned to the family in one society or another. These are too numerous to be discussed in detail. Special rights are frequently vested in the family instead of in individuals. Thus it is very often the unit for land ownership or for the exercise of particular rights and privileges. In some Madagascar tribes only the members of a particular lineage are allowed to kill cattle. Other lineages call them in to do this and pay them for it. Again, certain occupations, such as pottery-making or blacksmithing, may become the exclusive prerogative of particular families, the necessary knowledge and techniques being passed down in them from generation to generation. The variability of these functions suggests that they are of secondary importance in comparison with the more universal functions previously discussed. In many cases they seem to have been ascribed to family units simply as a matter of convenience. Certain things had to be done, and the family offered a convenient means for getting them done.

If we take the universal functions of the family, we find that there are only two absolute prerequisites for their successful performance. The family unit must include able-bodied adults of both sexes, and the association between these adults must be close enough and prolonged enough to permit of their training and their organization into an effective coöperative unit. Unless they live and work together for some time, they will not be able to reach satisfactory personality adjustments or to reduce their complementary activities to matters of habit. It is obvious that until such adjustments have been made and coöperation has become more or less automatic the family unit cannot perform its socially ascribed duties with any high degree of efficiency.

Such prolonged associations between individuals of opposite sex can be assured in either of two ways. A society may capitalize the sexual attraction between adults and do all it can to give permanence to mated relationships, or it may capitalize the associations formed on an asexual basis during childhood, reinforcing them and continuing them into adult life. Such asexual associations are most readily established between individuals brought up in the same functional family unit, i.e., real or socially designated brothers and sisters. In other words, the association of adults which is the necessary nucleus of any family as a functional unit may be based on either a conjugal or a consanguine relationship. Our own society has stressed the conjugal relationship as the foundation of its functional family unit to such a degree that we tend to think of marriage and the family as inseparably linked, but many other societies draw a clear distinction between the two.

In societies organized upon the conjugal basis we can picture the authentic functional family as consisting of a nucleus of spouses and their offspring surrounded by a fringe of relatives. In those organized on the consanguine basis we can picture the authentic family as a nucleus of blood relatives surrounded by a fringe of spouses. Under the first system it is the fringes of relatives which interlock and connect family with family. Under the second it is the marriages which, by their interlocking, link family to family. Under the first system the blood relatives of the spouses are of only incidental importance to the functioning of the family unit. Under the second, the spouses are of only incidental importance.

Both these systems represent modifications of the original, biologically determined human family group. If we may judge from the sub-human primates, the earliest human families probably corresponded to the nucleus of present families of the conjugal type. There was no recognition of blood relationships between adult individuals. Recognition of such relationship and its use as a basis for the ascription of social statuses must have been the first step in the evolution of families as we know them. It would seem justifiable, then, to consider those societies which organize their families on the consanguine basis as representing a higher point of evolution, in this respect, than those which cling to the conjugal basis.

Families organized upon the conjugal basis have certain inherent disadvantages for the performance of the functions universally ascribed to the family. Sexual maturity comes late in man, and actual mating is usually still further delayed by cultural and especially economic factors. This means that the individuals who must form the nucleus of the new conjugal family come to it with their personalities and habits already rather completely formed. There always has to be a period of adjustment, and some time must pass before the new family unit can begin to function effectively. Offspring of the union, as they grow up, are more and more integrated into the family unit. They begin to do part of the family's work very early. Even in our own rural communities the child of eight is already a distinct factor in the family's economic coöperation. The importance of children increases with age, and by the time they are fully grown their contribution is often as important as that of their parents. Whenever one of them marries and leaves the family, the coöperative unit is weakened and temporarily disrupted. Families built upon the conjugal basis are too variable in content to lend themselves to close and relatively permanent organization.

With relation to such functions as care of the aged, protection of its members' interests against outsiders, or most of the special functions, the disadvantages of the conjugal basis are even more marked. Conjugal families are strictly limited in size and come to an end with the death of the original partners. This means that the old may be left without support and that the individual may have insufficient backing or find himself with none at all. The short duration in time of conjugal families also makes them unsatisfactory agencies for the ownership of either property or privilege. When a society is organized on this basis, both must be reassigned in each generation, being either subdivided or passed on to some one of the offspring to the detriment of the rest. Repeated subdivisions of property, especially land, soon reduce the separate holdings to the point where they are almost value-less, while a corresponding distribution of privilege soon dis-seminates it so widely that it loses all social significance. If Europeans had allowed titles to be inherited by all children and passed on to all their children, every one of us would be a king a dozen times over. The short duration of families organized on the conjugal basis also deprives them of much of their potential value as reference points for establishing the status of individuals with regard to society as a whole. This function of the family is of little importance in simple societies but may become of great importance in complex ones where the rôles of individuals are clearly defined and require a considerable amount of preliminary training.

Most of the difficulties with regard to function which are inherent in family units of the conjugal type disappear when the nucleus of the family is made a group of real or socially ascribed brothers and sisters. In such units no time need be lost in the adjustment of adult personalities to each other. Such adjustments begin at birth and are completed during the formative period of the individuals involved. By the time brothers and sisters are grown up and ready to assume the nuclear rôles in the family unit, all questions of dominance and mutual adaptation will already have been settled and they will be in a position to work together smoothly and efficiently. The emotional attachments between them may be less strong than those existing between husbands and wives, but their association and coöperation will have the reinforcement of habit. Adult brothers and sisters may quarrel, but their disputes lack the vigor of those between hus-band and wife and are much less likely to lead to the disruption of the family unit.

The idea of unilinear descent seems to be almost inseparable from that of consanguine family organization. It is strongly stressed by nearly all societies which recognize the consanguine group as the nucleus for their authentic family units. The reasons for this linkage will be discussed later. With unilinear descent the consanguine family achieves a continuity which makes it admirably adapted to the performance of all functions. It persists for generations, its active nucleus being constantly recruited from below, and it can be extended to include a much larger number of persons than can any family organized on the conjugal basis. It can thus ensure support of the old and adequate backing to its members and is better adapted than the conjugal family to exploitative activities which require the coöperation of a large number of individuals. Its continuity makes it the ideal agency for the retention of property and privilege and a constant reference point for the ascription of individual status.

Families organized upon a consanguine basis can, therefore, perform all the functions possible to those organized upon a conjugal basis, with the exception of the satisfaction of sexual needs and the production of children. These functions are ruled out by the universal human pattern prohibiting incest. The consanguine groups can even perform most of the family functions more successfully. Nevertheless, the Nayar appear to be the only group who have taken consanguine relationship as the exclusive basis for their family organization. This is presumably because the factors which brought the conjugal family into existence at the sub-human level are still operative. Social systems have changed and evolved, but the innate qualities of human beings have remained very much the same. The consanguine family may be a more efficient functional unit as far as society is concerned, but it is less emotionally satisfying to the individual than is the conjugal unit. Man shares with other primates sexual jealousy and a desire for the exclusive possession of a mate. These tendencies can be inhibited by training, but they remain strong enough to ensure the continued existence of conjugal units side by side with consanguine ones in practically all societies.

Although nearly all societies recognize both conjugal and consanguine groupings, most societies tend to put their emphasis on one or the other, making it the basis for the authentic, functional family as far as their own social system is concerned. On the basis of shifting emphasis, it might be possible to arrange societies in a graded series with such devotees of conjugal organization as ourselves and the Eskimo at one end of the scale and the exclusively consanguine Nayar at the other. Most societies would fall between these two extremes but with a recognizable leaning toward one grouping or the other as the focus both for family functions and individual loyalties. Thus the Malagasy marriages are attended by a ceremony as formal as our own, and there is nearly as much effort to give them stability. In fact, the divorce rate is probably lower than it is in the United States. At the same time, the consanguine unit to which each partner belongs is the focus for loyalty and for a good deal of coöperative activity. Husband and wife have no rights over each other's property, although relatives do have such rights, and the woman usually sends any money she makes back to her own family to be taken care of. Each partner will work for the interests of his or her own relatives against those of the other partner, and even the children feel only the slightest bonds with their mother's family. In one legend the mother's brother takes in her supposedly orphaned son, treats him well, and rears him to manhood. The son reciprocates by returning to his father's family and taking his benefactor's cattle with him, thus giving an edifying example of family devotion.

It may very well be asked how the concept of consanguine groups as authentic, functional family units can be correlated with the almost universal institution of marriage and the equally widespread prohibition on marriage between brothers and sisters. Under such circumstances, how is it possible for the consanguine group to assume most of the functions assigned to the family in our own society? Wherever the consanguine pattern of family organization is strong, the establishment growing out of a new marriage will usually be set up near those of the relatives of one partner. In technical terms, the new unit will be either *matrilocal* or *patrilocal*, with the mother's people or with the father's people. Unfortunately, writers have applied each of these terms rather indiscriminately, lumping together social situations which are actually quite distinct. Thus they call a marriage patrilocal whether a woman marries the son of the family next door and moves fifty yards to her new residence or whether she marries a man from another village and moves to a place twenty miles away on the other side of a river. The fact that a woman goes to live with her husband's people is less important, for practical purposes, than the degree of isolation from her own family which this entails. If she goes on living in the same village with her own brothers and sisters, the consanguine unit is not seriously disrupted. Outside of the strictly localized work of house-cleaning she can continue to coöperate with them as fully as she ever did. She can have their help in cooking and baby-tending and keep her place in her consanguine family's work groups. Although she may have to live with her husband's family, she does not have to make much effort to adjust to them. At the first signs of trouble she can find shelter with her own male relatives, who probably do not like her husband's family anyway.

What is sauce for the goose is also sauce for the gander. Matrilocal residence, as long as it is in the husband's village, has very much the same qualities. The Iroquois situation affords a good example. Here the functional family unit was the *long house,* a group of real or socially ascribed brothers and sisters who occupied a single building. Each adult woman and her children had a compartment, while the whole unit was controlled and directed by an old woman. When a man married, he moved to the house of his wife's group, which was usually only a few steps from that of his own, but he still spent most of his time with his mother's group. He hunted and went on war parties with the men of this group, and there was always some socially ascribed sister ready to cook for him and keep his clothes in repair. He was socially obligated to do all he could for his sisters' sons, one of whom might inherit his office in the tribe, while his own sons lived with their mother's group and were held to him only by the ties of affection which might develop through personal contacts. Under such conditions it is not surprising that divorce was easy and frequent.

As long as the members of a consanguine unit continue to live in easy reach of each other, the marriage of any given member has little effect on the family's activities. When marriage entails the breaking of contact between the men and women of the consanguine group, the family's activities are disrupted, but even then it is possible to retain the consanguine unit as the focus of the family's loyalties and functions. One half of the total consanguine unit, nearly always the male half, continues to live and work together. Their sisters may marry and leave them, but they will be welcome whenever they choose to return, and new women can be brought in to take the places of those who leave. There are rare cases in which it is the man who leaves and goes to live far away with his wife's people, but this is exceptional. Baby-tending, cooking, and house-cleaning require no special familiarity with the locale. A wife who comes to a strange neighborhood can get her bearings in a few days and work there as efficiently as at home. Hunters and herders, on the other hand, must have a good knowledge of the region, as must warriors mustering for the defense of their territory. If they moved to a new region when they married, the knowledge they had of their home region would be rendered useless.

The position of the outside partner who goes to live far from home with a spouse's consanguine group is anything but a comfortable one. She, for it is usually a woman, is very much under the thumb of both her husband and his relatives. In most cases she has no standing with her husband's family until she has borne him a child. After that, as mother of a family member, she gains a certain position and security which increases with age and with her gradual incorporation into the family as a coöperative unit. The psychological stresses involved in the process of adaptation must be severe and must often increase the woman's attachment to her own family unit, which would appear brighter in retrospect. At the same time, the odds against the strange husband or wife are so heavy that all but fools submit and try to adapt themselves as soon as possible. If they cannot, they can always go back to their own families, so the situation is not quite as desperate for them as Europeans might picture it. Marriages under these conditions either break quickly or run with fair smoothness. It is only when the consanguine families of both spouses are present or when a society stresses the conjugal relationship so heavily that spouses have no outside functional groups to fall back on that marital battles can pass into the stage of trench warfare.

There are certain broad correlations between the type of family which any society selects for emphasis and certain other patterns in its social system. Societies which emphasize the consanguine family commonly show a greater interest in everything connected with descent than do those which emphasize the conjugal group. The reasons for this are fairly obvious. Descent is highly important for the determination of membership in consanguine family units and of little importance for determining membership in conjugal ones. In all societies there are certain blood relationships which constitute a bar to marriage, but there are relatively few societies in which particular blood relationships make marriage necessary. Even when there is insistence on the marriage of cross cousins, i.e., children of a brother and a sister, this pattern is practically always combined with a stressing of the consanguine group as the authentic family. It is a mechanism designed to constantly bring back into the consanguine group property or privilege alienated from it by previous marriages. The same considerations appear with even greater force in the case of brother-sister marriage, which was formerly countenanced in a few societies. Only three examples of this are known, in Egypt, Peru, and Hawaii, and in each case it was the practice of a small ruling group, designed to keep rank and privilege strictly in the hereditary aristocracy.

Given the nearly universal prohibition upon marriage between real or socially ascribed brothers and sisters, an emphasis on unilinear descent is an almost unavoidable accompaniment of the establishment of family units on the consanguine basis. The existence of such prohibitions makes it impossible for the consanguine group to perpetuate itself without outside matings. The society may choose to ignore such matings completely, as among the Nayar, but if it recognizes them the child must be definitely assigned to the family of one parent or the other. Failure to do this would result in making the individual equally a member of two functional family units, with resulting conflicts in his rights and duties with regard to each of them. The ascription to the individual of equal relationship in both the father's and the mother's families is very rarely found except in societies like our own where the authentic, functional family unit is the conjugal one. We can consider ourselves equally related to our father's and to our mother's families because, socially speaking, we are not closely related to either. We have few clearly defined rights or duties with relation to them, since nearly all our interests and coöperative activities are focused on our own parents, brothers, and sisters. Moreover, we know that even our relations with this small, closely knit unit will be changed and the ties which bind us to it somewhat relaxed as soon as we marry and set up families of our own.

The results of trying to trace family descent in both lines when the functional family was of consanguine type would be bad enough in the first generation and would increase in geometric ratio with each succeeding one. Thus it would make the individual a member of two families in the first generation, four in the second, eight in the third and sixteen in the fourth. In the average tribal group such an arrangement would mean that even by the fourth generation every individual in the tribe would belong to such a large percentage of the tribe's families that the social significance of family membership would become nil. We find that, with very few exceptions, wherever the consanguine group is also the functional family unit the relationship of the individual to either his father's or his mother's people is strongly emphasized, while the relationship on the other side of the house is allowed to lapse after the first two or three generations.

Why certain societies with consanguine family organization have chosen to stress the male and others the female line of descent is not clear. Either line, once it has become recognized and established, can perform the function of delimiting the consanguine group equally well. Moreover, both lines are equally easy to establish. It may be more difficult to determine the biological paternity of individuals than to establish maternity, but social paternity is only indirectly connected with biology. Most uncivilized peoples are less troubled about physical paternity than were the nineteenth century anthropologists of the evolutionary school. A good many of them do not even understand the biological rôle of the father in reproduction. For social purposes a child's father is his mother's husband and can be as easily determined as his mother. It also seems certain that matrilineal and patrilineal descent do not represent successive stages in the course of an inevitable evolution of social institutions. While a number of groups are known to have shifted from the female to the male line, there are clear indications that some other groups, certain tribes in British Columbia for example, have shifted in the opposite direction. We can only conclude that the selection of a particular descent line by a particular group has been due to historic causes which were probably highly complex and never exactly the same in any two cases.

Economic factors have no doubt had a considerable effect in determining the choice of a particular line, and it is easy to see how they might operate. All societies show a fairly rigid division of activities between men and women, and the tasks of providing food and raw materials usually fall more heavily upon one sex than upon the other. It would be natural for a consanguine group to try to retain those members belonging to the sex whose activities were economically most important. Thus in a society which was primarily dependent upon agriculture carried on by women, a consanguine group would suffer more inconvenience through the loss of its girls by marriage than through the loss of its boys. In a herding society where the animals were tended exclusively by men the reverse would be the case. When ownership of a natural resource, such as garden or pasture land, was vested in the family, there would be a still stronger incentive to retain persons of the sex who could exploit this resource and to make the spouses of such individuals come and settle with the consanguine group. At the same time such economic factors can very easily be counterbalanced by others of many different sorts. Thus the tribe depending on women's agriculture may have a pattern under which the social position of the various consanguine groups is determined by the number of heads their men bring home, leading each consanguine group to do all it can to retain and build up its male membership. Again, the women of the herding tribe might weave cloth which found a ready and profitable market. A particular line of descent might even come to be established through sheer imitation of some other group which was admired. However, in spite of all these variables there does seem to be a very rough and general correlation between the line of descent selected by a particular group and the sex which is of preponderant economic importance. Male-supported societies tend to be patrilineal, female-supported ones matrilineal.

There is a much clearer correlation between the line of descent in any society and the place of residence for married couples. Matrilineal descent is normally linked with matrilocal residence, patrilineal with patrilocal. There are a fair number of cases in which residence is not prescribed at all, but patterns of matrilocal residence with patrilineal descent or vice versa are extremely rare. In the cases where residence is not prescribed at all, there is usually an added emphasis on the conjugal group at the expense of the consanguine group. The reason for this correlation between descent line and place is fairly obvious. The main advantage of tracing descent is that it makes possible the assignment of individuals to particular consanguine units at birth. Such an assignment makes it possible to catch the individual young and to begin training him at once in coöperation with and proper attitudes toward the other members of his family unit. This training is easiest and most effective when he is in constant contact with the other members. It is better to bring him up with the people with whom he will later have to work, and the simplest way of ensuring this is to have the child's parents live with the consanguine family to which the child belongs.

Each of the basic types of family also shows certain correlations with particular patterns of dominance and control in the family unit and of attitudes toward marriage. I have been unable to find any exception to the generalization that where the conjugal family is the functional unit formal control of this unit is vested in the husband. This condition almost certainly derives from the biologically established dominance of the male, which is given full play under these circumstances. However, the formal attitudes toward marriage in societies of this type are highly variable. Such a strongly conjugal society as the Eskimo are notoriously casual in their attitudes toward marriage as an institution, the partners leaving at will, while some other conjugal societies are extremely strict. The reason for such a range of attitudes probably lies in the fact that, if the society's emphasis on the conjugal grouping as the functional family unit is strong enough, the continuity of marriage becomes self-enforcing. If the partners have no consanguine groups to fall back upon, their economic dependence upon each other becomes so complete that they cannot separate without serious inconvenience to both. They may come to dislike each other thoroughly, but continued life together is the lesser of two evils.

In societies organized on the consanguine basis the conditions are quite different. When the families of both partners are in easy reach, actual dominance of either partner in the marriage relationship is reduced to a minimum. In so far as it exists at all it will normally be vested in the partner through whom the children derive their family membership and with whose family the conjugal group will normally live. This may be the woman, and most of the so-called matriarchal, i.e., woman-ruled, societies show this condition. Under such circumstances the wife derives her power from the backing of her own male relatives, which prevents the exercise of physical dominance by the husband. In such societies divorce is usually easy and frequent, since either partner can leave the union without serious inconvenience. It is most frequent in matriarchal societies, since the presence of the husband is less vital to the well-being of the child than is the presence of its mother. His functions can readily be taken over by her male relatives, and her family will not make any great effort to keep him. When the child belongs to the father's family, there will be a more consistent effort to keep marriages intact, since the well-being of the child requires its mother's presence.

It is easy to provide a father substitute, but it may be very hard to find a wet-nurse.

The highest degree of female dominance in the marriage relationship would, all other things being equal, occur in societies having distant matrilocal residence. Here the man would be almost completely at the mercy of his wife's relatives, their control being tempered only by the ease with which he could run away. Actually, societies of this type are extremely rare. The highest degree of male dominance in the marriage relationship does demonstrably occur in those societies which have distant patrilocal residence. Here the physical dominance of the husband is enforced by the presence of his own and the absence of his wife's relatives. It is more difficult for a woman to run away than for a man to do so, and the strange wife is at the mercy of her husband's group to an extent unknown in the opposite situation.

It is in societies organized on the basis of patrilineal descent and distant patrilocal residence that we find the most elaborate development of formal machinery for ensuring the continuity of marriage relationships. The well-being of the child requires the presence of its mother during at least the first two or three years of its life. With close patrilocal residence breaking of the marriage bond does not really separate the child from either its mother or its consanguine family. If it is an infant she may take it home with her, but as it grows older its consanguine group can easily reassert their rights. If it is an older child it can see its mother as often as it wishes while still living with its own consanguine group. With distant patrilocal residence this situation is completely changed. In case of a separation a young child's consanguine group must either allow it to go with its mother or be party to its death, while if it does go with its mother it is likely to be lost to them permanently. The desire of the mother's consanguine group to increase its strength is enough to ensure the child a welcome, while her male relatives can provide for its economic needs and training. If it comes back to its father's group at all, it will come as a stranger.

The commonest mechanism for ensuring continuity to the

marriage relationship is that of making it a contract between the consanguine groups of the spouses rather than between the individuals actually involved. The man's group usually gives a consideration of some sort to the woman's group, i.e., a bride-price, and in return the woman's group abrogates part of her rights with them and relinquishes all rights in her children. The spouses are thus under pressure from both sides to continue the arrangement, since their separation will involve the honor and usually the finances of both the contracting groups.

Most of the correlations which have just been pointed out can be explained on a functional basis. Certain combinations of patterns are better adapted to particular situations than are others. However, the existence of such correlations lends only a very limited support to theories of functional determinism. It is plain that in the development of any social system there have been repeated opportunities for choice. Thus a society may base its family organization entirely on either the conjugal or the consanguine unit, or it may recognize both. If it does the latter, the possibilities of varying emphasis on one or the other of the two units and of the division and ascription of functions to each are almost unlimited. If a group chooses to stress the consanguine unit, it will almost inevitably be led to the development of patterns of unilinear descent, but it may trace this descent in either the male or the female line. There would hardly be an instance in the whole course of the development of any social system where alternate ways of meeting the functional requirements of a situation would not present themselves. Why any society has chosen to incorporate into its system a particular alternative can be explained only in terms of the total situation existing at the time the choice was made, i.e., in terms of historic causation. Functional considerations may and do serve to limit the range of workable alternatives, but they rarely if ever limit them so strictly that choice is excluded.

CHAPTER XI

MARRIAGE

The terms *marriage* and *the family* are often used as though they were synonymous, but this usage is incorrect for many social systems. The married partners, with their children, either real or socially ascribed, constitute what we have termed a conjugal group. The personnel and functions of this group may coincide with those of the authentic family in certain societies, but they do not do so for human societies as a whole. Marriage and the family are really distinct institutions and must be considered separately.

Marriage is a socially recognized union between persons of opposite sex. It differs from non-marital sexual relationships primarily through this factor of social recognition and through the increased duration in time which such recognition assumes. It derives its importance as a social institution from the fact that it provides a stable foundation for the creation and organization of a conjugal group. Its intrinsic functions of providing for the sexual needs of the partners and through these for the production of offspring are secondary to this. Both these needs can be met satisfactorily without the marriage institution. However, conjugal groups cannot exist without marriage, and we find that in many societies a union is not considered really a marriage until the conjugal group has come into existence, i.e., until a child has been born. Until this time, society gives only a tentative recognition to the spouses' relationship. In many cases marriages which are not productive of children are *ipso facto* dissolved, while in all societies, even our own, the termination of childless marriages is viewed with less disapproval than is that of marriages with children. In the first instance separation entails hardship only on the immediate parties, while in the second it means the disruption of a conjugal group with hardship to the children and very often for individuals outside the conjugal group. Whichever spouse the children go with in such cases, the relatives of this spouse must assume added responsibilities with regard to their care and training.

Practically all societies consider married life the most normal and desirable type of existence for adults. The spouses are expected to find in such relationships not merely regular satisfaction of sexual needs and coöperation in economic matters, but emotional response as well. There are a few societies where the claims of the consanguine group are so strong that it is taken for granted that spouses will not feel affection for each other, but in at least 90 per cent of the world's cultures the ideal patterns for marriage do call for it. Even when marriages are arranged by the parents and the young people have no opportunity of knowing each other in advance, there is usually a sincere effort to bring together individuals who will have the potentialities of happy life together. Thus in China there is a saying that a family should marry its sons and daughters to families whose doors are opposite its own, i.e., which have the same background and social position. Persons from families of this sort have a better chance of adapting to each other than those who come from markedly different backgrounds. When the young people have opportunities for meeting each other, their wishes are almost always consulted even when marriages are, in theory, arranged by the parents. Many societies believe that the parents have better judgment in such matters, but very few of them approve the forcing of children into unions which are actively distasteful to them. Such forcing occurs mainly in societies which practise child betrothal with exchanges of property, but even here there are usually provisions for escape.

While there is thus a nearly universal tendency to show consideration for the individual's wishes, there are very few societies in which young people are allowed a free hand in choosing their mates. Marriage brings the families on both sides into a series of new relationships, and it is natural that they should take an active interest in it. The commonest method of solving the difficulty is to allow a limited choice among partners whom the family consider desirable. Actually, such an arrangement entails no great hardship. It does not agree with our own patterns of romantic love, yet it is interesting to speculate in how far these patterns are themselves a result of culture. The concept of romantic love did not appear in Europe until the time of the thirteenth century troubadours, and these experts ruled at first that it was impossible to married people. Even as late as the eighteenth century it played a very small part in European marriage. All societies recognize that there are occasional violent emotional attachments between persons of opposite sex, but our present American culture is practically the only one which has attempted to capitalize these and make them the basis for marriage. Most groups regard them as unfortunate and point out the victims of such attachments as horrible examples. Their rarity in most societies suggests that they are psychological abnormalities to which our own culture has attached an extraordinary value just as other cultures have attached extreme values to other abnormalities. The hero of the modern American movie is always a romantic lover just as the hero of the old Arab epic is always an epileptic. A cynic might suspect that in any ordinary population the percentage of individuals with a capacity for romantic love of the Hollywood type was about as large as that of persons able to throw genuine epileptic fits. However, given a little social encouragement, either one can be adequately imitated without the performer admitting even to himself that the performance is not genuine.

Most societies are less keen on romance than on congeniality. They train their young people to believe that any well-bred boy and girl, once married, will be able to live together contentedly and will in time develop a real fondness for each other. In most cases this seems to be correct. The percentage of happy arranged marriages is probably as high as that of happy romantic marriages, and they are likely to be much more satisfactory to the families involved. At the same time, all societies recognize that there are couples who are unable to adjust to each other and who can never establish any relationship more satisfying than that of an armed truce. The institution of divorce is a recognition that congeniality and happiness are essential aspects of the marriage relationship. It is as much an expression of the basic values of marriage as is the institution itself. Divorce is a technique by which individuals who have failed to find these values in one union may be released to seek them in another. Mere separation will remove the irritations of an unhappy marriage, but unless the former relationship is definitely terminated the individual cannot enter into a new relationship. He is debarred from the advantages of marriage and doomed to an incomplete existence.

Although practically all societies recognize divorce, there is no society which approves it in principle. The ideal marriage is everywhere that in which the members remain together for life. Divorce is looked upon as a last resort, to be employed only when the relationship becomes intolerable. Of course this breaking point will depend a good deal upon both the individual and the culture in which he has been reared. There are certain American societies in which it is notably low, as when a California judge recently granted a divorce because a man's wife insisted on wearing yellow. There are other societies in which it is very high. In nearly all societies it is given formal recognition in a series of legal causes for divorce which may even be enumerated in the marriage contract. Thus in Madagascar the bride's family, in a formal address, recommend her to the care of her new husband and warn him that he may beat her, but if he breaks a bone, or pulls out her hair, or puts out an eye, they will claim her again. Conversely, he is entitled to send her away if she speaks disrespectfully of his parents, or commits adultery, or cannot cook rice well. Lastly, the parties may separate by mutual consent, in which case neither one receives any indemnity from the family of the other.

All societies devote much more ingenuity to safeguarding the marriage relationship and to providing for its continuation than they do to divorce, while none encourage divorce. In their simplest form these safeguards may be nothing more than freely expressed disapproval of spouses who separate, with a still stronger disapproval of outsiders who contribute to the separation. In the close-knit life of a primitive community this method is highly effective, while it remains flexible enough to take account of exceptional cases. If a marriage finally does break up, every one knows all the circumstances and puts the blame where it belongs. The more formal techniques for ensuring the continuity of marriage are highly variable. They include all sorts of religious, legal, and economic sanctions, with a wide range of combinations of these. It happens that our own society relies heavily upon religious sanctions, but it is somewhat atypical in this. Taking the world as a whole, the religious aspects of marriage seem to be rather poorly developed. The actual ceremony of marriage frequently includes an introduction of the family's new member to the ancestral spirits or an invocation of blessings upon the union, but its termination rarely results in supernatural punishments.

Most societies look upon marriage as a legal contract either between the individuals involved or between their respective families. This leaves the way to divorce open, since the failure of either party to live up to the terms of the agreement renders the contract null and void. Such contracts become more binding when they involve property as well as mutual rights and duties. The commonest form of such ratification of contract by transfer of property is that which is, often rather erroneously, known as wife-purchase. In this the husband, or the husband's family, makes a payment to the wife's family. The converse condition, i.e., payment by the woman's family to the man's family or the man himself, is extremely rare. The old European system of providing a dowry for each daughter is one of the closest approaches to it. While this dowry usually remained the property of the woman, it was an addition to the husband's working capital as well as a contribution to the comfort of the new family. Well-dowered girls had a much better chance of marriage than poorly dowered ones and a large enough sum would compensate the husband for almost any deficiencies in his wife's appearance or disposition. Direct payment to the husband is even rarer, but is found in a few Indian castes where there is a marked shortage of men. Hindu religion enjoins dire penalties on a father who fails to get his daughter a husband, and among the poor of these castes there are professional husbands who sell their services. Some of these men have as many as a hundred wives scattered in different villages and travel on a regular circuit, spending two or three days with each.

Wife-purchase is so foreign to the patterns of our own society, which leans rather toward husband-purchase, that we are prone to misunderstand its real significance. There are very few cases in which it degrades women to the level of chattels. A man may buy his wife, but there is hardly any society in which he can sell her again. The payment which he or his family makes to her family does not give him absolute rights over her. Although the purpose of the property transfer is interpreted somewhat differently in various societies, it usually has two main functions. It reimburses the woman's family for the loss of her services and, incidentally, makes it possible for them to replace her by another marriage. The bride-price which comes in is paid out again at a son's wedding. In this respect wife-purchase is really a substitute for daughter-exchange, a fairly common phenomenon among people of simple culture. Purchase has the same advantage over direct exchange that cash transactions have over barter. There is no need to wait for the other family to produce a daughter equal in age and value to your own. Moreover, it makes wives a highly desirable form of interest-bearing investment. With luck, the husband may get his money back several times over from the sale of his own daughters. In some parts of Africa the husband regularly relies on the first instalments paid on his daughter to meet the last instalments due on her mother, while in some tribes of northern California a still more curious arrangement prevailed. Here the price paid for a woman set the rock-bottom price for her daughters, and the husband's family would give all they could afford for her, counting it a sound investment.

The other and in certain respects even more important function of the bride-price is to establish the rights of the families involved in the contract over the children which may result from the marriage. In return for a consideration, the mother's family relinquishes all rights. This aspect of wife-purchase comes out very clearly in native law both in Madagascar and in many African tribes. The Mashona express it in a terse proverb: "The

children are where the bride-price is not." In Madagascar it is
the giving of property to the wife's family by the husband's
family which legalizes a marriage. The value of the goods exchanged is usually fixed by custom and actually it is usually
small, equivalent to the "consideration" of our own legal contracts. Although among the Tanala most of the clans give only
a spade, a large bead of a particular sort, and a shoulder cloth
for their wives, this establishes the family rights over the offspring. In the one clan which does not pay even this nominal
bride-price the children belong to the mother's family. If the
father strikes one of them, the mother will warn him; and if he
repeats the offense, she will go back to her own family and take
the children with her. The other Tanala feel that this practice
is disreputable and look down on the members of this clan as
living in shameless concubinage. Among themselves only illegitimate children belong to the mother's family.

The significance of the bride-price comes out even more
clearly in the laws of another Madagascar tribe, the Vezo Sakalava. Here the bride-price is considerable, sometimes as much as
ten or twelve head of cattle. In case of divorce, no matter what
the cause, the husband's family cannot claim either a refund or
the substitution of another woman. At the same time, the divorced
wife cannot marry again without her former husband's permission. Before he gives this he enters into an agreement with the
new husband by which he will receive the first children born from
the new union up to three. He is legally entitled to demand a
refund of the original bride-price instead, but he would be ridiculed for doing so. It would be felt that he was putting property
values above human values. These children are his return on the
original investment and have exactly the same social and legal
position as children of an unbroken marriage. It is not even
necessary for the first husband to adopt them in order to make
them his legal heirs. He claims them as soon as the nursing
period is finished, and they are reared by his own family. Men
seem to take exactly the same interest in these bride-price children as in their actual children and often develop a strong
affection for them.

Before passing on to other aspects of marriage, it might be well to say a word about marriage by capture. Early students of marriage attached great importance to this form, even considering it as the first step in the development of individual marriage as an institution. The capture of women and their taking as concubines by their captors is a common phenomenon, but this in itself does not constitute marriage. The women are slaves, and their sexual use does not alter their social status. Mohammedan law, which is unusually liberal in this matter, provides that a woman shall become free as soon as she has borne a child to her master, but even then she remains a concubine and lacks the rights of a legal wife. In Madagascar a slave concubine and her children remained slaves unless her master and their father freed them by a regular ceremony. If he neglected to do this, they might be sold to settle his estate. The woman would become a wife only if her relatives paid the husband one half of her ransom value. This freed both the woman and her children and gave them full family status.

It is difficult to see how marriage, as a social institution, could have developed out of the capture of women. There would be little need for any formal, social recognition of the relationship between captor and captive, since it would establish no new relationship between family groups and since the affiliations of the offspring would never be brought in question. The captor's property rights over the captive would be enough to ensure the continuity of the union, and it would be to the advantage of the captor to keep the decision as to whether it should be continued or broken off in his own hands. The captive, as an outsider, would have no rights deserving of the society's consideration, and it would not be likely to take steps to ensure to her her owner's care. Moreover, the regular getting of wives by the capture method would have inherent difficulties. It would limit the captor's choice almost as much as the captive's and, under primitive conditions, would necessitate a vigilance wearing to all concerned. Real marriage by capture does not exist in any society at the present time, and most of the marriage rites which have been interpreted as survivals of it are susceptible of other explanations. Sham fights between the husband's and wife's relatives, sham abductions and pursuits of the bride may be nothing more than dramatizations of the girl's modesty and her family's regret at losing her. Even among ourselves neither the girl nor her family are supposed to be elated on these occasions. The marriage may be the culmination of a long and well-conducted campaign, but it is customary for both the bride and her mother to shed a few tears and for the father to look solemn.

There seems to be no recognizable correlation between the techniques employed to stabilize marriage and the content of the married group. Theoretically men and women can be combined in marriage in four ways: 1 man—1 woman (monogamy), 1 man —x women (polygyny), x men—1 woman (polyandry), and x men—x women (group marriage). The term *polygamy* properly means simply plurality of mates and thus includes both polygyny and polyandry. We have come to use it as an equivalent for *polygyny* largely because polyandry is so foreign to our own social patterns that plurality of spouses at once suggests plurality of wives. All four of these possible combinations are recognized or permitted in one culture or another, but they differ considerably in their frequency.

Group marriage was given a large place in the old evolutionary theory of the development of marriage. It was logically necessary as a step between the original promiscuity which this theory assumed and any of the three other forms of marriage. We have seen that this original state of promiscuity is probably a myth, and at the present time group marriage is so rare that its very existence has been questioned. It cannot be denied that certain societies recognize and permit an arrangement by which a group of men and women live together as spouses. Certain writers have claimed that such an arrangement does not constitute group marriage because there is, in all the cases known, a main pair whose marital rights in each other take precedence over those of the other members of the group. It seems to the writer that this fact does not invalidate the arrangement as group marriage any more than the existence of a head wife among several wives makes it impossible to call such cases polygyny. Thus in thē Marquesas the household formerly consisted of a head couple and a series of other men and women who lived with them and had recognized sexual rights both with regard to the heads and with regard to each other. This arrangement differed from the ideal pattern of group marriage only in the fact that the connection of the subsidiary partners with the household could be more readily broken than the relationship between the main partners.

Something approximating group marriage has also been developed among the Toda in recent times. This tribe formerly practised polyandry, the number of women in the tribe being kept down by female infanticide. In connection with this system the tribe developed strong patterns against male sexual jealousy and held up the amicable sharing of wives as a virtue. Under British rule infanticide has been discouraged and the number of women correspondingly increased, but the attitudes toward wife-sharing have remained so strong that a group of brothers now take two or more women as common wives instead of taking one wife as formerly. However, the fact remains that group marriage is excessively rare, perhaps because it presents no practical advantages. It is hard to conceive of a situation in which it would be more advantageous than any of the other three forms, while it goes dead against the apparently innate tendency for human males to strive for exclusive possession of females.

Polyandry, although considerably more frequent than group marriage, is still quite rare. It seems to be rather uniformly correlated with hard economic conditions and a necessity for limiting population. Ethical concepts aside, the most effective method of limitation is female infanticide. The number of women of child-bearing age in any group determines the possible rate of increase, while the number of men has no effect on this rate. Polyandry, as an institution, serves to provide the surplus males with mates and also to ensure to the conjugal group the economic contributions of several males. Under certain conditions this last factor may be as important as the first. Any social worker will testify that even in our own society hard times often result in what is essentially a polyandrous arrangement, although the secondary husband is usually known as a boarder.

In most polyandrous societies the plural husbands are usually a group of actual or socially ascribed brothers. Tibetan polyandry is one of the classic examples. In Tibet all arable land has long since passed into family holdings. Many of these holdings have become so small that they barely suffice to support a conjugal group and could not do so if they were further subdivided. It has become customary for one son from each family to go into religious life, thus relinquishing his claim on the family land. The other sons marry a single wife, work the family holding for the support of this woman and her children, and pass the holding on to the children intact. In spite of female infanticide, the position of women is high. The wife usually takes charge of the finances of the family and may dominate her spouses. That Tibetan polyandry is primarily due to hard economic conditions seems to be proved by the fact that it is characteristic only of the lower classes. Tibetans of higher economic status tend to be monogamous, while rich nobles are sometimes polygynous.

Polygyny, i.e., plurality of wives, is considered the most desirable form of marriage in a very large part of the world's societies. It does not seem to be directly correlated with any particular set of economic conditions or even with the primary dependence of the society on the labor of either men or women. It exists alike in societies in which women do most of the work and every wife is an added asset to the conjugal group and in those in which men carry the economic burden and each wife is an added liability. Although such factors do not seem to influence the ideal pattern, they naturally limit its exercise. Where wives are an asset, even a poor man can be polygynous unless the bride-price is prohibitive, and actual plurality of wives tends to be common. Where wives are a liability, few men can afford the luxury of an extra wife. Thus, although the Greenland Eskimo permit polygyny, only a very good hunter can support more than one woman, and only about one man in twenty has a second wife. The same holds for most Mohammedan communities. Although a man is allowed four wives and an unlimited number of con-

cubines by Koranic law, poor families are nearly always monogamous and only the rich can take the full number of wives
permitted.

One factor which unquestionably does make for polygyny is
a shortage of men. Systematic male infanticide is almost unknown.
It would have no effect on population increase and would weaken
the power of the group for offense or defense even if it had no
economic consequences. However, due to the more active life of
men and the ascription to them of the more hazardous occupations, uncivilized groups usually show a surplus of women. Warfare, of course, contributes to this situation, but its effects are
probably secondary in most cases to those of the occupational
dangers. Although uncivilized tribes are usually at war with some
one, the actual losses are surprisingly small. Thus a chief of the
Mahafaly, in southwestern Madagascar, in telling me of an important war which had cost his people a large piece of territory,
said that his tribe *had had eight men killed!*

It seems probable that the widespread occurrence of polygyny
derives more from the general primate tendency for males to
collect females than from anything else. The other factors involved are only contributory causes. At the same time, polygyny
does not necessarily imply a high degree of male dominance in
the marriage relationship or even a low position of women in the
society. Polygynous societies are as variable in this respect as are
monogamous ones. While there are a few cases in which the wives
are completely dependent upon the husband, in most instances
their rights are well guarded. When the plural wives are congenial, the women of a polygynous household may form a block,
presenting a solid front against the husband and even dominating
him. The situation existing in polygynous families in Madagascar,
which is typical for a large part of Africa as well, is about as
follows.

There are some differences in the family arrangements from
one tribe to another, but the basic patterns are nearly the same
everywhere. A man's first marriage is normally a love match,
although there are a few tribes which require marriage with the
daughter of a father's sister. In either case, the first wife ranks

all subsequent wives and is the unquestioned head of the women's half of the conjugal group. The first plural marriage usually takes place three or four years after the original union and is, in a surprisingly large number of cases, instigated by the first wife. Women work in the fields as well as in the house, and when there are small children they often find the burden exceedingly heavy. No female help can be hired, and even the purchase of a slave woman is not a satisfactory solution. (Slavery has, of course, been terminated by French rule. We are discussing conditions of fifty years ago.) The husband would be entitled to use such a slave as a concubine, thus giving the wife as much cause for jealousy as would another wife, while the slave's interest in the establishment would be less and her coöperation less whole-hearted. The best solution is for the husband to marry another wife, and his failure to do so is either an admission of poverty or a sign of indifference to the first wife's interests.

Second wives are drawn from the women who are not attrac-tive enough to be chosen as first wives, from widows and from divorcées. A man must marry his brother's widow if she has children, his first wife having no say in the matter. Otherwise, he must have his wife's permission for the second marriage. Actually, they usually talk over the possibilities and finally agree on some woman who will be acceptable to both. In at least one case a man married a second wife because his first wife insisted on it. The woman was a close friend of hers whom the husband rather disliked. For all subsequent marriages the husband must have the permission of all his previous wives. As the number increases it becomes more difficult to get this, and the husband often has to resort to bribery, making the other wives gifts of money or cattle. The only exception to this rule is when the husband is detected in an affair with an unmarried woman. If it seems to be serious, his wives may insist upon his marrying her on the principle that she should share in the labors of the house-hold. Needless to say, her position after the marriage is not a happy one, and this curious form of revenge is a rather strong incentive to good behavior. Chiefs do not have to have their wives' permission for plural marriages, and they are the only men who collect large numbers of wives. Very few commoners have more than three.

When a man has three wives, each wife will have a separate house for herself and her children. The first wife usually keeps the original dwelling, and the husband considers her house as his real home and keeps most of his belongings there. However, he is required to spend one day with each wife in succession. If he spends one wife's day with another wife, it constitutes adultery under native law and entitles the slighted wife to a divorce with alimony amounting to one third of the husband's property other than land. Such an offense is considered more serious than misconduct with a woman outside the conjugal group, and the husband will be lucky if he escapes with a liberal gift to the offended wife. Conversely, adultery in our use of the term is considered the affair only of the wife on whose day the offense was committed. The other wives will be sure to tell her about it if they discover it first, but unless the husband is having a real affair they are more likely to make fun of her than to sympathize. Theoretically the injured wife is entitled to a divorce with alimony, but she will be ridiculed if she claims one on grounds of a single offense and is usually satisfied with a moderate gift.

For purposes of cultivation, the husband's land is divided among the wives as equally as possible. Each wife works her section and can claim the husband's assistance on her day. This economic claim over the husband goes so far that if he hunts or fishes on that day the wife has a right to half his take or to half the money received from the sale of any surplus. From the produce of her section of land each woman feeds herself and her children, also the husband on the day he is with her. If there is a surplus to be sold, one half of the proceeds go to the husband as ground rent. The other half is the property of the wife, and she usually banks it with her own family. In a well-organized conjugal group the women usually take turns working on the land while one of them remains at home to cook and tend the children. The whole family will eat first at one house and then at another, so that, if there are three wives, cooking and dishwashing will fall to the portion of any one of them only on every third day. In many cases the plural wives become strongly attached to each other, while there is always a tendency for the female part of the group to present a united front toward the husband. Wives will not infrequently carry on love affairs with the full knowledge of their fellow-wives without fear of betrayal. The female half of the family is thus able to control family policies to a considerable degree, and hen-pecked husbands are by no means unknown. If the husband tries to coerce one wife, the rest will resent it and make his life miserable by those unofficial methods with which all women are familiar. The wives receive added power from the fact that the husband is theoretically in complete control and cannot appeal for outside help without making himself ridiculous.

The condition just described may be extreme, but there are few polygynous systems in which the position of the male is really better than it is under monogamy. If the plural wives are not congenial, the family will be torn by feuds in which the husband must take the thankless rôle of umpire, while if they are congenial he is likely to be confronted by an organized feminine opposition. Among the sub-human primates the male can dominate a group of females because these females are unable to organize among themselves. He can deal with them in detail. The human male cannot dominate his wives in the same degree, since they can and do organize for both defense and offense. If all a man's wives want a particular thing, they can work on him in shifts and are fairly certain to get what they want.

The only form of marriage which is recognized and permitted in all social systems is monogamy. It coexists with all the other forms, although it is the preferred form in a relatively small number of societies. In those groups which recognize it as an alternative, its social significance varies according to what the preferred form may be. Thus in a polyandrous society monogamous unions may bring the members a certain prestige. A man who can support a conjugal group without help must be richer and more able than the average. Conversely, in a polygynous society monogamous unions may mean loss of prestige. If a man has only one wife, it will be tacitly assumed that he is too poor to buy or support a second. When this attitude is present, the first wife often feels the situation keenly and does all that she can to bring about a second marriage. She may not enjoy having a rival in the family, but she enjoys still less the idea that she is married to a failure.

An actual analysis of marriage in various societies shows that there are very few groups in which plurality of spouses is the general condition. Even when polygyny is the ideal, there are usually only a few men who can afford to have more than one wife. Thus among the Eskimo plural unions stand to monogamous ones in the ratio of about one to twenty. In the non-Christian civilizations such as those of India, China, or Islam, the ratio is almost as low. Although economic factors are mainly responsible for this condition, all groups can also show certain unions which are monogamous by preference. When the partners find complete emotional satisfaction in each other, they prefer not to admit additional spouses even when there is social pressure for them to do so. Such unions seem to provide the maximum of happiness to the parties involved.

There is no absolute scale against which the advantages and disadvantages of the various forms of marriage can be measured. Each form is an integral part of a particular economic and social system and, as such, will function better in connection with that system than with any other. Our own form of marriage works very well in its present setting, yet when it has been introduced into other societies the results have often been catastrophic. As far as the happiness of the individuals involved is concerned, there are a few persons in all societies who would not be content under any form of permanent mating, and a few at the opposite end of the scale who are able to find complete contentment in enduring monogamous unions. The bulk of all populations appear to fall between these two extremes. They can be conditioned to accept any type of union as natural and will find contentment in it as long as the other partners are not actively uncongenial.

CHAPTER XII

SOCIAL UNITS DETERMINED BY BLOOD

All social systems include certain units whose membership is determined by blood relationship. The extent to which such units are stressed differs greatly from one society to another. In some they are of only secondary significance, while in others they quite overshadow the conjugal units, becoming the primary focus for their members' interests and loyalties and the basis on which most coöperative activities are organized. In the latter case they are more nearly the social equivalents of the family as we know it than are the conjugal groups. Socially emphasized consanguine units of this type are known as *joint families*. This pattern of organization is so foreign to our own system that it may be well to begin our discussion of it with a concrete example.

Among the more primitive divisions of the Tanala tribe, in Madagascar, the joint family is the most important social unit. All stages in the development, stabilization, and final disintegration of such units can be observed here at first hand. The growth of a joint family begins with a conjugal group closely comparable in its composition to similar groups among ourselves. Although plural marriages are permitted, they are rare in practice, and such a group normally consists of a man, his wife, and their children. As the children grow up, such a group becomes a well-organized coöperative unit. When the sons marry, they bring their wives home, building new houses for themselves close to their father's dwelling. The daughters marry out of the family, but since all marriages are normally contracted within the village the separation is more apparent than real. The daughters' new residences are usually within two or three minutes' walk of their father's house, and they continue to coöperate with their original family groups to a considerable degree.

The father has complete control over his children and his sons' children as long as he lives. His orders to his married daughters take precedence even over those of their husbands, but he has no control over his daughters' children, who belong to their fathers' joint families. He organizes and directs the group's activities, settles disputes between the members, and has complete control of the finances. When they are at home in the village, all the male members of the family work together in the rice fields, and the product belongs to the father, who divides it among the sons according to their needs and keeps the surplus, or the profit from its sale, for himself. If the sons go away to work, they are expected to send him the lion's share of their wages. All these profits are commonly invested in cattle, the only form of interest-bearing investment known to the tribe. The father in return pays the bride-price for his sons' wives and makes them occasional gifts of needed money, but there is little opportunity for any of them to acquire wealth as long as their father lives.

The conditions under which the Tanala live make it highly advantageous for a number of men to work together as a coöperative unit. Their main crop is rice, cultivated by the cutting and burning method. The jungle can be cleared more efficiently by gang labor than by single individuals. Moreover, gangs of men were in a better position to repel enemy attacks, which were common prior to the beginning of French domination. Fifteen or twenty men working together can get a greater individual return for their labor than can the same number working separately, and this fact seems to have been important in establishing the joint family pattern.

Many Tanala men live to see their grandchildren full grown, and it is not uncommon for a patriarch to have ten or twelve able-bodied sons and grandsons under his control. When the old man dies, the members of this group continue to live and work together on much the same terms. The eldest son takes the place of the father as director and organizer, but with the important difference that he cannot demand contributions from his brothers nor sequester the surplus crop. Each of the brothers has full patriarchal rights over his own children and can now begin to enrich himself. The actual power of the eldest brother depends a good deal upon his own personality. To ensure him an added measure of control it is usual for the father to leave the bulk of his estate to the eldest son, thus enabling him to make loans to his brothers and generally control their financial activities. At the same time, he is expected to help his brothers freely in time of need and to contribute more heavily than the rest to family ceremonies. Although the other members of the joint family have no legal claim on the inheritance which the eldest has received, they do have a moral claim upon it and can always demand aid from him.

The habits of coöperation developed during the original father's domination are usually so strong that the family continues to function smoothly and efficiently under the eldest son's control. When he dies his eldest son succeeds to the post of family head, and from this point on there are likely to be splits in the group. Brothers from the first generation may outlive the eldest and are likely to be jealous of domination by a younger man, especially when they have acquired independent wealth through the exploitation of their own children. The size to which the family has grown will also have an effect. A joint family which includes only a small number of men will rarely split, while one in which the number exceeds the optimum for coöperative land-clearing is very likely to do so. There is also the factor of crowding, since each joint family occupies a clearly defined plot of ground in the village. A family which has grown too large for its plot may buy land from its neighbors if they have it to spare, but if it cannot do this it is almost forced to split. Common residence seems to be vital to the maintenance of the joint family as a genuine functional unit, and a household which moves away even to another part of the same village quickly drops out of the coöperative unit.

The founders of joint families receive special consideration in the ancestor cult, being worshiped by all their descendants in the male line. No matter how many times the lineage which they have founded subdivides, their names will still be included in the sacrificial rituals of all the resulting groups and their honor will increase rather than decrease with time. Men who do not found a new joint family are worshiped only by their own sons and grandsons, and their names are soon forgotten. There is thus a strong incentive for men to break away and found new joint families, but only a few are able to do so. The founder of a new line must have enough grown sons or grandsons to form an effective work unit and must also be wealthy in his own right. When he secedes from the joint family he relinquishes all rights in the family's town property and must be prepared to buy town property for the new family in either the same or a new village. As long as he lives with the original joint family he must submit to the control of its head. The purchase of town property is official notice to the tribe that a new family has come into being, and such property is thenceforth held by the family as a corporation. It is the visible symbol of the family's existence as a distinct unit, and no individual member can inherit or sell it. Among the Imerina, who have a very similar joint family organization, the symbol of the family is not a town lot but a common tomb, and no man can found a new line until he is rich enough to build such a tomb for himself and his descendants.

A very large joint family will sometimes found a new village. In such cases each head of a household takes up land at the new site and the original unit dissolves into a whole series of new joint families. Ordinarily the new units split off one at a time and at considerable intervals, those who stay behind retaining the town property and reorganizing on the new basis. A joint family may thus be continued through the line of eldest sons for many generations and comes to an end only when the supply of sons fails. When there are not enough men left to form an effective coöperative unit, the surviving households will sell or relinquish their town property and attach themselves to other families, the men going to live with their wives' people. The children are reared as members of the mother's joint family, and in two or three generations all memory of their father's unit will be lost.

The members of a Tanala joint family do not hold property in common except for the town lot which is the symbol of the

family's corporate existence. Since rice land must be allowed to
lie fallow for several years between crops, it is held by the village as a whole and new sections are allotted to each family annu-
ally. The size and value of these allotments is adjusted to the
needs of the family, and this serves to keep all the families on
very much the same economic level. Every house on the town lot
and every piece of portable property is individually owned and
can, in theory, be sold by its owner. At the same time, all family
members have a moral claim on each other's property. Nothing
of value would actually be sold to an outsider without the approval of the group. No household ever lacks food or other necessities, and all family members contribute in proportion to their
means toward the expenses of circumcision ceremonies, weddings,
and funerals, even when their own households are not involved.
Money is hoarded, and money loans between family members
are considered commercial transactions with interest a legitimate
feature, but everything else is lent and borrowed freely. On ceremonial occasions the head of the family will be decked out in the
finest clothing and jewelry that the combined resources of the
households can provide. The owners of this finery are content to
cut a poorer figure themselves, for the family head stands as a
symbol of the unit and outsiders will judge its wealth and importance mainly from him. The same thing holds for brides,
whose wedding outfits are borrowed piece by piece and returned
to their owners after the ceremony.

Within the family labor is pooled even more completely than
property. Members never receive pay for helping each other,
being assured of a return in kind whenever they need it. In spite
of the large size of some joint families this coöperation seems to
be spontaneous and to require no formal machinery for its enforcement. Slacking brings automatic punishment, since he who
does not help will not be helped, but the desire to maintain the
honor of the family is an even stronger incentive. The various
joint families within a village are always critical of each other
and may even be mildly at feud. Bad conduct by any individual
reflects upon his whole group even when actual injury is confined to the family. There is an ever-present fear of what the

neighbors will say. This means that necessary discipline within the group will be applied as quietly as possible and by informal means which will elude the attention of outsiders. It also means that the family will not stand by members who are obviously in the wrong or who are confirmed bad characters.

This desire to maintain the good name of the family even at the expense of individual members comes out clearly in two Tanala institutions, that of disownment and that of infanticide. Disownment is a terrible weapon, since it cuts the individual off from both his living family and his ancestors and condemns him to a vagabond existence in this world and the next. Such a sentence is considered more serious than death. It is employed only against disobedient sons whose behavior has become an open scandal, habitual thieves, or persons guilty of repeated incest. It is felt that in each of these cases injury is done to the entire community. Filial disobedience and incest arouse the wrath of the ancestral spirits, and punishment in the form of sickness for the former and crop failure for the latter are likely to be visited upon the whole village. The broader implications of theft are obvious. Only adult sons are disowned and even then only after repeated warnings. The ceremony is a solemn one, performed in the presence of the whole village, and the sentence is irrevocable. The ancestral spirits are notified, and the family makes gifts to the heads of all the other joint families as a means of reimbursing the village for the loss in its total man-power and also for their service as witnesses. The disowned man is driven out and will usually be killed if he returns. Any of his subsequent misdeeds which come to the ears of the village will not be held against his family, since they have formally disavowed him.

The practice of infanticide springs from a similar desire to maintain the family honor. Children are a distinct economic asset to their parents and are loved quite as much as among ourselves, yet a considerable number of infants are put to death. Whenever a child is born, a diviner is called in to determine its destiny in accordance with a calendar of good and bad days. Children born on three or four days of each calendar round are foredoomed to become thieves or sorcerers or to bring ill fortune upon the family group, and such children are killed as quickly and mercifully as possible.

Units very similar to the Tanala joint families just described exist in many other societies. The Iroquois households mentioned in an earlier chapter are good examples of such an institution with membership based on female instead of male descent. Moreover, the joint family type of organization is not necessarily limited to groups of simple culture. The normal Chinese family includes three or four generations of males with their wives and offspring, the whole group living in a single establishment and pooling its labor and finances under the direction of the oldest living male. Such groups often persist for centuries, sons who wish to break away being given their share of the common property in cash, while the establishment and land are retained by the corporation. Although such units are sometimes dissolved and their common resources divided among the male members, such action entails a serious loss of prestige and makes the members of other family groups reluctant to intermarry with them. Joint family organization is also characteristic of various civilized groups in India, and the institution has received recognition in British law.

Joint families are distinguished from other social units whose membership is determined by unilinear descent primarily by the factors of common residence and limited size. These make it possible for the joint family unit to assume most of the functions ascribed to conjugal family units among ourselves. In the establishment of families as functional social units blood relationship is important only as a reference point by which membership in the residential group is determined. Thus among ourselves a child who has been brought up in another household is not a true, functional member of the social unit into which he was born. For all practical purposes he belongs to the group with which he has been reared. This becomes painfully evident whenever such a person visits what we would call his own family. The ideal patterns of our culture prescribe certain attitudes between parent and child and between brothers and sisters, yet the visitor is actually a stranger and these attitudes have to be counterfeited, with resultant strain to all concerned. Moreover, it is extremely hard to fit such a visitor into the family work unit. The organization of any group for constant coöperation must be based upon its constant membership. Both the visitor and the visited feel that he should help, but both are at a loss as to just what he should do. Conversely, people who habitually live together, whether related by blood or not, develop mutual personality adjustments and bonds of affection and can be trained to complete and largely unconscious coöperation.

Limited size is as constant a feature of joint families as is common residence. It is characteristic of such units that when their membership increases beyond a certain point certain households break away from the group and found new units. It seems probable that there is an optimum size for the joint family in each society. This size would derive partly from factors connected with common residence and coöperative exploitation of resources, partly from psychological factors. The former no doubt vary from one society to another, but the latter must be fairly constant. There are ultimate limits to the number of persons with whom any individual can establish close contacts and personality adjustments. When the unit becomes too large for every one in it to know every one else well, there will be a natural tendency toward the formation within it of groupings of close acquaintances. Conflicts between the interests of such groupings are almost certain to develop, and the group will split.

The number of societies having the joint family pattern is comparatively small. However, the great bulk of the world's social systems include units whose membership is determined by descent through the male or female line. The factors which may have led to the selection of one or the other of these lines in particular societies have been discussed in an earlier chapter. Actually, which line happens to be selected is not of vital importance, since the groupings established by either show exactly the same random distribution of individuals of both sexes and all ages and have the same potentialities for social function. It is true that, as Lowie has pointed out, "A matrilineal society that consistently practises matrilocal residence with local exogamy cannot achieve a maximum of political solidaiity. Its fighting strength is made up largely of men from without, possibly from a dozen clans, hence potentially at loggerheads with one another." [1] However, this difficulty is not implicit for social units based on female descent. It can be avoided by keeping marriages within the local group (local endogamy) or by combining matrilineal descent with patrilocal residence or by the elimination of permanent marital unions. All the phenomena which we find associated with patrilineal descent groups may also appear with matrilineal ones, and it seems clear that the line of descent is a minor factor in the situation.

At the present time there is a good deal of confusion in regard to the terminology applied to such unilateral descent groups. In the earlier studies of these units great importance was attached to the line selected. Units in which membership was based on male descent were called *gentes* (*gens*, singular), while those based on female descent were called *clans*. There was no general term for such units irrespective of the line of descent. There has been an attempt to supply this lack by the introduction of a new term, *sib*, but this has not been generally accepted. The tendency at present is to use *clan* as synonymous with *unilateral descent group* and to refer to matrilineal or patrilineal clans when it is necessary to indicate the line. This usage will be followed in the present volume.

At the very outset of any discussion of clans as social phenomena, the dual nature of the clan must be made clear. It has biological and social aspects which are fundamentally distinct. According to the commonly given definition of a clan it is a biologically determined unit. If one adhered rigidly to this definition, any population could be divided into clan groups by the simple process of studying its members' ancestry and sorting them out on the basis of common unilateral descent. However, the groupings established in this way would have none of the social aspects of the clan. They would be mere collections of individuals unadapted to each other in either behavior or atti-

---

[1] Robert H. Lowie, *An Introduction to Cultural Anthropology* (Farrar and Rinehart, 1935), p. 258.

tudes. It is the recognition of unilateral descent groups as distinct units within the social body and the ascription to these units of certain functions with relation both to their component individuals and the society as a whole which transforms the clan from a biological into a social phenomenon. The particular functions ascribed to such units and even the recognition of their existence are aspects of culture. This means that although all clans are, by definition, biological equivalents, the clans within any two societies are never exact social equivalents. As a result, it is extremely hard to generalize about clans as social institutions.

In both its biological and its social aspects the clan is essentially an expansion of the consanguine family group. Instead of allowing the knowledge of relationship to lapse after two or three generations, this knowledge is perpetuated, so that cousins many degrees removed look upon themselves as fairly close relatives. Wherever the clan is recognized there are mechanisms for keeping this fact of relationship before the mind of the individual and stressing its importance. The clan unit will usually have a name and very frequently a symbol of some sort, such as a particular animal or object, which its members treat with respect. Its members will often have distinctive details of dress or ornament, so that clan affiliations can be recognized at a glance. The unity of the clan may be further emphasized by reunions or special ceremonial observances. Lastly, it is common for clan members to use the same terms of relationship toward each other that they use toward members of their immediate family groups. Thus a man will frequently call all clan members of his own generation brother and sister, all males in his father's generation father, if the group is patrilineal, all women in his father's generation father's sister, etc. This usage does not imply that the individual is in any doubt as to who is his real brother or father or aunt. It is merely a technique for emphasizing the fact that the whole clan is, in theory, one big family.

In spite of such attempts to emphasize the unity of the clan and its likeness to the consanguine family group, it can never actually replace this group as a functional unit. In the normal course of events any clan soon becomes too large for all its members to have direct personal contacts with each other. In the clan the mutual attitudes which give the close consanguine group strong solidarity and high capacity for coöperation become weakened and diffused. The clan member may be expected to feel affection for all other members and to take a lively interest in their affairs, but he cannot develop genuine attitudes of this sort toward persons with whom he has little or no contact. The best that he can do is to counterfeit such attitudes when they happen to meet. The situation can be readily understood by any reader who has had to entertain a cousin whom he has never met before. Such counterfeit attitudes may fulfil the requirements of good manners, but they provide no drive toward actual coöperation.

The patterns governing the behavior of clan members toward one another are nearly always modeled on those governing the reciprocal behavior of actual family members, but in the absence of genuine attitudes these patterns undergo a gradual attenuation. Thus the theoretical rights and duties of the clan head, if it has one, are nearly always a repetition of those of the family head. However, the clan head will never have as much real power over his clansmen as the family head has over his family. Even when he is absolute in theory, he will be limited in practice by a series of checks and balances. Similarly, the individual will not behave in the same way toward a clan brother or father that he will toward an actual brother or father. If there is a general pattern of respect and obedience toward fathers, the individual will accord these to his own father in the highest degree, will give somewhat less to a classificatory father who is closely related and well known to him and still less to a "father" who is a remote relative with whom he has had little contact. He may be in duty bound to help any man whom he calls brother, but he certainly will not help all "brothers" to the same extent.

The clan must be regarded, then, as an expanded and diffused family unit. Its functional potentialities depend primarily upon the emotional vigor of the bonds which unite its members and the opportunities which they have for coöperation. These, in turn are influenced by many factors. A society which centers its interests upon conjugal units and regularly gives the interests of spouses precedence over those of blood relatives can scarcely develop a strong clan organization. The degree of unity and *esprit de corps* characteristic of the clan will also depend to a considerable extent on the effectiveness of the techniques which the culture employs to develop correct attitudes in the clan members. It may be mentioned in passing that the actual unity and coöperative potentialities of clans cannot be judged from the degree of exactness with which their members' behavior to each other is prescribed. Societies vary enormously in the extent to which they formalize and verbalize behavior patterns. Exact rules of conduct do not necessarily imply any more emotional drive than do vaguely formulated patterns of mutual respect and assistance. In fact the group with thoroughly verbalized patterns may function less efficiently than the one without, since it is much easier to avoid the letter of the law than its spirit.

The factor of residence also has a strong effect on a clan's functional potentialities. When the clan group and local group coincide, a feeling of solidarity and patterns of coöperation may become highly developed. The clan can actually take over most of the functions of both the family and the local group. A similar condition exists when the clan is the nucleus of the local group, the balance of the grouping consisting of spouses drawn from other units. On the other hand, a clan whose members are distributed over a wide territory may consider itself as a distinct entity, but it cannot function as a unit under ordinary circumstances. Its members will rarely meet in a body, and although they may coöperate under special circumstances, as in the performance of a ceremony, their day-to-day coöperation will have to be with members of other clans among whom they live. They will have more interests in common with the other members of the various local groups with which they may be affiliated than with their clansmen.

The social significance of the clan varies widely in different societies. It would be possible to construct a graded series ranging from societies in which the clan is a highly organized, socially dominant unit only one step removed from the joint family to those in which the functional importance of the clan is hardly greater than that of our own family-name groupings. There seems to be no constant correlation between the degree to which clans are stressed and any other single element of the culture, or between such stressing and the general degree of cultural complexity. Clanless societies occur at all cultural levels.

It has frequently been claimed that strong functional clans are characteristic of societies in the middle zone of cultural development and that the pattern tends to become weaker toward the top and bottom of the cultural scale. This is at least open to doubt. The Eskimo, who are hunters of simple culture, lack the clan concept entirely, but the Australians, who stand on about the same level, have a highly developed clan organization with a wealth of clan functions. To pass to the other end of the scale, the Chinese have retained a form of clan organization in their family-name groupings or great families. These Chinese units do not have as many functions as do the clans of some other societies, but they are genuine functional units of considerable social importance. Each great family, at least in North China, has its own home territory with an ancestral temple and lands owned by the group as a corporation. Although the great family may include 200,000 or 300,000 individuals scattered all over China, all members are listed and the records are revised at regular intervals. Rich members make bequests to the family for the support of the temple and for the assistance of poor members. Many of these families maintain clubs in distant cities which serve as gathering places for their members and as mutual benefit societies. All members of the unit owe each other the assistance due to relatives, and they may not intermarry no matter how remote the actual blood relationship.

Although strong functional clan organization cannot be correlated with any particular stage of cultural complexity and certainly is not a stage in the unilinear evolution of society, it does seem to be correlated, in a very general way, with stability of culture and fixity of residence. Societies which belong to what we think of as the middle zone of cultural development usually provide both these conditions. Although their cultures are never completely static, the rate of change is usually slow. The membership of local units, especially in agricultural societies, also tends to be fairly constant. Even when such units are nomadic the result is simply a transfer of the total village from one site to another and an individual normally lives and dies among the same neighbors. Such conditions are favorable to the development of a heavy preponderance of ascribed as against achieved statuses, and the clan offers a convenient reference point for the assignment of such statuses to individuals. In a stabilized society, membership in a strong, well-defined social unit provides the individual with both economic and emotional security. His chances for advancement by his own efforts are strictly limited by the established social patterns, so that he has little to lose by fusing his interests and activities with those of his clan. Under conditions of rapid cultural change, the patterns which limit individual achievement always tend to break down. The able and ambitious man can go farther alone than as a member of a large consanguine group. He has less need of the help which the clan can offer and is reluctant to pay for it by taking care of a number of poor or socially insignificant relatives. When rapid cultural change is combined with urban life and high individual mobility, it becomes almost impossible for clans to function. Successful individuals can move away from their clansmen and, once out of reach, can ignore the claims of the clan. The larger the size of the political unit, whether in territory or population, the easier it is for the defaulter to lose himself. The persistence of clans as functional units in China may well have been due to the relative stability of Chinese culture and to the limited opportunities for individual advancement. Security was worth more to the average man than the opportunity to play a lone hand. Conversely, the rapid disappearance of large consanguine groups as functional units in the developing civilizations of Greece and Rome was probably due to the sudden expansion of political units and the wealth of individual opportunity which came with this in combination with a rapidly changing culture.

It has already been said that the clan is essentially an extension of the consanguine family unit and that its functions with relation to its members are normally much the same as those of the consanguine family. In the clan the mutual rights and duties of family members are spread over a larger number of individuals, with some resulting dilution. The clan relatives who are socially equated with immediate family relatives relieve the latter of a part of their duties and stand ready to take over completely in case of need. The result is an increase in the individual's security arising from the certainty of help in time of need. The clan, like the family, also acts as a buffer between the individual and the total society. It can perform this function more effectively than the family because of its greater numerical strength and economic resources. The pattern of clan responsibility for the behavior of clan members is a very common one. As long as the individual is unable to get away and leave his clansmen "holding the sack," this pattern is advantageous both to the individual and to the society as a whole. On the one hand, it protects the individual from the vengeance of stronger enemies and from extreme or unjust penalties for his offenses. On the other, the pattern is a most effective instrument for preventing the commission of offenses. No matter how united the front which a clan may present to outsiders, its members do not enjoy finding themselves embroiled with their neighbors or mulcted for some offense by one of their number. The clan members know each other well and are dependent upon each other for many services; hence they are in a good position to prevent overt offenses by bringing informal pressure on the individual. They are in a still better position to make the offender's life miserable if he offends in spite of them. The clansman who plans a crime may be sure that his clan will get him out of trouble if they cannot keep him out of it, but he can be equally sure that existence will be far from comfortable afterward.

Among the general functions which the clan may inherit from the consanguine family group there are two of outstanding importance: the regulation of marriage and the control of property. Although neither of these functions is ascribed to the clan in all societies, that of regulating marriage is so frequent that it may be called typical. Clans are usually exogamous units, i.e., their members are forbidden to intermarry. In a much smaller number of cases they are endogamous, i.e., their members are forbidden to marry outsiders. In either case, membership in the clan unit limits the individual's choice of spouses just as does membership in a family unit. This is the common principle which underlies exogamy and endogamy alike. Exogamous regulations derive directly from the incest prohibitions which are normally a part of all patterns of family organization. They emphasize the idea that the clan is really an enlarged family. Endogamous regulations commonly arise from a desire to keep property or privilege within the clan group and to emphasize the distinction between it and other clans. Either type of regulation serves to keep the reality of the clan unit before its members' minds and to delimit its membership with increased clarity. Where such rules are in force the clansman will know exactly who are clan members and who are not.

Control of property is a less universal function of the clan. Its occurrence seems to be most frequent in the case of localized clans, the members of which often hold land in common. However, Lauriston Sharp reports a case in northern Australia in which clans, the members of which are scattered through a number of local groups, still hold territories in common. These clan territories consist of scattered tracts of land and the clan members who live nearest to each tract will commonly be the ones to exploit it most, but any clansman normally has the right to hunt in any clan territory.[2] Even when patterns of individual ownership are well developed, it is not uncommon for the clan as a corporation to retain a sort of residual interest in its members' property and to be able to veto the sale of land or valuables to outsiders. This situation probably derives from the fact that as long as the patterns of mutual assistance between clan members remain strong there is a pooling of economic resources within the clan in practice if not in theory. The group can draw on the resources of its component individuals in time of need. The sale of property, especially land, to outsiders thus means a reduction in the capital of the clan as a corporation, and it is natural for it to take an interest in such transactions.

2 Lauriston Sharp, unpublished correspondence.

The fact that the clan is a corporation outlasting the life-span of an individual makes such units highly convenient instru-ments for the performance of functions which require continuity. The assignment of such functions to clans rather than indi-viduals is a common phenomenon of clan-organized societies. The range of the actual functions is, of course, extremely wide, often including very curious duties. Thus in Madagascar one clan of the Bara tribe is required to provide a human sacrifice at the death of the paramount chief. The man must be young, able-bodied, and in good health and a full clan member. When the chief dies, the elders of the clan assemble and decide who can best be spared. This duty is considered an honor to the clan, a recognition of its faithfulness to the reigning family, and it is said that the man who is selected never tries to escape. The task of providing certain public functionaries is also very frequently assigned to clans. While such assignments are generally inter-preted as honors and may become jealously guarded prerogatives, the practical advantages which accrue to the clan from them are often nil. However, the advantages which accrue to the total society are considerable. Let us suppose that the high priest of the tribe is always drawn from a particular clan. This means that that clan, as a corporation, must assume the duty of keeping the post adequately filled. It must attend to the training of indi-viduals in the duties of the office, select those who are compe-tent, and keep one or more trained individuals in reserve, ready to take over the office as soon as the acting priest dies or resigns. By assigning this function to the clan, the society ensures con-tinuity in the priesthood and the uninterrupted performance of the priestly duties.

The corporate qualities of the clan are also utilized by assign-ing it religious or magical observances which are considered vital to the well-being of the society. The care of sacred objects of significance to the whole group is usually assigned to a par-ticular clan or clans rather than to individuals. Similarly, the performance of rituals tends to be ascribed to clans even when these rituals are for the good of the whole society. Thus among the Pawnee the religious life of the tribe centered about a series of sacred objects and the rites performed in connection with them. The objects themselves have been rather erroneously called "medicine bundles." Actually, they were collections of sacred articles which, when exhibited and used in certain ways, established a link between mankind and certain supernatural beings. The nearest equivalent for them in our own culture would be a portable altar which had been consecrated. Each of the Pawnee clans was the custodian of one of these altars. It selected a member to be the guardian and priest of this altar, the office having a tendency to become hereditary. Priest and clan were together responsible to the tribe for the care of the altar, renewing the various parts as they wore out. The priest took charge of the ceremonies connected with his altar, and the clansmen were the main participants. The ceremonies of the various altars were performed in a fixed chronological order, running through the sacred summer season, and each of them had a different objective. Thus one altar ceremony encouraged the growth of corn, another prevented illness, and so on. Taken together, the full round of ceremonies brought supernatural aid to the tribe for all its common needs and activities. No one clan profited by this arrangement more than another. The custodians of the corn-growing bundle would have no better crops than any one else. However, the ascription of the various ceremonies to the various clans made each ceremony the focal point for the interest of a particular group and assured its proper and regular performance.

An almost identical arrangement is found among some of the Pueblo tribes, while rather similar ones could be cited from many different parts of the world. The altruistic element in the clan performance of rituals seems to reach its peak in certain Australian tribes where there is a strong development of totemism. Here each clan stands in a particular relationship to a certain plant, animal, or thing which is of economic importance to the tribe. Under ordinary circumstances the members of the clan do not utilize this totem, yet each clan has a ceremony to ensure the increase of its totem species by magical means. The clan derives no direct advantage from the performance of this ceremony, but the clan ceremonies as a whole are supposed to ensure the tribe a sufficiency of food.

The various clans within a society may have, in addition to their special functions with regard to the total group, special functions with regard to each other. The members of two clans may assist each other in particular ceremonies or in care for each other's dead. They may also emphasize this social relationship by an extension of their marriage rules, putting members of the other clan on the same basis as those of their own and either prohibiting or prescribing marriage with them. Such groupings of closely affiliated clans are know as *phratries*. They are of much less frequent occurrence than clans but are found in a considerable number of social systems.

One more type of grouping based upon blood relationship remains to be discussed, the *moiety*. Tribes as wholes are frequently divided into two units membership in which is determined by unilateral descent. These units are termed *moieties*, from the old English word meaning "a half." Such an arrangement is usually correlated with clan organization, certain clans belonging to one moiety and others to the other, but it may exist in clanless societies. It is nearly always used to control marriage, the moieties being definitely exogamous or, less frequently, endogamous. It also serves as a basis for the organization of competitive activities within the group, the members of the moieties playing against each other in games. Where both moieties and clans occur, the former are ordinarily more limited in their functions and of less social importance, possibly because the larger size of the moiety makes the establishment of well-defined attitudes between the members and their organization into a coöperative unit more difficult.

This discussion of social units determined by blood relationship should indicate once again the sharp distinction which exists between societies as aggregates of individuals and the social systems which organize the attitudes and activities of such aggregates into functional wholes. Although all societies recognize blood relationship and use it as a basis for delimiting the membership of certain social units, the particular type and degree of relationship utilized varies from one system to another. In the biological interrelations of its members, the aggregate offers the social system a wide range of relationships to choose from. The system ignores some of these and stresses others, its choice being governed less by factors inherent in the relationships than by cultural factors quite external to the relationships. Similarly, even when several societies have selected the same type of biological relationship for emphasis, the functions assigned to the units established in this way will vary from one society to another and will be determined primarily by cultural factors. The attempt to classify social units according to their biological composition is an inheritance from the early days of anthropological study. The value of such classifications as a basis for either the description or the study of social phenomena is distinctly questionable.

CHAPTER XIII

THE LOCAL GROUP

It has been said in a previous chapter that there are two social units which appear to be as old as the human species and which probably were present even at the sub-human level. One of these is the basic family unit composed of mates and their immature offspring. This served as the starting point for the evolution of all the current types of social units membership in which is determined on the basis of relationship through blood or marriage. The other of these ancient units was the local group, an aggregation of families and unattached males who habitually lived together. This served as the starting point for the development of all the current types of combined political and territorial units such as tribes and nations. For some reason, anthropologists have paid much more attention to the first type of grouping and its derivatives than to the second, although the local group has certainly been as important as the family in the development of social institutions. This focusing of interest upon the family may have been due in part to the European culture pattern of extreme interest in everything connected with mating and reproduction and to the greater variety of the social institutions which have been evolved from the family. The varying emphasis which various social systems placed upon marriage, the ways in which they limited it, and institutions like the joint family fired the investigator's imagination by their very contrast with anything to be met with in his own society. Local groups, on the other hand, are as familiar to us as any social institution of universal occurrence can be. They are, or at least have been until very recent times, as characteristic of European societies as of any others. They are still the basis of most of our political organization even though they are losing some of their former importance as functional social units. Moreover, their qualities are so much the same everywhere in the world that these qualities can be studied almost as effectively fifty miles from any large city as in the wilds of Australia. While an understanding of the local group is vitally necessary to the understanding of any social system, the task of collecting the necessary information does not necessarily lead the student into romantic regions.

There is not even any general agreement on a term for localized, socially integrated groups of fairly constant membership. They have been variously referred to as *hordes, villages,* and *bands. Horde* at once brings to mind the promiscuous hordes posited by the evolutionary sociologists as the starting point for the development of all social institutions or, worse yet, an unorganized mass of savages. *Village* suggests permanent habitations and settled life. The term *band* carries the fewest connotations for the average individual, so it will be used to designate all social units of the type under discussion.

Life in bands presents considerable practical advantages. Even hunting groups at the lowest level of material culture have a certain amount of property which is not in constant use and which the owners do not need to carry about with them. Also, any group of families includes a number of individuals such as old people, small children, and pregnant women who are less active than the able-bodied men. It would be a decided handicap to the hunter to have to keep such persons with him and regulate his speed of movement by theirs. Lastly, most human beings live in climates which make sheltered sleeping places desirable even if not absolutely necessary. The building of even the simplest shelter entails some time and effort and, other things being equal, it is much easier to return to the same shelter for several nights than to build a new one each night. The longer a shelter is to be utilized, the greater the labor which can profitably be expended in making it and the greater the degree of comfort which can be attained. Actually, it is the normal practice for the members of a band to establish a camp or village, a place where the women and children and surplus property are left and where the shelters of the various families are erected close together.

The factor of protection is also important. A few able-bodied men can be left in the camp as a guard while the rest go out to hunt.

Among hunters, the possible size of such units is restricted by economic factors. Ultimate limits to their growth are set by the amount of food and raw materials which can be obtained by exploiting the natural resources of a territory from a single center. This amount is, of course, influenced by both the potential resources of the territory and the techniques of exploitation known to the society. The zone of exploitation for a band is normally the territory the limits of which a man can reach in one day, returning to the camp at night. The exploitation of territory beyond this zone, while possible, becomes less and less profitable as the distance increases. The food within the exploitable zone will, of course, be most plentiful when the camp is first established, diminishing as the region is hunted out. Most groups at the hunting, food-gathering level hold much more land than they can exploit at any one time. They establish a camp, work out from it until food becomes scarce, and then move on to another camp, leaving the territory which has been hunted over to recuperate. Actually, most of them move in a fairly regular circuit, returning to the same camping places season after season. Any improvement in transportation facilities will add to the possible size of the band, since it will enable hunters to cover a wider territory from a single center and also make it possible to move camp more easily and frequently. Thus the introduction of the horse into Plains culture made it possible for many more families to live and move together.

Every hunting band claims certain territory and stands ready to defend it against trespassers. At the same time, the definiteness with which band territories are delimited varies considerably in different societies. There is some correlation between this and the nature of the game on which the group primarily depends. The value of land lies in what can be obtained from it. When the game is non-migratory, a certain area can be depended upon to yield a fairly regular annual return. Bands living under such conditions usually have well-defined territorial limits and

practise a primitive form of game conservation, being careful
not to take enough animals from any one part of their territory
to diminish the regular supply. They take vigorous action against
trespassers, since hunting by outsiders endangers the group's
future as well as present resources. When the main dependence
of the band is on a migratory species, such as the caribou in the
Barren Grounds or the buffalo in the northern Plains, exact delimitation of band territory becomes much less important and
trespass less injurious. In such cases the band territory becomes
little more than a vaguely defined range, the band hoping to in-
tercept the herd at some point in its wanderings and coming into
conflict with other bands only when the two actually meet.

The hunting band may be thought of as a village which is
frequently removed from one site to another. The camp of any
hunting group usually has a definite pattern of arrangement so
that certain families will always be close to each other and others
always at the far end of the camp. Thus among the Comanche
when a new camp site was reached the leader of the band
selected the site of his tipi and all the other families automatically took position with relation to it. If a certain family had
lagged on the march, their place would be left open for them.
The contours of the camp site would influence the arrangement
somewhat, but in choosing his own place the leader would try
to allow for these. Next-door neighbors in one camp would be
next-door neighbors in all camps.

Permanent settlement becomes possible whenever the territory within an exploitable distance can be relied upon to furnish
a regular and constant supply of food. We are accustomed to
think of settled life as necessarily correlated with agriculture, but
this is not the case. Hunters can rarely establish permanent settlements because of the nature of their food supply, but fishermen
frequently can and do. When the sea constantly brings a new
supply of food to the door, a band may occupy the same site
generation after generation. A regular and abundant supply of
wild vegetable foods will have the same effect. Thus in California
the regular crop of acorns and wild seeds made possible settle-

ments which were more permanent than those of many agricultural Indian tribes.

The best example of permanent settlements and a high culture in the absence of agriculture or any domestic animals of economic importance is that afforded by the coast tribes of British Columbia. Here the annual salmon runs and the abundance of wild berries provided a food supply as large and as thoroughly predictable as the results of agriculture in most uncivilized communities. Moreover, thanks to the development of techniques for food preservation, the group's cycle of activities was not unlike that of agriculturalists. Periods of intense labor, harvest seasons for the wild food supply, were interspersed with longer periods of community leisure. This made possible an extraordinary development of culture, especially on the esthetic and ceremonial side.

Groups who are dependent upon domestic animals for the bulk of their subsistence have more difficulty in establishing permanent settlements than do agriculturalists, but such settlements are not impossible to them. There are cattle-rearing tribes in Africa who are almost completely sedentary. All that is required for permanent settlement with dependence on domestic animals is sure and sufficient pasturage within the territory which can be exploited from a single center. It may be necessary for the village to shift from one site to another two or three times during the year, but such a life has none of the aspects of nomadism. A Masai band will have three or four villages which are occupied at different seasons. Each family will have a house in each village complete with necessary furniture, and when the band moves it entails nothing more than driving the herds and carrying a few personal possessions.

Conversely, the development of agriculture does not necessarily mean really permanent settlement. It may do nothing more than to slow down the rate of movement for the band. Primitive agriculture is often wasteful and rapidly leads to soil exhaustion. It is said that Iroquois villages had to transfer to new sites at intervals of about fifteen years, since by this time corn lands and firewood near enough to the village to be profit-ably exploited would be exhausted. The same holds for many tropical agricultural peoples. Tropical soils are usually poor, due to leaching-out of their mineral content by warm rains, and the best crops are obtained from land where primeval jungle can be cut over and burned. Without artificial fertilizers profitable crops can rarely be obtained from the same tract more than three years in succession. When the land within profitable reach of the vil-lage has been exhausted, the village as a whole moves to a new site. In Borneo the great communal houses which compose the village are taken to pieces and rafted to the new location so that not only the band and its personal property but even its dwellings are transferred from time to time.

Really permanent settlement becomes possible even for agri-cultural bands only when the resources of a particular area can be relied on indefinitely. This may come with the development of techniques for crop rotation and artificial fertilization or through settlement in particularly favored regions. The latter are usually river valleys, or, curiously enough, semi-arid regions. In river valleys the soil is usually rich to begin with and is con-stantly replenished with the silt brought down by floods. In semi-arid regions the soil has not lost its mineral content through rain leaching, and with the aid of irrigation it may produce good crops for generations. It is probably significant that the earliest high civilizations of the Old World were nearly all river-valley civiliza-tions, while those of the New World were nearly all developed in semi-arid regions.

Permanence of settlement, after all, has very little to do with the band as a social phenomenon. The frequency with which the group has to move has little influence on its size or on the rela-tions existing between its members. The growth of the agricul-tural village, like that of the hunters' camp, is limited by the amount of food which can profitably be obtained by working out from it. The amount of land which it can exploit is roughly de-termined by the distance to which its inhabitants can travel, do a day's work in the fields, and return to the village at night.

Land which lies farther off is hard to work, while guarding the standing crops becomes still harder.

What happens when the population of a band reaches the limit imposed by the natural resources will depend on many factors. If the territory it claims is rich enough, the unit splits, part of its members establishing a new band and setting up a new center to work out from. The same thing will usually happen when it is possible for the band to take in new territory, either by settlement of unoccupied land or by conquest. It must be repeated that the size of a band is set by the zone of exploitation about its settlement, not by the total territory available to its members. There is always an optimum size for the effective exploitation of this zone. When the band increases very much beyond this point the unit will split if new territory is available for it. When the band falls much below this point, its members must amalgamate with some other band or they will face extinction. If it is impossible for the band to split, the natural forces which deal with overpopulation will come into play to bring its strength back to normal. The first bad season will bring famine and the cutting-off of many members. However, most human groups seek to avoid such drastic conditions by a conscious or unconscious limitation of population through prevention of births or, more commonly, female infanticide. The actual methods by which limitation is accomplished are very diverse and need not be discussed here.

Being subject to such a variety of factors, it is natural that the actual size of bands should be highly variable. Where there is no reliance on trade and manufactures, the upper limit for agricultural groups seems to be 350 to 400. Even this requires unusually good soil and well-developed farming techniques, and such a size is rarely reached. Taking the world as a whole the average size of the band for agricultural peoples is probably between 100 and 150. Herding peoples with well-developed transportation facilities may, by frequent movements, live in units nearly as large as those of agriculturalists. The bands of hunters and food-gatherers are usually much smaller. In regions of scanty food supply they may be limited to ten or fifteen individuals, while under optimum conditions they rarely exceed 100 to 150.

So far we have been discussing the practical, primarily the economic, aspects of the band as a social unit. There are, however, psychological aspects which cannot be ignored. Whether it is a cultural survival from the remote period when all mankind lived in bands or whether it is due to innate tendencies, the average individual in all societies feels a need for membership in some compact social unit larger than the family. He is unhappy and unsure of himself unless he feels that a number of other individuals share his particular ideas and habits and are his friends. These attitudes are readily understandable in individuals who have been brought up as members of small, compact local units, bands as they commonly exist. Such persons are accustomed from infancy to having a crowd of other people about, develop an emotional dependence upon their neighbors, and feel insecure as soon as they find themselves alone or among strangers. However, the possibilty that the band type of social grouping rests upon something more than economics and conditioning cannot be too lightly dismissed. Something very like it is found even under circumstances which preclude close or constant social and spatial relationships between the members of the unit. Thus there are certain parts of the world in which the food supply is so scanty that the normal type of band residence is impossible. Each family has to spend most of its time alone and on the move. Nevertheless, groups of families which exploit contiguous territories look upon themselves as a social unit, assembling from time to time for ceremonial or social purposes. They constitute what sociologists call an *ingroup,* being conscious of common interests and loyalties and having a perfectly clear idea as to which families of their acquaintance belong to the unit and which do not.

A quite similar condition is found in Wisconsin farming communities. American farmers have inherited from northern Europe the pattern of life in isolated homesteads, and before the introduction of the telephone and automobile the loneliness of such existence was proverbial. Throughout much of the year the farm family met their neighbors only at church or perhaps on a Saturday afternoon in town. Nevertheless, groups of farm families formed and still form self-conscious social units. Such groupings are known to the members as *neighborhoods*. They have distinctive names such as Lost Lake or Hazel Ridge, and every farmer can give his own neighborhood and that of any other family which he knows moderately well. Neighborhoods are not correlated with any of the regular political groupings such as townships or school districts. In general, the families who form a neighborhood occupy adjoining farms, but an individual retains his feeling of membership even after he moves away and will be heartily welcomed whenever he comes back on a visit. Conversely, settlement among the group does not necessarily mean acceptance into the neighborhood. The newcomer is carefully looked over and not infrequently rejected. Although the neighborhood has no formal organization, it is an authentic social unit with a strong influence on the lives of its members. It sets the limits for their social activities, determining who will and will not be invited to parties, and maintains a considerable degree of coöperation. Neighborhood men help each other in threshing and hog-killing, while neighborhood women coöperate in all sorts of emergencies. Marriages are normally made within the group, and in the occasional Saturday night town fights the factions divide along neighborhood lines. It is clear that these neighborhoods are the social equivalents of bands in spite of the relative isolation of their component families.

It is not only among uncivilized peoples or in rural districts that the tendency toward the band type of organization asserts itself. Even city populations show a strong tendency to segregate themselves into local units. The cities of unmechanized civilizations are always divided into a series of wards or districts which are fairly permanent in population. Each ward will have a center of interest such as a market, the church of some saint to which its inhabitants are particularly attached, or a series of shops and factories employing mainly ward members. In many cases the inhabitants of each ward will tend to specialize in a particular industry so that there will be a rough correlation between the distribution of wards and that of individuals having common economic interests. As the inhabitants of each ward live and work mainly within it, they will be well known to each other and bound together by social ties of all sorts. Aside from the greater number of outside contacts, the situation in such a ward is not greatly different from that in a rural village. Even in mechanized cities this condition survives to a surprising degree. Any large American city, when one gets outside the business district, divides itself into units with distinct shopping centers. When the population is relatively stable, these units become self-conscious, replicas of the wards in the unmechanized city. Social ties are established between their members, common interests are developed, and the units assume more and more the aspects of village life. In every modern city it is possible to find local units which are self-contained for all ordinary social purposes. To their members the city as a whole is simply the zone of exploitation, the region which the males go out to daily, returning to their band at night with their spoils.

It seems probable that two sets of psychological factors are at work to produce this division of large population units into smaller units which correspond to the bands of those who are not city-dwellers. On one side there is the need for companionship and for the reassurance and emotional security which comes from belonging to a social unit whose members share the same ideas and patterns of behavior. On the other, there is the practical impossibility of establishing close contacts with or developing habitual attitudes toward any great number of people. An individual can know only a few persons really well, and to get this knowledge he must meet them often. Life as a member of a social unit large enough to offer variety in personal contacts yet small enough to permit of the establishment of personal relations with the majority of its members seems to be the most satisfying life for the bulk of mankind. There are, of course, certain individuals who fear intimacy and derive their emotional satisfaction from impressing casual acquaintances, but they are very much in the minority. Whether man's immemorial pattern of life in small, socially integrated local groups has produced these needs in the individual or whether the pattern is partly a reflection of such needs is a question which may be left to the psychologist. It is sufficient for our purposes that the average individual in all societies seems to be happiest when he is a member of a band.

If we try to evaluate the band in terms of its social importance, we are at once struck by the fact that the band *is* society as far as most of mankind are concerned. The writer realizes that such a statement at once raises the question as to what constitutes a society, a point upon which there is still no general agreement. If we go to one extreme and use the term to include all individuals who are in direct or indirect contact or whose activities affect each other in any way, the whole modern world must be considered a single society. American society would thus include the Chinamen who pick our tea and the West Africans who gather the palm oil for our soap. The concept thus becomes meaningless. If we take society to mean a group of individuals who are mutually interdependent, mutually adapted in their attitudes and habitual behavior, and united by a feeling of solidarity, the statement that the band *is* society for most of mankind is justifiable. Bands among uncivilized peoples are normally self-sufficient economically, internally well organized, with a strong *esprit de corps*, and capable of a satisfactory existence even in the absence of all external contacts. Even in unmechanized civilizations social units larger than the band rarely show these characteristics.

In the absence of easy and rapid communication the band is the only unit of population, aside from the immediate family, which can be organized into a constantly functional social entity. Mutual adaptations in attitudes and habitual behavior and the development of *esprit de corps* are impossible unless the individuals involved are in fairly close and constant contact. Until the rise of modern civilization it was impossible for either the individual or the band to have more than sporadic contacts with any one outside the immediate neighborhood. There was no postal service, and travel was always laborious and usually dangerous. Even in the unmechanized civilizations of to-day, a person who leaves his local group simply disappears over their social horizon. Similarly, an outsider who comes to the group, even if he is a fellow-national, is something from beyond the social horizon. He impinges upon the functional social unit, but he is in no sense a part of it. Socially speaking, he is on a par with the weather or any other purely external phenomenon. The society may include in its culture techniques for dealing with him, just as it includes techniques for meeting any other recurrent situation, but this does not make him a member of the society. He may be welcomed and honored or treated with fear, mistrust, or hostility, but he will not be treated like a regular member of the band. Authentic band members, even when personal enemies, are known quantities whose behavior can be predicted, while the stranger is an unknown quantity. His presence is always a disturbing influence, and the band usually tries to rid itself of him as quickly as possible or to assign him to a particular status in its social system, thus bringing him within the scope of the regular patterns of social behavior.

In spite of sporadic contacts with the outside world, the members of the band face inward. Emotional attachments, common interests, habits of coöperation, and even rivalries and disputes of long standing knit them together into a self-conscious, well-integrated whole. Even when the members of the band are conscious of a larger unit, such as the tribe or state, to which their band belongs, their mental picture of this unit is usually vague and their attitudes toward it are weak and indefinite. To the average band member such units are abstractions existing on a quite different level from the group of well-known individuals with whom he lives and works. Between this group and the larger unit there can be no question of divided loyalties. The individual's first duty is to his kin, then to his band, and only residually to anything beyond.

The close and continuous personal contacts which exist within the band provide the optimum conditions for the transmission of culture. Since under ordinary conditions the band is both socially and economically self-contained, its culture must be a complete one, including techniques for meeting all the ordinary exigencies of existence. The participation of individuals in the total culture is also much more complete than it can be in larger and more spatially-diffused units. The growing individual can learn all the ordinary techniques employed by the group's members simply by observing what is going on around him and gather all its ordinary lore by listening to conversations. Its patterns for social behavior come to him in simple, concrete terms of how he should act toward certain individuals, while the basic ideas and values of the culture present themselves simply as what all sane persons believe or how everybody feels about certain situations. The bulk of the culture's content is thus not only available for the individual's learning but it is also presented to him in the most readily assimilable form. Lacking contact with other societies and therefore any basis for cultural comparisons, he accepts the culture of his group automatically as the best and most natural way of life.

Actually, every band has a culture of its own. The various bands within a tribe may have closely similar cultures, but these will never be identical at all points. Thus among the Comanche each band had certain peculiarities of dress which served to identify its members in any company. Each band also had a favorite dance, these dances being quite independent of each other and bearing no relation to any round of tribal ceremonies. One band habitually made its clothing from antelope skins, although the rest preferred deer skins. One band made no pemmican, another made it without berries, while a third always added berries. Although in this tribe families could change allegiance from one band to another at will and inter-band marriages with patrilocal residence were fairly common, such cultural differences seem to have had no tendency to disappear. A family or individual who joined a new band would consciously copy that band's habits. Differences of culture from band to band did not present themselves to the individual as alternatives between which he might choose. It was mandatory upon him to follow the customs of the group with which he lived, and to do otherwise would be considered an affectation if not a sign of disloyalty.

In addition to such easily observed differences, the bands within a single tribe may differ profoundly in attitudes and basic culture values even when their cultures are almost identical in their superficial aspects. Thus two bands may be familiar with the same magical techniques and even tell the same legends about their use, yet the members of one band will be convinced of their efficacy and employ them constantly, while those of the other question their efficacy and rarely use them. Again, members of one band may be notoriously loose in their sexual behavior and those of another very strict when the mores of both bands are the same in theory. The existence of these band differences makes it extremely unsafe to generalize about the culture of any tribe as a whole until the cultures of several of its units have been studied individually.

The almost complete participation of the individual in the culture of his band and his unquestioning allegiance to its mores contribute to making offenses against these mores infrequent. Moreover, the extremely close relations existing between all the band's members makes it possible to deal with offenders effectively yet at the same time informally. A small local group can function smoothly in the absence of any formal techniques for punishing criminals. Even in one of our own isolated rural villages the law is commonly represented by a single justice of the peace or a constable, and these are symbols of the existence of law and order rather than active functionaries. The constable may arrest a few drunks in the course of the year, but such arrests are little more than the expected terminations of a successful evening. Far from being offended or suffering loss of social prestige, the local drunk would be disappointed if he was not arrested. All disputes between members of the community are commonly settled without appeal to the law, and persons who do appeal to it lose the sympathy of the group. They are bringing outsiders into a social situation which the group feels it is competent to handle, and such intrusion is quite naturally resented.

While universal and unquestioning acceptance of the band's mores is probably the most potent single factor in making its members law-abiding, there are other factors which affect the situation. Under the normal conditions of band life crimes against property are unprofitable. Since every item of personal property is well known to most of the group's members, the thief cannot use what he steals. It is unsafe for him even to keep it in his house, since neighbors are constantly dropping in. The only things which can be taken successfully are food for immediate consumption and money. Even then the individual's character, habits, and income are so well known to the rest of the community that he can rarely "get away with" it. Even in a modern American village a man who begins to miss his chickens usually has a fairly clear idea of who is taking them and lays traps accordingly. Similarly, any display of wealth after a robbery at once focuses suspicion on the one who displays it. There are very few cases in which the actual needs of all of a band's members are not provided for, if only through informal charity. There is thus no necessity for theft while the gold-fish-like life of the members of such a group makes it extremely hazardous. Actually, only fools or kleptomaniacs are likely to attempt it, and it does not become a real social problem. First offenders can be effectively dealt with by ridicule and loss of prestige. Those who repeat the offense are felt to be abnormal and are usually dealt with rather as public nuisances than as criminals. They are either killed by some irate victim, with the tacit approval of the community, or driven out.

The practical certainty of detection also has a deterrent effect on offenses other than those against property, but it must be remembered that many anti-social acts are not premeditated. This is particularly true of acts of violence and sex offenses, both of which are often committed on the spur of the moment with no weighing of consequences. The intimate contact of individuals within a band makes it easy to predict the results of situations existing between individuals and to employ informal techniques of social control for preventive as well as punitive purposes. Disputes which might lead to violent acts are known to all, and the group will usually take measures to settle them before they reach the point of outbreak. Similarly, incipient affairs can be detected and stopped before they lead to serious consequences. It is this, rather than the certainty of punishment, which makes the number of overt offenses within the band so small. Of course, the vigor with which preventive measures are applied will depend a good deal on the society's attitude toward the particular offense.

Some societies view violence between individuals with equanimity and countenance fights as long as they do not lead to serious damage. In fact they may encourage them as a method of bringing differences to a head and settling them, only taking pains to ensure fair play or to limit the violence to those immediately concerned. Other societies strongly reprehend all resorts to violence. Thus very few of my Tanala informants had ever seen a fight between adults, and none of them had heard of a case of murder in which both parties belonged to the same village. At the same time, the members of this tribe were as warlike as any other Malagasy and had a deserved reputation for courage.

The most effective weapon which the band employs against the potential or actual offender is ridicule. Although some atypical individuals may glory in wickedness when it brings them serious attention, no sane person likes to be considered a fool. The jeers of one's neighbors hurt even more than their serious disapprobation. The member of the band cannot escape from the pressure of public opinion, and it nearly always brings him to terms. If it fails, the band has still more terrible weapons in ostracism and expulsion. The seriousness of ostracism can be observed in any of our own small communities. There it usually results in the ostracized individual's moving away, but the member of a band normally cannot move away. He has to stay and try to live down his offense. Expulsion is usually used only as a last resort. The group acts in self-defense, getting rid of an individual who is a social liability without incurring the guilt of actually killing him. Even in unmechanized civilizations the average individual is so closely bound to his local group that expulsion from it is hardly less drastic than a death sentence. It means the loss of the individual's livelihood, of all his friends, and of his place as a member of society. Even when other bands are not actively hostile, they are sure to be suspicious and unfriendly. They will assume, *a priori*, that no man leaves his band for good unless he has to and will be reluctant to accept him into their own group.

Although offenses within bands are always extremely rare, it does not follow that their members are equally law-abiding as regards the larger social or political units to which their bands belong. Nothing brings out the social self-sufficiency of the band more clearly than does the practically universal application of one set of mores to dealings between band members and of another set to their dealings with outsiders. The stranger is not a member of society, and his person and property are considered fair game. While fear of a higher authority may prevent too direct action, the band member who gets the better of him is always applauded. The same individual who is scrupulously honest with regard to his neighbor's property may be a notorious thief on the outside and glory in his prowess. Any of my readers who served in the World War will remember the contrasting attitudes toward a man who stole from a member of his own company and one who stole from another company. The former was regarded as sub-human and gotten rid of as soon as possible, while the latter was considered something of a public benefactor. The same indifference to the interests of the larger unit of which the band forms a part comes out very clearly in its employment of expulsion both as a punishment and as a form of self-defense. This attitude is apparent in the old American pattern of "running people out of town." The community is only interested in getting rid of an undesirable and does not worry about the effects on other communities.

Under the conditions of band life the need for formal governmental machinery is reduced to a minimum. There are many cases in which bands function efficiently without any officials or even any formal assembly. The members of the band are so closely united by a common culture, common interests, and personal ties that no formal methods of ascertaining their will or of enforcing it are really necessary. Actually, every band has a council, although the people themselves may never think of it as a governmental agency. Thus in the Marquesan village in which the author lived for several months, every clear evening saw most of the inhabitants assembled at the old ceremonial dancing place. The natives thought of these gatherings as purely social affairs, yet in the course of the evening everything of current interest would be talked over and communal activities organized for some days ahead. There was no order of business, no presiding officer, and no method of taking votes, yet every one present obtained a clear idea of what was the will of the community and afterward acted accordingly. Every one was allowed a voice in the proceedings, but most attention was paid to heads of families and other persons of importance. In many of our own rural communities the evening assembly in the crossroads grocery store performs very much the same function.

In all bands actual rule is in the hands of a few individuals who are recognized as leaders. Without their approval nothing can be done. Such leadership is often as informal as that of the key men in an American community. It derives from personal qualities and the group's recognition of these qualities and has nothing to do with formal office. Since it depends in the fullest degree upon the consent of the governed, such leaders are usually careful to ascertain the will of the majority and to act in accordance with this. Even in the so-called matriarchal societies the majority of these leaders are always men. Women may be included, but if so they are persons of outstanding ability.

Although bands can function effectively without any formal officials, it is advantageous to have some one person who assumes responsibility for the execution of the band's decisions and directs its common activities. Almost every band has a head man or two or three head men who act as executives and coördinators. When there are two or three of these, each one usually takes charge of a particular communal activity. Thus one will serve as war chief and another as priest. These positions are frequently so informal that the people have no names for them, and, as in the case of the key men, tenure may be entirely dependent upon personal qualities. When the band is in frequent contact with outsiders, the desirability of having a head man is considerably increased. It is much simpler for a central government or for traders or other visitors who have business with the group to deal with a single individual who has a large measure of control over the band and will be responsible for its acts. Thus among certain American Indian tribes in which the pattern of having head men was very weak if it existed at all, contact with traders and European governments led to the development of band chiefs with considerable power.

The effectiveness of informal methods of government under the conditions of band life makes the development of formal governmental machinery unnecessary, but it does not preclude it. The actual processes of government are strikingly the same in all small local groups, yet the formal aspects of government vary considerably. Even among ourselves one village may have a regular government with a full set of officials from mayor down, while another of equal size remains unincorporated. The degree to which government is formalized in the band seems to be more a matter of the culture patterns of the group than of anything else and does not seem to bear any direct relation to the actual needs of the community.

Both the Negroes of Africa and the Malagasy, whose culture is similar in many respects, seem to have a certain flair for formal organization. In particular, they have been interested in the development of law and legal procedure. Even the most trivial disputes between band members are usually settled in a local court with the full paraphernalia of justice. In spite of such constant resorts to the law, the essential solidarity of the local group is shown by the extreme unwillingness of the group to refer such disputes to higher authority. Many African tribes have a well-developed central government, yet this is only appealed to as a last resort. The village court is convened as often as seems necessary. The village chief or head man usually presides, while the whole community acts as an informal jury. Accusations are made, witnesses examined, either the principals or their attorneys plead the case, and the head man hands down his decision in accordance with what he feels to be the will of the spectators. Although these have no official place in the trial, they guarantee fair play, and it is a bold judge who dares to go against them. Such trials break the monotony of village life and are enjoyed by all. A dispute between two old women over a hen may provide amusement for half a day, while the wisdom of the head man's decision will be discussed long afterward.

In this region it is also customary to delegate large powers to village head men and to surround their official activities with considerable pomp and circumstance. How much this signifies as regards real power depends primarily on the character of the man who holds the office. He is a symbol of the corporate existence of the local group and as such will be given exaggerated respect and prompt obedience before outsiders. At the same time, he is well known to all members of the group in his unofficial moments. Fellow-villagers catch him off guard, and his wives discuss him with other men's wives. He lacks that remoteness and mystery necessary in all cases in which great power attaches to office irrespective of the man who holds it. Actually, if he is a weakling he will be completely under the control of the village key men, while in any case he will be largely dominated by public opinion. He is as much a part of the community as any other individual and as emotionally dependent on his neighbors' goodwill.

In sharp contrast to this African pattern, many American Indian bands seem, to the superficial observer, to lack all formal organization. They have no regular legal procedures and, in many cases, no officials. At the same time, disputes between their members are settled quietly and effectively, group mores are preserved, and the necessary work of coördinating and directing their members' activities is accomplished. They seem to be quite as successful in the actual business of living as the most thoroughly organized African village. Actually, the superficial differences between the two are much greater than the real ones. When both systems are observed in action, it becomes apparent that the band with a high degree of formal organization ignores or evades many of its formal patterns in practice, while the band without formal organization is actually a well-organized whole. The control of natural leaders does not depend upon official titles, nor the efficacy of culture patterns in shaping behavior upon the degree to which they are conscious and verbalized. Such a tribe as the Comanche attached tremendous importance to individual freedom of action. Disputes between members of a band were phrased as so many distinct events to be settled according to the personalities involved, yet case histories show the existence of rather definite patterns for dealing with particular types of disputes. Again, there was reluctance to accord formal recognition of a leader's power, but a genuine recognition of it was reflected in attention to his advice and submission to his will. The Comanche band was better organized than it was willing to admit, while the African village is often less organized than it wishes to appear.

There is one last aspect of life in the band which remains to be mentioned. Although such groups usually contrive to present a united front to outsiders, they are often divided internally into two or more factions, each of which heads in a particular key man or group of key men. Although such factions are rarely given formal recognition, they are an important factor in the life of many groups. They seem to be especially common in American Indian bands, but it is impossible to say to what extent the phenomenon derives from culture patterns or from the natural rivalries of ambitious men. If reports are to be believed, there are certain cultures in which the bands are genuine homogeneous wholes with no factional splits. Among American Indians the pattern of factions is certainly deep-seated. In some cases two factions have survived for generations, changing leaders and the bases of their disputes and winning some individuals from each other, but remaining distinct social entities in constant opposition to each other. This opposition seems to be their main reason for existence, their policies and the declared grounds for opposition shifting with the circumstances. In many cases any cause which is espoused by one will immediately be resisted by the other. The whole matter of these factions, their causes and functions, is an interesting and still almost unexplored field for study.

In spite of its superficial differences from one culture to another, the band is the most constant of all social phenomena and, in many respects, the most uniform. It lies at the very foundation of all existing political and social systems. Its disintegration is one of the most revolutionary results of the rise of modern civilization. With the present ease of travel and communication, both rural and urban local groups are losing their old qualities as closely integrated, self-conscious social units. As a result the patterns of government and social control which have been evolved through thousands of years of band living are becoming increasingly unworkable. Moreover, the change has been so rapid that the average adult is still a person who was conditioned in childhood to life on the band basis. He has been trained to look to his neighbors for reassurance and moral backing, and when these neighbors are removed he finds himself at loose ends. The modern city, with its multiplicity of organizations of every conceivable sort, presents the picture of a mass of individuals who have lost their bands and who are trying, in uncertain and fumbling fashion, to find some substitute. New types of grouping based on congeniality, business association, or community of interest are springing up on all sides, but nothing has so far appeared which seems capable of taking over the primary functions of the local group as these relate to individuals. Membership in the Rotary Club is not an adequate substitute for friendly neighbors.

Although the disintegration of local groups in our society may progress even further than it has, the author is inclined to regard it as a transitory phenomenon. The sudden rise of the machine and of applied science has shattered Western civilization and reduced Western society to something approaching chaos. However, unless all past experience is at fault, the society will once more reduce itself to order. What the new order will be no one can forecast, but the potentialities of the local group both for the control of individuals and for the satisfaction of their psychological needs are so great that it seems unlikely that this unit will be dispensed with.

CHAPTER XIV

TRIBE AND STATE

In the absence of easy and rapid means of communication the local group is the only unit of population which can be organized into a closely integrated, constantly functional society. However, there is an almost universal tendency for the members of bands to recognize the existence of a larger social entity, the tribe, and to differentiate in their attitudes and behavior between bands which belong to their own tribe and those which do not. In its simplest form the tribe is a group of bands occupying contiguous territories and having a feeling of unity deriving from numerous similarities in culture, frequent friendly contacts, and a certain community of interest. More or less elaborate superstructures of formal tribal organization may be erected upon this basic condition, but tribal groups can exist and function without them.

Tribes commonly come into existence through increase in the population of a single original band and the consequent formation of new bands. This process has been described in the preceding chapter. At the moment of division the new band and its parent will be identical in culture and language and the members of both will be connected by numerous ties of personal acquaintance and family relationship. If the two groups occupy adjoining territories after the division these individual ties will not be broken off immediately. Friends and relatives will visit each other, and new personal ties will be developed generation after generation. Such informal intercourse between the groups will keep alive the memory of their common origin and the feeling of unity between them and will also retard the development of marked differences in language and culture. As more and more bands split off it becomes impossible to maintain such personal relationships between all the tribe's members, but the tribe will still be bound together by a series of interlocking relationships. Thus the members of band A may have no direct contact with those of band C, whose territory lies at a distance from their own, but the members of both A and C will be acquainted with persons in band B, which occupies the intervening territory. As long as all the bands occupy contiguous territory social relations can be maintained between them and with these a general community of language, culture, and interest.

The tribe is always a territorial unit. If one of its bands is cut off from the rest, the members of the new unit will be unable to maintain personal relations with their fellow-tribesmen and the memory of a common origin will soon fade. Cultural and linguistic differences will develop, and within a few generations all feeling of unity between the two will be lost. Thus there is good evidence that the Shoshoni and Comanche were originally a single tribe. The time of their separation cannot be fixed, but it probably did not occur before 1600. A band or bands from the original unit drifted southward, lost touch with the parent body, and became the Comanche. By 1880 the southern group had lost all memory of their northern relatives, and young Comanche who went to Indian schools were amazed to encounter there boys who spoke their own language with only slight differences in vocabulary and pronunciation. During the time that they had been separated the culture of the two divisions had diverged much more than their language and each division had assumed all the aspects of a distinct tribe.

It seems probable that the nucleus of a tribe is always formed through the increase and splitting of an original band, but bands of foreign origin may come to be included. The best known example of this in America is the Kiowa tribe, which includes a band of Apache origin. This band is considered an integral part of the tribe and has been assigned a place in the arrangement of its ceremonial camp. Its members have assumed many elements of Kiowa culture but have retained their own language. In Madagascar also genealogies show that the members of a tribe are often of diverse origin. A tribe which held more territory than it needed would frequently allow a band of foreign origin to settle within its borders in return for their promise to aid in war. Within a few generations such a group came to be considered an integral part of the tribe even when it maintained numerous peculiarities of culture. It is difficult to tell how important this process of amalgamation has been in the formation of tribes in general. Language and culture are easily changed, and the memories of uncivilized peoples are usually short, so that absolute proof of it can be obtained in only a few cases. However, there are often peculiarities of tribal organization which can be explained more readily on this basis than on any other. Thus the peculiar dual organization of the Creek Indians may well have arisen through the fusion of two originally distinct groups.

The thing which really distinguishes a tribe from a simple aggregation of bands is the feeling of unity among its members and the distinctions which they draw between themselves and non-members. Occupation of a continuous territory, with the opportunities which this provides for social intercourse, is necessary to the perpetuation of such attitudes, but it does not necessarily create them. The band on one side may be a member of your tribe, while that on the other, equally close in space, is a member of another tribe and a hereditary enemy. Community of language, culture, and origin also are not enough to transform an aggregation of bands into a tribe. They contribute to ease of intercourse and make the development of a feeling of unity more likely, but they do not necessarily produce it. Deep-seated hostility may exist between two bands from the moment of their separation. Lastly, although a strong central authority may be able to bring together under its rule a number of bands and to force them to coöperate, it cannot transform them into a tribe. Such bands may live together in peace and even work together, but lacking the feeling of unity the organization will dissolve into its component units as soon as the central control is removed. The existence of the tribe rests upon psychological factors. Lacking these it can never become a genuine functional entity while, when they are present, it can function without formal machinery of any sort.

The Tanala Menabe of Madagascar are a good example of how a tribe may function in the complete absence of formal organization. The largest political unit native to their culture was the village. Groups of villages occupying contiguous territories constituted what we may call sub-tribes, while a number of these sub-tribes formed the total tribe. The tribe as a whole had a very clear idea of what units did and did not belong to it, although some of those which were included differed more in culture from one another than they did from units in certain of the neighboring tribes. When a new village was formed it immediately became politically independent, selecting its own head man and settling its own disputes. There was no central authority in the tribe or sub-tribe, but the villages within a sub-tribe would not make war upon each other. Although they did not normally aid each other in offensive warfare or in repelling simple raids, they were under a quite informal obligation to unite against serious attacks from the outside. The comparative isolation of the village units and their pattern of marriage within the village made contacts between members of the sub-tribe rare and the chances for offenses between members of different villages correspondingly slight. There was no machinery for handling such offenses, but in practice they were extremely rare. Even when they did occur they were compounded in informal fashion, in marked contrast to offenses within the village, which were settled by regular legal procedure. Both the villages involved would be anxious to avoid an open break and to maintain the sub-tribe's united front.

Warfare and especially cattle-stealing were common between sub-tribes, but this condition had been adjusted to the wider tribal concept. Such wars were in the nature of family affairs. They were never pushed to the extermination of the vanquished group and usually ended with a formal admission of defeat. Even the cutting off and carrying away of the heads of fallen enemies was deprecated, although it was approved in warfare outside the tribe. The captives taken in such wars were on a quite different level from those taken from neighboring tribes. They were very rarely sold outside the tribe and still more rarely abused. While marriage with slaves of foreign origin carried a social stigma, marriage with Tanala slaves did not. In fact it might be sought after if the captive was of good family. Although prisoners were never exchanged, they were freely ransomed, and if they died unransomed their bodies were returned to their relatives for burial in the village tomb. Marriages with captives and the relations which they formed with their captors while waiting for ransom led to the establishment of personal ties between members of different sub-tribes and thus contributed to their feeling of unity.

The Comanche afford another example of tribal solidarity without formal organization. The tribe was divided into a large number of bands which were politically autonomous. It had no tribal chiefs or regular council, and it is doubtful whether all the bands were ever brought together in a single assembly. Even the Sun Dance was only participated in by a part of the tribe. At the same time, there was a strong feeling of tribal solidarity. Any Comanche was sure of a welcome in any band, and there was an almost complete absence of inter-band warfare or even horse-stealing. When one of the bands finally broke away from the tribe and aided the whites against the rest, the feeling toward it was much more bitter than that toward any of the tribe's hereditary enemies. Its members were considered traitors, and a certain social stigma still attaches to their descendants. In spite of the political autonomy of the bands and certain minor cultural differences between them, they were knit together by a series of personal relationships which cut across band lines. Friendships might be formed between men of different bands, inter-band marriages were not infrequent, and families might change their allegiance from one band to another while remaining on amicable terms with the members of their original band.

The tribes just described have no formal organization, no tribal ceremonies or periodic assemblies, and no symbols of tribal unity. At the same time, they have a very real feeling of unity and draw a clear distinction between tribesmen and outsiders. This condition is made possible by the existence of individual relationships which link the members of one band with those of another. It seems probable that such relationships are always

the main agency in establishing tribal solidarity and that the
more formal methods of emphasizing this solidarity are in the
nature of afterthoughts. Any arrangement which serves to bring
the members of different bands together, thus enabling them to
establish informal relationships, is an agent in promoting tribal
solidarity. Tribal ceremonies and assemblies thus make a dual
contribution. They emphasize the reality of the tribe and
strengthen the concept of unity by the induction of emotions
between the individuals present. At the same time they bring
together individuals from different bands and give them an opportunity to know each other. The second is probably quite as
important as the first. Thus our own rural churches seem to owe
their efficacy as agencies for social unification as much to the
informal "get-togethers" after the service as they do to their
members' common creed and common participation in the service.
The formal activities of tribal assemblies strengthen the concept of tribal unity, but the establishment of individual relationships beyond the limits of the band reduces this abstract concept
to concrete personal terms, making it much more real to the
individual.

Marriages between members of different bands link the two
groups together by a combination of informal and formal relationships. Such marriages are nearly always permitted and are
not infrequently insisted upon. They lead to the shifting of individuals from one band to another and at the same time establish
ties of formal relationship between a number of persons in both
groups. The woman who marries and moves to her husband's
band is a living link between it and her own. She has friends and
relatives in both and shares the interests of both. In addition, the
marriage creates formal ties between her husband and her father,
between her father and her children, and so on. When the organization of the tribe includes clans, fraternal orders, or any other
non-localized social units, these also help to strengthen the feeling of tribal unity. Like the inter-band marriages, they establish formal relationships between persons belonging to different
bands and thus help to draw the tribe together into a self-
conscious whole.

Although there may be little opportunity for formal relationships between members of different bands to find expression in overt behavior, they are highly important in maintaining the feeling of unity. Any individual who is linked to any member of a band by their mutual participation in a socially recognized pattern of reciprocal rights and duties cannot be excluded from the band's concept of society. Such individuals may not be active participants in band activities, but they are included in its system of statuses and rôles. Their position is much like that of an absent member of the band. Both are functionally latent members of society, and as such the band's attitudes toward them are much the same as their attitudes toward active members. The visitor who comes to a band where he has relatives may be personally a stranger, but he is not socially a stranger. He can immediately be assigned to a place in the society and will find his rôles with relation to other members of the society fairly well defined from the start.

The assignment of social status to persons living outside the band helps to break down the distinctions between bands and to draw them together into larger social units. Since the same individual may be an active member of one band and at the same time a latent member of a number of other bands, the attitudes and behavior patterns which find their most complete expression under the conditions of band life are extended in an ever-widening circle until the whole tribe is included in their scope. This extension is inevitably accompanied by dilution. Attitudes between tribe members have a weaker emotional context than those between band members, and the patterns of reciprocal behavior, lacking the reinforcement of frequent overt expression, become curtailed and formalized. Nevertheless, the presence of these patterns provides a basis for effective coöperation, while the attitudes provide the stimulus toward it. Together they transform the aggregate of individuals and bands into a social entity with potentialities for function.

Intra-tribal attitudes and behavior patterns are always reciprocal. They are acquiesced in by all who come within their scope. The attitudes and behavior patterns which govern the dealings of the tribe with outsiders usually lack these elements of reciprocity and acquiescence. They are comparable in this respect to those which govern the tribe's exploitation of its environment. Although neighboring tribes may develop recognized reciprocal patterns, thus extending their concepts of society to include each other, it is more usual for the tribe to consider all outsiders on a par with non-human phenomena. Since they are not members of society, the rules governing the interrelations of human beings, i.e., society members, simply do not apply to them. The same group which is honest and kindly in its internal dealings may be treacherous and callously cruel in its dealings with outsiders. Thus the members of a Marquesan tribe were more than ordinarily kind and considerate among themselves and viewed the eating of a tribe member very much as we view cannibalism. Their stories of individuals guilty of this crime reflect the same horror as our own tales of ogres and cannibal witches. At the same time, members of other tribes were eaten without a qualm. Although the eating of enemy warriors had certain elements of ceremonialism and revenge, alien women and children were eaten simply because they liked the meat. Members of other tribes were hunted much as pigs were hunted, and captives were treated with unconscious cruelty. If they had more captives than were needed for the feast, they broke their legs to prevent escape and kept them until they were needed.

The fact that the tribe sets the limits of society makes it easier for it to function as a unit in dealings with outsiders than in anything else. Its reactions to outside attack or to opportunities for outside loot are automatic, and no formal techniques are needed to ensure concerted action. The tribe can function effectively for offense and defense without any sort of central authority. The presence of such authority may increase efficiency by coördinating the group's efforts, but it is not really needed. The most universal and probably the oldest of the tribe's functions is that of making war. Making peace, on the other hand, is a much less universal tribal function. It requires some sort of constituted central authority and a considerable degree of control by the tribe over its component bands and individuals. In the absence of such control wars are easy to begin but almost impossible to stop. Our own frontier history is full of cases in which peace, made in good faith on both sides, was broken through the acts of irresponsible individuals. Most Indian tribes had no effective techniques for preventing determined men from going on the war-path, while our own government was unable to control its frontier population.

Such unorganized tribes as the Tanala and the Comanche are little more than offensive and defensive alliances between a group of bands. They can scarcely be said to have any functions with relation to their component bands and individuals. Membership in the tribe gives these an added security, but that is about all. Before the tribe can begin to function in the control of its members there must be some degree of formal organization and a central authority. Even when these are present it seems to be the normal pattern of tribal organization to leave as much to the local groups as possible, respecting their autonomy and dealing with them rather than with individuals. The band is a far more efficient agent for social control than any remote authority can possibly be. In offenses and disputes within the band the tribe usually keeps hands off. It does step in to settle disputes between bands or between individuals from different bands, since in these cases the techniques of band control become inoperative. Moreover, such disputes are a genuine concern of the tribe since they are likely to lead to feuds and the tribe's ultimate disruption. They are most easily settled when there is a strong central authority, but even when this is lacking there will usually be an attempt to settle them amicably, with the other bands bringing pressure to bear on both parties to come to some sort of an agreement. However, this requires at least a tribal council before which the case can be heard. Among the Comanche the tribe had no technique for formal intervention, but the feeling of unity made the bands themselves very reluctant to come to an open break. The old men, who were the official peacemakers in intra-band disputes, would visit back and forth and try to bring about a settlement by the same informal methods used within the band.

The formal organization of tribes, and with it the degree to which they can control their members, varies so much that it cannot be used as a criterion for determining what constitutes a tribe and what does not. The real test is whether the members of the tribe consider themselves a single society, and this seems the only valid reference point for distinguishing between *tribe* and *state*. The tribe is a social entity, while the state, as the term will be used here, is a *political* entity. Some states actually have less formal organization than some tribes, but in the absence of the tribal feeling of unity the minimum of organization necessary to their survival is much greater than that for the tribe. They must have at least a formal council, while most of them have a fairly strong central authority with power to coerce their members. While most of the tribe's activities are automatic and largely unconscious, those of the state are deliberate and conscious. To a much larger degree than the tribe, the state must deal with internal conflicts of interest and with organized internal opposition, and the central authority must have enough power to override these if the state is to function.

States may come into being either through the voluntary federation of two or more tribes or through the subjugation of weak groups by stronger ones, with the loss of their political autonomy. In either case war seems to be the main agency in producing the state. Neighboring tribes may live together amicably and even develop a marked degree of economic interdependence while maintaining complete political autonomy. Such interdependence can even exist in the face of not too serious warfare between the tribes, trade being carried on through the medium of truces or neutral groups. Its advantages to all concerned are obvious enough to ensure its continuance in the absence of any central authority. Confederacies usually owe their origin to the fear of a common enemy and to a realization of the advantages to be derived from concerted action against this enemy. They are much more characteristic, at least in their inception, of groups which are on the defensive than of those which are on the offensive. No tribe surrenders its political autonomy willingly, and if it does so freely it must feel sure of important returns. The advantages of confederation are much more obvious in the case of defeated tribes than in that of victorious tribes. The former can see the need of increased strength and the advantages of coördinated effort, while the latter can get along well enough without either and commonly look upon allies as something of an encumbrance.

Most federations begin as defensive alliances, gradually developing organization and increasingly strong central control as the necessity for these become apparent. In its inception the central authority has somewhat the aspects of a high command, coördinating the efforts of the allies and bringing in reserves from groups who are not immediately threatened. If the danger continues long enough, the allies develop such a mass of habits and techniques of coöperation that the alliance continues after the original stimulus to it has been removed. Thus the famous League of the Iroquois began as a defensive measure, and even then, if the native traditions are to be believed, it was hard to persuade the various tribes to join. The Iroquois had been harassed for generations by their Algonkin neighbors, and Dekanawide, the promoter of the League, advertised it as a way of bringing peace. Once formed it soon put an end to the Algonkin menace and then embarked on an amazing career of conquest. This was rationalized, in thoroughly modern fashion, as "a war to end war," since obviously the League could only be sure of peace when all its potential enemies had been exterminated.

Confederacies thus owe their origin to a community of interest, even if this is of a very limited and specific sort. The function of the central authority is that of directing and coördinating the voluntary activities of the federated tribes. It derives its powers from the consent of the governed, and any attempt to coerce the tribes is promptly resented. However, the presence of common interests makes it possible for the central authority to perform its functions with a minimum of machinery and of delegated powers. Since the component tribes are always jealous of their rights, the government of a confederacy must be democratic in fact if not in theory. The most usual pattern seems to be that of a council of tribal representatives with no chief or with one who is merely an executive. The lack of a strong central authority makes it difficult for confederacies to act quickly and also renders them liable to disruption through internal disputes. However, they are highly resistant to attack. Any outside interference strengthens their members' feeling of unity and willingness to coöperate, making such states much harder for an enemy to break up or subdue than those created through conquest.

States based upon the principle of confederation are rare in spite of the fact that defensive alliances are common. The transformation of such alliances into organized political units seems to require special conditions. The patterns of confederate governments are, almost without exception, projections of those of the tribal governments with which their members are familiar. While these patterns always have to be somewhat modified to meet the new conditions, there is a clearly recognizable continuity. Thus the Iroquois had a single basic pattern of formal control which extended from the household through clan, village, and tribe to the League itself. They themselves recognized this continuity, referring to the League as the Long House and emphasizing its similarity to a household. Again, the confederations of the Tuareg, with their noble and servile tribes, were a direct projection of the tribal organization with its noble and serf families. This adherence to preëxisting governmental patterns suggests one reason for the rarity of confederacies. Tribes which have no formal governmental machinery and those in which the government centers in a chief with autocratic powers will both have great difficulty in forming them. The former have no models for confederate organization unless they try to imitate that of some confederacy with which they are familiar. Thus some of the Algonkin tribes tried to imitate the League of the Iroquois, but with poor success. Autocratic tribal patterns are not applicable to confederate conditions. Autocratic central control is incompatible with the voluntary association of tribes which is the essence of the confederacy. It presupposes a surrender of autonomy to which the various tribes, and especially their chiefs, will usually be unwilling to submit. It seems that the only tribes which can successfully confederate are those whose preëxisting governmental patterns are at once conscious and formal and democratic. Such tribes are rare, and the possibilities of confederation are correspondingly limited.

Conquest states are much more numerous than confederacies. In fact most existing political units larger than the tribe have originated in this way. While confederacies may occur at any level of economic development, conquest states are nearly always associated with patterns of settled life and a degree of technological advance which makes it possible for a population to produce an economic surplus. They are unknown among hunting peoples and practically unknown among nomadic herdsmen, although the latter have frequently formed conquest states by the subjugation of agricultural groups. The hunter cannot produce enough surplus to make his subjugation and exploitation worth the effort. Decisive wars between tribes at this level result in the expulsion or extermination of the vanquished and the occupation of their hunting territories by the victors. With nomadic herdsmen the conditions are somewhat the same. Tribes at this level can produce a surplus, but they are highly mobile, with all their wealth in portable form. They can flee from their territory in case of attack, and even if they submit to the victors they can slip away so easily that it is very difficult to exploit them.

The only tribes which can be organized and exploited successfully are those who are able to produce enough surplus to repay the conquerors' efforts and who are at the same time sedentary. Conquest states are characteristic of societies which rest upon agriculture or manufactures or both. They replace the older patterns of expulsion or extermination as soon as the conquerors realize that the conquered are worth more to them alive than dead, or, it might be more accurate to say, as soon as the conquerors realize that they are worth more as subjects than as slaves, for it is the essence of the conquest state that its rulers exploit societies rather than individuals. The conquest state represents a relinquishment of the quick profits to be derived from loot and individual enslavement for the slower but in the aggregate much greater profits to be derived from tribute or taxes.

Really successful exploitation requires the maintenance of a delicate balance. The conquered society must be allowed to keep much of its original organization or it will be unable to function or to provide for its own wants, still less to produce a surplus. At the same time, the more completely it is left intact the easier it is for it to revolt and the greater the difficulty of watching and controlling it. The conquerors always wish for the maximum profit, yet if taxes or tribute are too high, the subject society is paralyzed and its contributions to the conquerors automatically cease. The conquered must be controlled and cropped regularly, yet the process must be carried on in such a way that they will neither lose the will and capacity for production nor be driven to desperation and revolt. The threat of force must always be present, but the use of force must be reduced to a minimum. Punitive expeditions are costly, interrupt the flow of tribute, and are likely to lead to revolts in other parts of the state.

The successful organization of a conquest state thus presents a whole series of problems which are lacking at the tribal level. All tribes have successful techniques for dealing with enemies, but dealing with subjects is a different matter. The development of methods for ruling and exploiting conquered societies requires not only inventive ability but a long process of trial and error. It is not surprising therefore that conquest states which have once been established tend to retain very much the same type of formal organization through repeated conquests and changes in the ruling group. A tribe which has had no previous experience of rule must accept the patterns which it finds or the state will dissolve into chaos before it can develop new ones. Thus when the Arabs suddenly became masters of the Near East they were forced to take over the governmental forms of the empires which they had conquered, and within two or three generations their tribal chiefs had become Oriental monarchs. Similarly, the Mongols in China had only one alternative to the adoption of the existing governmental machinery. This, the extermination of the Chinese and the turning of their territory back into pasture land, is said to have been seriously debated, but as soon as the decision was made the result was inevitable. Within three generations the Mongols had adopted Chinese administrative patterns as a whole and had become merely another Chinese dynasty.

All the Old World conquest states conform to a few main patterns of organization. This uniformity is probably due to historic causes rather than to the strict limitation of possibilities. The problems which the conquest state presents are fairly uniform, yet each of these can be met in more than one way, and the choice which a ruling group has made serves to establish patterns which may long survive its disappearance. Thus the vital problem of control can be met either by the dispersal of the conquerors through the conquered area or by their concentration in a particular territory, with the development of techniques for distant control. Both these systems have advantages and disadvantages. The dispersal method, under which the ruling group becomes a widely distributed aristocracy, makes it possible for them to watch the conquered and to collect tribute with a minimum of formal governmental machinery. At the same time, it scatters the conquerors' military force, thus diminishing their power for direct action, and sows the seeds of dissolution in the conquest state. In the absence of rapid and easy communication the aristocrats cannot maintain touch with each other, and this results in a gradual weakening of their *esprit de corps* and a breakdown of their original culture. Since they are in much closer contact with the conquered peoples among whom they live than they are with each other, they soon develop divergent interests and cultural differences. Unless the central authority is unusually strong, the state will break up in a few generations, the aristocrats fusing with the conquered groups among whom they have settled and leading these groups against each other.

This process is primarily an example of acculturation. The cultural fusion of conqueror and conquered becomes inevitable as soon as the conquerors lose touch with each other. Cultures cannot be maintained intact without a nucleus of individuals who are in constant association. The conquerors may make a conscious effort to maintain their old culture for the sake of social prestige and may succeed in maintaining most of its outward forms, but they cannot maintain its subtler and more vital elements. It is characteristic of aristocrats the world over that they are reluctant to take care of their own children. Any one who has had to take care of two or three infants simultaneously will understand why. This arduous business is turned over to slaves or servants from the conquered group, which means that the child is exposed to the culture of this group during its most formative period. It learns the language of the conquered before it learns its own and unconsciously absorbs most of their attitudes. Since most of the child's later dealings will be with the conquered, this is a distinct advantage to him, but it spells the destruction of the conquerors as an integrated social and cultural unit. The Normans in the British Isles provide a fine example of the dispersion of a conquering group and its results. Within a few generations those who had settled in England became English, those in Scotland Scottish, while those of Ireland were more loyal to their new land and greater haters of the English than the Irish themselves.

Dispersal of the conquering group and its transformation into a non-localized aristocracy was characteristic of most of the conquest states which arose in Europe after the fall of the Roman Empire. The invading tribes were themselves loosely organized and unaccustomed to strong central control within the group, while by the time of their invasion much of the Roman governmental machinery had broken down. They thus had no satisfactory models for the organization of centralized conquest states, while at the same time the pattern of dispersal was more compatible with their old cultural values of personal independence and individual initiative. In Asia most of the conquest states developed along a different pattern. The conquerors settled in a particular section of the conquered territory, thus providing a base from which the entire territory was exploited. In contrast to the European pattern of exploitation by individual aristocrats who might coöperate but who worked essentially for their own interests, the Asiatic pattern was, in most cases, that of the exploitation of the conquered by the conquering society as a whole.

The immediate advantages of the Asiatic pattern were that

it gave a concentration of military power, enabling the ruling group to strike a quick and hard blow, and that it helped to maintain the social and cultural unity of the ruling group. The child, even if cared for by foreign slaves, formed most of his associations with people of his own tribe and received its culture as a whole. In time the conquerors might take over elements from the conquered cultures, especially when these were more advanced than their own, but they could maintain their native values intact. The relation of the conquerors with their subjects was one of suspended hostilities. They were a tribe surrounded by a ring of enemy tribes who had been temporarily beaten into submission, and the realization of this helped to unify the ruling group and to maintain its social integrity. The rulers might be wiped out by a rising of the conquered population or the arrival of new conquerors, but they were unlikely to be quietly absorbed into it.

Under such conditions the successful exploitation of the conquered required a good deal of formal governmental machinery. Until this had been developed the position of the conquerors remained precarious and the profits from their domination uncertain. The development of this machinery was a slow process. The earliest Near Eastern conquest states followed the pattern of leaving the conquered societies intact and with almost complete autonomy. All that the rulers demanded from them was the regular payment of tribute, failure to pay being punished by plundering raids. An outside attack on the ruling group or dissensions within it always meant the end of tribute and usually a series of revolts. Thus when a new king came to the throne of Assyria his first task was usually to reconquer his father's empire and to reduce the subject tribes to a proper state of terror. With this terror went a deep-seated hatred which was renewed by each raid and which would flare into revolt at the least promise of success. Such states could be maintained only by strong kings backed by tribesmen who had kept their fighting ability.

To give such states any permanence it was necessary to develop techniques for exerting quiet, continuous pressure upon the conquered and for nipping revolts in the bud. It was also necessary to develop techniques for collecting tribute, for appraising the actual ability of the conquered to pay, and for dividing the income among the conquerors. In time the Near Eastern conquest states developed extensive bureaucracies with local governors appointed by the central authority, services of information, tax-collectors, and accounting departments, all of which focused upon the ruler of the conquering group. Theoretically they received their powers from him and were responsible to him, but actually they were largely self-perpetuating and acted to circumscribe the powers of the ruler and of the ruling tribe. Once firmly entrenched, the bureaucracy went on generation after generation and changes of dynasties or even of ruling groups had little effect upon it. Big officials would be removed at such times, but the small ones would continue to carry on their duties, serving the new rulers as they had the old.

Asiatic conquest states, with very few exceptions, were based on the theory of absolute rule. Each grade of officials had complete authority over those of the grades below and with it assumed responsibility for their good behavior. It was a military organization projected into the handling of civilian affairs and was probably an outgrowth of the original pattern of military domination by the conquerors. Since, at least in their inception, all these states rested upon force, there was no need for the rulers to consult the wishes of the governed. The problem of government was that of the quick and effective application of force to recalcitrant subjects. This required not only responsible officials but also a centralized authority which could make prompt decisions. Although the conquering group might have democratic patterns when it seized control, such patterns were poorly suited either to conquest or subsequent rule. A revolt might gain serious headway if no action could be taken until tribal representatives had been assembled and what to do debated. The result seems to have been in all cases the strengthening of central control even within the tribe and the metamorphosis of the tribal chief into a theoretically absolute monarch. If the conquest was that of an established state whose members were already accustomed to the absolute pattern, the process was naturally accelerated.

The conditions existing within conquest states were also peculiarly favorable to the functioning of this pattern. Tribal chiefs, although they may be absolute in theory, can hardly be so in practice. They are in too close contact with their subjects and united to them by too many ties of relationship and common interest. They are an integral part of the tribal society and thus subject to the pressure of public opinion. The ruler of a conquest state stands apart from all his subjects except his own tribesmen from the beginning. He does not have to consult their wishes, and his lack of contact with them transforms him into a symbol of the central authority. He is the mysterious and impersonal source of orders which must be obeyed. In time this attitude tends to extend itself even to his own tribesmen. As military leader the tribal chief usually receives the lion's share of the loot or subsequent tribute, and with this he is able to build up a personal following which is loyal to him rather than to the tribe. The conquered also feel that their loyalty is to him rather than to the conquering group as a whole, since it is from him that benefits and punishments come. The loyalty of the conquered and the presence of a palace group of guards and officials both help to remove the king from the direct and informal pressure of his tribesmen's opinion. The ordinary man cannot get to him, while the tribe as a whole cannot take action against him without danger of attack from the subjects. Even if these feel no great loyalty to the king, a split in the ranks of the conquerors offers a good opportunity for revolt. In most of the Asiatic conquest states the members of the ruling group ultimately became as subject to the will of the king as any of the conquered, retaining at most a few special privileges.

The problem which confronts the rulers of conquest states is essentially that of maintaining a steady flow of income with the minimum friction and the fewest possible resorts to force. The earlier conquest states lacked machinery for the direct control of individuals or local groups, making it necessary for them to leave the conquered societies a high degree of autonomy. Under such conditions it was to the conqueror's interest to perpetuate the cultural differences between the conquered peoples and to keep alive their mutual hatreds. The development of any united will among the subjects was discouraged, since it was almost certain to lead to action against the conquerors. The pattern was that of divide and rule, since the greater the dissensions among the subjects the greater the dependence of each conquered group upon the central authority.

One of the earliest methods of assuring division and dependence was that of *mitimœ*, the shifting about of conquerèd populations. The usual method was to carry off part of a defeated tribe and settle them in distant territory where they would be among strangers. At the same time part of some other conquered tribe would be settled on the land which they had vacated. The Babylonian captivity of the Jews is a good example of this technique. The old inhabitants of the region would usually dislike the new-comers who had been settled on what they felt was their land and would be eager to report to the central authority any signs of incipient revolt. At the same time, the exiles would be dependent upon the central authority for protection against their neighbors and could be trusted to watch them and report on them.

Such shifting about of populations and fanning of mutual hatreds made for the security of the conquerors, but they did not make for the smooth functioning of the state. Ties between conqueror and conquered which derived entirely from the conquered tribes' fear of each other were tenuous and easily disrupted. It was desirable to bind the conquered peoples to the central authority by a broader community of interest and to make them more contented with the *status quo*. The development of conquest state patterns shows an increasing attempt to replace the threat of force with encouragements to willing submission. In this development the increasing effectiveness of techniques for centralized control of individuals and local groups no doubt played a part. These made possible the integration of larger and larger groups of individuals into functional societies. When they had become well developed, the central authority of the state was able to take over most of the earlier functions of the tribe; and since the tribe, with its potentialities for revolt, was politically dangerous, the central authority sought to eliminate it.

We have already seen that the essential feature of the tribe is the feeling of unity existing between its members. This can survive the complete elimination of all formal aspects of tribal organization, as the history of many conquests clearly shows. Really to unite a conquered group with their conquerors, it is not enough to destroy their formal organization. Bonds of common culture and interest must be established. The subjects do not become genuine members of the state until they share in its community of will. The later conquest states realized this and developed various techniques for hastening the establishment of such bonds. The first move in this direction came, probably quite unconsciously, with the pattern of taking hostages. Members of leading families in the conquered tribe were carried off and kept as security for its good behavior. Since such hostages were of no value dead, they were usually well treated. Child hostages in particular, being brought up among the conquerors, absorbed much of their culture and formed personal relationships with members of the conquering group. When they returned to their own people they formed a link between the two societies. The political possibilities of this situation were soon realized, and all the later conquest states followed the pattern of keeping hostages at court as honored guests rather than prisoners, and rearing child hostages with the children of the conquering nobility. In many cases marriages between the leading families of the conquered groups and their conquerors were also encouraged. This not only helped to unite rulers and subjects by ties of blood, but wives given by the conquerors could exert influence on their husbands and report on their behavior. It is said that the Chinese emperors made considerable use of this technique, presenting royal concubines to the chiefs of conquered tribes or those of doubtful allegiance. These ladies were chosen for brains as well as beauty and were highly effective diplomatic agents.

The last stage in the evolution of such techniques for unification came with the extension to selected elements or individuals among the conquered of formal membership in the ruling group. This was not only an aid to unification but also served to alienate from the subject groups the individuals who would be their nat-

ural leaders in case of revolt. The advantages of such membership were usually great enough to ensure its ready acceptance,
while refusal could only be construed as a disloyal act. Even if
not directly punished, it revealed the person's sentiments and
marked him as one to be watched. The extension of Roman citi-
zenship is one of the best examples of this technique, and its
efficacy cannot be doubted.

In spite of some 6,000 years of experimentation, the problems of organizing and governing states have never been perfectly solved. The modern world, with the whole experience of
history to draw upon, still attacks these problems in many different ways and with indifferent success. One thing seems certain.
The most successful states are those in which the attitudes of
the individual toward the state most nearly approximate the attitudes of the uncivilized individual toward his tribe. If the members of a state have common interests and a common culture,
with the unity of will which these give, almost any type of
formal governmental organization will function efficiently. If the
members lack this feeling of unity, no elaboration of formal governmental patterns or multiplication of laws will produce an
efficient state or contented citizens. How such unity may be
created and maintained in great populations and especially in
fluid ones where the individual's close, personal contacts are
reduced to a minimum is probably the most important problem
which confronts us to-day.

CHAPTER XV

SOCIAL SYSTEMS

At the very outset of any general discussion of social systems it is necessary to reëmphasize the distinction between such systems and societies. Societies are groups of individuals who live and work together, their coöperative existence being made possible by mutual adaptations in the various members' attitudes and behavior. Social systems consist of the mutually adjusted ideal patterns according to which the attitudes and behavior of a society's members are organized. A society is an organization of individuals; a social system is an organization of ideas. It represents a particular arrangement of statuses and rôles which exist apart from the individuals who occupy the statuses and express the rôles in overt behavior.

It is extremely hard to keep this distinction clear in our thinking. As we have seen in the chapter on "Status and Rôle," many statuses are assigned to individuals on the basis of easily determined biological factors such as sex, age, and various kinds and degrees of biological relationship. Thus in our own society the statuses of father and son carry a mixture of social and biological associations. We think of the pattern controlling the interrelation of persons in these two statuses as something which derives from the biological relationship and cannot be divorced from it. As a matter of fact, the father-son pattern presumably did develop through the stabilization and transmission of forms of behavior developed by fathers and sons as a result of the constant contact into which they were brought through their mutual attachment to the mothers. However, once these patterns had been established, the blood relationship became simply a reference point by which certain individuals were assigned to certain statuses. Even for this the social recognition or assumption of the existence of the blood relationship became vastly more important than the relationship itself.

Thus in our own society physical paternity without social recognition of the fact, as when a boy's actual father is his mother's secret lover instead of her husband, gives father and son no status with regard to each other. Father status relative to the boy will be ascribed to his mother's husband and, if the mother and lover keep the secret, the social relation between the husband and his wife's son will be exactly the same as that between a legitimate father and son. Illegitimate but socially recognized paternity does establish statuses for father and son, although the pattern is rather vague in our present system. It was definite enough in Europe in the Middle Ages, but the statuses in such cases were quite different from those for a father and his son born in wedlock. The statuses for a father and his legitimate son are clearly defined in our system, since here the biological relationship is not only recognized but approved. At the same time, these statuses may frequently be ascribed, *via* adoption, to individuals who stand in no blood relationship to each other. Lastly, the statuses of a father and his legitimate son whom some one else has adopted are different again. The pattern for this relationship happens to be vague in our system, but it may be quite definite in other systems where adoption is more frequent. Thus in the Marquesas, where practically every child was adopted, the real or putative biological father had well-defined rights and duties toward his son even after the adoption.

It can be seen from the foregoing that even in such a close and easily determined relationship as that of father and son, social factors have come to outweigh biological ones in the ascription of status. This is even clearer when we observe the statuses assigned on the basis of more remote biological relationships. Such relationships are not, in themselves, responsible for any type of social interaction between the individuals who stand in them. There is no implicit reason why a man should be in closer or more continuous contact with a blood relative, say the daughter of his father's sister, than with any other woman belonging to the same age group and consequently no implicit reason for his developing particular attitudes or forms of behavior with regard to her. If the society has a pattern of patrilocal marriage, he may only see her at rare intervals and have much less necessity for mutual adjustment with her than with a dozen biologically unrelated girls who are members of his own band. However, almost any social system will have a definite pattern for individuals who stand, or are socially assumed to stand, in this particular biological relationship.

In short, the development of social systems with their formal patterns for the interrelations of individuals has resulted in a greater or less divorce between biological relationships and social relationships. The individual is socially ascribed to particular statuses, biological relationships serving merely as a reference point. With the exception of the relationship between nursing mother and child, any one of the requisite sex and age level can be substituted for the blood relative without interfering in any way with the full expression of the social pattern. Even the emotional attitudes which we are accustomed to think of as intimately associated with biological relationships can be assumed easily and readily by unrelated individuals who are socially assigned to the corresponding statuses. Thus the affection between adoptive parent and child is often as deep and as real as that between blood parent and child.

This dissociation between social relationships and biological relationships is made still more evident by the important rôle which statuses ascribed with relation to non-biological factors play in all societies. Our own social system includes hundreds of these, the teacher-student or employer-employee statuses being good examples. Sometimes participation in a pattern of this sort may even carry a very high emotional context. Thus among the Comanche the most important social relationship was probably that into which two men entered voluntarily. They might be remotely related by blood or marriage, but this was rarely the case. Every adult male normally had a brother-in-arms, the two men selecting each other on the basis of mutual congeniality. The establishment of such a relationship was given no ceremonial expression. Individuals grew into it so gradually that it would be impossible to say where ordinary friendship ended and the brother-in-arms relationship began. At the same time, it was given full social recognition, and the reciprocal rights and duties of the brothers-in-arms were defined with unusual exactness. In fact this pattern was more conscious and more thoroughly verbalized than the patterns for such socio-biological relationships as that between father and son or husband and wife. The emotional context of this relationship was also deeper, the brother-in-arms being considered closer than any blood relative, even a father or brother. It was to his brother-in-arms that a man turned first in any difficulty, and it was his brother-in-arms whom he saved first in time of danger.

We must think of social systems, then, not only as distinct entities but as entities only remotely related to the biological relationships existing between the members of a particular society. Social systems are really systems of ideas. The recognition of this fact does not call for any mystic or supernaturalistic attitudes toward them. It is quite on a par with the distinction which we constantly make between an organization of any sort, say a coöperative society, and the constitution and by-laws of the organization. The social system influences the attitudes and behavior of the individuals who share its component ideas, but it would be ridiculous to impute to it any consciousness or volition. These remain exclusive attributes of the society's component individuals.

Perhaps the nature of a social system can best be understood if we compare it to a geometric figure, a bit of "nothing intricately drawn nowhere." Actually, there is nothing else within the range of common experience which would be so closely comparable. A geometric figure consists of a series of spatial relationships which are delimited by points. These points are established by the relationships and can be defined only in terms of the relationships. They have no independent existence. Each of the patterns which together compose a social system is made up of hypothetical attitudes and forms of behavior, the sum total of these constituting a social relationship. The polar positions within such patterns, i.e., the statuses, derive from this relationship and can only be defined in terms of it. They have no more independent existence than do the points of the geometric figure. Any status, as distinct from the individuals whom society may designate to occupy it, is simply a collection of rights and duties. Thus the status of employer derives from the relationship between employer and employee and can be defined only in terms of the attitudes and behavior which the total pattern for this relationship ascribes to this one of its two polar positions. The question "What is an employer?" can only be answered by explaining what an employer does for his employees and what he receives in return. The status of employer is a constant in our social system, while actual employers come and go in our society. Employers are a host of individuals old and young, male and female, irritable or easy-going, and employees are equally varied. The range of variation in their actual attitudes and behavior toward each other, in spite of loose conformity to the ideal pattern for the relationship, is even wider. Nevertheless, *the employer* and *the employee* and the pattern from which these statuses derive exist as an integral part of our social system and are only superficially affected by their varying agents and expressions.

Since patterns find expression only through the medium of the individuals who occupy the statuses which they establish, it is the statuses which are first brought to the attention of the investigator. All societies have names for many of the statuses in their systems and are accustomed to express their patterns, when these are at all conscious or verbalized, in status terms. In describing such a relationship as that of father and son, they will tell first what one does and expects, then what the other does and expects. As a result, most investigators have shown a tendency to treat statuses as though they were fixed points between which various behavioral relationships might develop. This tendency is increased by the fact that so many statuses are ascribed to individuals on the basis of biological relationships present in all aggregates. The fallacy of regarding statuses in this way comes out very clearly when we try to apply our own status terminology to the statuses in other social systems. Thus we have a single term, *uncle,* which we apply indiscriminately to the brothers of both parents and the husbands of both parents' sisters. This usage reflects the fact that in our particular system there is a single pattern for the child's relation with these four male relatives. In other systems the same four groups of relatives, i.e., father's brother, mother's brother, father's sister's husband, and mother's sister's husband may be sharply distinguished, with a different pattern for the child's relation with each group. Moreover, none of the four patterns will agree in all respects with our own uncle-child pattern. To lump these four statuses together under our own term *uncle* is to completely misrepresent the situation. In some cases the patterns for father and father's brother may be the same, i.e., the two relationships may be social equivalents. Again, the pattern for mother's brother may be totally different from that for father's brother. It may even agree more closely with our own pattern for the father relationship than does the pattern for this relationship within the particular system.

If we attempt to apply to other social systems the terms which we have developed for certain groupings of individuals, such as the word *family,* we are likely to be led still further astray. From the social, as distinct from the biological, point of view, a family is a group of interrelated statuses determined by the presence of a complex series of mutually adjusted patterns. These patterns will never be exactly the same in any two societies, and even the criteria by which individuals are assigned to family status may vary widely from one system to another. Thus the family unit may be extended to include remote degrees of biological relationship in the line of one parent and cut off short in that of the other parent. It may have spouses as its nucleus, or it may center about a group of brothers and sisters whose spouses are never really incorporated. The functional relations of the family's members to each other and of the family unit to the total society may also be highly diverse. In short, the family is never the same thing in any two systems.

Like diversity can be shown to exist for all social institutions. No two institutions belonging to different systems are ever identical, although they may present numerous similarities. While these similarities may be used as a basis for classification, the constant presence of differences means that the assignment of particular institutions to particular categories must depend on the judgment of the investigator. For example, both the Central Algonkins and the Iroquois recognize groupings based on unilateral descent, but aside from this the two institutions have little in common. The Central Algonkin institution's functions are mainly religious, and it resembles certain non-hereditary societies found in tribes farther to the west more than it resembles the Iroquois institution. Are the similarities in this case of sufficient importance to outweigh the numerous differences and to justify classing both institutions together as clans? All classifications of institutions are based not only on the recognition of similarities between those in different systems, but also on an ignoring of their differences. Investigators are prone to forget this and to speak of the categories which they themselves have established as objectively real. They will make solemn generalizations about the characteristics of clans when all they are really doing is stating the basis on which their classifications are established. Instead of these characteristics growing out of a particular institution, any institution which lacks this particular combination of characteristics is not classed as a clan and is therefore excluded from the discussion. Classifications of institutions are convenient tools for descriptive purposes, and they have been used as such in the preceding chapters, but they can aid us very little in understanding the real significance of institutions.

The logical starting point for investigations of society is thus the study of particular social systems as wholes. The recognition of such systems as entities distinct from societies simplifies the problem somewhat, since it makes it possible to ignore the wide range of individual variation in the expression of the system's patterns and to concentrate upon these patterns and their interrelations. However, the problem still remains sufficiently complex. The first task confronting the investigator is that of ascertaining what the patterns are. Societies vary greatly in the degree to which their patterns are conscious and verbalized. Thus the members of one society may be able to tell the minutiæ of behavior prescribed by a particular pattern, say that connected with the statuses of chief and commoner, while members of another society can give only vague generalities. The best way to establish the patterns is by a combination of statements and case histories. Either of these classes of evidence is unsatisfactory when taken alone. Certain patterns may be almost unconscious, while many cases may be atypical. In case histories the way in which the community felt about a particular episode is, if anything, more important to our study than the actual behavior, since this makes it possible to determine in part how far the behavior differed from the accepted pattern. To give a concrete example, it would never occur to a Comanche to tell an investigator that in case of an attack on the camp it was expected that a son-in-law would help his mother-in-law to escape before he tried to save himself or his property, or that if he failed to do this she could order her daughter to leave him. The informant would only say vaguely that a son-in-law should respect and help his mother-in-law. At the same time, in an actual case of this sort the sympathy of the group was all with the abandoned mother-in-law. It was felt that the man had shirked his duty and that the mother-in-law was quite justified in dissolving the marriage.

The investigator's picture of the social system as a whole must be built up through a piecemeal gathering of the component patterns and observation of their mutual relationships and adaptations as revealed in their actual exercise. The average member of any society cannot help the investigator in this. It is only in highly sophisticated societies such as those of China, of Greece in classical times, or of modern Europe that any one realizes that the patterns which govern social interactions constitute a system. Even then it is only the philosopher or sociologist who troubles his head about the matter, and even he must deduce the system from observation of the patterns in action. Given equal facilities for this, an investigator brought up outside a particular society can gain quite as clear a picture of its system as one brought up within it. In fact, he can frequently gain a clearer one, since his investigations will not be hampered by prejudices or by an unwillingness to admit the presence of particular patterns which he feels are not commendable. All systems include certain patterns which are at variance with the professed mores of the society, but which are patterns nevertheless. For example, a society which strongly reprehends illicit relations between the sexes will frequently have fairly definite patterns for such relations. The society does not approve of sin, yet at the same time it provides the individual with guides to sinning.

Not only does the average individual fail to apprehend the patterns which govern the life of his society as a system, but he is rarely if ever familiar with all the patterns themselves. He has to know a certain number of them if he is to do his part as a member of the society, but there is no necessity for him to know all of them. Thus the average man has to be acquainted with the pattern for the parent-child relationship and usually has an opportunity to learn it through experience as well as instruction, but he does not need to know the pattern governing the relations between a chief and his councilors or between two priests in the service of a particular deity. Unless he has more than the average amount of curiosity he will not trouble to learn these even when given an opportunity to do so. The patterns which compose the system are transmitted to the individual as so many discrete units, and the knowledge and exercise of these patterns at any given point in the society's history is divided up among the society's members just as are the knowledge and practice of all other elements within the society's culture.

This at once brings up another and perhaps the greatest difficulty which confronts the investigator of social systems. Even when a complete picture of such a system has been obtained, the working of the system cannot be understood unless it is studied in relation to its broader context, i.e., the environment and culture of the society. Social systems can only function as parts of a larger whole, the total culture of the society. It is possible for an investigator to isolate the social system from the rest of culture for descriptive purposes by a process of analysis and selection comparable to that by which the anatomist isolates a nervous system from the rest of an organism. However, the isolation is artificially imposed, both organisms and cultures constituting functional wholes. Viewed from this aspect, a social system is simply a segment of a culture, that fraction of the whole which provides the members of a society with designs for group living. In this respect it is on a par with those other segments of culture which provide the group with techniques for getting its food or protecting itself from enemies. Since social systems are never apprehended as wholes by those who live under them and never function except in relation to the total culture, it is an open question whether they can be considered as constituting a distinct class of phenomena. The utility of the concept for descriptive purposes is obvious, but from the standpoint of the student of function such groupings of patterns appear to be something which the investigator interposes between two genuinely operative things: the pattern, which is known to individuals and influences the behavior of individuals, and the culture, which provides for the total needs of the society.

The problem of the reality of social systems is a philosophic rather than a practical one. The important thing is that the complex of mutually adjusted patterns which we term "a social system" develops and functions in constant relation to the rest of culture and that the patterns must be adapted to this setting quite as much as to each other. The total culture, in turn, must be adapted to the natural environment of the society, since man may develop many and diverse techniques for mastering and exploiting his environment but can never escape from it. Every social system is, therefore, part of a vastly larger configuration all of whose component elements are interrelated. It can be understood only when it is studied with relation to this configuration whose other elements impose constant limits upon its growth and operation.

The way in which the content of a configuration operates to limit and shape the patterns of a social system can best be illustrated by a concrete example. Let us assume that a society which has a simple hunting economy settles in a region where the food supply is so scanty that only five or six persons at most can be supported by exploiting the territory from a single center. Under such conditions patterns of extreme economic specialization and constant interdependence are unworkable. The specialist and his products would rarely be at hand when needed. There can be a moderate development of specialization and exchange, but each man must at least know how to get food and how to make the minimum equipment necessary for survival. The institution of slavery is unworkable, since a slave sent out hunting has too good an opportunity to escape, while one kept in camp cannot produce enough to repay the expense of supporting him. The narrow economic margin of the group, poor development of manufactures and trade, and the difficulty of transporting property make the development of marked economic inequalities between individuals or family lines improbable. Patterns of aristocracy based on wealth are therefore unworkable. If the food supply is too scanty to support units of population larger than single families of conjugal type, the joint family pattern is unworkable. It is impossible for sons, grandsons, and great-grandsons and their wives and children to live and work together constantly; hence, while the closeness of these relationships may be recognized, no constantly functional grouping can be based upon them. Lastly, it is impossible to put into effect patterns of autocratic rule in such a society. The economic surplus is not large enough to support a king, still less the officials necessary to enforce his orders, while the high mobility of the individual families makes it easy for them to escape from control.

Let us suppose that a single new element, say domesticated horses, is introduced into this configuration. Certain social patterns which were previously unworkable at once become workable. The potential food supply is increased, and it becomes possible for larger units of population to live together. This, combined with the increased ease of transportation, opens the way for increased specialization and trade. Slaves can now be used to advantage either for herding or as specialized craftsmen. At the same time, the ease of escape, especially when herding, acts as a preventive to the development of patterns of extreme severity in dealing with slaves. They must be treated well enough to make their lot endurable. With the possibility for larger population units, joint family organization becomes possible and is even advantageous, since it ensures the coöperation of a large number of men for war or hunting and reduces the labor of herding the horses. One man can take care of fifty almost as easily as he can of three or four. Individual and family inequalities in wealth may develop, and a wealth aristocracy pattern becomes workable. Patterns of autocratic rule are, however, still difficult to put into effect because of the high mobility of the population. Lastly, the situation is particularly favorable for the operation of patterns of warfare and social distinctions based on war prestige. Horses make it possible for hostile groups to strike at a distance and escape readily and at the same time increase the economic profits of raiding. Horse herds are easier to get away with than any other form of loot. The introduction of any other new element into the configuration will similarly open up new possibilities for the operation of social patterns or render existing patterns disadvantageous, leading to their ultimate modification or abandonment.

The factors cited in the above examples influence social patterns mainly through their effects on the economic life of the group. However, there is at work another series of factors which are only indirectly connected with economics. It has been pointed out in an earlier chapter that it is the sharing of a certain body of ideas and values which gives any society its *esprit de corps*. Apparently almost any combination of ideas and values can perform this function effectively, but if such elements are to have meaning and to serve as rallying points for the emotions of the group's members they must constantly be reaffirmed in practice. Thus no society could hold as one of its basic values the superiority of women over men and their inherent right to male deference and consideration and at the same time make wife-beating an integral part of its ideal pattern for the marriage relationship. The presence of a particular body of ideas and values within a culture limits the operation and especially the development of certain social patterns quite as genuinely as do particular natural environments or the presence of particular techniques for exploiting them.

We have spoken hitherto of the negative, limiting factors which simply by their presence render certain patterns unworkable and by this means passively shape and direct the development of social systems. Let us turn now to the positive factors, those which stimulate the development of social systems and the elaboration of their patterns. These factors would seem to be of two sorts: the innate qualities of members of the species *Homo sapiens* and the situations which are a constant accompaniment of life in aggregates. The innate qualities of human beings have already been discussed at length in Chapter XI. There we attempted to show that such qualities do exist and that they are responsible for certain trends in the development of social systems. These trends are reflected in the varying frequency of occurrence of certain institutions. Thus it was pointed out that the greater frequency of polygyny and monogamy as contrasted with polyandry or group marriage probably derives from certain physiological qualities of our species. At the same time, the existence of socially recognized institutions and patterns not in agreement with these trends proves that their working-out can be inhibited by cultural factors.

There are a number of situations which are a constant accompaniment of life in aggregates. Thus there is the close biologically determined association between mother and infant, an association which goes back to the very beginnings of mammalian life. There is the association between mates and, growing out of this, the almost universal association between males and their offspring. There are the associations which are sure to be formed between individuals of the same sex on the basis of common interest and congeniality, i.e., friendships. There is the presence in all aggregates of individuals of different sex and age with differing potentialities for service to the society and for interaction with each other. There is the necessity for coöperation and for the organization of the activities of individuals in such a way that there will be a minimum of mutual interference. Arising out of this there is the need for leadership and direction in the society's activities.

Lastly, there is the constant clash of personalities and the conflicts of interest both between individuals and between the individuals and the group.

All these situations are present in all societies and beget problems which must be solved if social life is to continue. These problems and the trends resulting from the innate qualities of human beings are the constants affecting the development of social systems. However, the diversity of social systems proves that the problems may be solved in a great variety of ways. Thus leadership of some sort is a necessary accompaniment of organized social life, yet the patterns for leadership and the bases on which leadership status is assigned may be of many sorts. There may be a single leader in all activities or different leaders for different activities. Leaders may function constantly or only in emergencies. Their position may be given elaborate ceremonial recognition or only informal recognition. Leadership status may be assigned to the old men as a whole, as among certain Australian tribes; to active warriors of proved ability, as among the Comanche; to an elected council, as among the Iroquois; or to a hereditary chief, as among the Maori. In Australia obedience is assured by the personal influence of the old men, probably with the threat of magic in the background. Among the Comanche the ruling warriors maintained their position by a combination of generosity and persuasion and flattered their followers by a mock humility. Among the Maori the chief derived his almost absolute authority from the supernatural power which was supposed to have come to him through his high descent, and the exercise of this authority was backed by religious sanctions. All of these various arrangements met the need for leadership adequately, and all of them seem to have been equally effective. It is evident that, given the necessary adjustment between the patterns in a particular configuration, any one of a long series of patterns can meet a particular social need.

The great variety of patterns and social systems is no doubt due to the large number of variable factors which influence their development. The passive, limiting factors imposed by the total configuration within which the system develops and must function are inherently variable, as we have already seen. However, the dynamic factors which make for the development of patterns are also inherently variable. There is abundant proof that social patterns and institutions may be borrowed from one society by another like any other elements of culture. The spread of the Rotary and other business men's clubs from the United States to Mexico and the Orient is an example of this. Even complete patterns for such intimate social relationships as those associated with marriage and family life can be transferred from one system to another. Many societies have substituted formal patterns of monogamy for polygynous ones when they accepted Christianity. Such borrowed patterns are always somewhat modified and reinterpreted by the receiving group. Moreover, the preëxisting social system and culture of the receiving group have a selective effect, preventing the acceptance of patterns which are thoroughly incompatible with the existing configuration. At the same time, the influencing of borrowing on social systems cannot be ignored, and the opportunities for borrowing depend upon contacts which are chance-determined. Thus it must be considered pure accident that the contacts of the Mexican Indians were with Spanish culture, while those of the Indians of the United States were mainly with English and French culture. This difference in contacts meant that different sets of social patterns were made available for borrowing in each case and had important effects on the further development of the Indian social systems in each case. Modern Mexican social systems are all a blend of Spanish and Indian patterns which have been modified and reinterpreted.

Even when no outside influences are at work, an element of pure chance may enter into the development of social patterns. Thus the Mohammedan rule that a man may marry the divorced wife of an adopted son can only be accounted for by the fact that the prophet wanted to marry the divorced wife of his adopted son and had a revelation that it was permissible. This pattern was completely at variance with the pre-Mohammedan Arab ideas on the subject. Had the lady been less attractive or Mohammed more ascetic, it is highly improbable that the pattern would ever have come into existence. Again, there is one clan among the

Tanala, in Madagascar, which prohibits the taking of sisters as plural wives, although all the other clans permit it. This prohibition was barely fifty years old at the time of my visit. It derived from a case of poisoning between sisters who were plural wives, the circumstances and names of the parties still being clearly remembered. There is a general Tanala belief that sisters are more likely to be jealous of each other than wives who are not related, but only this one clan has given the belief expression in its formal patterns. Apparently the poisoning incident brought feeling to a head, resulting in a definite ruling. It should be noted in this connection that the sister-jealousy pattern itself is probably culturally determined. The Comanche hold exactly the opposite view and encourage the marriage of sisters, saying that they are less jealous than strangers. Both groups can cite plenty of examples in support of their respective theories so there is probably no sub-cultural basis for either.

Although there are a series of constants which affect the development of all social systems alike, it can be seen from the foregoing that these constants are only a few of the many factors which contribute to the formation of such systems. The specific form of any pattern or institution is mainly the result of social inventions, culture contacts, and the total environment, natural as well as cultural, in which the pattern or institution develops and functions. Since all of these factors are inherently variable, patterns and institutions, when treated as discrete phenomena, can only be explained on a historic basis. In most cases our knowledge of their history is so brief and so incomplete that they cannot be explained at all. All that we can do is to observe and describe the operation of such patterns and their functional interrelationships.

Although we may be able to determine the trends which influence the development of all social systems, knowledge of these can give us little ability for prediction in the case of specific societies. The influence exerted by the total configuration, by culture contacts, and by individuals is too strong. Ability to predict, if it can ever be achieved, must be based on the observed compatibility or incompatibility of particular patterns or institutions.

Even then the valid predictions will be mainly on the negative side. We may be able to say that the presence of a particular set of patterns will render a certain pattern unworkable and thus prevent its development or introduction, but we will not be able to say that the presence of a particular set of patterns will inevitably lead to the development or acceptance of some other pattern. There may always be other elements in the total configuration which will prevent this. While negative predictions can be based on generalizations arrived at through observation of series of different configurations, positive predictions must be based on intensive study of particular configurations and must take into account elements quite outside the social system. An example may make this clear.

It was pointed out in an earlier chapter that the formation of conquest states is compatible with patterns of settled life and technical development which make possible the creation of an economic surplus, but incompatible with patterns of nomadic hunting life. The reasons for this were also indicated. On the basis of this generalization it can be predicted with a high degree of probability that any tribe which attempts to establish a conquest state among nomadic hunting peoples will fail. However, this generalization does not make it possible for us to predict that the same tribe will succeed in an attempt to establish such a state among settled agriculturalists. To do this we must have a mass of additional knowledge as to the relative numbers of men on the two sides, their weapons and fighting ability, the personalities of leaders, and the political situation in the various groups. All these factors will be different in each instance, and knowledge of them in one case will not help us at all in another case. Again, we can predict that a society with highly developed polygynous patterns will present greater resistance to the introduction of Christianity, with its insistence on monogamy, than to the introduction of Islam. However, there is sure to be some resistance in either case, and the actual acceptance or rejection of the new religion will be influenced by a number of other factors. Christianity may come backed by official pressure or baited with social and economic advantages great enough to ensure its acceptance even when this entails the complete revamping of the preëxisting social system. Conversely, the pagans' hatred of their Christian rulers may be so strong that they flatly refuse to accept Christianity even when it would be compatible with their preëxisting social institutions.

Classifications of social institutions and systems are useful tools for descriptive purposes, and generalizations with regard to the interrelations of patterns and institutions help to bring some order out of chaos and to increase our understanding of social processes. At the same time, a real understanding of these processes must depend upon the study of the total configurations of which social systems form a part. Such configurations include three distinct elements: the personalities of the individuals who compose the society, the natural environment to which the society must adapt its life and the culture of the society; the whole mass of techniques for living whose transmission from generation to generation ensures the society's continued existence. Of these three elements the last appears to be by far the most important, and the chapters which follow will be devoted to a discussion of its qualities.

CHAPTER XVI

PARTICIPATION IN CULTURE

The reader who has come thus far will have a fairly clear idea of the meaning of the term *culture*. It has already been defined in various ways and used in numerous connections. He should also have a clear idea of the nature of society and should realize that culture and society are mutually dependent. Neither can exist as a functioning entity without the other. It is the possession of a common culture which gives a society its *esprit de corps* and makes it possible for its members to live and work together with a minimum of confusion and mutual interference. At the same time, the society gives culture overt expression in its behavior, and hands it on from generation to generation. However, societies are so constituted that they can only express culture through the medium of their component individuals and can only perpetuate it by the training of these individuals. It is with the participation of these individuals in the total culture of their society that we will deal in the present chapter.

It has been pointed out in an earlier chapter that no one individual is ever familiar with the total content of the culture of the society to which he belongs. Even in the simplest cultures the content is too rich for any one mind to be able to apprehend the whole of it. The patterns of division of and specialization in activities make it possible for the individual to function successfully as a member of his society without such complete knowledge. He learns and employs certain aspects of the total culture and leaves the knowledge and exercise of other aspects to other individuals. At the same time, every person is usually familiar with elements of his society's culture which he will never be called upon to express in action. Thus a lame man may be thoroughly familiar with the behavior appropriate to men on war parties although he himself can never take part in one. The same situation may hold for whole categories within the society. Thus all men may know the taboos incumbent upon pregnant women, although obviously they will never be called upon to practise them. To come closer home, the conventions governing male and female costume are quite different, yet each sex has a fairly clear idea of what is appropriate for the other. A surprising number of women help to buy their husbands' clothes, while husbands not infrequently veto their wives' lipsticks or bathing suits or advise them to imitate the costume worn by Mrs. X.

These factors increase the degree of the individual's participation in culture, but it never reaches completeness. If we observe the culture of any homogeneous society, we will find that the content of this culture can be divided into three categories these being derived from the extent to which the elements within each category are shared by the society's members. As in all classifications, there may be some difficulty in assigning certain elements to their places in this three-fold division, but the position of most of them will be plain enough.

First, there are those ideas, habits, and conditioned emotional responses which are common to all sane, adult members of the society. We will call these the *Universals*. It must be understood that this terminology applies only to the content of a particular culture. An element classed as a Universal in one culture may be completely lacking in another. To this category belong such elements as the use of a particular language, the tribal patterns of costume and housing, and the ideal patterns for social relationships. This category also includes the associations and values which lie, for the most part, below the level of consciousness but which are, at the same time, an integral part of culture.

Second, we have those elements of culture which are shared by the members of certain socially recognized categories of individuals but which are not shared by the total population. We will call these the *Specialties*. Under this head come the patterns for all those varied but mutually interdependent activities which have been assigned to various sections of the society in the course of its division of labor. In all societies certain things are done by or known to only a designated part of the population, although they contribute to the well-being of the whole. Thus all the women within a tribe will be familiar with certain occupations and techniques, while the men will be familiar with a different series. As a rule, the men will only have a rather vague general knowledge of the things which belong in the women's province and vice versa. Under this head there can also be classed the activities which the society has assigned to special craftsmen or functionaries such as the smith, carpenter, doctor, and priest.

The cultural elements which fall into this class are, for the most part, manual skills and technical knowledge. The greater part of them are concerned with the utilization and control of the natural environment. Although such elements are not shared by the entire society, the benefits arising from them are shared, and all members of the society will have a fairly clear idea as to what the end product of each specialized activity should be. Thus a husband may have only a general idea of the processes involved in making bread, but he will be keenly conscious of whether it has been made properly or not. Again, the average man does not know the techniques of the smith and regards his skill in metal-working with some awe, but he has a clear mental picture of what constitutes a good knife or hoe and will be both resentful of inferior workmanship and suspicious of innovations. The same thing holds for the activities of the doctor or priest. The uninstructed do not know the full details of their procedure, but every one has a general knowledge of how healing or sacrificing should be done and of the results to be expected from it. Any departure from the accustomed procedure or failure to achieve the expected results brings an emotional reaction.

Third, there are in every culture a considerable number of traits which are shared by certain individuals but which are not common to all the members of the society or even to all the members of any one of the socially recognized categories. We will call these *Alternatives.* The elements of culture which may be included in this class have a very wide range, varying from the special and often quite atypical ideas and habits of a particular family to such things as different schools of painting or sculpture. Aside from the nature of the participation in them, all these Alternatives have this in common: they represent different reactions to the same situations or different techniques for achieving the same ends. The cultures of small societies living under primitive conditions usually include only a moderate number of such Alternatives, while in such a culture as our own they are very plentiful. Examples of such Alternatives for ourselves would be such things as the use of horses, bicycles, railroads, automobiles, and airplanes for the single purpose of transportation overland; our variety of teaching techniques; or our wide range of beliefs and attitudes toward the supernatural.

Beyond the limits of culture there lies still a fourth category of habits, ideas and conditioned emotional responses; that of *Individual Peculiarities*. These include such things as one person's abnormal fear of fire, due perhaps to some accident of his early experience, a craftsman's individual tricks of technique or characteristic muscular habits, or a purely personal doubt regarding some generally accepted article of faith. Every individual has certain peculiarities of this sort whether he is a member of a primitive tribe or a modern urban community, and the sum total of such individual differences within any society is enormous.

Individual Peculiarities cannot be classed as a part of culture, in the sense in which the term is ordinarily used, since they are not shared by any of a society's members. At the same time they are of extreme importance in cultural dynamics since they are the starting point of everything which later becomes incorporated into culture. There is always some one individual in a community who is the first to discover, invent, or adopt a new thing. As soon as this new thing has been transmitted to and is shared by even one other individual in the society, it must be reckoned a part of culture. Individual Peculiarities occupy somewhat the same position with regard to culture that individual mutations occupy with regard to a biological species. Most Individual Peculiarities, like most physical variations, are never transmitted at all or are transmitted to only a few individuals and ultimately disappear. However, if the Peculiarity is of a sort advantageous to its possessor, it may be transmitted to an ever-widening circle of individuals until it is accepted by the whole society.

It is easiest to apply the foregoing classification to elements within cultures of the sort carried by small, closely integrated social units such as the local groups described in a previous chapter. When we turn to larger units such as tribes, or more especially modern states, we find a vastly more complex situation. While ethnologists have been accustomed to speak of tribes and nationalities as though they were the primary culture-bearing units, the total culture of a society of this type is really an aggregate of sub-cultures. Within tribes or unmechanized civilizations these sub-cultures are normally carried by the various local groups which go to make the total society and are transmitted within these groups. In a few cases there may also be sub-cultures which are characteristic of particular social classes and which are transmitted within them, but this arrangement is much less characteristic than the local one. Every sub-culture always differs in some respects from all the rest, and the total culture consists of the sum of its sub-cultures plus certain additional elements which are a result of their interaction.

If we attempt to apply our three-fold classification to a tribal culture we will find that, in comparison with any of the sub-cultures which compose it, it shows fewer Universals and a marked increase in Specialties. The peculiarities of the various sub-cultures must be listed as Specialties rather than Alternatives since they are not presented to the individual as traits toward which he can exercise choice. Each individual accepts the patterns of his own sub-culture as proper guides to behavior and rarely attempts to imitate the patterns of other sub-cultures even when he is familiar with them. In fact, the presence of such differences usually makes him cling more tenaciously to the habits of his particular sub-culture, since these become a symbol of his membership in his particular social unit.

When we take such a culture as a whole, the number of Alternatives will also show some increase over those within a given sub-culture, since all the Alternatives within all the sub-cultures will be included. However, as long as the contacts between the social units which bear the sub-cultures are not very close or frequent, the total number of these Alternatives will bear little relation to the number of them which are submitted to any given individual for choice.

The sub-cultures within a tribal culture must of necessity be adapted to each other and have a considerable number of elements in common, else it will be impossible to maintain a feeling of tribal unity or for the tribe to function as a unit. However, the degree of adaptation necessary will depend largely upon the amount of contact between the units bearing the sub-cultures and especially upon the degree to which they are interdependent. Thus the various sub-cultures within a Plains Indian tribe could exist and develop with little reference to each other. The bands bearing them were economically self-contained and came together only at fairly long intervals. When, on the other hand, the groups which bear the sub-cultures are in close and frequent contact, or when the products of certain of these groups are necessary to the rest, there will have to be a much greater degree of adjustment. In particular, changes in any one of the sub-cultures will be strongly influenced by the situation existing in the rest.

Even when there is close contact and marked interdependence between the groups which bear sub-cultures, it is still possible for the sub-cultures to maintain their integrity. They become adapted to each other and to the total social structure, each of them performing certain functions with relation to the whole. Once a satisfactory adaptation has been achieved, there is no incentive for the individuals who share a particular sub-culture to give up their distinctive habits. These habits constitute Specialties, from the point of view of the culture as a whole, and are an integral part of it. While they may subject those who share them to jests and good-natured ridicule, as when the peasants of one village laugh at the costume of those in the next, they have the reinforcement of general recognition. As long as the groups which bear the sub-cultures remain conscious of themselves as distinct entities and retain their hold on the individuals who compose them, the sub-cultures will persist.

It is only when the hold of the local group or social class upon its members is broken, as it is beginning to be in our own society, that the sub-cultures tend to merge and disappear. The first effect of this merging is that the distinctive features of the sub-cultures cease to be Specialties and become Alternatives, i.e., are thrown open to individual choice. As competing Alternatives, most of them will finally be eliminated, with a consequent loss to the total content of the culture. However, until this elimination has taken place there will be a marked increase in the number of culture elements made available to any individual within the society.

The incomplete participation of all individuals in the culture of their societies is reflected in the presence within all societies of differential lines for the transmission of various culture elements. These lines correspond not only to the membership of the social units which carry particular sub-cultures but also to the various socially established categories of individuals within each of the functional social units. Thus certain elements are transmitted in family lines. The members of one family may be taught to say a particular form of grace at meals, perhaps the Lord's Prayer in German, and this custom may be handed down within it for generations, while other families transmit a grace of a different sort. Similarly, in all cultures the knowledge of the Specialties assigned to women will be transmitted almost entirely in the female line, while knowledge of those assigned to men will be transmitted in the male line.

One of the most interesting aspects of this differentiation of lines of cultural transmission, and one very frequently overlooked, is that the various age categories within a society also correspond to lines of cultural transmission. While the growing individual learns much from his elders, he learns even more from his contemporaries, as many baffled parents can attest. His contacts with his contemporaries are normally closer and less formal, and the heroes whom he strives to imitate are usually not adults, whose interests and activities lie largely beyond his ken, but individuals within his own general age category. In particular he will copy those who are slightly older than himself and more expert in the activities socially ascribed to the particular category.

Even in our own culture there are many elements which are transmitted almost exclusively within certain age brackets. For example, adults very rarely teach children to play marbles, this particular item being transmitted from boy to boy. Similarly, the techniques employed by adolescents in their first romantic advances to each other are constantly transmitted from older to younger adolescents without penetrating either the adult level or the child level. Although individuals naturally carry a knowledge of these techniques with them when they pass into the higher age groups, they would never think of employing them, still less of teaching them to their offspring. It seems quite possible that even the antagonism between adolescents and their elders and those questionings of certain values which we call "the revolt of youth" represent simply culture elements which are differentially transmitted in the adolescent line.

Let us turn now to the possible application of our classification of culture elements to some of the problems which confront the anthropologist. In a study of any culture the Universals and Specialties are the elements which strike the investigator first and which it is easiest for him to get information about. The traits in these two categories affect the life of the whole society directly and continuously so that every one either knows them or can refer the investigator at once to specialists who do know them. Moreover, this part of any culture bears the stamp of social recognition, and members of the society will talk about it freely. The only exceptions to this seem to be in the case of individuals who are sophisticated enough to know something about the investigator's own culture and to wish to present their own society to him in a favorable light.

It is much more difficult to learn the Alternatives. Many of the traits which belong in this group may be shared by such a small part of the population that they are likely to be overlooked. Others will usually be at variance with the ideas and values which are approved by a majority of the society's members, so that the people who do share them will be reluctant to talk about them. In either case few of them will come to light until the investigator has succeeded in establishing close and informal relations with many individuals in the society which he is studying.

The longer an investigator lives with any tribe and the better he comes to know them, the more Alternatives will be brought to his attention. Thus when I was studying the Comanche and asked for the process of making buckskin, I was told only the method which my particular informant preferred. Other informants checked the accuracy of this account point by point, and it was not until some time later that I learned that it was only one of three methods all of which were still in use in the tribe. Some women were familiar with all three, some with two and some with only one. Several women had deliberately experimented with the different processes, finally settling down to a constant use of the one which seemed to give the best product with the least labor. Even in such a vital matter as the individual's search for supernatural power, the Comanche recognized the possibility of several different approaches to the Beings, and different men would seek to obtain power from them in different ways.

Most of the descriptions of cultures which are now extant are heavily weighted on the side of the Universals and Specialties. This is due partly to the difficulty of obtaining information about the Alternatives, partly to a quite natural desire to make the description as coherent as possible. The only Alternatives which will be noted will usually be those which have large numbers of adherents. As a result, the participation of the average individual in the culture of his society is made to appear much more complete than it actually is, and the differences between different groups of individuals are minimized. Any one who has come to know a "primitive" society well can testify that its members do not show the dead level of cultural uniformity which these reports suggest.

The ability of all cultures to incorporate numerous Alternatives without serious interferences with their functioning is of vital importance to the processes of cultural growth and change. These processes will be discussed elsewhere. Suffice it to say that in spite of the occasional realization of brand-new needs by a society, with the consequent introduction into the culture of elements with new functions, the bulk of all cultural changes are in the nature of replacements. The newly introduced element takes over the user or functions of a preëxisting element. Its general acceptance by the members of a society will depend very largely on whether it performs these functions more efficiently. Thus men had cutting tools long before they had metal, and the introduction of the new material was by a process of gradual replacement. Stone knife and metal knife were, for a time, used side by side. Even the forms of the older tools were carried over and copied in the new medium. Again, our own need for transportation was already met by a variety of appliances at the time the automobile was invented. The new appliance was accepted because it was superior in one way or another to each of the preexisting ones, but it still has not replaced any of them completely.

When a new element is offered to any society, full acceptance is always preceded by a period of trial. During this period both the new trait and the old trait or traits with which it is competing become Alternatives within the total culture complex. They are presented to individuals as different means to the same end. In all cultures the Alternatives serve as a proving ground for innovations. If the new trait meets the need more adequately than the old one and if it can be successfully adapted to the total pattern of the culture, it will be taken over by more and more individuals until it finally achieves general acceptance and wins a place among the Universals or Specialties. Simultaneously, the trait or traits which it is replacing will lose adherents until it finally drops out of the culture. The waning use of the bicycle in our own culture in competition with the automobile is a case in point. If the new trait cannot meet the test, it never reaches the Universals or Specialties. The individuals who have accepted it gradually relinquish it and ultimately it will be forgotten. Bridge and mah jong may serve as an example of this in our own culture. They had the same social and recreational functions and required about the same degree of attention. The old trait, bridge, appeared to be seriously threatened for a time, but it reasserted itself and mah jong dropped out.

In all cultures the Universals and Specialties represent the traits which have been successfully assimilated. The changes necessary to adjust them to each other and to prevent interference in their overt expressions have been made and the situation has temporarily stabilized. Many of the Alternatives, on the other hand, may be in process of assimilation. New traits, especially if they have been borrowed from other cultures, have to be modified to fit the preëxisting patterns, and whether they can be successfully modified is as important to their ultimate acceptance as any factors of immediate utility. While they are Alternatives they lack the stabilizing effects of full group participation and offer a fair field for modifications and improvements. The society's attitude toward them is quite different from its attitude toward the Universals and Specialties. Most of the Alternatives are frankly on trial, with no long-established associations or rationalizations to protect them and must stand or fall on their own merits.

Although certain traits may remain in the zone of Alternatives indefinitely, neither achieving general acceptance nor dropping out of the culture, the bulk of the elements in this category are always on their way into or out from the solid core of Universals and Specialties. It seems that the only traits which can survive indefinitely as Alternatives are those which have only a superficial influence upon the behavior of the society. Half a dozen ways of playing solitaire, two or three versions of an amusing story, or several conflicting theories as to the nature of the stars may persist side by side for generations. Even two techniques for the manufacture of identical products may persist in this way if they are of approximately the same efficiency. However, if one of them is markedly more efficient, the other will ultimately be forced out. When it comes to socially important ideas and values, the competition is much keener and always results in the elimination of one or the other Alternative. When different groups which do not constitute socially recognized categories of individuals within the society come to hold divergent views with regard to such matters as sexual morality or the private ownership of the group's natural resources, one view must ultimately triumph and drive out the other.

While the Universals and Specialties within any culture normally form a fairly consistent and well-integrated unit, the Alternatives necessarily lack such consistency and integration. Many of them are in opposition to each other, and some of them may even be at variance with elements in the first two categories. Actually, all cultures consist of two parts, a solid, well-integrated, and fairly stable core, consisting of the mutually adapted Universals and Specialties, and a fluid, largely unintegrated, and constantly changing zone of Alternatives which surrounds this core. It is the core which gives a culture its form and basic patterns at each point in its history, while the presence of the fluid zone gives it its capacity for growth and adaptation. If we study any culture continuum we will be able to detect a constant process of give-and-take between these two parts, with traits moving from one to the other. New traits, beginning as Individual Peculiarities, gain adherents, rise to the status of Alternatives, and finally pass into the core as they achieve general recognition. Old ones, as soon as they are brought into competition with new ones, are drawn into the zone of Alternatives and, if they are inferior, finally drop out of the culture. This exit, in turn, takes place by way of the Individual Peculiarities. Some die-hard individual may insist on driving a horse and buggy after all the rest of his society have automobiles, and the trait will not finally disappear until his death.

The proportion which each of these two parts of a culture bears to its total content may vary greatly at different points in its history. In general, the more rapid the contemporary rate of change, the higher the proportion of Alternatives. The proposition is stated in this form simply because most of the stimuli to change, as well as the bulk of the new traits by the acceptance of which it is accomplished, normally originate outside the culture. When a culture is changing very rapidly, as our own is at present, the Alternatives may become so numerous that they quite overshadow the Universals and Specialties. Each new trait, as soon as it is accepted by any part of the society, draws certain traits which were formerly Universals or Specialties out of the core of the culture into the fluid zone. As the content of the core is reduced, the culture increasingly loses pattern and coherence.

Such a fluid, disorganized condition within culture has inevitable repercussions upon the society which bears it. It is the common adherence of a society's members to the elements which form the core of their culture which makes it possible for them to function as a society. Without a wide community of ideas and habits the members of the group will not react to particular stimuli as a unit, nor will they be able to coöperate effectively. Such coöperation really rests upon the predictability of the other individuals' behavior. When there are very few elements of culture in which all the members of a society participate, i.e., when the proportional size of the culture core has been greatly reduced, the group tends to revert to the condition of an aggregate. The society is no longer able to feel or act as a unit. Its members may continue to live together, but many forms of social intercourse will be hampered by the impossibility of predicting the behavior of individuals on any basis other than that of their known personalities. Even economic coöperation will be seriously interfered with, due to the lack of fixed standards of integrity and fair dealing. It is obvious that this condition puts the society at a marked disadvantage, and it is probable that there is a point below which participation cannot fall without a resulting collapse of both the society and the culture.

The difference between folk cultures and modern civilizations, or between genuine and spurious cultures, as Sapir calls them, is primarily a matter of the proportion which the core of Universals and Specialties bears to the fluid zone of Alternatives. Folk cultures are borne by small, closely-integrated social units or by aggregates of such units which have already worked out satisfactory mutual adjustments. In such cultures, new items are not appearing with any great frequency and the society has plenty of time to test them and to assimilate them to its preëxisting patterns. In such cultures the core constitutes almost the whole.

In modern civilizations, on the other hand, the small, closely integrated social units are being broken down, giving place to masses of individuals who are much more loosely interrelated than the members of the former local groups and classes. The very size of these masses confers a considerable degree of anonymity upon the individual and protects him from the pressure toward cultural conformity which neighbors exert in a small group. Coupled with this there has been an extraordinarily rapid increase in the total content of civilized cultures. Due to the organization of research and invention, new items are appearing with such frequency that our society has had no time to really test them, still less to bring them into readily assimilable form. Many of these new items are of a sort which will necessitate radical changes in other phases of our culture. Thus the mechanization of agriculture or the acceptance of organic evolution as an established fact entails a series of compensating changes in other aspects of our life and thought which it will require years to accomplish. In modern civilizations, therefore, the core of culture is being progressively reduced. Our own civilization, as it presents itself to the individual, is mainly an assortment of Alternatives between which he may or frequently must choose. We are rapidly approaching the point where there will no longer be enough items on which all members of the society agree to provide the culture with form and pattern.

The disruptive trends in our own culture have not yet had time to work themselves out completely. In our rural districts the local groups still retain a good deal of their former function as culture-bearing units. There are often striking differences in the ideas and habits of communities living only a few miles from each other. The older generation in such communities shares a fairly consistent sub-culture, but the younger generation shows the influence of the new conditions. The young people are usually at odds with their elders and critical of the old standards without having any definite new standards to substitute for these. The facts of common residence and economic dependence force the young people to an outward conformity with the community patterns, but they no longer accept these as natural or inevitable. They have ceased to give emotional allegiance to the culture of their parents and are ripe for change, but the wider society with which automobiles, movies, and the press have brought them into contact has, as yet, no coherent pattern of life to offer them.

In cities the results of cultural disintegration are even more marked. Here the local groupings have already almost disappeared, while the now evolving interest and congeniality groups have not yet developed to the point where they can serve as culture-bearers. The individual has to make constant choices from among the wealth of culture Alternatives presented to him, and after he has chosen there is no way for him to establish contacts with other individuals whose choices have been similar. Without the backing of a group of like-minded people, it is impossible for him to feel absolutely sure about anything, and he falls an easy prey to any sort of high-pressure propaganda.

Such a condition is fatal to the effective operation of democratic institutions, since these depend upon a high degree of cultural participation, with the united will and consciousness of social as apart from individual interests which this confers. A low degree of cultural participation makes the rule of organized minorities not only possible but almost a necessity if society is to be maintained as a functioning entity. The members of such minorities do have a number of ideas and values in common, and the knowledge that these are shared by a number of other members reinforces them in every individual. Such minorities are capable of concerted action, while the bulk of the population, lacking common attitudes and values which might serve as rallying points, can do nothing against the minority or for themselves.

The situation which confronts us to-day is not altogether unique. Something very much like it existed during the later phases of the Roman Empire. Here also the rural local groups were broken down, in this case by economic forces which drove the peasants out of existence. In the cities the old Roman culture, which had served as a unifying core for the empire during its period of growth, passed into solution as it was compelled to compete with new elements drawn from the diverse cultures of a multitude of subject peoples. Although the Roman situation was not complicated by any revolution in technology, the derangement of the economic system was probably as great as that from which we are now suffering. During the empire's growth, Roman culture adapted itself to the conditions created by a constant inflow of loot and tribute and a seemingly inexhaustible supply of slaves. These conditions made it possible for the society to maintain its unemployed on doles. One is reminded of the present European and American systems, with their dependence on selling to societies which have not yet been mechanized. When, under the later empire, the inflow of wealth began to dwindle, the sufferings of the lower classes became acute, but their members did not have enough cultural unity to do anything about it. There were no plebeian movements comparable to those in the early Roman state, and, in spite of half-hearted attempts to right things from above, conditions became increasingly bad until both the society and culture practically collapsed.

Out of the chaos of this collapse there finally emerged a new type of culture and a reintegrated society which were built about the ideas and values which had persisted through the period of confusion among certain sections of the population. The strongest of these was the idea of personal loyalty to a commander, which always survived in the army and had been strong among the barbarian invaders. The ideas held by the Christians, for long an organized minority, served as a second focal point about which culture and society could reintegrate. Together they recrystallized the fluid culture of the period of Roman decline and barbarian invasion into that of medieval Europe with its Feudal System and its Church Triumphant.

That our own culture and society will eventually stabilize and reintegrate can hardly be doubted, but two things will have to happen first. We shall have to develop some sort of social unit which can take the place of the old local groupings as a bearer and transmitter of culture and ensure a similar high degree of individual participation. There must also be some diminution in the flood of new elements which are being poured into our culture from the laboratories of the scientists and technologists. The breakdown of our present economic system would solve both problems. The descendants of those who survived would be forced to return, for the most part, to life as peasants in small communities, while research would cease through lack of the economic surplus and trained personnel which it requires.

None of the problems involved in the present situation are really insoluble, and, if our culture and society collapse, they will not fall from lack of intelligence to meet this situation, but from lack of any united will to put the requisite changes into effect. What the modern world needs far more than improved production methods or even a more equitable distribution of their results is a series of mutually consistent ideas and values in which all its members can participate. Perhaps something of the sort can be developed in time to prevent the collapse which otherwise seems inevitable. If not, another "dark age" is in order, but we can console ourselves with the knowledge that the darkness is never of very long duration. Unless all history is at fault, our descendants of half a thousand years hence will once more have achieved a consistent, patterned culture and an integrated society. However, it is quite impossible to predict what forms these will assume. There is no way of knowing which of our present Alternative values will survive the present turmoil, or what new values may be developed to serve as crystallization points for the new culture patterns. The Roman philosophers thought and wrote very little about military loyalty, accepting it as a matter of course, and the ideas of the Christians seemed to them utterly illogical and ridiculous.

CHAPTER XVII

THE QUALITIES AND PROBLEMS OF CULTURE

Any investigator of culture is at once confronted with the problem of its reality. Do cultures actually exist, or are they simply abstractions which the investigator derives from his studies of individuals? A fairly good case can be made out for either view. The culture of any society consists of the sum total of the ideas, conditioned emotional responses, and patterns of habitual behavior which the members of that society have acquired through instruction or imitation and which they share to a greater or less degree. In trying to determine the content of any culture the investigator must admittedly abstract these elements from the personalities of the society's component members. Whether the results which are thus arrived at correspond to a genuine entity which may be considered as having an existence distinct from that of this aggregate of personalities is a question which could only be solved by a lengthy philosophical investigation into the nature of reality as well as into the qualities of culture. Such an investigation lies quite outside the scope of this book. Suffice it to say that cultures can be treated as though they were realities. They can be studied and analyzed, and certain valid generalizations can be made with regard to them. Beyond this point it is unnecessary for us to inquire.

At the very outset of any investigation of culture we must recognize that it is something which lies entirely outside the range of physical phenomena. The form, the content, and even the existence of cultures can only be deduced from the behavior to which they give rise. The term *behavior* is here used in a very wide sense to include not only ordinary acts but also the manufactured products which may result from certain series of acts and the externalizations of culture through speech. Culture itself is intangible and cannot be directly apprehended even by the individuals who participate in it. The student of culture is thus in a position somewhat like that of the student of atomic physics. Both must deduce the existence and nature of things which are themselves completely outside the range of direct observation by observing the effects which they produce.

This distinction between culture and its manifestations in the behavior of the individuals who act as its agents is a hard one to grasp. Perhaps it can be made clearer by a few examples. If all the radios in the world and even all the literature relating to them should be destroyed by some selective cataclysm, say a miracle worked by a man who had to live next door to one, radios would still persist as an element within our culture. The overt expression of this element would have been temporarily interrupted, but thousands of individuals would have retained the knowledge of how to build radios, including the motor habits and skills necessary to the task. Millions of people would remember the radio as a useful or at least diverting object and feel a need for it. New machines, constructed on the basis of this knowledge with the purpose of meeting this need, would be on the market within a fortnight.

Again, the first European immigrants to America, when they crossed the Atlantic, had to leave most of their tangible possessions behind. They also left behind many of the more formal aspects of social life and, as individuals, lost many of their social statuses. Thus they were removed from all the functionaries who enforced law and order in the old country, and the man who had been a policeman or magistrate there might be simply a farmer or lumberman here. Nevertheless, such immigrant groups brought their culture with them practically *in toto*. If they lost any of it, the loss was confined to a few special skills such as those associated with, say, paper-making. Even such losses were only temporary, for knowledge of the results of such skills and a desire for the product survived, and a paper-maker would be encouraged to immigrate. Once on the new continent, the immigrants set about recreating the outward manifestations of their culture, whether this happened to be English, French, or Spanish.

Each cultural group did its best to duplicate the conditions in the country which it had left, with only such changes as the new natural environment imposed. Even the new problems presented by this environment were solved by each group in a different way, according to its cultural ideology. Thus the Spaniards enslaved the Indians without attempting to compete with them in agriculture or handicraft. To them the New World offered an opportunity for every white man to achieve his primary desire of becoming a gentleman with a landed estate and servants of his own. Again in accordance with their cultural ideology, the Spaniards took large numbers of Indian concubines and recognized their children by these concubines. The French and English went into direct economic competition with the Indians, since in their culture patterns profits were held more important than dignity. The French accorded the Indians a considerable degree of social equality, mixed with them freely, and recognized the half-breed offspring. The English refused the Indians such equality and were contemptuous alike of "squaw men" and half-breeds.

It will be clear from the foregoing that culture is essentially a socio-psychological phenomenon. It is carried in the minds of individuals and can find expression only through the medium of individuals. At the same time, it differs in numerous respects from the individual personality. While it corresponds rather closely to the ideas, emotional values, and habitual behavior patterns which make up the bulk of the personality, it does not include any of the rational functions. Although culture provides the individual with most of the concepts which serve as the basis for his rational activities, the actual processes of thought and reasoning are individual and not cultural. Conversely, the adherence of many individuals to a culture reinforces the strength of its ideas and values in each of them and gives these a super-individual quality. It is therefore impossible either to explain any culture completely in terms of individual psychology or to explain it without constant reference to individual psychology. In culture, society and the individual meet and each makes its own contribution.

The rôle of individual personalities in the perpetuation of

culture is brought out very clearly by the way in which any culture can survive the interruption of its expression in overt behavior and the elimination of the society which originally carried it. As long as any individual who has been reared under a particular culture is still alive, the culture will survive if only in latent and mutilated form. An ethnologist can recover from the last survivor of a tribe the basic elements of his extinct society's culture plus the particular skills in which this survivor had been trained. It is even possible to recreate many of the outward manifestations of such latent cultures as when, under the direction of such a survivor, a canoe of the ancient type is built or some one is trained to perform an ancient dance.

At the same time, no culture can survive either the dissolution of the society which bore it or the interruption of its expression in behavior for a period longer than the life-span of the last individual trained to it. Culture can be transferred from one individual to another or from one society to another only through the medium of its overt expressions. All culture is learned, not biologically inherited, and it is only through the medium of behavior that it can be externalized and made available to new individuals for learning. Of course this externalization may be through the medium of language as well as through that of physical acts. The knowledge of how to conduct a war party may be transmitted in society for several generations in spite of the fact that white domination has made actual war parties impossible.

The super-individual quality of culture is illustrated by its ability to perpetuate itself and to survive the extinction of any of the personalities which share it or of all those which have shared it at any given point in its history. It can do this because of its dominant rôle in shaping the personalities of the new individuals whose birth within the particular society brings them under its influence. The child is born without a personality, and in the course of his development one is created in him by the interaction of his inherent potentialities and his external surroundings. As a member of any society, the child's environment consists almost entirely of the overt expressions of that society's culture and of personalities which that culture has already shaped.

Contact with these, aided by the more active factors of instruction and imitation, establishes within his personality the characteristic cultural complex of associations, emotional values, and habits. In other words, he acquires the culture of the society in which he is reared. As he, in turn, becomes part of the environment in which new personalities are being developed, he transmits this complex to them. Culture is completely external to the individual at birth, but in the course of his development it becomes an integral part of his personality. Most of it sinks into the personality so deeply and becomes so completely incorporated with the other elements that it lies below the level of consciousness, motivating and directing the individual's behavior without his realizing that it is doing so.

It seems that the transmission of culture has somewhat the same quality as the apostolic laying-on of hands. Its genuine transfer from individual to individual or from one generation to the next can only be accomplished by personal contacts. The material manifestations of any culture may outlast it for thousands of years and provide the student with a more or less accurate idea of what certain of its aspects were like, but a culture dies as soon as the direct line of person-to-person transmission is broken. Even the literature of a people cannot convey their fundamental ideas and values in such form that they will become an integral part of the reader's personality. These are the vital sparks within any culture, the things which give it life and ensure its overt expression. Without them a culture, no matter how well its content may be known, is simply a subject for anatomical study. No new excavations or finds of long-hidden manuscripts will make it possible for us to bring classic Greek culture to life again. We can read the plays of the Greeks, but we cannot reach the deeper meanings or participate in the emotions of the audiences which saw these plays acted for the first time.

The ability of culture to perpetuate itself through the medium of an ever-changing series of individuals is responsible for another of the outstanding differences between it and the isolated personality. The personality passes through successive stages of growth and integration to a more or less complete stabilization and its final extinction in death. Cultures have no such pre-destined life cycle. The spectacular rise and fall of certain civilizations should not blind us to the fact that most cultures have never fallen. They and the societies which bore them have gone on quietly, enriching their content by inventions and borrowings, changing their form, and achieving a better and better adaptation to their particular settings. Only a few cultures have ever mounted to a peak or followed this peak by a decline. The decline of cultures, when it does occur, can usually be traced to causes outside themselves. Cultures, like organisms, may become so accurately adapted to a particular set of conditions that, when these conditions change, they are unable to make the necessary readjustments quickly enough. This failure results in paralysis and ultimate collapse. Even cultures which collapse do not die as long as the society which bears them retains its continuity. Those parts of the culture which are adapted to the new conditions survive, and, after a period of retrenchment and confusion, the culture reorganizes itself along new lines and once more begins the upward climb.

This difference between culture and the individual personality is easily explained by the difference in the foundations upon which each rests. The personality is dependent upon the brain and nervous system of the individual. Its life cycle is simply one of the aspects of the life cycle of the human body. Culture, on the other hand, rests on the combined brains of all the individuals who compose a society. While these brains individually develop, stabilize, and die, new brains constantly come forward to take their places. Although both societies and cultures have frequently been blotted out by forces external to themselves, neither a society nor its culture can conceivably die of old age.

Since the personalities which bear culture are constantly being renewed, its psychological attributes correspond most closely to those of young personalities which have not yet become set. Every society includes both old, stabilized personalities and young ones in all stages of formation. The older members of a society usually acquire new ideas or change established habits only with difficulty. To the young, unformed personalities all habits and ideas are equally new and all can be incorporated with ease. The man of seventy may learn to drive an automobile, but he rarely gets to the point where he feels really comfortable behind the wheel. His seventeen-year-old grandson takes autos as a matter of course, learns with ease, and soon comes to drive automatically. An old Indian has great difficulty in assuming the ways of the white man and especially in comprehending the values of white culture. He has to overcome emotional resistance at every point where the new ways clash with the old. An Indian boy, given the necessary contacts, can assume the culture of the whites or the culture of his tribe with equal ease.

Because of this constant presence of personalities which are still in the formative period, cultures have an almost unlimited capacity for change. They can be rebuilt bit by bit by adding new elements, working these over to fit the rest of the culture, and dropping elements which have become poorly adapted to existing conditions. In time a culture may, without any break in its continuity, achieve a form and content totally different from that with which it began. The modern Welshman of Mediterranean stock is linked to the earliest Neolithic inhabitants of Wales by an unbroken line of both biological and social heredity. His ancestors in every generation have had a culture which was adequate to meet all the needs of which they were conscious and have transmitted this culture to their offspring. However, if we compare the life of a Neolithic Welsh community with that of a modern Welsh factory town the two will be found to have very few elements in common. In the course of 4,000 years Welsh culture has been completely made over. The difference between its first and last phases is as great as that between either one of them and Chinese or Zulu culture.

This brings us at once to another of the distinctive qualities of culture. It is a continuum extending from the beginning of human existence to the present. As a whole, it represents the social heredity of our species. Particular cultures are strains of social heredity, corresponding in many respects to the divergent strains of biological heredity which constitute different varieties within a species. Like these strains of biological heredity, cultures have crossed and recrossed in the course of their development, fused and divided. The condition is infinitely more complex than that existing in the biological field. In the crossing of biological strains all the inherited factors on both sides are fused in the hybrid. In cultures, on the other hand, there is a constant process of selective borrowing. One culture can take over from another single traits or complexes of functionally related traits, the result being an extreme mixture of elements from diverse sources.

Throughout the length of the cultural continuum, therefore, traits are constantly being added and other traits lost. However, the difficulties do not end here. The adoption of a trait is always followed by a series of modifications both in it and in other pre-existing traits. The reasons for this will be discussed in a later chapter. Every trait which has formed a part of any culture during any period in its history thus leaves its mark upon the culture. Its effects on the total culture may endure long after the trait itself has been eliminated. Thus the custom of wearing a long sword on the left side was responsible for the custom of mounting horses from the left. The sword-wearing has long since disappeared, but the left-side mounting remains.

The situation which exists in a given culture at a given point in its history is thus a direct result of all the changes and vicissitudes which the culture has undergone prior to that time. It is conceivable that if we knew the entire past of any culture we would be able to explain its entire content in terms of historical cause and effect. However, most of the past of all cultures is hopelessly lost to us. Written history goes back at most 6,000 years, becoming increasingly local and fragmentary. Behind this we have the evidence of archæology, which can reveal only a few phases of any people's existence, and even this feeble light soon flickers out, leaving the beginnings of culture in complete darkness. When we come to study specific cultures we find that, outside a few areas of high civilization, most of them have no history which might be helpful to us. The written records, if they exist at all, are usually woefully inadequate, while traditional records are commonly an inextricable mixture of fact and fancy.

It follows, then, that when an anthropologist speaks of the form and content of a culture what he really means is the form and content of a cross-section of the culture continuum taken at a particular point in its length. For practical reasons this section can only be taken from the proximal end of the continuum. It may be either thick or thin, depending upon the length of time for which satisfactory records are available, but it can never represent more than a very small part of the whole.

Every culture is not only a continuum but a continuum in a constant state of change. There is a popular belief that the cultures of "primitive" peoples are static. This seems to have arisen partly through the wishful thinking of certain of the early anthropologists, who hoped to find in these cultures living fossils which would throw light on our own remote past, and partly from a lack of historical records. Actually, wherever such records exist, changes in the "primitive" culture are discernible. The rate of change varies enormously from culture to culture and also within the same culture at different periods in its history, but it is improbable that there has ever been a culture which was completely static at any time.

The cross-section of the culture continuum which it is possible for the anthropologist to study thus bears much the same relation to the whole that a short section of motion-picture film, clipped out at random, bears to the entire picture. It is a part of a continuous movement which has been artificially caught and fixed. Such a section of film will give only hints of the total action and will show some of the actors in strange and grotesque attitudes, perhaps poised in the air in the middle of a leap. Similarly, the section of culture cuts across and artificially fixes a series of changes which are in all stages of completion and makes conditions which are really transitory appear permanent. A few examples may make this point clear.

At the time that Marquesan culture was first studied and recorded, the custom of adoption had been developed to the point where practically all children were adopted. The infant was often asked for before it was born and was turned over to its adoptive parents when it was a few months old, the real parents relinquishing all rights to it. Moreover, the real parents were required to make a substantial gift to the adoptive parents, this being rationalized as a reimbursement to them for the expense of rearing it. The social pressure was so strong that it was almost impossible for the real parents to refuse to give up the infant. Such a refusal would be punished by universal ridicule and might even give rise to a feud between the two families.

These practices must have been developed in the Marquesas subsequent to the settlement of the islands and seem to represent a sort of hypertrophy of tendencies traceable in most of the other Polynesian cultures. There can be no question that the loss of the child caused considerable grief to its parents, especially the mother. Women nursed their infants for some months before giving them up and thus had time to become strongly attached to them. Many women and even a fair number of men were not in favor of the custom, and the women reacted to it, as individuals, by refusing to bear children. The Marquesans' knowledge of both contraception and abortion made this easy. As a result, the population was declining even at the time of the first European contact. The situation was a socially unhealthy one, and it seems probable that the sentiment against wholesale adoption would have increased until the custom was modified or eliminated.

Again, in 1870–1880 the practices of the Comanche with regard to inheritance were in a chaotic condition. There is good reason to believe that the whole problem of inheritance was new to the culture. The Plateau tribes from whom the Comanche had separated themselves when they entered the Plains were accustomed to destroy all a man's property at his death. This entailed few hardships and no serious economic loss, since the property was limited to clothing and a few weapons and utensils. When the Comanche took over the Plains culture and acquired horses, inheritance became a real problem. Some individuals owned very large herds, in one case 2,000 animals. To slaughter the entire herd at the death of the owner was strongly against native sentiment and also prejudicial to the interests of the tribe. Since animals were freely loaned, several individuals might be dependent upon one man's herd for their mounts and would be seriously handicapped in hunting and war if these were killed. Stories indicate that there were some cases of wholesale killing during the early period, but by 1870 it had become customary to kill only a man's favorite horses and distribute the rest among the surviving relatives. No rules governing this distribution had been developed, with the result that there was usually hard feeling among the heirs. Everything indicates that the culture was moving toward a settlement of the problem partly through bequests, a new pattern, and partly through recognition of the rights of certain relatives to take their choice in a fixed order. However, neither of these methods had as yet received general recognition.

At whatever point we take our cross-section of the culture continuum we will find certain changes completed, others well under way, and still others just beginning. All these different and often conflicting trends will be reduced to some sort of rough working order, since otherwise the culture as a whole could not function. However, we will look in vain for the close integration and perfect coördination posited by certain current writers on culture. The fewer the changes actually under way at any point in the continuum, the more closely the situation is likely to approximate this ideal condition, but no culture can achieve perfect integration and complete internal adjustment as long as it is a living, growing thing. If we could study the whole continuum, a deeper consistency of form and pattern might be revealed, but this is pure conjecture.

Given the cross-section of our culture continuum, with the limitations which the fact that it is only a section entail, let us see what we may hope to find out about it. The first problem is that of determining its content and internal organization. Although anthropologists are accustomed to speak of these aspects of culture with considerable glibness, they actually know very little about them, and it is extremely hard to determine them by the techniques now at our disposal. The task which confronts the investigator is not unlike that which confronts the psychologist in his study of individual personalities. Both must deduce the qualities of the thing which they are studying from its overt expressions in behavior, but the anthropologist is handicapped by the necessity for introducing an additional step at the very beginning of his work. While the psychologist can observe the behavior of his subject directly, the anthropologist must base his conclusions upon the ideal patterns of the culture with which he is working. In the chapters dealing with society we have already discussed these patterns as they apply to particular social relationships and have shown how they may be determined. Societies, which are the carriers of culture, are so constituted that they can only act or be acted upon through the medium of their component individuals. This means that the actual behavior which expresses a particular culture pattern may vary considerably with the individual who is expressing it. At the same time, the members of the society will have a fairly clear idea as to what is the proper response to any familiar situation, and the variations in individual behavior will tend to cluster about this norm. From a comparison of these norms with the expressed ideas on the subject, the ideal patterns of the culture may be deduced with reasonable accuracy. However, the necessity for establishing such patterns by deduction introduces a source of error with which the psychologist does not have to contend.

Even when the ideal patterns of a culture have been determined, the anthropologist's work has only begun. These patterns represent only the outer levels of culture, corresponding roughly to the conscious level of the individual personality. The associations, emotional evaluations, and drives which give cultures their vitality and seem to be responsible for much of their organization all lie below the pattern level. In his attempts to bring these to light the task of the anthropologist is much like that of the psychologist in his probings of the sub-conscious. In both cases the investigators' findings really consist of a series of interpretations, and the facts on which these interpretations are based are frequently susceptible of more than one explanation. The very nature of cultural material precludes the use of controlled experiment as a method of checking such interpretations, so all analyses of cultural elements below the pattern level are supported only by the judgment of the observer. This judgment, in turn, can hardly fail to be influenced by the observer's own personality and cultural background. No matter how hard he tries to maintain complete objectivity, his own personality will make certain explanations of the observed patterns more congenial to him than others and throw certain aspects of the culture into undue relief.

Observations of the same culture by several individuals of different personalities and backgrounds, with a comparison of their results, may provide some check on this personality factor; it is doubtful, however, whether it can ever be completely eliminated. While the pattern levels of cultures can be approached with a fair degree of objectivity, the lower levels can be approached only by subjective techniques which correspond more closely to those of the literary artist than to those of the physical scientist. Although the work which has been done upon these lower levels is stimulating and suggestive, none of its present results can be considered conclusive. It is probable that any real advance in this direction must await further developments in the field of psychology. When the content of the lower levels of individual personalities can be studied by exact methods and expressed in exact terms, we may be able to apply the same techniques to culture, but the solution of the more complex problem must wait upon that of the simpler one.

Determination of the form and content of cultures is primarily a means toward other ends. Descriptions of cultures in terms of their elements are valuable mainly as a basis for comparative studies which may lead to the establishment of valid classifications of cultures and the discovery of genetic relationships between them. In themselves they do not contribute toward the understanding of culture dynamics. At the same time, determination of culture content is an absolute prerequisite to all effective studies of these dynamics. It bears very much the same relation to them that anatomical studies bear to physiological ones. Just as it is impossible to understand the life processes of an organism without constant reference to its structure, it is impossible to understand the processes of cultural growth and change or the functioning of a culture at any point in its history without a thorough knowledge of its content and organization.

To understand cultural processes we must both know content and observe this content in action.

There are two aspects of the problem of culture dynamics. There are the processes of growth and change, which give cultures their form and content at any particular point in their history, and there are the processes of interaction of cultural elements at this point. The first group of processes can be understood only if they are approached by the historical method, i.e., by observations of the culture continuum carried on over the longest possible interval. The second group of processes does not require such historical studies, but if we are to draw valid conclusions with regard to either we must have a much more extensive knowledge of the deeper levels of culture content than we now possess. Every culture is, as a whole, a response to the total needs of the society which bears it. Outside the relatively small fields of biological survival and cultural continuity, these needs are conditioned by those deep-seated psychological elements which lie below the pattern level. How important the solution of these needs is to the successful functioning of culture can be seen by comparing the actual content of any culture, even the simplest, with the minimum content which would be necessary to biological and social survival.

The bulk of all cultures consists of what are, from the practical point of view, embroideries upon the fabric of existence. Neither the presence nor the functions of these elements can be adequately explained on physical or social grounds. They represent responses to psychological needs which are, in turn, shaped and directed by a long series of culturally established associations and interests. Thus personal decorations do not contribute in any direct way to the biological survival of the individuals who exhibit them. In fact they may even lessen the individual's chances of survival. It is said that in certain Melanesian tribes the custom of body scarification takes a regular toll of life through the resulting infections. At the very least it entails much pain and physical disability. Even in less drastic cases the socially approved forms of decoration often diminish the subject's efficiency and impose a quite unnecessary handicap on physical activities. The African woman who wears twenty pounds of brass wire on her ankles must expend that much more energy as she goes about her tasks. At the same time, these practical disadvantages are outweighed by the satisfaction which any individual takes in knowing that he is being admired, or at least approved, by the other members of his society. His decorations serve to meet a psychological need which is more vital to him than his desire for physical comfort.

The effectiveness of any element of culture for meeting such psychological needs depends much less on its own inherent qualities than upon the associations which have been established within the culture with regard to it. Thus no young lady in our own society feels an overwhelming desire for a gold nose-stud. In fact, if she was given one her first move would probably be to have it changed into an ear ornament, since our culture associates the attachment of decorative objects with ears and not with noses. The same stud which would excite ridicule when worn in the nose would excite admiration, and satisfy its wearer's psychological need for the same, if it were worn in the ear. To say that the function of such an object is to excite admiration is a simple, objective statement of fact which ignores all the more important and vital aspects of the situation. The same thing holds even when the object performs the social function of indicating its wearer's status in the group. Any form of decoration can perform either of these functions adequately if it has become the focal point for the necessary cultural associations. We cannot understand the real relation of such an element to the rest of the culture unless we know what these associations are and, to a lesser degree, why they have become attached to it.

It is the deep-seated psychological elements within culture which give human life its meaning and make it something more than a brute struggle for biological survival. They permeate the total fabric, controlling the direction of his growth and bending all its component elements to their use. Until we arrive at a more complete understanding of them, no study of culture in terms of its overt expressions, history, or the obvious functions of its elements can really penetrate below the surface. The ultimate realities of culture are still hidden from us, but it has become possible to draw a few superficial conclusions as to its processes. What these are we shall see in the succeeding chapters.

CHAPTER XVIII

DISCOVERY AND INVENTION

Discovery and invention are the obvious starting points for any study of cultural growth and change, since it is only by these processes that new elements can be added to the total content of man's culture. Although developed cultural traits can be transmitted from one culture to another and most cultures owe the bulk of their content to this process, every culture element can ultimately be traced to a discovery or invention, or to a more or less complex combination of various discoveries and inventions which arose at a particular time and place. The process by which culture elements are borrowed, commonly known as *diffusion,* will be discussed in a later chapter. For the present we will concern ourselves only with the problem of how they come into being.

The first requirement of such a study is a clear understanding of the terms which are its tools. Although there have been many attempts to define what constitutes an invention or a discovery and to establish a valid line of demarcation between the two, none of these have been altogether successful. The popular usage of both is extremely loose, yet both carry certain fairly uniform associations which must be taken into account in any attempt to define them more accurately. Failure to do this will result in constant confusion when the terms are in use. The first of these associations, and one which is common to both terms, is that of newness. Elements of culture are only referred to as inventions or discoveries during the early period of their history, while they are still novelties. No culture element is classified as an invention or discovery after it has achieved general acceptance and has come to be taken more or less for granted. Thus no one in our own society would refer to soap as an invention except in connection with some research into its early history. Conversely, the new cultural feature of radio is constantly referred to as an invention or, when certain of its principles are under discussion, as a discovery.

The terms *invention* and *discovery* both carry the further implication of being elements which have originated within the bracket of a particular combined society and culture. I think every one would agree that an element which one society has borrowed from another would never be termed an invention or discovery of the receiving group. We recognize French inventions and discoveries and German ones, even though we dispute the priority of some of these over similar ones made in our own society. An invention or discovery is thought of as having a direct genetic relationship to a particular society and culture. It is something which has originated with a member or members of this society and which has assumed form and function in constant relation with that society's culture. These factors distinguish such elements from the borrowed ones, which come to a culture with form and functions already developed and which must therefore be modified to integrate them with their new cultural context.

Given these common features for discoveries and inventions, it remains to establish some valid line of demarcation between the two orders of phenomena. The popular distinction, which is based on motivation and makes discoveries a result of accident and inventions a result of intention, is far from satisfactory. Thus although we are accustomed to speak of the discovery of a new chemical element, the process which goes to making this discovery is as deliberate and thoroughly motivated as the invention of improving features for a phonograph. A gap in the atomic series is noted, the probable qualities of the missing member of the family of elements determined by a comparison of those which stand close to the gap, and the techniques which should lead to the isolation of the new element tested and progressively modified. The final discovery comes as a climax of perhaps years of directed endeavor.

Even in discoveries which *are* accidental, the important factor from the cultural point of view is not the mere recognition of a hitherto unknown phenomenon, say that certain kinds of black stones will burn, but the perception of the implications of this observed phenomenon and a realization of its potentialities for use. Unless there is this application of rational processes, the discovery remains an isolated bit of information. Such informaiton may become a part of the total knowledge, i.e., culture, transmitted by a society, but it has no social significance. An example of this in our own culture would be the great number of chemical compounds which are known to exist and which can even be produced at will but for which no uses have been found. The knowledge of these compounds is a latent element in our culture. It will become an active, functional element only if or when some inventor discovers a way of combining this knowledge with other knowledge to produce a socially significant result.

The facts just stated would seem to provide us with a valid basis for distinguishing between discoveries and inventions. We may define a discovery as any addition to knowledge, an invention as a new application of knowledge. To give a concrete example, on an individual rather than a social basis, when a small child pulls a cat's tail and gets scratched, this particular sequence of cause and effect is a discovery as far as the child is concerned. The observed fact that cats will scratch when their tails are pulled is an addition to his store of knowledge. If the child pulls the cat's tail when some one else is holding it, so that that person will get scratched, this is in the nature of an invention. The knowledge is employed in a new way to achieve a particular end. If the child is then spanked, he will have another discovery to his credit.

Since it is the application of knowledge, i.e., invention, which is functionally important to culture, we will refer to all new active elements which are developed within the frame of a particular culture and society as inventions. Although much of the knowledge employed in such inventions may have been accidentally acquired, this fact has no special bearing on our present discussion. Every new application of knowledge calls for an exercise of those rational functions which, as has been pointed out in previous chapters, are the exclusive possession of individuals.

Societies, as such, are incapable of thought and therefore of invention. At most the conditions of social life may make it possible for a certain limited group of individuals to work on a problem together, stimulating each other's minds by an exchange of ideas and contributing various elements to the final invention. It is never the entire society which joins in such activities, and a thorough analysis of the results can usually break them down into ascribable individual contributions. In short, there can be no inventions without inventors.

Granted that individuals are the only agents in invention, it becomes important to ascertain what stimulates them to invent. Of course we can answer glibly that it must be either an inner urge or the expectation of reward or, more probably, a combination of the two, but the question deserves further investigation. At the very outset we must realize that our own condition with regard to inventors and inventions is quite atypical for societies in general. Invention in our own culture has become an industry, organized upon very much the same pattern as other industries. Successful invention, at least in theory, brings the inventor abundant economic rewards and a social prestige which seems to be more intimately bound up with the extent of these rewards than with the real value of the inventor's contribution to society. In most societies this economic stimulus is either unimportant or lacking. Where all goods are produced mainly for the personal consumption of the producer, the economic advantages which can accrue to him through an improvement in technique are almost negligible. Even when the society has developed patterns of specialized production and economic exchange, the return of improvements must remain small as long as all objects are produced by individual craftsmen using hand methods. Uncivilized people have no patent offices, and even if the superiority of an inventor's product or technique is recognized his invention will be utilized by other craftsmen in the same field before the inventor can "cash in" on it.

There remains the question of the inventor's rewards in prestige rather than wealth. Although this stimulus must always be present in some degree, one questions whether it is of great importance under ordinary circumstances. Under normal conditions every culture provides its members with techniques for meeting all the needs of which the society is collectively conscious. The solution which a particular culture offers to a particular need may not be a very efficient one, but it must be at least adequate or the culture and society will be unable to function. The average member of a society takes his culture very much for granted, and unless a new element is of obvious advantage he will usually be chary in accepting it. Anything which departs too far from established patterns will be viewed with suspicion and is more likely to bring its inventor ridicule than prestige. We must remember that the high-pressure salesman with his techniques for developing a consciousness of new needs in a society is as much a special product of our culture as the electric razors and cigar-lighters which he attempts to sell.

The only time when invention can bring the inventor any very large prestige returns in a primitive society is when the society has become conscious that some of its needs are not being met adequately. At such times the whole society will be on the lookout for a satisfactory solution and the man who finds it will be rewarded accordingly. However, such crisis situations are rare under normal conditions. They may arise when a society finds itself in a new natural environment which renders certain of its economic techniques inoperative, as when a fishing tribe is forced to move away from the coast, but even then the best answer is usually borrowing rather than invention. An immigrant tribe will rarely find itself in a region which has previously been uninhabited, and it is much simpler for the tribe to take over the solutions to local problems which have already been worked out by the aborigines than to try to invent new ones for itself. Even deliberate organized invention takes time, while meals must be provided immediately.

The crisis situations in which the inventor receives the highest degree of recognition and reward seem to be those in which the very existence of a society and culture are threatened by some other society. The situation of the Plains Indian tribes after their final defeat and confinement to reservations would be a case in point. Although the white culture made available a new set of culture patterns which were adapted to the new conditions, acceptance of these would have meant the destruction of the whole of Indian culture and society. The Indians realized this, and the result was a frantic search for some way out. Messiahs such as the founder of the Ghost Dance religion were welcomed and honored, and their social and religious inventions were immediately accepted by tens of thousands of individuals. Such stimulations of invention in these non-material fields is by no means limited to the case just cited. It is a common phenomenon of contact between white and native groups with the threat to native cultures and societies which this entails. One could cite examples of such Messianic movements, which are in the last analysis inventions, from points as diverse as Greenland, Africa, and Melanesia.

Prior to the sudden onslaught of the whites such crisis situations must have been rare. If we are to get any just idea of the possible influence of the prestige motive on invention we must consider it as it operates under conditions where an effective adaptation to environment, both natural and social, has already been achieved. Under such circumstances a society is not likely to be conscious of any very acute needs which its current culture is unable to satisfy. At the same time, every society has a certain group of directed interests which are, in themselves, a part of its culture. Thus certain of the Plains tribes were profoundly interested in everything which pertained to supernatural power, which they felt to be of great importance to their existence. The Malagasy had no concept which really corresponded to this Indian one, but were interested in divination as a method of ascertaining a future which they believed to be mechanistically determined. Another tribe might have a deep interest in dancing, or wood-carving or some other form of esthetic expression. Because of this differential interest, any group will be much more receptive to inventions within a particular field than to inventions within some other field which they do not consider of particular importance. Inventors who make contributions along the line of interest will be rewarded with prestige, while those who make contributions along lines which have been given a lower social evaluation will be met with indifference or ridicule. The importance of prestige as a stimulus to invention thus varies not only with the society and culture but also with the field to which inventive ability is applied in each case.

In spite of this fact it appears that all cultures include examples of at least minor inventions in all fields. It is impossible to account for this on the assumption that the inventor is simply a tool which society employs to satisfy its needs and rewards for efficient service. It is also impossible to account for it on the basis of the individual's desire for economic returns or prestige, since many inventions must have brought their inventors little of either. Social recognition of needs and hope of reward are certain stimuli toward invention, but they are not everything. There must be other things which lie in the psychology of the inventor, an inner urge of some sort which leads him to try to produce new things without reference to their social implications.

Every individual is conscious of deficiencies in his culture at one point or another. Although personalities are largely shaped by their cultural setting, the infinite variety which they present in all societies proves that they are not completely shaped by it. Every individual finds that the patterns of his culture make him uncomfortable at some point, but most individuals are willing to accept these discomforts as inevitable. It is only the atypical person who tries to do something about it. The degree to which the discomfort which spurs him to action is consciously shared by other members of his society will control in very large measure the support which his attempts receive and his rewards for finding a successful solution. Positive action of this sort comes hard to all individuals, and the person who consciously attempts to modify the culture in which he has been reared, if only by the addition of a minor technique of some sort, is usually stimulated to do so by a more than ordinary degree of discomfort. In short, he must be maladjusted in comparison with other members of his society. Our own folk belief that inventors are queer seems to rest, like many other folk beliefs, on sound observation.

Conscious inventors of this type stand out from their fellows both in their perception of cultural lacks and in their deliberate attempt to remedy them. They constitute the vanguard on the road to cultural advance, but their efforts are too often nullified by getting too far ahead of their society. History affords many examples of valuable and quite workable inventions which the inventor's society has failed to accept. As we say, "The time was not yet ripe." The fact that such inventions could be made and made repeatedly is in itself a complete refutation of the frequent claim that the inventor is simply an unconscious agent of society, dominated and directed by it. Society would not, conceivably, employ agents to produce something which it was unconscious of any need for and which it refused to accept.

Because of this tendency to outrun his society, the conscious inventor's contribution to cultural growth has probably proved less in the long run than that of another type, viz., the unconscious inventors. These add to the content of culture without any realization of general needs unmet and largely without any feeling that they are doing so. Their inventions are, as a rule, of little individual importance, but they loom large in the aggregate. The main stimulus to this type of minor invention seems to lie in the craftsman's pleasure in the exercise of his profession. To the really skilled workman the creation of new objects is always something more than labor. It provides an esthetic outlet and endless possibilities for novel experience. Although this attitude is hardly compatible with modern machinery and mass production, some vestiges of it survive even there. A factory worker who was a friend of the writer's never tired of telling of the peculiarities of the machines which he tended in a barbed wire factory, the individual problems which they presented, and, incidentally, of his own skill in solving these problems.

In cultures where all industries are carried on by hand methods this love of the individual for his trade is much more marked. Actually, it is probably a prerequisite for all really good craftsmanship. In most cases it is combined with a quite natural aversion to the monotony of exact repetitions. There are numerous stories of native workmen who will charge more proportionally for three or four objects, say chairs to form a set, than for any one of them, simply because of their dislike of repetition. The skilled workman gains a thorough knowledge of the materials and techniques employed in his craft and with this a realization of their unexploited potentialities. He escapes monotony by setting new problems for himself and solving these in much the same spirit that one solves a chess problem. Even when, for market reasons, the end products have to be all very much the same, he can satisfy his urge for variety by employing various techniques and seeing how much he can speed up the work. In short, *he plays with his art.*

It is probably in this sort of virtuosity, rather than in the matter of important inventions, that the desire for prestige exerts its strongest influence. A major invention may very well lie so far outside the previous experience of a society's members that they cannot understand it. They may admire it, but the fact that this admiration is unintelligent and too frequently directed to the wrong things is constantly a fly in the ointment. A minor improvement in craftsmanship, on the other hand, can bring the most emotionally satisfying of all responses. It may not be admired by many people, but those will be fellow-craftsmen whose admiration is worth having.

Minor inventors of this sort are, for the most part, contented men who are seeking satisfaction for no needs more vital than those of amusement and a desire for professional admiration. Needless to say, they function best under placid conditions where a little more time can be spared from the sheer business of making a living and where there are few urgent matters to divert them from their work. If we can judge at all in a field where the historic records are so inadequate, the old saying, "Necessity is the mother of invention," is less than half true. The periods of steadiest cultural advance have been those when necessity did not press too hard on the average man. The sudden appearance of some necessity may bring to the front an inventor who has been quietly working on the problem for years and ensure his invention prompt acceptance, but the aftermath is usually one of confusion and maladjustment. Necessity gives the conscious inventor his chance, and he leaves it to future time to bridge the gap between himself and his society. The unconscious inventor builds slowly and solidly, each step growing out of those which have gone before, and the structure which he creates is valid and functionally integrated at every point in its development. The aftermath of an emergency invention may be almost as bad as the condition it sought to remedy, especially when the invention in question is in the fields of religion or social organization rather than in those of technology. Unconscious inventions are usually too small and too closely related to the culture's past to cause more than a ripple in the whole continuum.

Before leaving this matter of the inventor for that of his inventions, an example may serve to show the way in which cultural and social forces play upon and help to direct the line of his work and shape the results. There are very few cases in which the actual process of invention has been observed in any society other than our own. The making of inventions is always sporadic and unpredictable, and only chance could place an observer on the spot at the proper time. The example which I am about to record was not witnessed at first hand, but it occurred within the memory of many individuals still living at the time of my visit, and I believe the account which they gave of it to be substantially correct. At least all the witnesses agreed on the major details. It must be considered atypical in that the inventor was not born a member of the society, although he had been largely accepted at the time of his invention.

In about the year 1900 a Gilbert Islander settled in the island of Hiva Oa in the Marquesas group. He took a native wife and began to earn his living as a fisherman. Even twenty years before, his fishing activities would have been resented as poaching. Under the old Marquesan patterns this was carried on as a semi-communal activity. There was a sacred place at the shore where the fishing canoes were kept, and the men of the community served as fishermen in rotation, with a formal division of the catch. In each fishing place there was a resident priest who directed the activities and, incidentally, watched the canoes. By the time our hero arrived all this had broken down and fishing had become individual. All canoes had always been personal property, but under the old conditions this had meant little. The owner always gave his permission for the canoe's use and, probably, received a little more of the proceeds in return. Under the new conditions the idea of individual ownership was strengthened, but canoe-stealing became endemic and was a great nuisance to the more industrious members of the community. The canoe watcher had passed with the fisher-priest, and the complete breakdown of the old religion had destroyed the efficacy of magically supported taboos. Many a man who came down to the beach for a night's fishing would find his canoe gone and would only recover it several days later when some one stumbled on it abandoned in some neighboring cove. We may imagine that the Gilbert Islander, being a stranger, was subjected to more annoyance in this respect than the local fishermen. The Marquesans combine with their light-fingered tendencies an almost sophomoric delight in practical jokes and hazing.

Whatever the reason, the visiting fisherman invented a new type of detachable outrigger. This contrivance was quite different from the outrigger of his home islands and, as far as I know, from that used in any other part of the Pacific. The float was indirectly attached to the cross pieces which held it to the canoe. The uprights which connected the float with the cross pieces were made from staves of European casks and were fitted solidly into the float at the bottom. They were pierced with holes a few inches below the top and through these holes the ends of the cross pieces passed. Both uprights were lashed to the cross pieces, and the cross pieces in turn lashed to the canoe, with a single continuous piece of rope. When the owner beached his canoe, he undid the lashings, laid the float and cross pieces side by side, wound the rope around them and carried the whole up to his house on his shoulder. Since the canoe could not be used without an outrigger, it was quite safe from theft, while when he wanted to use it himself he could put on the outrigger in five minutes. The canoe itself was quite safe unwatched, since to have damaged it would have been considered an offense against property of a much more serious sort than any casual borrowing for use.

The invention had so many advantages that it spread like

wildfire. By the time of my visit the native type of outrigger had gone out of use so completely that there was said to be only one canoe which still had it left in the group and this was on the most remote island. The new contrivance had one practical disadvantage. The older type of outrigger had had an arrangement of small sticks for its uprights, which the natives explained as an adaptation to landing through heavy surf. If an outrigger of the old type struck bottom when the canoe was riding a wave in, the sticks snapped and the canoe could still ride in without capsizing. If an outrigger of the new type struck bottom, the canoe was thrown end over end. However, European supplies and the declining population combined to make fishing less important in the native economy and the disadvantage was compensated for by going out only on calm nights. A curious repercussion of the invention was its influence on the form of the canoe models which the natives had long been accustomed to make for the European trade. The pre-invention models show a fair imitation of the actual outrigger of the period. The post-invention models show only a travesty of the real outrigger, the size of the uprights being increased out of all proportion so as to give the carver more space on which to expend his skill.

The foregoing may serve to show not only the motives which may underlie an invention but also the highly complicated factors which may influence its development and acceptance by a society. The breakdown of certain aspects of the old culture had produced a mild crisis with regard to canoe-stealing. A pattern of casualness toward the "borrowing" of other people's property had always been present in the culture, but particular conditions had weakened the factors which previously inhibited it. It may also be mentioned that it would have been effectively inhibited as far as canoes were concerned if the people had had the pattern of living at the beach, a perfectly possible procedure, and keeping their canoes in their own front yards. As a stimulus to invention the danger of theft was given more point by the inventor's purely personal status as a foreigner. It seems safe to assume that in making the invention his intentions were purely individualistic and primarily economic. One is permitted to doubt whether it ever occurred to him that he was meeting an unsolved problem of the society in which he found himself. The economic aspects of the invention were obvious: no canoe, no fish. It may also be doubted whether the desire for prestige played any important rôle in this case, although the invention did bring a certain measure of it. Characteristically the natives spoke of him with grudging admiration not because he had invented something which was useful and which had been widely copied but because he had gotten the better of them. Except for those of our own professional type, all inventions are probably surrounded by an equally complex collection of circumstances and one which will never be alike in any two cases.

Let us leave the inventor and turn to a consideration of his products. There have been numerous attempts to classify inventions, none of them altogether successful and all depending for their utility upon the particular problem in which they are to be employed. There is the simple division of inventions into religious, social, and technological. This is useful for descriptive purposes, yet there are practical difficulties in drawing lines between even such elementary divisions. Almost every religious invention has numerous purely social aspects. The revelation, if such happens to be the starting point of the new cult, nearly always includes regulations for human relationships as well as for the relationship between believers and the supernatural. It may even include fairly complicated rules as to how the faithful should dress, what food they should eat, and how they should kill their meat. Moreover, such a classification is of little value for the study of the dynamics of culture. The classification most useful in this appears to be the simple one of *Basic inventions* and *Improving inventions*.

A Basic invention may be defined as one which involves the application of a new principle or a new combination of principles. It is basic in the sense that it opens up new potentialities for progress and is destined, in the normal course of events, to become the foundation of a whole series of other inventions. The bow would be a good example of such an invention. It involved the use of a new principle and became the starting point for a whole series of Improving inventions, such as those which culminated in the laminated bow, cross-bow, and so on. A more modern example of such a Basic invention would be the vacuum tube, whose potentialities for use are only beginning to be understood. An Improving invention, as the name implies, is a modification of some preëxisting device, usually made with the intention of increasing its efficiency or rendering it available for some new use. Thus the modern hand telephone instrument is an Improving invention superimposed upon the Basic telephone invention. Although certain inventions are clearly Basic and others as clearly Improving, the assignment of many others rests upon the observer's judgment of when any modification is important enough to be said to involve a new principle. Perhaps the best test is a pragmatic one, classing any invention as Basic when it becomes the starting point for a divergent line of inventions and Improving when it does not.

It is impossible to establish any constant correlation between this classification of inventions and our previous one of inventors. In the great majority of cases Basic inventions are probably the work of conscious inventors, but exceptions could no doubt be found. A new principle, say that of fixing a particular dye by the addition of a colorless mordant, might come into use by accident and later be applied in a number of different ways without ever being grasped as a principle. Numerous examples of this sort could be cited in the technology of uncivilized peoples. At the same time, the influence of the conscious inventor in the production of Basic inventions is certainly paramount. By their very definition such inventions imply a considerable departure from the *status quo,* and the individual who is consciously interested in producing something new is much more likely to hit upon a new principle or combination of principles than one who is not. Improving inventions, on the other hand, may derive from conscious or unconscious inventors with equal facility. Under our own system of organized invention the conscious element has certainly become the dominant one in the improvement of all devices. However, it is interesting to note that institutions devoted to organized invention have produced far fewer Basic inventions in proportion to their total output than have unorganized inventors as a whole. It seems that the unorganized inventors are more likely to wander into unpromising by-paths of experiment from which they frequently bring back something worth while. The very studies which have led to a number of the Basic inventions made in recent times have been of a sort which the inventor's contemporaries considered a waste of time.

Although a certain romantic interest attaches to Basic inventions just as it does to conscious inventors, the bulk of cultural progress has probably been due to the less spectacular process of gradual improvement in preëxisting devices and the development of new applications for them. In fact Basic inventions seem to be valuable mainly as the starting point for series of Improving inventions. Very few of them are efficient or satisfactory in the condition in which they first appear. Thus the first automobiles were little better than toys or scientific curiosities. They did not begin to play their present important rôle in our culture until they had been refined and perfected by literally hundreds of Improving inventions.

A sufficient number of Improving inventions can even transform an appliance into something quite different from the original and with totally different applications. Thus the wheel appears to have been, in its inception, a development of the roller and something employed exclusively in transportation. As the potentialities of the device were recognized, it was turned to other uses, as for drawing water for irrigation and for the manufacture of pottery. Still later came a realization of its potentialities for transforming direct into rotary motion and for transmitting power, until this transportation appliance became an integral part of thousands of devices which were in no way related to transportation. Again, the bow, beginning as a weapon, or more probably as a toy, not only underwent a series of modifications which perfected it for its original use but, through a divergent line of inventive evolution, became ancestral to the harp and ultimately to all stringed musical instruments. In both of these cases the development of the new appliances rested upon a long series of Improving inventions no one of which seemed to be of tremendous importance in itself but which, in the aggregate, produced something fundamentally different from the original appliance. For this reason it is extremely hazardous to class any appliance as the result of a conscious Basic invention unless its actual history is known. The new principle which gives it its Basic quality may have crept in little by little, entering by such gradual degrees that its point of first appearance can hardly be detected.

Hitherto we have discussed the inventor and his inventions from the point of view of their own qualities, but the picture would be quite misleading if we stopped there. There is a constant and intimate association between the inventor and his products and the cultural setting in which inventions are produced and must function. We have defined an invention as a new application of knowledge, a definition which at once implies that the knowledge must precede the invention. Although the knowledge incorporated into a new invention may derive in part from a fresh discovery, most of it always derives from the culture of the inventor's society. Every inventor, even the one who produces a Basic invention, builds upon this accumulation of previously acquired knowledge, and every new thing must grow directly out of other things which have gone before. Thus no inventor reared in a culture which was ignorant of the wheel principle could conceivably produce even such simple appliances as the potter's wheel or lathe. The wheel would have to be invented first. The content of the culture within which the inventor operates thus imposes constant limitations upon the exercise of his inventive abilities. This applies not merely to mechanical inventions but to invention in all other fields as well. The mathematical genius can only carry on from the point which mathematical knowledge within his culture has already reached. Thus if Einstein had been born into a primitive tribe which was unable to count beyond three, life-long application to mathematics probably would not have carried him beyond the development of a decimal system based on fingers and toes. Again, reformers who attempt to devise new systems for society or new religions can only build with the elements with which their culture has made them familiar. It is ridiculous to try to understand the form and content of such sects as Christianity and Mohammedanism until we know the cultural background from which they sprang.

The culture not only provides the inventor with the tools which he must use in invention but also controls, to a very large extent, the direction of his interest. Series of evaluations are an integral part of all cultures and differ from one culture to another. The things which one society considers important and is interested in may be totally different from those which another society is interested in. Thus Hindu culture, prior to its contact with modern Europe, felt a deep interest in philosophy and very little interest in the perfection of mechanical appliances. Conversely, the modern European displays a lively interest in mechanical gadgets of all sorts and very little interest in philosophical speculation. These culturally established interests of a society inevitably focus the inventor's attention and efforts. He unconsciously turns his mind in the same direction in which the minds of other members of the society are turned. Moreover, it is only along these lines that invention can bring him any recompense of favorable emotional response or added prestige. Contrast the attitude of our own society toward a man who invents an engine of super-efficiency and toward one who develops a new and more effective teaching technique. The former will make the headlines and a fortune, the latter will be lucky if he receives recognition in a technical journal. Of course there are occasional "queer" individuals who do not exercise their inventive talents along the culturally indicated lines, but their way is always a hard one and their opportunities of making lasting contributions to culture are slight indeed. Society meets their most successful inventions with a bland "What of it?" and turns back to the things which it considers important.

This brings us at once to another of the influences which culture exerts upon invention, that of selection. From the point of view of culture dynamics, the successful invention is simply the one which is accepted by society and incorporated into culture. Other inventions, no matter how adequately they may achieve the purpose which their inventors imagined for them, are in the class of the successful operation under which the patient died. This matter of acceptance seems to be controlled much more by the factor of the society's directed interests than by any factors of practical utility. A society will not accept a new invention simply because it works better than something which they already have if it lies in a field which the society considers unimportant. The actual gains do not seem to them to be sufficient to repay for the annoyance of changing established habits or making the alterations in other elements of culture which the acceptance of any new element always entails. Thus a society which has existed contentedly for generations on a hand-labor basis and fixed its attention on speculations regarding the nature of the universe and man's relation to it will feel no great urge to adopt labor-saving appliances, even those which exhibit a high degree of efficiency. It will feel still less urged to accept them while they are still subject to the frequent breakdowns and uncertain performance which attend the early stages of most inventions. The first failure will end even casual interest, and one more invention will have been stillborn.

It can be seen that the factors which control socially successful invention are highly complex. Many of them are also inherently variable, making any accurate predictions regarding the progress of culture through invention completely out of the question. Individuals capable of making Basic inventions, with the vistas of cultural enrichment which these open up, are not produced in accord with any known rules. Even when they do appear, they must owe the opportunity to exercise their gifts to a happy combination of circumstances. It is interesting to conjecture what Mr. Edison's contribution to culture would have been if he had been born a serf in central Europe in the twelfth century. Although every invention must be preceded by a particular accumulation of knowledge and accompanied by a situation in which it will have some utility to society, there is abundant evidence that a perfect setting for an invention will not automatically lead to its development. Thus in Yucatan during the Maya New Empire there was extensive trade and travel, a fine system of hard-surfaced roads, and every incentive to improve transportation. The principle of the roller was known, as is proved by the recent discovery of one used for packing the road surface. However, this perfect setting did not produce the wheel. As far as any one can tell, invention is subject to pure chance on its positive side and to a long series of variables in its other aspects.

In our own civilization invention itself has become a focus of interest as long as it confines itself to mechanical lines. Social and religious invention is still frowned upon, but this attitude may change as the necessity for advance in these fields becomes increasingly apparent. However, there has never been a time in history when individuals were afforded a better opportunity to add to the material aspects of a culture. In most societies the way of both the inventor and his inventions are hard, and surprisingly few inventions survive to be actually incorporated into culture. For every invention which has been successful in the cultural and social sense there have probably been at least a thousand which have fallen by the wayside. Many of these have been successful in the practical sense, being actually more efficient than the appliances which were used before and continued to be used after. However, society rejected them, and if they have not been completely forgotten they survive simply as antiquarian curiosities. We know that the Alexandrian Greeks had a steam-engine which was effective enough for one to be installed on the Pharos and used to haul up fuel for the beacon. Leonardo da Vinci's note-books provide a perfect mine of inventions, many of which show a surprising similarity to modern ones. Perfectly feasible repeating rifles and machine-guns were developed during the first hundred years that hand firearms were in use. All of these inventions failed to "take."

It seems that any invention which fails of acceptance by society within the first generation after it appears may be set down as a total loss. Even when, as in Europe, there are methods for recording it and preserving it as a latent element within the culture, it is rarely if ever revivified. The examples cited above had nothing to do with the modern inventions which they foreshadowed. The inventor works from his own knowledge and his own sense of needs and rarely pores over archives. The same things are invented again and again and rejected again and again until changes in the culture continuum have prepared a place for them. The process is slow and, from the point of view of the inventor, most discouraging. In the progressive enrichment of its culture no society has ever employed even a tithe of its members' inventive ability. There are few cultures which can show more than a mere handful of traits which have been invented by members of the societies which bear them. All cultures have grown chiefly by borrowing, a process which will be discussed in the next chapter.

CHAPTER XIX

DIFFUSION

We have seen in the previous chapter how the particular culture within which any inventor works directs and circumscribes his efforts and determines whether his inventions will be socially accepted. Because of this the number of successful inventions originating within the confines of any one linked society and culture is always small. If every human group had been left to climb upward by its own unaided efforts, progress would have been so slow that it is doubtful whether any society by now would have advanced beyond the level of the Old Stone Age. The comparatively rapid growth of human culture as a whole has been due to the ability of all societies to borrow elements from other cultures and to incorporate them into their own. This transfer of culture elements from one society to another is known as *diffusion*. It is a process by which mankind has been able to pool its inventive ability. By diffusion an invention which has been made and socially accepted at one point can be transmitted to an ever-widening group of cultures until, in the course of centuries, it may spread to practically the whole of mankind.

Diffusion has made a double contribution to the advance of mankind. It has stimulated the growth of culture as a whole and at the same time has enriched the content of individual cultures, bringing the societies which bore them forward and upward. It has helped to accelerate the evolution of culture as a whole by removing the necessity for every society to perfect every step in an inventive series for itself. Thus a basic invention which has been made at one point will ultimately be brought to the attention of a great number of inventors and its potentialities for use and improvement thoroughly explored. As more minds are put to work upon each problem the process of culture advance is accelerated. The rapidity of progress during the past century is certainly due in large part to the development of means for easy and rapid communication plus techniques for ensuring to the inventor the economic rewards of his labors. Patents have made secrecy unnecessary. They impose a temporary tax upon the use of inventions but make the idea available to all. Any invention which is made at the present time is promptly diffused over a wide area and becomes part of the store of knowledge available to hundreds of inventors. Prior to the development of the present conditions it took centuries for any new element of culture to diffuse over the same territory to which it is now extended in a few months or years.

The slow cultural advance of societies which are left to their own abilities is well illustrated by the conditions in isolated human groups. Perhaps the outstanding example is the Tasmanians. These people were cut off from the rest of mankind at least 20,000 years ago. When they reached their island they seem to have had a culture which, in its material development at least, correspond roughly to that of Europe during the Middle Paleolithic. They were still in this stage when Europeans first visited them during the eighteenth century. During the long period of isolation they had no doubt made some minor advances and improvements, but their lack of outside contacts was reflected in a tremendous culture lag. To cite a much less extreme example, the culture of some of our own isolated mountain communities still corresponds in many respects to that of the pioneers of a century ago. The first settlers of these isolated regions brought this culture with them, and their unaided efforts have contributed little to it. In general, the more opportunities for borrowing any society has the more rapid its cultural advance will be.

The service of diffusion in enriching the content of individual cultures has been of the utmost importance. There is probably no culture extant to-day which owes more than 10 per cent of its total elements to inventions made by members of its own society. Because we live in a period of rapid invention we are apt to think of our own culture as largely self-created, but the rôle which diffusion has played in its growth may be brought home to us if we consider the beginning of the average man's day. The locations listed in the following paragraphs refer only to the origin points of various culture elements, not to regions from which we now obtain materials or objects through trade.

Our solid American citizen awakens in a bed built on a pattern which originated in the Near East but which was modified in Northern Europe before it was transmitted to America. He throws back covers made from cotton, domesticated in India, or linen, domesticated in the Near East, or wool from sheep, also domesticated in the Near East, or silk, the use of which was discovered in China. All of these materials have been spun and woven by processes invented in the Near East. He slips into his moccasins, invented by the Indians of the Eastern woodlands, and goes to the bathroom, whose fixtures are a mixture of European and American inventions, both of recent date. He takes off his pajamas, a garment invented in India, and washes with soap invented by the ancient Gauls. He then shaves, a masochistic rite which seems to have been derived from either Sumer or ancient Egypt.

Returning to the bedroom, he removes his clothes from a chair of southern European type and proceeds to dress. He puts on garments whose form originally derived from the skin clothing of the nomads of the Asiatic steppes, puts on shoes made from skins tanned by a process invented in ancient Egypt and cut to a pattern derived from the classical civilizations of the Mediterranean, and ties around his neck a strip of bright-colored cloth which is a vestigial survival of the shoulder shawls worn by the seventeenth-century Croatians. Before going out for breakfast he glances through the window, made of glass invented in Egypt, and if it is raining puts on overshoes made of rubber discovered by the Central American Indians and takes an umbrella, invented in southeastern Asia. Upon his head he puts a hat made of felt, a material invented in the Asiatic steppes.

On his way to breakfast he stops to buy a paper, paying for it with coins, an ancient Lydian invention. At the restaurant a whole new series of borrowed elements confronts him. His plate is made of a form of pottery invented in China. His knife is of steel, an

alloy first made in southern India, his fork a medieval Italian
invention, and his spoon a derivative of a Roman original. He
begins breakfast with an orange, from the eastern Mediterranean,
a canteloupe from Persia, or perhaps a piece of African water-
melon. With this he has coffee, an Abyssinian plant, with cream
and sugar. Both the domestication of cows and the idea of milking
them originated in the Near East, while sugar was first made in
India. After his fruit and first coffee he goes on to waffles, cakes
made by a Scandinavian technique from wheat domesticated in
Asia Minor. Over these he pours maple syrup, invented by the
Indians of the Eastern woodlands. As a side dish he may have
the egg of a species of bird domesticated in Indo-China, or thin
strips of the flesh of an animal domesticated in Eastern Asia
which have been salted and smoked by a process developed in
northern Europe.

When our friend has finished eating he settles back to smoke,
an American Indian habit, consuming a plant domesticated in
Brazil in either a pipe, derived from the Indians of Virginia, or
a cigarette, derived from Mexico. If he is hardy enough he may
even attempt a cigar, transmitted to us from the Antilles by way
of Spain. While smoking he reads the news of the day, imprinted
in characters invented by the ancient Semites upon a material
invented in China by a process invented in Germany. As he absorbs the accounts of foreign troubles he will, if he is a good
conservative citizen, thank a Hebrew deity in an Indo-European
language that he is 100 per cent American.

The foregoing is merely a bit of antiquarian virtuosity made
possible by the existence of unusually complete historic records
for the Eurasiatic area. There are many other regions for which
no such records exist, yet the cultures in these areas bear similar
witness to the importance of diffusion in establishing their content. Fairly adequate techniques have been developed for tracing
the spread of individual traits and even for establishing their
origin points, and there can be no doubt that diffusion has
occurred wherever two societies and cultures have been brought
into contact.

In view of the tremendous importance of this mechanism for

the enrichment of culture, is is rather surprising that so little is still known about the actual dynamics of the diffusion process. Most of the students who have been interested in this field have considered the study of diffusion little more than a preliminary to historic reconstructions. They have spent much time and effort in tracing the distribution of culture elements, but have been content with the formulation of two or three basic principles of diffusion which were immediately applicable to their historic studies. Such studies are by no means the mere satisfactions of idle curiosity which some of their opponents would have them to be. The content of a culture at any point in its history can only be explained in terms of its past, and any light which can be thrown upon that past contributes to our understanding of the present. Even the study of the functions of the various elements within a culture becomes largely meaningless unless we can determine the factors to which these elements owe their form and consequently their potentialities for function. This matter will be discussed at length in a later chapter. For the present we need only point out that the more exact our knowledge of the dynamics of the diffusion process the greater will be the possibility of making valid historic reconstructions from trait distributions.

A real understanding of the dynamics of diffusion can be arrived at only by observing the process in actual operation. A thorough study of the current spread of any new culture element, the factors responsible for this spread, the reactions which the new element has evoked in different societies, and the adaptations which the acceptance of the new trait into various cultures has entailed would do more to put diffusion studies on a sound basis than twenty studies of trait distributions at a given point in time. Unfortunately there is hardly a single study of this sort extant. In the discussion which follows we must, therefore, raise far more questions than we can answer. Nevertheless, there are a few generally recognized principles of diffusion, and we may begin our investigation with these.

The first of these is that, *other things being equal, elements of culture will be taken up first by societies which are close to their points of origin and later by societies which are more remote or which have less direct contacts.* This principle derives from the fact that the diffusion of any element obviously requires both contact and time. It is impossible for any trait to spread to a culture unless there is contact with some other culture which already has it. Thus if we have three tribes, A, B, and C, with the territory of B intervening between that of A and C and preventing any direct contact between them, no new culture trait which A may develop can reach C until after it has been accepted by B. From this it also follows that the trait will be received later by C than by B.

There is abundant historic evidence of the general validity of this principle. Thus the alphabet, which seems to have been invented in the general region of the Sinai peninsula, was taken up first by the Semitic groups which immediately adjoined this area and transmitted by them to the Phœnicians. These carried it by sea to the Greeks and Romans, from whom it was diffused into northern Europe. It did not appear in Scandinavia until about 2,000 years after its invention and reached this region by way of a series of intermediary cultures each of which had had certain effects on the alphabet's development.

From this principle of the diffusion of traits to more and more remote localities a second principle emerges, that of *marginal survivals*. Let us suppose that a new appliance has been developed by a particular society and is spreading to the neighboring societies in an ever-widening circle. At the same time it may very well be undergoing changes and improvements at its point of origin. These improvements will, in turn, be diffused to the neighboring societies, but since this diffusion will begin at a later point in time, the improved appliance will have a tendency to lag behind the original one in its spread. Long after the new appliance has completely supplanted the ancestral one at its point of origin, the ancestral one will continue in use about the margins of the diffusion area. This principle may be illustrated by the present distribution of telephone types in the United States. The earliest telephones had cranks for calling central. At the present time the crank telephone is still used in the more remote rural districts but has completely disappeared in the cities. The desk type of telephone, with automatic call, is used over an intermediate zone, while the hand telephone, first used in New York in 1927, is still largely confined to city use. Lastly, dial telephones are making rapid headway in the large cities, but are only beginning to spread to the smaller ones and have not reached any rural districts. The example may not be considered a perfect one, since the diffusion of the telephone has obviously been influenced by such atypical factors as the monopoly of telephone service and desire of the company to use old equipment already in existence, but it does serve to illustrate the principle.

The simile most commonly applied to the diffusion process is that of the ripples sent out by dropping a stone into still water. The last ripples will still be moving outward when the center has once more become quiet. While such a constant and uniform spread of traits from a single center in order of their development may be used as a hypothetical case to illustrate the principle, actual historic records show that it never occurs in fact. Even traits which originate in the same center spread irregularly and travel at different speeds. A few examples will make this clear.

Everything indicates that the cultivation of maize in America was a culture trait which originated in Mexico. From there it spread widely over the Mississippi Valley and eastern United States and also took firm root in the Southwest. While in the East it reached New England, the Dakotas and the peninsula of Michigan, in the West it barely penetrated southern California. This in spite of the fact that this region was in fairly close touch with the Southwest, where maize culture was highly developed and where there were adequate techniques for growing the crop under semi-arid conditions. Again, the California Indians, outside a small area in the south, failed to take over pottery although they were close to an area of high pottery development and although the rather sedentary life of most California tribes would have given it great utility. Our present fairly accurate knowledge of Southwestern time sequences proves that tribes on the margins of the California area must have been exposed to both maize and pottery for at least 1,500 years, yet they failed to accept either.

Such reluctance to accept new elements of culture slows down their rate of spread even when it does not completely inhibit their diffusion in certain directions. A group which is reluctant to take over a new trait interposes a bar between the origin point of that trait and more remote groups which might be quite willing to accept it if given the opportunity. Even if the reluctance of the intermediary culture is finally broken down, much time will have been lost. Because of this varying coefficient of receptivity, traits always spread from their origin points irregularly and certain traits may be diffused with amazing speed while others diffuse slowly, if at all. One of the most striking examples of extremely rapid diffusion is that afforded by the spread of certain New World food crops, especially maize, during the first 300 years following Columbus's discovery. By the end of this period these crops had penetrated practically all areas in Europe, Asia, and Africa in which they could be raised and in many places had profoundly altered the patterns of native life. Thus the Betsimisaraka of Madagascar, who could scarcely have received maize before 1600, have a myth that it was given to them by the Creator at the same time that he gave rice to the Plateau tribes of the island. They meet any suggestion that it might be a fairly recent introduction by the simple statement that it cannot be, since the people could not live without it.

The spread of tobacco after the discovery of the New World is a still more striking example of rapid diffusion and has the advantage of being well documented. For once, popular traditions seem to be correct in their ascription of the introduction of smoking into England to Sir Walter Raleigh. At least the first mention of it there is in connection with the return of his Virginia colonists, and we know that Ralph Lane, the first governor, presented Raleigh with an Indian pipe in 1586 and instructed him in its use. This launched the custom of smoking in court circles, and from there it spread to the common people with amazing speed. It should be noticed that tobacco had also been introduced into

Spain by Francisco Fernandez in 1558, but it came in the guise of a medicine and there was considerable delay in its acceptance for purely social purposes.

These two points of introduction became, in turn, centers for the diffusion of tobacco over the Old World. England was the main donor to northern Europe. Smoking was introduced into Holland in 1590 by English medical students, and the English and Dutch together spread the new habit by sea into the Baltic countries and Scandinavia and overland through Germany into Russia. By 1634, forty-eight years after its first appearance in northern Europe, it had become a nuisance in Russia and laws were enacted against it. Nevertheless its spread eastward continued unchecked, and within 200 years it had crossed the steppes and mountains of Siberia and was reintroduced into America at Alaska. This rapid diffusion is the more remarkable since in much of this northern region the plant had to be obtained by trade over great distances.

From Spain and Portugal tobacco was diffused throughout the Mediterranean countries and into the near East. The dates here are less certain, but Sultan Murad of Turkey passed laws against its use in 1605. The Dutch and Portuguese together carried it to Africa and southeastern Asia. In far-off Japan it was accepted so quickly that by 1605 it was found necessary to limit the amount of ground which could be devoted to its cultivation. In South Africa tobacco became the regular medium of exchange between the Dutch and the natives, a cow being valued at its over-all length in tobacco leaves. In spite of frequent official opposition and drastic laws, the new element of culture spread almost as fast as men could travel.

It has been observed that while elements of culture may be diffused alone they are more likely to travel in groups of elements which are functionally related. This point is also illustrated by the spread of tobacco, since with the plant there were diffused various methods of using it. The linkage of these methods with the various lines of diffusion can be traced back even to the New World. The Indians used tobacco in different ways in different regions. Those of the eastern coast of North America smoked it in elbow pipes, which became the prototypes of the modern English briars. Although this form of pipe underwent various modifications along the northern route of diffusion, all the people who derived their tobacco habit by way of England have remained predominantly pipe-smokers. The Indians of Brazil, with whom the Portuguese had most contact, preferred cigars, as did some of the Antillean groups. The Mexicans, on the other hand, preferred the cigarette and gave it to the Spaniards. From them it passed to the other Mediterranean cultures, a fact reflected in our own preference for Turkish and Egyptian cigarettes. Since the Portuguese and Dutch acted simultaneously in the diffusion of tobacco to southeastern Asia, that region received both the pipe and the cigar, and the two still exist side by side there in many localities. Some tribes even preserve complete neutrality by rolling their tobacco into cigars and then smoking these in pipes. In Africa, where the Dutch won in the struggle against the Portuguese, the pipe became the regular appliance.

In the course of its diffusion tobacco even developed two new methods of use, the water-pipe and snuff. The water-pipe originated in the Near East and never diffused far beyond that region. Snuff seems to have originated in Spain and grew out of the medicinal application of tobacco. It had no prototype in America. Some of the Antillean and South American tribes did use snuff, but it was not made from tobacco. On the other hand snuffs of one sort or another had been used in Europe for centuries. Apparently this was a result of a mistaken attempt to reach the brain through the nasal passages. The first tobacco sent from Portugal to France was in the form of snuff, and the habit of taking tobacco in this way became established at the French court and spread from there to the whole of European polite society. In fact, it seems for a time to have threatened the existence of smoking in higher social circles. Toward the close of the eighteenth century the high tide of snuff began to recede, and it now survives only in marginal areas and even there is at a social disadvantage.

The last chapter in the diffusion of methods of smoking is curious enough to deserve special mention. The cigarette, in spite of its general acceptance in the Mediterranean area, did not spread to northern Europe or the United States until very recent times. It was not introduced into England until after the close of the Crimean War, when the custom of cigarette smoking was brought back by officers who had learned it from their Turkish allies. It reached the United States still later, within the memory of many persons now alive, and there encountered vigorous opposition. Although there seems to be no proof that the cigarette is any more harmful than the virile corn-cob or the chewing tobacco which was the American pioneer's special contribution to the tobacco complex, laws against its use are still to be found on many statute books. It was considered not only harmful but also effeminate, and traces of the latter attitude survive even to-day. He-men who enjoy their cigarette can console themselves with the knowledge that many a "hard-boiled" Aztec priest must have indulged in one before beginning his "daily dozen" of human sacrifices.

It should be plain from the foregoing that no simple mechanistic interpretation of diffusion will prove adequate to the needs of even the rather limited field of historic reconstruction. Diffusion required not only a donor but also a receiver, and the rôle of this receiver is certainly the more important. As we have seen in the case of the California Indians with regard to maize and pottery, exposure to a culture trait is not necessarily followed by acceptance. Diffusion really includes three fairly distinct processes: presentation of the new culture element or elements to the society, acceptance by the society, and the integration of the accepted element or elements into the preëxisting culture. Each of these is influenced by a large number of variable factors most of which still require study.

The presentation of new elements to a society always presupposes contact. The society with which this contact is established may, of course, be either the originator of the new culture element or simply an intermediary in its spread. This factor can have little influence on the process. However, the nature of the contact is of tremendous importance. Such contacts vary from those in which two societies and cultures are brought into a close relationship as wholes to sporadic trade contacts or those in which a single individual from one society settles in another society. Complete contacts are decidedly rare. It is difficult to find examples of them except in the case of conquering groups who settle among and exploit the conquered or in that of immigrant groups such as we still have in many parts of America. Such contacts have a somewhat different quality from those involved in the ordinary diffusion process, and the process of culture change under these conditions is usually termed *acculturation*. Apparently the use of this term, which was first applied to the study of changes in immigrant groups, is based on the rather naïve belief that one of the societies thus brought into contact completely abandons its former culture and completely accepts that of the other. Actually, such close and complete contacts always result in an exchange of culture elements. In the long run both the originally diverse societies and their cultures will fuse to form a new society and culture. In this final product elements from both will be represented, although they may be represented in widely varying proportions. Thus the Italians in America usually lose their identity as a distinct society by the third or fourth generation and accept the culture in which they then find themselves. At the same time this culture is not the same which their ancestors encountered on arrival. It has been enriched by the American acceptance of such originally Italian elements as a popular interest in grand opera, spaghetti dinners, and superior techniques for racketeering.

Taking the world as a whole, the type of contact which makes acculturation possible is more likely to arise through conquest and the settlement of the conquering groups among the vanquished than through anything else. In such cases the normal numerical superiority of the conquered is likely to be balanced to a considerable extent by the superior prestige of the conquerors, so that the two cultures stand on fairly equal terms in their contribution to the new culture which always arises under such conditions. Such hybrid cultures usually present the aspects of a chemical rather than a mechanical mixture. In addition to traits drawn from both the parent cultures they possess qualities foreign to both. However, we must return to the more normal forms of culture contact and the dissemination of culture elements which these make possible.

It goes without saying that contacts between cultures can only be established through the medium of individuals. We have pointed out in a previous chapter that no individual participates completely in the culture of his own society. This means that under ordinary conditions the full culture of the donor society is never offered to the receiving society. The only elements made available to them are those with which the contact individuals are familiar. Thus if a trade relation exists between two tribes, the trade being carried on by men, the product of the women's industries in one tribe may become familiar to the other tribe, but the techniques will not be transmitted with it. The men who do the trading, even if they do not guard these techniques as valuable commercial secrets, will have only a vague idea of how the things are made. If the receiving tribe becomes accustomed to the use of this product and then finds the supply suddenly cut off, it may develop quite different techniques for the manufacture of equivalent articles. It is interesting to conjecture whether the extreme diversity of techniques of pottery manufacture in the Melanesian region may not have arisen in this way. There are many tribes here who regularly use pottery without manufacturing it, and it is easy to imagine the members of such a group working out a method of making the familiar and necessary pots if their normal source was removed.

The differential which is introduced into diffusion by this varying participation of individuals in their own culture is just as strongly operative when the contact-individuals from the donor group settle among the receiving group. The trader, missionary, or government official can transmit no more of his culture than he himself knows. If the contact-individual is a male, he usually can transmit very little from the female half of his own culture, and the female elements which he can transmit are likely to be heterogeneous and to bear little functional relation to each other. I knew a French official who was the envy of all his colleagues because he had been able to teach his native mistress how to starch and iron his white shirts. His knowledge of this technique had been acquired by accident, and he knew no more about other aspects of housekeeping than the average male. Conversely, if the contact-individual is a female she can transmit female techniques but is most unlikely to pass on such purely masculine items as a new form of metal-working or a new war magic. It is easy to imagine situations in which, due to this contact differential, many elements from certain sections of a culture will have been presented and even accepted while few or none have been presented from other sections. Thus the natives of an island which has been a regular port of call for whaling vessels may have absorbed a good many of the culture elements connected with the industry and even a fair number of the habits and attitudes of whalemen. They may learn to build whaleboats and dress in European garments gotten from the whalers, while they still have no idea that drawing-rooms exist, still less of the behavior appropriate to them. To cite a less extreme case, a native group might have had close contact with half a dozen missionaries and their wives without receiving any inkling of the evolutionary theories which now influence so much of European thought or of modern European trends in dress and interior decoration.

When two societies are in long-continued contact, as in the case of two tribes who live side by side and are generally on friendly terms, sooner or later the entire culture of each will be made available to the other. The long series of contacts with individuals, each of whom is a partial participant, will have a cumulative effect. When, on the other hand, the contacts of one society are exclusively with selected groups of individuals from the other society, the receiving group may never be exposed to the totality of the donor group's culture. This situation holds true to a very large extent for regions to which whites come as traders or administrators, but never as artisans or laborers.

A second factor which exercises a strong influence upon diffusion is what, for lack of a better term, may be called the inherent communicability of the culture elements themselves. This has nothing to do with the attitudes of the receiving group or with its preëxisting culture configurations. Although this aspect of the diffusion problem has never been studied, it seems probable that we are dealing here with something which is fairly constant. In a previous chapter we have pointed out that culture is itself a socio-psychological phenomenon and that the various forms of behavior which we are able to observe and record are simply its overt expressions. Certain elements of culture can be much more readily expressed than others, whether this expression takes the form of ordinary acts or verbalizations. Since it is only through the observation of these overt expressions that culture elements can be transmitted from one individual to another or from one society to another, it follows that those culture elements which can be most readily and completely expressed will be those which are the most readily available for acceptance. Among the varied elements which go to make up the totality of a culture, the techniques for food-getting and manufacturing take precedence in this respect. These can be made clear to a bystander without the medium of speech. If he wishes to acquire such techniques, all he has to do is to imitate the worker's movements carefully and exactly. Although he may lack the proper muscular control at first, this can be acquired through practice. The same holds for manufactured objects. Even when the techniques have not been observed, the members of the receiving culture can fix the details of the object firmly in their memory and proceed to reproduce it at leisure. The tendency which the Japanese still show to study and reproduce imported objects would be a case in point.

As soon as we pass from such simple culture elements as techniques and their material products, we encounter increasing difficulties in communication. Although it is quite possible to describe such an element of culture as the ideal pattern for marriage and even to express it in non-verbal behavior, this expression is much less complete than that which is possible with regard to such a culture element as basket-making. The most thorough verbalization has difficulty in conveying the series of associations and conditioned emotional responses which are attached to this pattern and which give it meaning and vitality within our own culture configuration. In all our overt expressions of such a pattern these things are taken for granted, but the individual to whom we are attempting to convey a sense of the pattern can know nothing of them. Even when language difference has ceased to be a serious barrier to the conveyance of such patterns, it is extremely difficult to put them across. This is even more true of those concepts which, while a part of culture, find no direct expression in behavior aside from verbalizations. There is a story of an educated Japanese who was trying to understand the nature of the Trinity and after a long discussion with a European friend burst out with: "Oh, I see now. It is a committee." Such a remark gives a shock to any good Christian. The Trinity certainly is not a committee, but it may bring the point home to the reader if he pictures himself as trying to explain to this Japanese student just how and why he was in error.

Lastly, we have in all cultures those vital attitudes and values which lie largely below the level of individual consciousness and which the average member of a society rarely tries to verbalize even to himself. The practical impossibility of making such elements available for borrowing by the members of some other society is obvious. This part of any culture simply is not susceptible to diffusion. It can never be presented in sufficiently concrete and objective terms. Such things as religious or philosophical concepts can be communicated after a fashion, although probably never in their entirety. Patterns of social behavior can also be transmitted in the same uncertain way, but the associations which give them genuine potentialities for function cannot be transmitted. A borrowing group may imitate their outward forms, but it will usually be found that it has introduced new elements to replace those which could not be genuinely communicated to it. The institution of marriage as it exists among our own Southern Negroes would be a good example of such incomplete transmission of a pattern and its consequent modifications. As a matter of fact, the material techniques and their products are probably the only elements of culture which can be completely communicated, and it is significant that it is usually these elements which are accepted most readily and retained in most nearly their received form. It is obvious that such inherent differences in communicability must be of tremendous importance in diffusion, especially through their influence upon completeness of transmission and rate of transmission.

Our discussion hitherto has dealt with donor cultures and the qualities of culture elements. Let us turn now to what is the real core of the problem of diffusion, the reactions of the accepting group to the elements presented to it. In its acceptance or rejection of these elements a society exercises free will. There may be a few exceptions to this in cases in which a socially dominant group seeks to impose its culture forcibly upon a subject society, but these are less important than they might appear. In the first place, such a dominant group rarely, if ever, attempts to impose its culture as a whole. It is content with the imposition of a few selected elements, such as outward adherence to its religion or the custom of wearing trousers. Obviously no amount of force can introduce into another culture any element which is not constantly and directly reflected in overt behavior. The conquered can be forced to attend church regularly, and it may even become a habit with them, something which produces no emotional response, but they cannot be forced to accept the new faith emotionally or be prevented from praying to their own gods alone and in private. At the same time, the very use of force makes the proscribed elements of the native culture symbols of revolt and this inspires a stronger attachment to them. Under a veil of superficial compliance a persecuted group can maintain its own ideals and values intact for generations, modifying and reinterpreting the superficial elements of culture which are forced upon it in such a way that they will do these no violence.

With very few exceptions, therefore, every new element which a society incorporates into its culture, it accepts of its own free will. This acceptance, in turn, is controlled by a large number of variable factors. The only constant in the situation is that such elements are always taken at their face value. A society can apprehend only those parts of a total complex which can be communicated to it plainly and directly. Thus a woman from one tribe who copies the design which she has seen on a basket made by some other tribe does so simply because its esthetic qualities appeal to her. She knows nothing of the symbolism which may surround this design or of what the original makers consider appropriate or inappropriate uses for it. Similarly when a new appliance, say a rifle, is presented to any group, they accept or reject it not on the basis of its associations and functions in the donor culture but on the potentialities for use which they perceive for it in their own. This perception never extends beyond the limits of immediate utility. There is no perception of the modifications in preëxisting patterns which the adoption of the new element will entail. In fact it is doubtful whether any mind is ever able to foresee any but the most immediate of these. Even in our own culture no one could have foretold the profound changes which have come in the wake of the acceptance of the automobile, changes which have affected our social patterns even more deeply than they have affected our economic ones.

The factors which control the receptivity of a society toward any new element of culture are, after all, very much the same whether this element originates inside or outside of their culture, i.e., whether it comes to them through invention or through diffusion. The main difference between these two processes lies in the fact that, if society rejects an invention, that addition to the sum total of culture is permanently lost, while if it rejects an element presented by diffusion this element is not lost but remains in the hands of the donor culture and may crop up at a later time when the society's reaction to it may be quite different.

New traits are accepted primarily on the basis of two qualities, utility and compatibility: in other words, on the basis of what they appear to be good for and how easily they can be fitted into the existing culture configuration. Both these qualities are, of course, relative to the receiving culture and are influenced by such a long series of factors that an outsider can hardly ascertain all of them. We have mentioned elsewhere that culture change is mainly a matter of the replacement of old elements by new ones and that every culture normally includes adequate techniques for meeting all the conscious needs of the society's members. When a new trait presents itself its acceptance depends not so much on whether it is better than the existing one as on whether it is enough better to make its acceptance worth the trouble. This in turn must depend upon the judgment of the group, their degree of conservatism, and how much change in existing habits the new appliance will entail. Even in the simplest form of diffusion, that of mechanical appliances, superiority cannot be judged simply in terms of increased output. There are pleasant and unpleasant forms of work, and even such a simple change as that from the use of adzes to axes for tree-felling entails a change in muscular habits which is unpleasant for the time being. In many parts of Oceania the natives have been receptive to European plane irons, which they could haft and use like their original stone adzes, but have refused to accept the vastly more efficient axe simply because they did not like to work with it.

Very much the same situation holds with regard to the problem of compatibility. The acceptance of any new culture element entails certain changes in the total culture configuration. Although the full extent of these changes can never be forecast, certain of them are usually obvious. If the new trait is of such a sort that its acceptance will conflict directly with important traits already present in the culture, it is almost certain to be rejected. One cannot conceive of techniques of mass production being accepted by a culture which had a pattern of uniqueness. There actually are societies which believe that no two objects should ever be the same and never make any two things exactly alike.

One very good example of such a conflict is afforded by the reactions of the Apache to peyote, a narcotic cactus used by many Indian tribes to induce visions and through these to put the individual in closer touch with the supernatural. The Apache attach as much importance to visions as any other tribe, but each individual hoards the power which comes to him through his supernatural experiences, and such power can be stolen by other medicine men. The regular pattern of peyote use is that of eating it in a group ceremonial. After a tentative and partial acceptance of the new idea the Apache rejected it. The opportunities for stealing power which contact in the assembly would provide, especially if an individual were under the influence of the drug and thus off guard, were too dangerous. It was felt that a man was likely to lose more power than he could gain. As a result, the use of peyote in this tribe has become infrequent and even then is limited to men of no importance who have little power to lose.

Most conflicts between new elements and preëxisting elements are less direct and obvious. In the matter of compatibility as in that of utility there is a broad zone of uncertainty. There are new elements which may be recognized as slightly superior to existing ones and other elements which may be seen to be somewhat incompatible, but not enough so as to make their acceptance impossible. Very often the advantages and disadvantages are so evenly balanced that the acceptance of the new trait may seem desirable to certain members of the society and undesirable to others. The ultimate acceptance or rejection of elements which fall within this zone is controlled by still another series of variable factors about which we know very little. One of the most important of these is certainly the particular interests which dominate the life of the receiving group. A new trait which is in line with these interests will be given more serious consideration and has a better chance of adoption than one which is not. A slight gain along the line of these interests is felt to be more important than a larger one in some other line in which the group takes little interest. Thus the Hindus have always been highly receptive to new cults and new philosophic ideas as long as these did not come into too direct conflict with their existing patterns, but have shown an almost complete indifference to improved techniques of manufacture. The material world was felt to be of so little importance that minor advances in its control were not considered worth the trouble of changing established habits.

There are other factors beside those of the receiving group's interests and evaluations which may help to weight the scales for or against a new element of culture. One of the most important of these is the prestige of the donor group. There are many different grades and kinds of prestige. Occasionally one encounters a society which seems to have a genuine inferiority complex with regard to some other and to consider everything which this admired society has superior to the corresponding elements in its own culture. Such a group will borrow almost anything from its model that it has an opportunity to borrow. An example of this would be the indiscriminate acceptance of elements of European culture by the Japanese during the latter half of the nineteenth century. Such an attitude usually ends either in thorough disillusionment or in the disappearance of the borrowing society as a distinct cultural entity.

Such a condition is unusual. Donor prestige is usually of a much more limited type, referring only to certain aspects of culture. The average society believes in its general superiority to the rest of mankind, but at the same time admits that some other society or societies are superior in particular respects. Thus although Americans feel a certain condescension toward French culture as a whole, it has become almost an article of faith that the French are superior to us in the designing of women's wear. When an American woman is called upon to choose between a Paris model and a Chicago model, this feeling is strong enough to give the Paris model a distinct advantage. Conversely, a style which was advertised as originating in Germany would get less consideration than even the Chicago one, since we believe that dress-designing is not along the line of Germany's best efforts. In other words, Paris styles are aided in their American diffusion by French prestige, while Berlin styles are hampered in their American diffusion by a lack of prestige. Even in primitive society there are always neighboring tribes who are admired in certain respects and other tribes who are despised. Any trait which comes from the admired source will at least be given serious consideration, while one which comes from the despised source must be markedly advantageous to win acceptance.

A further factor which influences the acceptance of new culture elements is the prestige of the individuals under whose auspices the new thing is presented to the society. In diffusion as in invention, acceptance of a new trait begins with a single individual or at most a small group of individuals. It makes a great deal of difference who these innovators happen to be. If they are persons whom the society admires and is accustomed to imitate, the way for the general acceptance of the new trait is smoothed from the start. If the innovators happen to be personally unpopular or of low social status, the new element immediately acquires undesirable associations which may outweigh any intrinsic advantages. Thus in our own society no one would try to launch a new and daring style through the cheap dress shops. It would not take even in the social group which patronizes these shops, since the wearing of the new style would then be a mark of a social status about which its holders were not enthusiastic. The same style launched from the highest point in the social ladder which its designers could reach would be eagerly accepted by the cheap-shop patrons.

Lastly, there is the factor of what can only be termed "faddism." It is an observed fact that certain new elements of culture will be eagerly accepted by groups when there are no discernible reasons of either utility or prestige. Major elements are unlikely to be introduced into any culture in this way, but a whole series of minor ones may be. We ourselves have witnessed the arrival and departure of such items as the ankle watch, sunburn initials, etc. Moreover, such fads are by no means limited to effete civilizations. Primitive tribes also have their changes of fashion and their borrowing of intrinsically useless items of culture which happen to catch their fancy. Thus among the Bara of Madagascar the past twenty years have witnessed the introduction of fantastic haircuts among the men, while prior to this time there was a rather simple uniform mode of tribal hairdressing. The style is said to have owed its origin to an enterprising Imerina barber who settled in the Bara territory and sought an outlet for his professional gifts. The young men who accepted it were severely ridiculed at first, but once done it could not be undone and they thus had a strong incentive to make converts to the new idea. Beginning with no utility and a rather negative prestige. it has now become firmly established as a part of Bara culture.

All this will indicate the great number of variable factors

which enter into both the presentation and the acceptance of new culture elements. Until we know more about the operation of these factors we can have only a very imperfect understanding of the diffusion process. The last step in this process, that of the changes and readjustments which inevitably follow the adoption of any new trait, will be treated in the next chapter.

CHAPTER XX

INTEGRATION

We have seen in the previous chapter that, due in part to the difficulties of communication, culture elements are never transferred from one culture to another in their entirety. Every culture trait, even the simplest object or manufacturing technique, is really a complex of elements including various associations and ideas as to how it should be used. The receiving society can be conscious of only so much of this complex as can be made available to them through concrete acts or verbalizations. Even then they are likely to borrow only the core of such a complex, those parts of it which are most concrete and tangible and which they therefore find it easiest to imitate. In its new cultural setting this borrowed core becomes the center of a new complex of associations and uses; in other words, the receiving society develops new interpretations for it and shapes it to serve new ends. One of the classical examples of such a reinterpretation of borrowed culture elements is found in our own Southwest in the case of the Pueblo and Navajo rituals. Much of the paraphernalia of Pueblo religion is striking, and their masked dances impress even European observers. The Navajo have copied many of these features of Pueblo religion, since these were things which they could readily observe and imitate. At the same time the meaning of these performances, even if partially revealed to them, was not accepted. While the Pueblo rituals are concerned primarily with various aspects of fertility, rain, and food-getting, among the Navajo these objectively borrowed rituals were turned mainly to the healing of disease, a matter in which the Navajo were deeply interested. The borrowing society not only modified the accepted traits but completely reinterpreted them.

Further, since every culture is a configuration whose parts

are mutually adjusted to each other, the introduction of any new culture element at once upsets the balance. During the early stages of its acceptance, while it is still an Alternative, it is always in active competition with some other element or group of elements; and before it can become part of the core of the culture, i.e., a Universal or Specialty, there must be a new series of adjustments. This feature of mutual adjustment between culture elements will be termed *integration*. It has both its dynamic and its static aspects. By the *process of integration* we mean the progressive development of more and more perfect adjustments between the various elements which compose the total culture. By *degree of integration* we mean simply the extent to which such adjustments have been perfected at any given point in the culture continuum.

The interrelations of the elements within any culture are so complex that it is extremely difficult to study integration in its static aspects. Two elements which appear unrelated may actually be closely related through their mutual adjustment to a series of other elements. This fact appears plainly enough when we study integration in process, observing the new modifications and adjustments between existing traits which always take place when a new element is accepted into the culture configuration. It will be best, therefore, to begin our discussion with a concrete example of the effects produced on the Tanala culture configuration by the introduction of a single new element, the cultivation of irrigated rice. The following account is, in part, a historic reconstruction, but the events are so recent and are so well authenticated both by native stories and by the presence of clans whose cultures are still in all stages of change, that I believe the order and nature of the events recorded to be essentially correct.

The Tanala are a hill tribe of western Madagascar who have already been mentioned several times in this book. Their old joint family organization has been described in Chapter XII and their tribal organization, or rather lack of it, in Chapter XIV. Prior to about 200 years ago the economic basis of their life was the cultivation of dry rice by the cutting and burning method. Under the local conditions this method gave a good crop the first year and a moderately good one from the same land five to ten years later. After this the land had to be abandoned until it had once more produced a fairly heavy growth of jungle, twenty to twenty-five years as a minimum. Since the newly cleared land produced the best crops, the usual native method was to utilize all the original jungle which could be profitably exploited with the village as a center, then move the village to a new locality and begin the process again. Under these conditions there was no opportunity for individual ownership of land to develop. The village as a whole held a territory within which it moved from site to site, and forest products such as game taken from this territory belonged to the man who obtained them. Joint families owned the crops growing on jungle land which they had cleared, but the division of land for this use was made as equitable as possible. According to one account, the village elders staked out equal frontages of land to be cleared and assigned one of these to each joint family. The family members, working in a group, then cleared back from the line as far as they thought necessary to provide for their needs. If a family had had bad luck with its crops one year, it would be given an advantage the next. As a result, no marked inequalities in wealth between the joint families ever developed. As there was no market for any surplus, there was no attempt to cultivate more land than was actually needed, and the product was divided by the joint family's head, each household receiving according to its needs.

The cultivation of wet rice appeared first among the clans on the eastern edge of the Tanala territory, having been borrowed from the Betsileo. It began as a simple adjunct to dry rice, the new crop being planted in naturally wet places in the bottoms of the valleys. From the first this work seems to have been done by households rather than joint families, the task being too small to necessitate the coöperation of the whole group. Later came small systems of terraces, also borrowed, but by the time this improvement was accepted the pattern of household cultivation of the new crop had become thoroughly established, so that joint families, as such, rarely built terrace systems or shared the produce.

Even before the introduction of wet rice the Tanala had well-developed patterns of personal property, and these, in combination with the idea of family rights to land during the brief period in which it bore a crop, opened the door to individual ownership of land and the exclusive right of a household to the rice patch it cultivated. Since rice terraces were actually growing crops throughout most of the year and had to be kept in repair even between seasons, the land which they occupied never really went out of use and therefore never reverted to the village to be reassigned. Only a limited amount of land could be utilized for this purpose due to soil, height of water available for irrigation, and other natural factors. Hence those households which had not had the energy and foresight to take up rice land at first soon found themselves permanently excluded. Insensibly there grew up within what had formerly been a classless society a class of landholders, and with this went a weakening of the joint family organization. Loyalty to this unit had been maintained largely by the economic interdependence of its members and their constant need for coöperation. But a household could tend its fields of irrigated rice unaided, and its head felt a not unnatural reluctance to share the produce with persons who had contributed nothing toward it.

The rise of individual land tenure did not effect the expropriated very seriously at first, since they could continue with the older method of exploiting village land not available for irrigation. However, land within easy reach of the village would be increasingly exhausted, and the landless households had to go farther and farther afield to find jungle. Often their fields were so far away that they could not possibly go and return in the same day, so they developed the custom of building combined granaries and sleeping quarters there. These distant fields also became increasingly household rather than joint family enterprises. Perhaps the breakdown of the joint family patterns of coöperation had already progressed too far when the system was instituted, or the joint family may have been unwilling to risk any large number of men so far from home. This camping-out was dangerous, since a hostile war party could cut off a small group with ease.

One of the greatest stresses within the culture arose in connection with the periodic moving of the village. This was a deep-rooted custom, but now the villages were split into the landless, who needed to move, and the landowners, who had a capital investment in the locality and were unwilling to move. A further breakdown of the joint family system resulted. Under the old conditions villages not infrequently split and formed new units, but such splits were always along joint family lines. At most, a man who stood at the head of three or four households within the lineage would secede with his group and found a distinct lineage in the new village. Now when villages split it was the expropriated who moved, so that the immigrant group formed a cross-section of the original lineages. In the new locality the same process went on again until the land which had formed the range of the original mobile village was dotted with descendant villages each held in place by the irrigated fields about it.

The combination of increasingly settled life and breakdown of the joint family into its component households had still further results. The mobile villages had been socially self-contained, endogamous units. The settled villages were much less so. The joint family retained its religious importance, based on the worship of a common ancestor, after it had lost much of its functional importance and even after its component households had been scattered. Family members from different villages would still be called together on some ceremonial occasions, and this going and coming helped to break down the old patterns of village isolation. Intermarriages became increasingly common, especially among the clans of the Menabe division whose pattern of cross-cousin marriage often made such matings necessary. Thus the original pattern of independent village groups was increasingly transformed into a tribal one.

The new conditions also had important repercussions on the patterns of native warfare. The mobile villages had always fortified themselves with a simple ditch and stockade, but there was little point in expending a vast amount of labor on a site which would presently be abandoned. An enemy war party, using surprise, had a fair opportunity of taking such a village, seizing a rich booty of cattle and personable young women, and driving the group out of its territory, which could then be added to the enemy's own range. In fact this was a normal procedure whenever a village felt itself crowded. Now that permanent residence in a village was assured, the villagers could set themselves seriously to the work of fortification, and by the time the Europeans arrived some of the eastern villages, which had gotten wet rice first and hence been settled longest, had made themselves impregnable to anything short of artillery. I was told of one village which was protected by three concentric ditches each twenty feet wide and of the same depth, straight-sided and with hedges of prickly pear planted between. The Tanala probably copied this form of defense from the Betsileo, although they had not adopted it while they still followed the mobile pattern. The new conditions made what was already a well-known foreign trait desirable, and it was accepted accordingly.

Since the natives had no siege machinery, these great fortifications reduced war to a stalemate. It was impossible for an attacking party to take a village except by treachery, and the large, determined war parties of the earlier period degenerated more and more into small groups of raiders who aimed to cut off stragglers. This tendency was increased by an increase in the value of slaves. The presence of Arab, European, and Imerina slave-traders, who gave guns in exchange, had something to do with this, but their activities were never carried on on a large scale. In part, at least, this increased importance of slaves was correlated with the new crop. Under the old system slaves were of little economic value, while now they could be put to work in the rice fields. With the rise of slavery there came an increasing need for techniques of ransom and other relations involving captive slaves, and these were gradually developed. In particular, a technique arose for regularizing the relations between a slave woman and her master, her family paying half her market value and thus promoting her to the status of a legal wife. In this way still further bonds were established between villages, even when these belonged to different clans, and the whole tribe was drawn more and more together.

The last step in this drama of change came less than a century ago. In the early mobile period Tanala organization was highly democratic. The head of one of the lineages in a village acted as a magistrate and executive, but there was no formal investiture of any sort and he had no real power. Outside the village there was no recognized authority of any sort. The settled tribes to the east, on the other hand, had had kings for some centuries and were in process of developing a sort of feudal system which cut across the old clan-locality lines and strengthened the central authority. About 1840 one of the Tanala clans established domination over several of the other northern clans, declared itself royal, and announced that the hereditary head of its senior lineage was now King of the Tanala Menabe. Incidentally the control of this king always remained rather weak and he never really controlled any of the groups who were still mobile. Over the settled clans he was able to exercise some real authority, but the kingdom came to an end before adequate machinery for government could be developed or borrowed. This first king introduced two new elements of culture, both taken from the Betsileo. He built himself an individual tomb, thus breaking a long-established Tanala custom, and after his death the Tanala accepted the belief that the souls of their kings passed into snakes.

It was a far cry from the mobile, self-contained Tanala villages with their classless society and strong joint families to the Tanala kingdom with its central authority, settled subjects, rudimentary social classes based on economic differences, and lineages of little more than ceremonial importance. However, the transformation can be traced step by step and at every step we find irrigated rice at the bottom of the change. It created a condition which necessitated either a modification of preëxisting patterns or the adoption of patterns already developed in the neighboring tribes who had had a longer time to meet these problems. The introduction of the new crop produced a series of maladjustments, first in the culture elements which were in most immediate contact with it, then in other and more remote elements. To the student of the static aspects of integration these maladjustments are of great importance, since they throw into relief the interrelations of the elements concerned, interrelations which would not otherwise be obvious. Thus the dependence of the joint family pattern upon the necessity for coöperative labor and the check upon the accumulation of individual wealth which the old method of agriculture entailed become clear only when we observe the breakdown of this pattern under the impact of the new conditions. Again the relation of the joint family pattern to the social isolation of villages becomes plain only through the decrease in this isolation which accompanied the abandonment of the joint family as the basis of village fission and the creation of new communities.

The example also serves to illustrate the way in which, during any process of cultural change, disintegration and reintegration go on side by side. Certain parts of the culture had already achieved a working adjustment when others were just beginning to feel the disruptive effects of the new element. Thus the conflict between the factors of land exhaustion and capital investment in irrigated rice fields had been temporarily compounded by the development of techniques for using more distant lands before the patterns of village isolation had been seriously affected by the new conditions. The cultural transformation produced all sorts of stresses, with individual discomforts and interest conflicts of a new type, but in spite of these the society survived intact and the bulk of its members were still adequately fed and clothed. Moreover, only one clan in the entire tribe rejected the new culture element which was the root of the disturbance.

This clan, the Zafimaniry, lived on the edge of the Betsileo territory and were one of the first Tanala groups to take up irrigated rice culture. According to their traditions, they raised it for a considerable time. Then an enemy attack which came when the men of the various households were scattered on their individual holdings resulted in heavy loss. Perhaps the clan was already becoming conscious of the social difficulties which acceptance of the new technique entailed. If so, this incident brought matters to a head. The tribe tabooed the raising of wet rice and they still refuse to raise it in spite of the depletion of their jungle and mild government pressure during the past generation. Some years ago a group of Betsileo were settled in their territory to exploit land which was available for irrigated rice and which was not in use. Although these immigrants had the backing of the European authorities, the Zafimaniry attacked them, broke down the rice terraces, and drove them out.

Such rejection of a trait which has already achieved a considerable measure of acceptance is unusual. More commonly the receiving group is too conscious of the immediate advantages of the new element, the factors which have been responsible for its acceptance in the first place. They cling to it at the same time that they bewail its results. The desire to have one's cake and eat it too seems to be a universal human characteristic. However, no matter how great the disturbance which the new element may set up, the society survives and eventually succeeds in reaching a cultural accommodation. It seems that no element which is sufficiently compatible with a culture to be received at all can permanently disrupt a culture or destroy a society. Both possess an amazing vitality and an almost infinite capacity for change and adaptation. When the difficulties resulting from the acceptance of a new trait become apparent, the inventive ability of the society's members is at once brought into play and both the new trait and the preëxisting traits are progressively modified until they have been brought into agreement.

The disruptive effects of the acceptance of any new culture element and the difficulties attendant upon the reintegration of the culture configuration will, of course, differ profoundly from case to case. There are certain elements the adoption of which hardly causes a ripple. Thus a new form of ornament or the acceptance of a habit like smoking will usually have little effect on the culture as a whole. The situation which it creates can be met by minor changes in the elements upon which it immediately impinges. Any element the acceptance of which involves an important change in economic life will, on the other hand, entail a long series of compensating modifications. The securing of food, shelter, and survival to a society's members is the most basic function of any culture, since without these no society can survive. It is here that culture is in most intimate contact with the hard facts of the material world, facts which cannot be changed, still less ignored. The techniques connected with the satisfaction of these basic biological needs thus become the foundation upon which the whole elaborate superstructure of the culture is reared. Any change in this foundation shakes the whole fabric and entails a large measure of reconstruction. At the same time, economic techniques are more easily communicable and more obviously advantageous or disadvantageous than any other elements of culture which can be offered for acceptance. Their relation to the rest of the culture fabric is rarely obvious to those who share the culture, and societies are thus constantly trapped into accepting elements which are highly disruptive.

Such elements as a new ornament and the cultivation of irrigated rice might be taken to represent the opposite ends of the scale. Most new culture traits are more disruptive than the first and less so than the last. In this respect they present an infinite series of gradation. No two elements will ever be exactly the same in their disruptive effects upon even the same culture, nor will the same element have identical effects in any two cultures. In general, the extent of the changes which the acceptance of a new element entails will be directly proportional to the importance in the preëxisting culture configuration of the traits with which it comes into conflict. The results of the introduction of Christianity into various native societies serve to illustrate this point. Due to the peculiar conditions under which this element is usually introduced, any extensive adaptive modifications in the element itself are rendered difficult. The European missionary always labors to propagate his particular creed and ritual in complete and unchanged form. He is always backed by European prestige if not by more active agencies, and if the natives accept the new faith at all they must take it very much as it is offered to them.

In such a culture as that of Samoa, where religion seems to

have been of rather minor functional importance in pre-European times, the introduction of Christianity has had few disruptive effects and its integration has been easy. The chiefs have come to dominate the new faith much as they dominated the old and have been able to turn it to much the same uses. The change has hardly touched the preëxisting patterns of native life. However in Madagascar the introduction of Christianity has had profound disruptive effects. Here much of the native life was influenced by the original ancestor worship, and fear of the ancestors' displeasure was the main stimulus to socially acceptable behavior. When this stimulus was removed the whole culture configuration was disrupted, and although it is now in process of reintegration certain values seem to have been permanently lost. Thus theft, which was almost unknown in pagan times, has become a commonplace in Christian groups. The fear of hell and the police are a poor substitute for the fear of the ancestral ghosts who knew everything and punished the evil-doer with sickness on earth and exclusion from the ancestral village in the hereafter. Again, it is possible to tell immediately upon entering a native village whether the inhabitants are Christian or pagan simply by the condition of the houses and streets. Pagan villages are clean, since the ancestral spirits approve of this and punish slackness. Christian villages, where this sanction has been destroyed, are normally filthy.

This brings us at once to the question of how great a degree of cultural integration is necessary to survival. No culture, of course, will ever be in a perfect state of integration, i.e., have all its elements in a condition of complete mutual adjustment, as long as change of any sort is under way. Since change of some sort, whether due to invention or diffusion, is always going on, this means that no culture is ever perfectly integrated at any point in its history. Integration thus becomes a matter of degree and presumably there is a point below which it cannot sink without the paralysis of the culture and the consequent destruction of the society as a functioning entity. However, this point is rarely if ever reached. All cultures possess an amazing capacity for change and adaptation. It seems that they are able eventually to integrate any new culture element or series of elements which are not in such direct and complete opposition to basic elements in the existing configuration that the society rejects them from the first.

In this the fact that culture is a socio-psychological and not a physical phenomenon once more comes to the fore. The degree of integration which is required for its successful functioning is in no way comparable to that necessary to the successful functioning of an organism. Cultures, like personalities, are perfectly capable of including conflicting elements and logical inconsistencies. There are only two points in the entire culture configuration where such inconsistencies and lack of mutual adjustments can have a paralyzing effect. One of these is in the core of the culture, that mass of largely sub-conscious values, associations, and conditioned emotional responses which provide the culture with its vitality and the individual with motivations for exercising and adhering to its patterns. The other is in the most superficial zone of culture, that of the habitual patterns for overt behavior. Maladjustments in the first of these leads to constant emotional conflicts within the individual, conflicts between individuals who have made a different choice of values, and a loss of the group's *esprit de corps*. Maladjustments in the second result in constant interference and lost motion, not to mention a chronic state of irritation.

The elements which compose the core of any culture need not necessarily be consistent in all respects. In fact there are plenty of instances in which a particular society holds values which seem to be quite incompatible. Societies, like individuals, are capable of ambivalent attitudes. The Apaches are a good example of this. They combine respect for relatives, genuine affection for them, and a high degree of economic and social dependence upon them with a considerable degree of fear of them. However, such cases are rare. In most instances the conflicts between elements in the core of a culture are more apparent than real. Values which are logically inconsistent with each other or which introduce potentialities of conflict are adjusted by limiting their expression to particular culturally recognized situations. Thus in our own culture the high value which we attach to human life *per se* and the high value which we also attach to war would seem to be diametrically opposed. The average member of our society is able to recognize both without emotional conflict simply by exercising the first with relation to members of his own society and the second with relation to members of other societies. Similar adjustments can be found in all cultures, even the ambivalent attitudes serving to balance each other and prevent the disruption of the society.

The possibility of serious conflicts being produced in the core of any culture as a result of diffusion is relatively slight. We have already pointed out that there are inherent difficulties connected with the expression of the elements which form this part of culture. In many cases they cannot even be adequately verbalized. The chances of their being perceived by individuals reared in another culture are therefore small, and their chances of adoption by a whole society still smaller. The core of any culture is thus largely immune to direct disturbance through the introduction of new elements in fully developed form. It will, of course, be indirectly affected by any important changes in the total culture configuration, but these effects are of a sort which allows time for adjustment.

The content of the culture core is subject to change, like all other parts of culture, but the changes are normally much more gradual than those which take place in the culture's more superficial elements. Certain basic elements may be abandoned if some transformation in the outward aspects of the group's life persistently interferes with their expression in overt behavior. Thus the high value attached to war and personal courage in the cultures of all our Plains tribes can hardly fail to wane when war has been eliminated for several generations. However, this loss is rarely followed by the adoption of new elements which have been developed in other cultures. Thus the loss of the war value in the Plains has not been compensated for by an adoption of the work value of the whites. These tribes are still unconvinced regarding the honorable nature of labor or its desirability for its own sake. Changes in the basic values of a group seem to come almost entirely from within and to be less the result of competition between new and established elements than of conflicts between established elements and an external situation which the society and culture are powerless to modify. Any one who has worked with non-Europeans in process of acculturation can testify how few of the European values win genuine emotional acceptance. Even when the members of such a group have assumed all the trappings of white civilization, some unexpected happening will reveal that the core of the old culture is still alive and vigorous.

Since the changes in the cultural core are slow and more or less evolutionary in their character, they rarely entail serious conflicts. Old elements are abandoned and new ones developed in close and constant relation to the existing configuration. If the developing elements come into serious conflict with firmly established parts of this configuration, their further growth will be checked until such time as changes in the configuration have made its resumption possible. This part of culture can, therefore, maintain a high degree of integration through any normal process of cultural change. It can progressively adapt itself to new conditions and at the same time maintain its integrity, bending elements which have been accepted into the more superficial levels of the culture to a reaffirmation of the old values. Thus the Dakota, in accepting Christianity, have used the white custom of church donations to reëmphasize their old tribal pattern of honoring individuals by making gifts in their behalf. Such donations are phrased as being made in honor of so-and-so, and both this individual and the giver participate in the resulting prestige. The original white concept that the donor thus acquired merit in heaven and compensated for past misdeeds seems to have hardly been transferred at all.

It seems probable that as long as any society can maintain its integrity the core of its culture can escape disruption through the sudden introduction of new elements. However, serious disruption is likely to occur when two societies and cultures are in process of genuine fusion. In such cases there is certain to be a period during which growing individuals are exposed to two sets of values each of which may be internally consistent but which are at the same time sharply opposed in certain of their elements. Such conflicts are often reflected in conflicts within the personalities of the unfortunate individuals who have fallen heir to such a situation, and in increasing indifference to social values. However, the values which the two systems have in common will tend to persist even in such cases and will provide the foundation for the evolution of a new core of mutually adjusted elements.

Conflicts between a culture's patterns for overt behavior might be expected to have more immediately disastrous results than conflicts within the culture core. Unless the actual behavior of a society's members is adjusted in such a way as to prevent mutual interference and constant oppositions, the society simply cannot function. At this point it is necessary to emphasize again the distinction between culture patterns and the actual behavior of a society's members. The behavior itself is much more flexible than the patterns which influence it. It is always adjusted both to the pattern and to the actual situation in which the individual finds himself. This makes the compounding and adjustment of pattern conflicts relatively easy. All individuals possess a happy capacity for thinking or believing one thing and doing another. For this reason, conflict between two patterns does not necessarily result in the immediate rejection of either, but it does lead to immediate modifications in the behavior for which these patterns theoretically serve as a model. These immediate modifications in behavior will react on the patterns, in the long run, and lead to their modification and mutual adjustment. Behavior patterns are actually the easiest of all culture elements to modify, and most cultural change begins with them.

In addition to the core of the culture and its actual behavior patterns there are always many other elements conflict between which will not result in either emotional conflicts within the individual or interference with the necessary activities of the group. Inconsistencies in this zone are constantly present, but the individuals who share the culture are usually serenely unconscious of them. The desire for logical consistency within a culture is limited to highly sophisticated groups. It cannot develop until a people has ceased to take its culture entirely for granted, as is the common way of mankind. Even then the attempt to achieve consistency is usually left to specialists such as priests. The average individual can hold a whole series of conflicting beliefs as long as the behavior patterns which are related to these beliefs do not themselves involve direct conflict. Thus the average Protestant American of the early nineteenth century held three distinct and mutually contradictory beliefs with regard to the state of souls in the after life. He believed that the dead slept until the Day of Judgment, when soul and body alike would be resurrected. This was the concept which had the strongest backing in church dogma. He simultaneously believed that souls went directly to heaven or hell at death and that the blessed had no desire to return to earth, while the wicked were unable to do so. Lastly, he believed that souls, especially wicked souls, might appear to the living as ghosts and injure the living, although he had no clear idea as to just how they might injure them. The logical inconsistency of these beliefs did not trouble him in the least. The same man could be profoundly moved by a sermon on the Day of Judgment, speak of beloved relatives as awaiting him in heaven and look forward on his deathbed to immediate reunion with them, and have a lively fear of graveyards after dark.

One school of anthropologists have devoted much time and erudition to proving that uncivilized peoples do not think logically. This is essentially correct, the only error being that neither do civilized ones. Both can apply logic when it is necessary for the attainment of particular ends, but neither civilized nor uncivilized apply it habitually or, under normal conditions, use it to test the mutual consistency of the elements of culture to which they have been reared. The desire to reduce ideas to logical order is probably as much culturally conditioned as is the desire to reduce words to a particular order and make them into a poem. We have been trained to the belief that logical consistency is desirable, but in most cases the only effect of this is to make the individual angry rather than mildly surprised when the inconsistencies of his own beliefs are pointed out to him. After all, this capacity for inconsistency has its uses. It is the thing which makes it possible for men to achieve integrated personalities and at the same time survive in an unstable and constantly changing environment. The rare individual who is genuinely consistent in thought and act is always a burden to his friends and, if he carries this tendency to its logical conclusion, is likely to end his days in an asylum.

It must be remembered that culture is a socio-psychological phenomenon, not an organic one. If it can be said to exist at all, it consists of the elements which are shared by the personalities of the individuals who participate in it and which receive emotional reinforcement from this sharing. It is idle therefore to assume *a priori* that the elements which compose a culture must have a higher degree of mutual adjustment and logical consistency than the elements within any successfully adapted personality. To perform its functions successfully a culture need only be integrated to the point where it has eliminated paralyzing conflicts in emotional responses and overt behavior. It can successfully incorporate all sorts of logical inconsistencies and even emotional conflicts of a minor sort just as an individual personality can incorporate them.

It is quite true that the more perfectly the elements of a culture are adjusted to each other the more smoothly and efficiently these elements can function. This no doubt accounts for the observed tendency of cultures which are shielded from disturbing contacts and the diffusion of new elements to develop a more and more perfect state of integration. However, the culture configuration is itself only a part of a larger configuration which includes the total environment of the group. Its elements must adapt themselves to this larger configuration as well as to each other. The process of integration is constantly going on in all cultures and, carried to its logical conclusion, would eventually result in perfect internal and external adjustment with the consequent elimination of all necessity for change. Actually, this condition of perfect adjustment is never reached. Either some new element is added to the culture complex through invention or diffusion or there is a change in the society's environment, disturbing the state of balance and making cultural modifications necessary.

Actually, the value of a high degree of culture integration to a society must always be relative to the society's environment. In a stable environment, the greater the degree of cultural integration the better. However, the higher the degree of mutual adjustment and consequent interdependence between the elements which compose a culture, the more far-reaching the effects of any changes in the content either of the culture or its environmental setting. The increased efficiency which comes with a heightened degree of integration is balanced by a corresponding loss of the ability to alter the culture rapidly and with a minimum of discomfort to the society's members. The situation is comparable in certain respects to that existing in the case of those organisms which have achieved an adaptation to a particular environment which is so perfect that when that environment changes they are unable to readapt to the new conditions and simply disappear.

Perhaps an example may make this clear. The Pawnee had an extremely rich, internally consistent, and well-integrated culture. The elements which gave it its wealth of content were thoroughly adapted to each other and mutually interdependent to a very large degree. Comanche culture, on the other hand, was comparatively poor in content and full of all sorts of minor maladjustments which were due in large part to their recent arrival in the southern Plains and their extensive borrowings from the various groups with whom they were in contact. It seems safe to say that prior to the arrival of the whites Comanche culture was less efficient in providing for the needs of its society than Pawnee culture. Material needs were adequately met, but there was a great deal of friction between individuals. When the arrival of the whites produced profound changes in the environment of both groups, the well-integrated Pawnee culture held out for a time and then practically collapsed. The adoption of the culture elements necessary to the new conditions disintegrated the whole structure. The Comanche culture, in spite of the sudden elimination of their central war activity and their accustomed economic activities, did not collapse. New elements were adopted readily and integrated easily. Although stresses and emotional conflicts were not lacking, these never became as extreme as they did in the case of most of the other Plains tribes. Even the Ghost Dance, which was fundamentally an expression of despair, won only a few followers. Within two generations the Comanche had achieved a fairly good adaptation to the new conditions without the sacrifice of their cultural or social integrity. Their attitude toward the local whites is one of amiable avoidance. They have accepted elements from their culture with discrimination and have reinterpreted these in such a way that the greater part of their own values have remained intact. Thus the present peyote ritual prescribes the use of "Bull Durham" for the sacred cigarettes and of "Arbuckle" coffee for the morning feast in exactly the same terms that it prescribes the construction of the lodge fire. Again, the acceptance of the automobile was accompanied by the development of a taboo against parking one behind a medicine man's house. This arose immediately from old ideas that grease and passing behind a medicine man were both prejudicial to his powers.

In the example just cited new culture elements have been taken over without modification in their superficial form and incorporated into the preëxisting configuration by a process of reinterpretation. Their integration has been achieved not by changes in the elements as they were objectively received but by a selective ascription of functions and the addition of a new associational context. The possible ascription of functions is, of course, limited by the new element's inherent potentialities for use, but it rests upon a selective process in which certain of these potentialities are employed and others ignored. The fact that new elements can be adapted to a preëxisting culture configuration by the addition of an associational context is another proof of the relative looseness of the mutual interdependence of culture elements. Actually we know that what are, from the purely objective point of view, identical elements or complexes of elements may be an integral part of two or more widely different culture configurations. Thus the material culture of the Tlingit and Haida tribes appears to be identical. The only known difference is that the Tlingit sometimes employ maple wood for utensils, while this material is not available in the Haida territory. At the same time, the Tlingit and Haida culture configurations are markedly different in a number of respects. Again, the horse and hunting complexes of the Plains Indians were strikingly similar throughout the entire area. The tribal differences which did exist in the horse complex were limited to such minor items as whether the carrying frame or *travois* was oval or round and the relative height of saddles. Similarly, the surround method of hunting buffalo was universally employed, the only recognizable tribal differences being in the degree of discipline imposed upon the hunters. Nevertheless, these uniform elements were integrated in the various configurations in which they occurred with a wide variety of types of social organization and even of religious ideas and practices. Some of the tribes that used them had a well-marked clan organization, others a simple family organization; some of the tribes had patterns of pseudo-aristocracy with inheritance of rank and office, others were essentially equalitarian; some were patrilineal, others matrilineal. Again, religion ranged from the carefully guarded, purely personal powers of the Nez Percé to the thoroughly socialized clan powers and public rituals of the Pawnee.

It is clear that what we call integration in a culture can have little in common with any organic phenomenon. It can exist with surprisingly little modification in the objective aspects of the elements which have been integrated, which means that the mutual adaptations of culture elements cannot be deduced from a study of their form. Understanding of the principles of integration can be achieved only by studying it actually in process, and very few investigations of this sort have so far been made. As in the case of diffusion, our present state of knowledge raises more questions than it answers.

CHAPTER XXI

HISTORIC RECONSTRUCTIONS

Before we leave the discussion of culture content and the processes of culture change, some attention should be given to the matter of historic reconstruction. Since the content of a culture at any point in its development is very largely determined by past events, any method which makes it possible for us to ascertain these events is of great value for an understanding of the present. However, the anthropologists' techniques for such reconstruction are still faulty. Until we know more about the actual processes of invention and diffusion, all conclusions as to the points of origin of various culture elements, the routes by which they have spread, and especially the rates at which they have spread must remain tentative.

The best evidence for historic reconstructions is, of course, that provided by contemporary documents and archæological finds. However, such evidence is always incomplete, and it is entirely lacking for many cultures. The only universally applicable approach to the problem is that of the study of trait distributions and the subsequent analysis of these distributions. From this it is possible to ascertain, with varying degrees of probability, the various contacts which any given culture continuum has had with other continuums and even, in a still more tentative way, the sequence in which these contacts have occurred.

The first step in such a study is, of course, the actual mapping of the distribution of a particular trait or complex of traits. This is complicated by the fact that the possibility of an independent origin for similar traits in different cultures can never be completely excluded. There are wide differences of opinion regarding the importance of this factor. Thus certain schools of anthropological thought completely discount its influence and hold that the presence of similar traits in two cultures is always an indication of contact irrespective of the distance which may separate these cultures in either time or space. This theory does not, of course, exclude the possibility of indirect contacts through intermediary cultures or of the borrowing of the particular trait by both cultures from some third one. It simply means that they base their conclusions on the assumption that every trait of culture has originated but once and at only one point. At the other end of the scale lies the Evolutionary school, now largely defunct, which holds that similar elements of culture arise spontaneously under similar conditions of environment and culture advance. The truth undoubtedly lies somewhere between these two extremes. Independent invention has been more frequent than the extreme Diffusionists admit, less so than the Evolutionists believe.

The independent development of similar traits within two cultures may be due to either *convergence* or *parallelism*. In convergence the trait is developed independently out of two totally distinct culture backgrounds. An excellent example of this would be the fire piston, a contrivance which uses the heat generated by the sudden compression of air to ignite some inflammable substance. This appliance was invented by some group in southeastern Asia and is still used by many of the Malayan tribes in this region. Needless to say, these groups have no comprehension of the physical principles involved. The possibility of producing fire in this way must have been discovered by accident and the apparatus perfected by subsequent experiments. A similar appliance was developed in Europe during the early nineteenth century, but in this case it grew out of a deliberate attempt to apply a principle which had been discovered in the course of experiments in physics. The principle was understood before a practical application for it had been developed. Another case of convergence would be the erection of huge pyramidal structures in both Egypt and Mexico. The origin and purpose of these structures was quite different in each case. The Egyptian pyramid was evolved from the *mastaba* type of tomb and was always a mortuary structure, while the Mexican pyramid was evolved from a house platform and was primarily a foundation for the temple or altar erected on its top. Nevertheless, the superficial resemblance of the two is rather striking.

In *parallelism,* two societies have received a common element of culture at some point in the more or less remote past or have made the same basic invention. Through a series of improving inventions this original element has then been developed into closely similar forms in the two areas. A good example of such development based on independent discovery of the same principle in two areas is the blow-gun in South America and Malaysia. In both cases the development of this appliance must have begun with the discovery that small objects could be propelled by blowing them through a tube, a principle which we too employ in our bean-shooters. This discovery was made easy by the presence in both regions of long-jointed species of bamboo. In both regions the possibilities of the new discovery were recognized and more and more perfect adaptations developed, probably through unconscious experiment. It was found that certain guns worked better than others and these were copied and the more successful variants produced in the process copied again. In this way wooden guns with bores of nearly the same diameter and much the same type of arrow were developed in the two regions. It is interesting to note that recent experiments have shown that the caliber of these guns is actually that which gives the greatest range, sizes above or below it rapidly losing efficiency. Examples of parallelism based on the reception of the same element by two cultures and its subsequent independent development are hard to find. The great difficulty lies in proving that the developments really have been independent, since the contact which gave the same element to both in the first place is likely to be continued. However, it seems to be proved for the development of certain grammatic forms in some languages of the Indo-European group.

Convergence and parallelism are of importance to the present discussion only as they introduce a possible factor of error into the plotting of trait distributions. This error can be largely although not completely eliminated by taking certain factors into account. The first of these is that of the apparent probability of contact between the two cultures in which a similar trait occurs. To establish this their separation in both time and space must be considered. It is obvious that separation in time constitutes the most complete bar, yet its importance has frequently been overlooked. Thus the numerous attempts to prove a connection between the Mayan and Egyptian civilizations have uniformly ignored the time interval separating them. Egypt was already a Roman province when the Mayas erected their first dated monument. If there had been any contacts between the two civilizations after this time, there could hardly fail to be some historic record of them. Moreover, elements of classical culture would almost certainly have been transmitted with those of Egyptian culture, since the Egyptians of this period were not seafarers, while the classical peoples were. Elements of culture can only be carried across a time gap by some intermediary culture which receives from the older and gives to the younger. Since time is one of the primary factors in culture change, this intermediary is unlikely to pass on the element as it received it. When, therefore, we find closely similar elements in cultures separated by a wide time interval, the probability of their diffusion is not great.

Separation in space is a less effective bar to diffusion than separation in time, and in evaluating its importance a number of factors must be taken into account. Space is important only with respect to the influence which it has upon contacts. A thousand miles of sea may present little hindrance to contact between groups familiar with navigation, while fifty miles will be an effective bar to groups without boats. When contacts seem unlikely, the probability of similarities being due to convergence is greatly increased. Perhaps it would be more correct to say that the probability of diffusion is decreased, since the possibility of independent invention is more nearly a constant than are opportunities for borrowing. Thus one of the more primitive tribes in Borneo is said to have a concept of personal supernatural guardians which is reminiscent in several respects of that held by our own Plains tribes. In view of the distance between the two localities and the complete lack of direct or indirect contact prior to the arrival of Europeans, it seems highly improbable that there is any connection between the culture of the Plains and that of Borneo. On the other hand, the numerous similarities between the guardian concept in the Plains and the Eastern woodlands can be explained more readily on the basis of diffusion than on any other. The two groups were close to each other in space and were in constant contact on the margins of their respective areas.

Of course the possibility of irregular and more or less chance diffusion of isolated elements between distant localities which have no regular contacts can never be ignored. This is especially the case when there is some mobile group which may act as an intermediary. We know that within the historic period some very curious trait distributions have arisen through the activities of white traders. Thus there is a particular type of silver brooch whose present use is limited to the Indian tribes living about the western Great Lakes and one tribe in the interior of the Philippines. This particular type of brooch seems to have been invented by the Scottish Highlanders, although more remote origins might be found for it. In the sixteenth and seventeenth centuries the French made these brooches in large numbers for the Highland trade, and consignments of them were also included in shipments sent to America for the Indian trade. Apparently they caught the fancy of the tribes living about the Great Lakes and these soon learned to make them for themselves, preserving the original form but adding decorative incised designs drawn from their own art. The Spaniards also took brooches of this type, obtained from the same French manufacturers, to the Philippines. In the Philippines only one tribe became interested in these brooches, but they also learned to make them and still do so. Europeans long since ceased to make or use them, and if we did not have historic records we would certainly assume that the present distribution of this trait is due to convergence.

A further and perhaps more important check on the identification of traits is derived from the qualities of the traits themselves. Independent invention seems to be rare enough so that when there have been any opportunities for either direct or indirect contacts the presence of a trait in two cultures is more likely to be due to diffusion than to convergence. The probability of diffusion increases in direct ratio to both the degree of resemblance in the traits under consideration and the complexity of these traits. The greater the complexity, the greater the difficulty of invention and consequently the smaller the probability of independent origin. This is especially true in the case of complexes of traits which recur in two or more cultures in closely similar form. The probability of diffusion varies inversely with the functional interdependence of the traits which form such a complex.

An example may make this clear. The fact that the Marquesans and the Maori of New Zealand both used canoes does not imply that these two groups were ever in direct contact or even that they both received the canoe from some third culture. The canoe principle is a fairly simple one which might very well have been discovered independently by several societies. However, when we come to analyze the particular types of canoe used by the Maori and Marquesans, a number of similarities become evident. In both cases the canoe consists of a dugout body to which are added side planks and bow and stern pieces. These increase the efficiency of the canoe, especially in rough weather, and their addition to the dugout body calls for no great degree of inventive ability. The possibility of independent origin is not destroyed by this resemblance, although its probability is diminished. Actually, the probability of independent origin is still further reduced in this case by the presence of this type of construction in many other parts of the Pacific. While it might be invented two or three times, it is hard to imagine it being invented twenty or thirty times, especially when its distribution among a series of seafaring peoples can be so readily explained on the diffusion basis.

The presence of the five-piece canoe in both localities would thus establish a fairly strong presumption of some sort of direct or indirect culture contact. As we continue our analysis of the two canoe types this presumption becomes increasingly strong. The two show likeness in many details which are in no way related to increased efficiency. Thus in both the bow piece projects horizontally for some distance beyond the end of the dugout body and terminates in a carving. In both the end of the stern piece curves upward into a tall, thin vertical fin, not unlike the forward end of the runner of an old-fashioned sleigh. Lastly, in both, the seam between the body of the canoe and the side planks is covered on the outside with a batten which is lashed on in the same way and decorated at the lashings with tufts of feathers from the same species of sea bird. The stern fin actually detracts from the efficiency of the canoe, making it harder to steer and more liable to capsize in a strong wind, while the feather decorations can have only an esthetic or magical purpose. The chances of all these unessential features being invented independently and in this particular combination are not one in several million. In the case of the feathers alone, the natives of the two groups had a great number of species to choose from. The whole series of resemblances, taken together, make the probability of the common origin of the two canoe types so high that it amounts almost to a certainty. In any purely distributional study the investigator would be quite justified in classing these two canoe types together.

After trait distributions have been established the real work of the historic reconstructionist begins. This work consists in determining the relative frequency of past contacts between particular cultures, the nature of these contacts, and the chronological order of the contacts. Conclusions with regard to any of these matters can, again, be expressed only in terms of probability. The frequency and nature of past contacts is derived from a study of the whole group of culture elements which are common to the cultures under consideration, with a check against such other factors as distance and probability of contact. Thus, to revert to our Maori-Marquesan example, the close similarity of the two canoe types is almost indisputable evidence of contact of some sort. However, if this element were the only one common to the two cultures, it would be safe to say that its presence was due to some chance contact of brief duration. Even a drift canoe carried from one locality to the other by ocean currents might conceivably account for it. However, when we make a complete analysis of the two cultures in question we find a long series of similarities extending not only to manufacturers but to such things as religious concepts, social patterns, and even language. Many of these resemblances are quite as striking as those in the canoes. Moreover, many of the elements are of a sort which it would be difficult to transmit without long and intimate contact between the two groups. We must conclude, therefore, that at some point in their history these two cultures were either the same or stood in a very close relationship to each other. Here geographic factors come into play to influence the conclusions. The localities where these two cultures existed in historic times were so far apart that even direct voyages from one to the other must have been beyond the ability of the natives. The largest of their seagoing craft, even those described from the traditional period, could not have carried supplies for such a trip. However, there are in both localities what appear to be fairly authentic traditions of immigration from an intervening locality, the Society Islands. In this case the necessary voyages were within the scope of possibility. It seems highly probable, therefore, that the common elements of Marquesan and Maori culture were derived by both from the Society Islands. Moreover, the similarities are so numerous and the contact required for their transmission is so close that there is a high degree of possibility that their presence is not due to diffusion in the ordinary sense. It seems much more probable that both the Marquesan and Maori cultures spring from a common source in the culture of the Society Islands. In other words, their similarities are due to a common origin. They represent divergent developments of a single ancient culture which was carried by immigrants to both the Marquesas and New Zealand and underwent subsequent divergent modifications in the two localities.

This brings us at once to the second of the reconstructionist's problems, that of establishing time sequences. In the case just under discussion, the historic culture of the Society Islands differed more from that of either the Marquesas or New Zealand than these differed from each other. In fact it showed more numerous resemblances to the cultures of western Polynesia and Hawaii than it did to either the Marquesas or New Zealand. Since everything points to the Society Group, or at least some other group in the immediate region, such as the Australs, as the starting point for the Marquesan and Maori migrations, it seems almost certain that a culture of Maori-Marquesan type once existed in this region. If so, it could only have existed there prior to the development of the modern Society Island type of culture. The affiliations of this modern type, as revealed by a further study of trait distributions, seems to indicate that its presence was due either to the diffusion of various culture elements from western Polynesia or, more probably, to actual migrations from that region.

In making this time reconstruction we have employed the principle of marginal survivals. This has already been discussed in Chapter XIX. The elements common to Maori and Marquesan culture are marginal survivals with relation to the Society Island center of emigration. They have lingered on in these more distant localities after their replacement in the central locality. In this case the geographic conditions make the assumption that these traits actually are marginal survivals appear valid. However, it is obvious that the area which is taken into consideration in a study of trait distributions will have a great deal to do with this aspect of the evidence and consequently with the investigator's conclusions. Thus a trait which appears to be central and is therefore presumably late with respect to a particular area may appear marginal and therefore presumably early when the studies are extended to a wider region. To cite a single example, the limited occurrence of domiciliary mounds in the Mississippi Valley and the steady diminution in their numbers as one goes toward the margins of this area would certainly suggest that they were a late development here. However, if we extend the region to include Mexico, a good case could be made for them as marginal survivals of an ancient type of construction which there developed into the temple pyramid. The relative rarity of mortuary mounds in Mexico and their frequency in the Mississippi Valley suggests that, if mound-building was diffused to the Mississippi Valley from Mexico, the domiciliary mound may very well have been the first form transmitted and the adaptation of this type of earth construction to mortuary purposes may have been a later and local development of the basic trait of mound-building.

Another difficulty which attends the application of the marginal survival principle is that, although there have unquestionably been certain cultures which took and for a time maintained the lead in cultural advance within a particular area of communication, we have abundant evidence that such leadership may pass from one group to another. Thus northern Europe was very definitely a marginal area with respect to the elements of civilization developed first in the Near East and later in the Mediterranean region. Throughout its entire history prior to the nineteenth century it was a receiving rather than a donor culture. During the nineteenth century it suddenly forged ahead and became predominantly a donor, elements from it being diffused over the very regions and cultures from which it had previously borrowed most of its content. Again, new elements of obvious utility may arise in any culture at any time and move out from this center with little reference to the wider diffusion trends of the period. In Chapter XIX we used the simile of the ripples from a stone thrown into still water. A better simile for the actual situation would be that of the condition created by a group of boys throwing stones into the pond and sending ripples of all sizes crossing and recrossing each other. The actual spread of culture elements throughout the world cannot be represented by a few sets of concentric circles surrounding a limited number of centers and overlapping only along their edges. It would have to be shown by a vast number of circles drawn about thousands of centers and overlapping and interlacing in every conceivable way.

Unfortunately, the rates of dissemination of new culture elements are so variable that it is extremely difficult to establish centers of diffusion from trait distributions alone. If we find a particular trait common to a series of cultures which are not in direct contact, it is safe to assume that they either have been in contact at one time or have had contacts with some common donor. However, we can never be certain that this donor was located anywhere near the center of the area which the trait distribution delimits or that the cultures which lie around the margins of the area received the trait at anything like the same time. The center of dispersal may have been anywhere within the area, even on what is now its margin, or even completely outside it. Thus the flintlock gun shows a well-marked distribution in West Africa, but its use has completely died out in Europe, its point of origin. This uncertainty regarding centers of diffusion as well as rates of diffusion detracts greatly from the utility of the marginal survival principle as a tool for establishing chronological relationships. With our present very faulty knowledge of diffusion processes the historic reconstructionist can posit contacts between cultures or dissemination of culture elements to a series of other cultures from some undefined point. However, he cannot establish this point, still less the time of contact and reception. There are a few cases in which he can say that certain elements are older or newer in a culture than others, or that contacts have been remote or recent, but even these conclusions are not susceptible of complete proof. The chronological aspect of historic reconstruction is by far the weakest.

The inadequacy of the present techniques available for historic reconstruction will be made evident if we apply them to a case in which we have fairly complete historic records, ignoring these records until we have made our reconstruction. In this attempted reconstruction we will draw on the evidence which other sciences can provide, as the wise reconstructionist always does. We will even take archæological evidence into account, ignoring only the finding of actual remains or representations of the cultural element under discussion. Although this may be considered unfair, it must be remembered that for most of the reconstructions made to date no such direct evidence has actually been available.

The element which we will take as the basis of our study will be the domestication of maize, our conclusions being based on its current distribution. We can see at once that this plant is domesticated in most Old and New World localities where the climate makes it economically profitable. This very wide distribution at once suggests that maize must be one of the oldest of domesticated plants, and this conclusion is borne out by the testimony of the botanist, who tells us that it is the most highly specialized of all the domesticated seed grasses, having been developed through human agency to the point where it is dependent upon human care for its survival. We will also refer to him to determine its probable place of origin, and he will tell us that it is not very closely related to any other known plant but may be of American origin. However, this evidence must not be considered conclusive, since plant genera often have stray members turning up in unexpected parts of the world. The best check which offers is the correlation of the high degree of specialization of the plant with the archæologically indicated age of agriculture in the Old and New Worlds. Since this technique is much older in the Old World, the probability that maize is of Old World origin is greatly increased and the matter is clinched by the fact that the early agriculturists of this region domesticated a very wide variety of food grasses and made them their basic crop, while the American Indians had no domestic grasses with the exception of maize.

The origin of maize having thus been established in general terms, we seek to find its exact point of origin. Since it is a tropical plant, Europe and northern Asia are ruled out. Southeastern Asia can also be tentatively excluded, since the plant is of little economic importance here. Africa seems the best possibility, and that this is the origin point is indicated by several factors. Maize is of greater economic importance here than in any other part of the Old World and is basic to the native economy of many tribes. It is so thoroughly integrated with the rest of their culture that it seems, *a priori*, that they must have raised it for a long time. Still more conclusive is the fact that Africa lies close to the place at which we know agriculture developed and has accepted from this center the cattle half of the old grain-and-cattle complex. The Africans could not accept the grain half of this complex, since the crops which it included were unsuited to a tropical environment. What would be more natural than for them to domesticate some promising local plant to take the place of wheat? There seems to be good evidence that the natives of the Asiatic tropics did so in the case of rice. To be sure, the Africans did not use the plow in their maize culture, but this could easily be accounted for by the fact that it is poorly adapted to the habit of the plant.

Having established Africa as the origin point, let us see what part of Africa. We see at once that the plant is raised primarily in the plateau, but does best with a considerable amount of rain and humidity. Its point of origin is thus to be sought on the western edge of the plateau and, in view of spatial realtions with the southwestern Asiatic agricultural center, not too far south. The evidence points to the northeastern part of French Equatorial Africa, although it is somewhat marginal for the distribution of the plant on that continent. This conclusion is reinforced by the extensive evidences of an agricultural neolithic occupation here.

To summarize, maize was probably developed in northern French Equatorial Africa shortly after the establishment of neolithic culture in that region and diffused from there to the rest of Africa, southern Europe, and finally to southern Asia. It remains to account for its presence in America. First of all, we find maize cultivation most highly developed in a section of America which lies relatively close to Africa, and application of the same methods used for the Old World seems to show that its diffusion to the rest of the continent proceeded from this point. There are other food plants in America, notably beans and squashes, but these are botanically in no wise related to maize. Moreover, we know that Old World agriculture and the civilizations based upon it are much older than New World agriculture and civilization. We conclude, therefore, that maize was in some way introduced into America from Africa. Perhaps some Phœnician vessel was driven across the Atlantic with maize in its stores.

To those who know the actual history of maize this reconstruction must appear humorous, but it has been arrived at by the best methods and checked by more evidence than is usually available for such reconstructions. The only difficulty is that in this case we have historic records which show that maize was unknown in the Old World until after the discovery of America, that it was introduced first into western Europe, where it had little effect on the local economy, and that it spread first through the Mediterranean region. The full process of its diffusion and integration into a whole series of cultures took place within about 200 years. If such a rapid spread has been possible in the case of one culture element, especially one which profoundly affected the life of many of the societies which accepted it, it may very well have occurred in the case of other culture elements as well.

Our present research techniques make it possible for the historic reconstructionist to establish with a high degree of probability whether particular traits have been diffused. From such diffusion he can conclude, with much less probability, that certain cultures have been in contact at some point in the past and can even hazard a guess as to the length and closeness of this contact. From the latter he can also arrive at certain conclusions as to the probable movements of societies and the common origin of closely similar cultures. However, as soon as he tries to establish anything more than the most rudimentary chronological sequences for these events he finds himself completely in the dark. At most he can conclude with a moderate degree of probability that certain of these events took place prior to others. He thus finds himself very much in the position of a historian who is presented with the facts of a people's past without any of the dates. Under such circumstances the historian might be able to arrange some of these facts in chronological order, basing his conclusions on what appeared to be probable sequences of cause and effect. He would hardly be so reckless as to use these unproved sequences as a basis for generalizations in regard to the processes of history. The reconstructionist should be equally careful in the use of his own sequences for this purpose. Most of the current criticisms of historic reconstructions are based less on the reconstructions themselves than on the uses to which they have been put.

The author has no intention of questioning the value of "historic reconstruction" as an aid to the understanding of current cultural situations. What he does question is the value of reconstructions arrived at by our present faulty techniques. Any improvement in these techniques will bring us nearer to a solution of the problem of culture origins and, as such, is to be applauded. The current attempt to apply statistical methods to the study of trait distributions seems to him to be a long step in the right direction, but, although these methods can increase the probability of conclusions, they cannot in themselves establish their validity. The results of statistical studies will still require correction for those variable factors which we know influence the diffusion process but of which we know almost nothing more. Whether the influence of these factors can ever be reduced to exact terms or made susceptible to mathematical treatment remains to be seen.

CHAPTER XXII

CLASSIFICATIONS

In all the natural and physical sciences the development of classifications of materials has been one of the first steps toward putting research on a sound basis. It has served to bring some order out of chaos, to make the problems which confront the investigator more apparent, and to aid in delimiting fields of research. In every case the earliest attempts at classification were unsatisfactory and had to be modified as knowledge increased, yet even these helped to clarify the situation. In every case also the most satisfactory and universally useful classifications have been found to be those which were based upon the presence of characteristics indicating genetic relationships. When these had been established, the rest became easy.

Cultural anthropology has lagged in the development of classifications for its materials. Although there have been various attempts, no really satisfactory groupings have so far been developed either for cultures as wholes or for the elements of which these cultures are composed. This lag has been due to the extreme complexity of the material and the inapplicability of the methods developed in other sciences. There have been two praiseworthy attempts at the establishment of classifications for cultures as wholes, but the problem still remains unsolved.

The first of these attempts was that of the *Evolutionary school.* The investigators of this group proceeded upon the assumption of a unilinear evolution of culture in the course of which each developing culture had passed through a series of roughly equivalent stages. The leaders of this school never posited identity of these stages with regard to each culture continuum as a whole, since they recognized the limitations imposed by environment, lack of raw materials, and other factors. The main

382

weakness of their approach lay in their ignorance of the principles of diffusion and of the functional interrelations of elements within the culture configuration. The former led them to think of each new element which appeared in the culture continuum as a direct derivative from the preëxisting elements. The latter led them to believe in the evolution of institutions as something which might occur without direct and constant reference to their context. For classificatory purposes they posited a series of evolutionary stages which they named Pre-Barbarous, Barbarous, and so on, assigning a certain cluster of generalized culture elements to each stage and grouping cultures under these headings according to the number of such elements which were present. By a comparative study of the cultures assigned to the various stages they hoped to extend the number of criteria and also to solve problems connected with the general development of culture. The system failed of its purpose, since it soon became evident that the same culture often included elements which had been assigned, *a priori*, to different stages. Moreover, the order of cultures in the series varied according to the criterion adopted. As a result this system of classification was soon abandoned by anthropologists, although it lingered for a time in the field of sociology.

The next attempt at classification was that embodied in the concept of *culture areas*. This system is still current and, in spite of certain obvious shortcomings, has proved of considerable utility. In contrast to the evolutionary system just discussed, it was developed directly out of studies of trait distributions and gave full recognition to the importance of diffusion. Actually, the concept grew out of the observed similarities in the artifacts of tribes living within particular geographic areas and found its first utility as a guide to the arrangement of museum materials. In its development the American group of anthropologists, notably Wissler and Boas, has been more active than any other, possibly because American Indian cultures lend themselves rather readily to classification on this basis.

The classification of cultures by areas rests, ultimately, on the assumption of genetic relationships between the cultures assigned to each area. The theoretical explanation of the observed conditions is roughly as follows. Various geographical areas present marked differences in climate and economic resources. Any society which settles in one of these environmental areas must develop cultural adaptations to the local conditions if it is to survive. In time these adaptations will become increasingly complete and exact, so that its culture will diverge more and more from the cultures of tribes living in different geographic environments, even though these have the same remote basis. Thus if a single original tribe splits and part of its members settle in a mountainous, wooded region while the other part settles in a flat, arid one, in the absence of communications each of these groups will develop its own type of culture, which will be adapted to its surroundings. There is plenty of evidence that such changes in culture in response to new environments do occur.

Hitherto we have been referring to the changes which take place in culture when a tribe settles in an unoccupied territory of a new sort. When such a tribe moves into a new environment already occupied by groups which have been there long enough to have developed the necessary cultural adaptations, it is much easier for it to take over these well-adapted elements of culture than it is for it to develop new adaptations on the basis of its culture's previous content. In other words, it copies the methods of life which it finds already established in the region, and usually it copies rapidly, since its existence is at stake. The way in which a group of white men visiting the Arctic promptly accept such elements of Eskimo culture as seal-hunting and the wearing of skin garments would be a case in point. Of course it is not necessary for the newcomers to take over all elements of the preëxisting culture. They need only accept such elements as are of immediate utility in their new surroundings. However, the acceptance of these elements will produce a more or less extensive derangement in the newcomer's culture configuration. The culture configuration of the old settlers will be adapted to include these elements, and there is thus a strong tendency for the newcomers to modify their culture configuration still further by the acceptance of additional and already adapted elements from the culture of the old settlers.

Hence, any type of culture which has once become established in a particular environment tends to persist there in the face of immigrations and population changes. Each new group entering the area takes over a large part of the culture which it finds there and abandons a corresponding part of its original culture. This continuity of culture type is not broken even by the development of new elements within the area or by the borrowing of elements originating beyond its borders. Elements originating within it must, if they are to achieve acceptance in even one society, be adjusted to the elements which are common to all the culture configurations within the area, and their acceptance by other societies is thus made easy. It seems to be a fact that such elements spread to the limits of the area with considerable rapidity, although they frequently stop short at these limits. This is especially the case with techniques for utilizing particular aspects of the area's environment. It is obvious that these techniques will not spread to groups living in environments which lack these aspects. Thus an improved method of constructing wooden houses might spread with great speed through the tribes living in contact throughout a wooded area, but its diffusion would stop short at the borders of treeless plains. This rapidity of transmission within an area also holds for the diffusion of traits originating outside. These are presented first to border groups who, if they receive them at all, soon adapt them to the area configuration, thus making their acceptance by other groups in the area easy.

Whether the explanations which have just been given are correct or not, the tendency for particular types of culture to persist in particular areas and for the cultures of a group of tribes living in a particular environment to have a large number of elements in common cannot be questioned. The reality of culture areas can be proved both by studies of current trait distributions and, in many cases, by archæological or historical evidence. The main objections which have been raised by the opponents of this method of classifying cultures are based on the difficulties of applying the system to all parts of the world and on the fact that such classifications group together cultures which differ markedly with respect to certain elements. Both of these objections are admitted, but we will deal with them separately.

With regard to the difficulties involved in a universal application of the culture-area concept we must distinguish at the start between those present in relatively static situations and those produced by current or recently completed population movements. As regards the first, the close relationship between the natural environment and the cultures within an area has already been stressed. Geographic environments usually cannot be sharply delimited. Thus in North America the lines dividing the Plains from the Eastern woodlands, the Northern barren ground, and the arid Southwestern plateau were all vague and irregular. In each case the borders of the area presented a mixed environment which was susceptible to partial exploitation by the techniques which were fully adapted to exploiting each of the distinctive neighboring environments. Where such mixed environments exist, we normally find cultures which are susceptible to diffusion from both of the neighboring regions and which are correspondingly mixed in content. The assignment of such cultures to one or the other of the adjoining areas is always a matter of doubt, to be decided on the number of similarities which they show to each. A group of tribes living in such a marginal environment may even present a greater number of similarities to each other than they present to the generalized culture types of either of the adjoining areas, in which case it is safest to classify them as a separate unit. A good example of this would be the settled, agricultural, earth-lodge-building tribes who lived along the Eastern edge of the Plains and who seem to have shared more cultural elements among themselves than they shared with either the tribes of the Eastern woodlands or the nomads of the High Plains.

Another difficulty involved in the use of the culture-area classification is that we may have distinct types of culture existing within the same environmental area. This difficulty also is not insurmountable. It disappears if we focus our attention on the culture, the thing with which the classification is concerned, rather than on the geography. It must be remembered that the aspect which any environment offers to an immigrant group depends upon a combination of its actual qualities and the exploitive techniques with which the group is already familiar, i. e., it is the result of an interaction between natural environment and culture. Thus the coal and iron regions of Pennsylvania presented a totally different aspect to their aboriginal Indian inhabitants from that which these regions presented to European immigrants. To the first it was an undesirable region, unsuited to their type of agriculture and comparatively poor in game. To the second it was a source of potential wealth and as such eminently desirable for settlement. A group which enters a region with developed techniques for exploiting some phase of the natural resources which it provides is shielded from the urgent necessity which leads an immigrant group which lacks such techniques to take over the preëxisting culture.

This applies with double strength in the case of groups whose techniques enable them to exploit some aspect of the environment which has previously been neglected. They need not come into direct competition with the earlier inhabitants and so find themselves at only a slight cultural disadvantage. Actually, there are a few cases in which we find two distinct types of culture coexisting within the same environmental area. The classic example of this is our own Southwest, where we have a type of sedentary agricultural culture, exemplified in the Pueblo tribes, and a type of nomadic hunting and wild-plant-gathering culture exemplified by the Apache and, in early times, by the Navajo. Although these two types of culture interpenetrated each other and the societies which bore them frequently clashed, neither cultural group made any serious effort to dispossess or expel the other or to assume the other's type of culture. They were exploiting different aspects of the same environment, using different techniques for the purpose, and hence were not in direct competition. The significant fact is that neither the Pueblo nor the Apache culture type extended beyond the limits of the Southwest into an environment of markedly different character. We might say that there was a Pueblo culture area and an Apache-Navajo culture area which happened to be geographically superimposed upon each other.

Lastly, within a single environmental area we may find cultures of two or more types which show a broken and irregular distribution. This is especially likely to be the case in island regions, like Polynesia, and is apparently due to migrations of groups who have settled the area irregularly, their points of settlement being controlled by accidents of wind, tide, and aboriginal resistance. Once settled, the difficulty of communication has shielded the cultures of each type from the leveling effects of diffusion.

So much for the difficulties which attend the application of the culture-area classification to reasonably static culture conditions. When we attempt to apply it to those in which movements of peoples are actually in progress or recently completed, it breaks down entirely. In a few parts of the world there are areas in which the cultural conditions are reminiscent of the physical ones found in a geological shatter belt. Here groups from different areas have fought, interpenetrated, and settled with the result that several cultures, each of which has close affiliations with the type characteristic of a neighboring area, exist side by side. It is significant that this condition seems to be almost entirely limited to geographical marginal regions of mixed environment. In these the techniques developed for each of the more clearly marked neighboring environments are adequate for survival, and the immigrant groups can therefore retain their cultural integrity, at least for a time. If they exploit different aspects of the marginal environment, they may retain it almost indefinitely, the various cultures finally reaching a condition of symbiotic interdependence. One of the best examples of this would be the western Sudan with its mixture of Negro and Islamic cultures and its tacit ascription of particular activities to particular cultural and social units.

Let us turn now to the second of the basic objections to the use of the culture area classification. This is that the categories established on this basis always include groups which are markedly different in certain respects. Linked with this is the claim that this type of classification gives much too much weight to those aspects of culture which are directly connected with the exploitation of the environment and uses them as its main criterion. To the first we can only reply that any classification of cultures must group together some which differ markedly in one respect or another. No two tribes or even local groups have identical cultures any more than any two individuals have identical physical characteristics, and the broader the categories established within any system of classification the greater the variation among the members of the category is likely to be. The whole problem becomes one of the nature and degree of the differences which can be ignored for classificatory purposes, since the only classification which would be entirely free from this objection would be one in which every local group and even social class was given independent recognition, i.e., no classification at all.

As to the stress which the culture-area classification admittedly lays upon similarities in the techniques for exploiting the environment, we here pass at once into the highly controversial field of evaluations of importance. If we are seeking to imitate the natural sciences and to base our classification upon elements the presence of which indicates genetic relationship, this stressing of material techniques is fully justified. These techniques are the elements of culture which are most readily perceived on contact and, as a rule, most easily accepted. Moreover, their practical utility and constant relations with the natural environment tend to protect them from modifications which would make them unrecognizable. A borrowed technique may, in the process of its integration be given a new context of associations, but the qualities which make it of service to the adopting culture will normally be left intact.

With regard to cultures, the problem of genetic relationships presents two aspects, in contrast to the single aspect of the same problem in the natural sciences. There is the problem of establishing common origins for two or more culture continuums and that of establishing common origins for elements within different culture configurations. In other words, both independent development and diffusion have played a part in establishing the current content of all cultures. There is no trustworthy method for distinguishing between the elements within a culture which owe their presence to one of these factors and those which owe it to the other. If we were seeking proof of the common origin of two societies with their associated culture continuums our surest guides would probably be, first, basic similarities in language and, second, similarities in the elements which compose the sub-conscious core of each culture, i.e., its fundamental values and emotional associations. These seem to be the parts of culture which are least susceptible to change as long as a society maintains its existence as a distinct entity. However, we know from direct observation that language distributions are only superficially related to those of any other elements of culture, and classifications based upon them are useful only for linguistic studies. Languages of the same stock may be spoken by groups who have hardly another element of culture in common. As for similarities in the culture cores, the difficulties of analyzing this part of any culture are so great and the results depend so much upon subjective judgments that this part of culture must be ruled out as a basis for establishing genetic relationships.

In the present state of our knowledge and techniques, genetic relationships can only be established on the basis of quantitative similarities. The greater the number of elements which two cultures have in common, the greater the probability of their common origin or, at least, close and long-continued contact. We know so little of the factors governing the development or acceptance of new elements or of the relative persistence of elements of different sorts in culture configurations that we are quite unable to apply qualitative methods. We may be able to do this in a very general way when we know the differentials for elements of various sorts as regards both acceptance and persistence, but these remain to be established. For the present we can only say that the greater the number of elements of any sort which two cultures have in common the closer, presumably, is their genetic relationship.

It may well be asked what is the justification for trying to stick to genetic relationships as a basic for classification. Cultural material is intrinsically so different from that dealt with in the natural sciences that the approach to classification which they have found most useful may be quite useless for cultural studies. In organisms, genetic relationships are reflected in structural similarities which are of great functional importance. In cultures they do not appear to be. If we could determine which elements are vital in all cultures and give all culture configurations their form and orientation, these elements would offer a really valid reference for developing a system of classification. Unfortunately, this brings us back at once to the still unanalyzable core of culture. The key to such a classification may lie there, but we shall not have it in hand for some time to come.

Meanwhile, the quantitative genetic basis for classification appears most promising. We must have some method for arranging material in intelligible order, and no other basis of classification promises as much. Classifications based upon a limited selection from among the more superficial elements of culture may be useful for specific studies, but they cannot be generally useful. Protests against the present culture-area type of classification, which approaches most nearly to the suggested type, have come largely from individuals who felt that this did not allow sufficient importance to social organization. Before these protests can be taken seriously, the protestants should demonstrate that they have something better to offer. Certainly classifications based upon the presence of certain formal types of social organization bracket together cultures which, in their total configurations, are far more diverse than any to be found within a single culture area. Each of their various types of "social structure" can be found integrated with widely different sets of economic techniques and even of values in one culture configuration or another. When we find two tribes which appear to be nearly identical in both their techniques and values, one tribe having its individual relations organized on a simple family basis with strong patriarchal control while the other has functionally important matrilineal clans, it seems fairly obvious that the formal type of social organization is not the central feature in either configuration. In fact it probably has less influence on the total configuration than the techniques for dealing with that stubborn reality, the natural environment.

All such attempts to build classifications upon a single obvious aspect of culture fail to take into account the fact that the inter-relations of the elements within every culture configuration are at once extensive and loose. Every element within the configura-tion is more or less adapted to every other and must function in relation to the rest, but few elements are completely adapted to each other. In fact their mutual adjustments seem to lie less in modifications in their intrinsic form than in the attachment to them of mutually congruous interpretations and emotional con-texts. But this matter has been discussed before.

It is the author's belief that the culture-area classification has the widest applicability of any now available. However, its utility might be increased by certain modifications. The most im-portant of these would be a change in the focus of interest from the geographic factor to the genetic one, as this was revealed by quantitative similarities in content. This change would necessi-tate the abandonment of the term *area,* with its constant geo-graphic connotations, and the substitution of some other, possibly the neutral word *type.* Such a substitution would in no way con-flict with the observed fact that most culture types show a fairly continuous geographic distribution and are functionally related to particular environments, while it would make it possible to include in the correct categories cultures in shatter belts or isolated areas. Nearly all the world's cultures could be fitted into such a type classification if it was made simply on the basis of quantitative similarities. There would, of course, be certain cul-tures for which these similarities were so evenly balanced that their assignment would be open to question. The zoölogist has somewhat similar cases in which a species' resemblances are evenly divided between two genera. He meets the problem by establishing a new genus with a single member, and the anthro-pologist might follow a similar procedure.

The actual establishment of such a complete classification of cultures must await a far more complete knowledge of culture contents and the appearance of some anthropological Linnæus. However, McKern in his recently developed classification of archæological material has taken a long step in the right direction. In archæology the problem is simplified by the fact that the materials are largely limited to tangible objects and are thus vastly easier to analyze and compare, but his system is based upon exactly the principle of genetic relationship determined by quantitative similarity which we have already outlined. In this system the smallest recognized unit is the *Focus,* determined by the content of a series of sites which are similar in practically all respects. This unit would correspond to the single culture of the ethnologist, with its inclusion of closely related sub-cultures borne by particular local or social groups within a single functional society. The next larger unit is the *Aspect,* composed of a series of Foci which show a large preponderance of common elements. The next larger unit is the *Phase,* composed of a series of Aspects, and the largest the *Base.* When the number of similarities falls below a certain percentage, a site is classed as a new Focus or a group of Foci are classed as a new Aspect.

So much for attempts to arrive at a satisfactory classification of cultures as wholes. The classification of elements within culture presents a quite different problem. Some sort of classification is immediately necessary even for the presentation of descriptive data, and for many years the authors of such studies have been accustomed to group their materials under such headings as Material Culture, Social Organization, and Religion. A certain conventional arrangement for presenting the material has even been developed, material culture, i.e., the objects made and used and the techniques associated with them, usually coming at the beginning of the report. This form of classification really derives from one which we have developed with relation to the elements present in our own culture and is based, consciously or unconsciously, on recognized resemblances in primary functions. Thus all groups have techniques for manufacturing objects of one sort or another and for exploiting the resources of their environment. They also have rules governing the interrelations of individuals and techniques for dealing with the supernatural. It is therefore possible, if the secondary functions and interrelations of culture elements are ignored, to describe practically the whole content of any culture under one or another of the familiar headings. It is only when we begin to penetrate more deeply into the culture that the inadequacies of this system become evident.

The fact that the content of any culture can be analyzed and placed in such compartments, perhaps with the aid of an occasional *tour de force,* has led certain writers to attach more importance to these arbitrary divisions than they really deserve. One writer speaks of the "universal patterns" in culture which are thus revealed. Actually, there are no universal patterns, only a series of universal needs which each society has met in its own way. These needs can be grouped under three headings, biological, social, and psychic. The *biological needs* are those which derive from man's physical characteristics. They include such things as the need for food and shelter, for protection from enemies, whether human or animal, and the need for reproduction to perpetuate the species. These needs are common to men and animals and are of a particularly immediate and pressing sort. Unless the culture provides adequate techniques for meeting them, neither the individual nor the group can survive. At the same time these needs are more closely related to the natural environment than any others, and the specific form in which they present themselves may be largely determined by it. Thus the type of food and shelter required by the members of a society will vary with the region in which they live. It will not be the same for Polynesians and Eskimos. The natural environment will also have a strong effect, through the materials which it offers, upon the techniques which a society develops for meeting these needs. There are areas in which no food crops can be raised, areas without metallic ores, and so on.

The *social needs* of human beings arise from man's habit of living in groups. Similar needs must be present, in rudimentary form, for all gregarious animals, but the close interdependence of the members of a human society gives them a much greater importance for man. The first and most vital of these needs is that of preserving the solidarity of the group. Closely connected with these are the needs for reducing friction between individuals and minimizing open clashes, for training individuals to particular statuses in the social system, and for coördinating their activities and providing the group with leadership and direction. These needs are only remotely influenced by the natural environment and present themselves to all societies in very much the same form. At the same time, their effective solution depends more upon the adequate training of the individual and his conditioning to social life than upon anything else, so that a great number of workable solutions are possible.

Lastly, there are the *psychic needs,* which are extremely difficult to define but real nevertheless. One of the most important functions of any culture is to keep a majority of the people who share it happy and contented. All human beings have desires for favorable response from other individuals, for things which are unattainable (or for easy roads to attainment), and for psychological escapes. In the long run the satisfaction of these needs is probably as important to the effective functioning of a society as that of any of the needs of the other two categories, although they are less immediate and pressing. However, these needs are in themselves vague and general, being given point by the individual's cultural conditioning, and the responses to them which various cultures provide are almost infinitely varied. Depending on his training, the individual can obtain a warm sense that he is looking well and exciting admiration by wearing a bone through the nose, a new loin-cloth, or the latest products of a fashionable tailor. He can escape from reality equally well by immersing himself in a game of chess, hiring a medicine man to make a charm, or anticipating a better social status in his next incarnation. Utility imposes fewer restrictions on this aspect of culture than on any other with the possible exception of language, and the diversity of forms is correspondingly great.

Each of the categories into which the content of culture is ordinarily divided corresponds roughly to a particular category of these needs. Thus most of the elements which we would group under material culture are associated with the satisfaction of the biological needs for food, shelter, and protection. Again the category of esthetic activities is associated with the satisfaction of psychic needs. Since all these needs are of universal occurrence, it might seem that a universally applicable system for classifying culture elements could be developed on the basis of such correspondences. Unfortunately, the more thoroughly we investigate the functions of any culture element the more difficult its classification upon this basis becomes. Every element actually has numerous functions, and these are frequently related to needs which are in different categories. In most cases it is possible to distinguish what appears to be the element's primary function, the others being of less importance or less constantly exercised, but conclusions on this point must depend largely on the observer's judgment. We shall treat this multiplicity of functions at greater length in the next chapter.

It seems doubtful whether the present classification can be refined to any great extent, but as it stands now it is mainly useful to students of trait distribution. It does serve to gather together culture elements which are superficially similar and saves the labor of working through a whole report. Aside from this it is of very little significance. It is not even a safe guide to the arrangement of descriptive material, since the very processes of analysis and differentiation which it entails mask the actual interrelations of culture elements and make it extremely difficult for the reader to see them in their proper settings. The adequate presentation of cultural material even in simple descriptive terms offers a problem which is still unsolved. While the integration of culture elements is always loose, their interrelations are extensive. It is possible to start at any point in the culture fabric and to trace these interrelations and interactions over a wider and wider range until the whole configuration has been brought in. However, this method always gives the reader a false perspective, making it appear that the entire culture has been built about or is focused upon that particular segment of the configuration which has been chosen as a starting point. This effect is still more pronounced when those elements of culture which are less closely related to the particular segment are omitted or mentioned only in passing. There is an urgent need for the development of some new convention by which the total content of a culture and the interrelations of the elements within this content can be shown simultaneously.

There is also a genuine need for some purely objective classification of culture elements which can be used as an aid to analytical studies. In particular there is need of a more exact terminology. Even if such a classification takes into account only the overt expressions of culture, it will be a distinct help in the study of both diffusion phenomena and function. The following classification is offered as a possible starting point for further efforts along this line.

The individual acts and objects which constitute the overt expression of a culture are commonly referred to as *traits*. Any one of these traits can be analyzed into a number of still smaller units, which in the absence of any generally accepted term we will call *items*. Thus the bow is a culture trait, yet a comparative study of bows from several different cultures will reveal differences in the sort of wood used, the part of the tree from which the wood is taken, the shape, size, and finish of the completed object, the method of attaching the string, and the material used for the string. As far as a particular culture is concerned, the bow is a trait; the various details of wood, form, and string are items within the trait. Similarly a song may be considered a trait, yet it can be analyzed into words and melody, while a dance can be analyzed into rhythm and movements.

Although the traits which compose the overt expression of a culture can be isolated artificially, they are actually integrated into a functional whole. First, every trait is intimately associated with some other trait or traits to form a larger functional unit commonly known as a *trait complex*. The traits within such a complex are all more or less interrelated and interdependent from the point of view of both function and use. A number of such trait complexes are, in turn, combined to form a still larger functional unit which, since no term has so far been coined for it, we will call an *activity*. Lastly, the sum total of these activities constitutes the complete overt expression of the culture.

This classification of overt culture expressions by *item, trait,*

trait complex, and *activity* rests essentially on the basis of inter-relation in function and use, which in turn presupposes a certain degree of mutual adaptation in form. The possible application of such a classificatory system may be made clearer by an example drawn from Comanche culture. If we take the bow as a starting point, we find that it embodies a number of items such as the use of Osage orangewood taken from the heart of the tree, rectangular cross-section, length of not over three feet, high polish, and sinew bowstring attached in a particular way. While these items have little individual significance, they all contribute in some way to the successful functioning of the bow and together give Comanche bows a distinctive character, making it possible to identify them in a series of bows drawn from different cultures. The bow as a whole is combined with three other traits, the arrow, the combined bowcase and quiver, and the method of shooting with the bow to form a larger unit within the culture, the bow-and-arrow complex. The various traits within this complex are easily distinguishable and each of them can be analyzed into a series of items, yet they are closely dependent upon each other and can function effectively only as parts of this or some other complex. The bow-and-arrow complex is then combined with the horse complex, the tracking complex, and others to form the hunting activity. Lastly this activity is combined with a number of others relating to war, transportation, social life, dealings with the supernatural, and so on to form the total overt expression of the tribe's culture. The whole structure might be likened to a pyramid with the items, which are the most numerous, at the bottom and the number of units diminishing with each succeeding tier.

This classification represents an extreme simplification. The number of subdivisions could be expanded almost indefinitely. It is questionable, however, whether such an increase would make for greater accuracy. In any attempt to apply such a classification to the overt expressions of a particular culture, the subjective judgment of the observer cannot be excluded. The phenomena are so complex that it is almost impossible to develop any purely objective standards which will be applicable in all cases. The various divisions blend into each other imperceptibly, and in many instances the particular element can easily be classed as either an item or a trait, while a group of closely related elements can be considered as constituting either a trait or a trait complex.

A possible way out of the difficulty might be to abandon our strict adherence to the overt expressions of culture and to take as traits those elements which the individuals who share the culture are conscious of as distinct entities. However, the value of this approach is largely nullified by the practical difficulty of such determinations and by the factor of differences in culture participation. Thus the average Comanche certainly thought of the bow as a single entity, a thing which he could use in certain ways. A professional bow-maker, on the other hand, was fully conscious of all the items which went to make up a bow since he had to assemble them into a useful whole. To the average man the bow was a trait, to the specialist a trait complex. Similarly, the average man in our own culture thinks of his watch as a unit, a single trait, while to the watchmaker it is an elaborate complex of traits.

In this particular type of classification there is more or less interlocking between the categories due to the fact that a unit from one of the lower divisions may be shared by two or more units in the division above. This sharing becomes more marked as the units become larger. The same item may be shared by two or more traits, as when we find a particular type of irregular curve used, for esthetic reasons, in the design of canoe prows, house roofs, and headdresses, or when a particular material, glass for example, enters into a large number of different appliances. However, most items are so dependent for their functional significance upon the trait as a whole that they cannot enter into any other combination. Thus such an item as the characteristic length of a bow is quite inseparable from the bow.

Traits have a more independent existence, and it is common to find the same trait incorporated into two or more complexes. Thus to take the Comanche bow-and-arrow complex, the bow, in addition to its use with the arrow, might be used as part of a fire-making or drilling complex. The arrow was also part of a game complex in which it was thrown by hand. Even the movements employed in shooting were also part of a dance complex.

The same trait complex as a whole may also be incorporated into several different activities. In this tribe the bow-and-arrow complex was an integral part of the hunting activity, the war activity, and the sport activity. It might even be considered a part of the religious activity, since, although it was not used in any ritual, men who had a certain class of supernatural beings as their personal guardians were required to carry it as their only weapon. The horse complex was incorporated into the hunting, war, sport, and transportation activities. Such examples could be multiplied indefinitely. This sharing of items, traits, and trait complexes among the units of the next higher category seems to be a constant feature of the overt expressions of all cultures.

The validity of the foregoing system of classification may be questioned, but its immediate utility will be evident when we come to discuss certain of the problems connected with the study of function in culture and especially that of the relation of function to form. In closing we wish to emphasize once more the practical value of classifications as an aid to investigations of all sorts. Definitions and classifications are among the most valuable tools of the research worker, and anthropology is still sadly lacking in both.

CHAPTER XXIII

FUNCTION

The study of function in culture is one of the most recent and most promising developments in anthropological research. It has directed attention to an extensive and hitherto largely unexplored order of phenomena and promises important contributions toward the understanding of culture. Unfortunately, the functional approach has not yet been synthesized with the earlier approaches, although movements in that direction are already evident. Its present isolation derives partly from the fact that functional studies have grown out of the work of a somewhat divergent group of anthropologists, the *French School,* and partly from the functionalists' use of a peculiar terminology. These two items are closely related. The French School has certain basic postulates with regard to the nature of society and the complete submergence of the individual in society which have never been accepted by the members of other schools. The categories of phenomena and the terminology which have been developed on the basis of these postulates are extremely difficult to equate with those in more general use. To cite a single example, the functionalists employ the term *social system* to include a wide and rather vaguely defined sector of culture, assigning to it not only the patterns governing the interrelations of individuals within the society but also those aspects of economic life and religion which have a direct and obvious effect upon these interrelations. Members of other schools use the same term in the sense in which it has been used in the present book, i.e., as referring only to the mutually adjusted patterns governing the interrelations of individuals.

This difference in basic postulates and confusion in terms has resulted in much misunderstanding and a tendency for each group to under-estimate the importance of the other's contribution toward the understanding of culture. The author believes that the techniques now employed in functional studies are essentially sound although, like all other current techniques in anthropology, they require further refinement. Certainly no group of workers in the field of culture have made more important contributions during the recent period than Dr. Malinowski and his followers. At the same time, it seems possible to apply these techniques and realize their advantages without accepting the basic postulates of the French School, just as the techniques of psychoanalysis can be employed and therapeutic benefits derived from them without the acceptance of the conceptual scheme originated by Freud. Studies of the functions of cultures or culture elements are in no way incompatible with the concepts regarding the nature of culture and society which have already been set forth in this book. Real progress toward the understanding of culture processes will come only with the synthesis of all possible lines of attack upon these problems.

The first step toward such a synthesis would seem to be the development of a terminology comprehensible to the workers of all the schools. While terms and definitions may not be important in themselves, they are necessary tools for exact analysis and investigation. The term *function* seems to be used with considerable looseness even by certain of the functionalists. Actually, every element of culture has qualities of four distinct, although mutually interrelated kinds: i.e., it has *form, meaning, use,* and *function.* Before we can understand its significance to the total configuration of which the element is a part these must be distinguished and defined. It is further necessary to define the category of elements within culture to which these qualities may be said to pertain. Since this is one of the most basic aspects of the problem, we will deal with it first.

In the previous chapter a classification of culture elements into items, traits, trait complexes, and activities was suggested and the basis of this classification explained. The close interrelation between the elements in each of these categories and those in the larger and more inclusive categories was also pointed out.

Thus a number of items, in combination, constitute a trait; a number of traits, a trait complex; a number of trait complexes, an activity. The smallest combination of elements to which the qualities pertinent to functional studies pertain is probably the trait complex. It is possible to analyze such a unit into its component traits and items and to study these individually, but the average member of any society regards the trait complex as a whole, and it operates as a whole. With respect to form, meaning, use, and function the contributions of the component elements are so thoroughly interdependent that it is unnecessary to try to separate them. Perhaps the situation as regards function can be made clearer by a biological analogy. Any bodily movement is the result of a number of coördinated and mutually interdependent muscular responses. In the laboratory these responses can be isolated and studied individually, yet they have no real significance or utility except in relation to the total movement. It is this movement, as a whole, which constitutes the organism's response to a stimulus. Similarly, it is the trait complex or the group of trait complexes forming an activity which constitutes a society's response to need stimuli. It must be stressed once more that culture is a psychological phenomenon and that its component patterns correspond to the reactions of an organism rather than to the parts of an organism.

The *form* of a trait complex will be taken to mean the sum and arrangement of its component behavior patterns; in other words that aspect of the complex whose expressions can be observed directly and which can, therefore be transmitted from one society to another. It is believed that such a definition is in fairly close agreement with the ordinary usage of this term in anthropology. Thus it is customary to speak of the *form* of a ceremony or technique as something which can be established objectively and through direct observation. This definition at once establishes a distinction between *form* and *meaning*. The *meaning* of a trait complex consists of the associations which any society attaches to it. Such associations are subjective and frequently unconscious. They find only indirect expression in behavior and therefore cannot be established by purely objective methods. *Form* and *meaning* represent the passive qualities of the trait complex as contrasted with *use* and *function,* which are its dynamic qualities.

The terms *function* and *use* have been employed interchangeably even by certain members of the functional school, but the author feels there is a very real distinction and that there will be constant confusion unless this is made clear. The difference between use and function is most obvious in the case of material expressions of culture such as tools and utensils. Thus the primary use of an axe is for chopping, that of a spade for digging, but any one will feel the inappropriateness of applying the term *function* to such utilizations. The use of any culture element is an expression of its relation to things external to the social-cultural configuration; its function is an expression of its relation to things within that configuration. Thus the axe has a use or uses with respect to the natural environment of the group, i.e., to chop wood. It has functions with respect both to the needs of the group and the operation of other elements within the culture configuration. It helps to satisfy the need for wood and makes possible a whole series of woodworking patterns. To take another example, the use of a medicine may be to reduce fever, its function to restore individuals to health. The function of a trait complex is the sum total of its contribution toward the perpetuation of the social-cultural configuration. This function is normally a composite which can be analyzed into a number of functions each of which is related to the satisfaction of a particular need. This usage of the term is parallel in many respects to the usage already assigned it in linguistic studies.

It remains to make clear the relation existing between these various qualities of the trait complex. If such complexes developed *in vacuo,* form, meaning, use, and function would grow up together in close and constant relationship and would be completely interdependent. However, even when complexes originate within a culture they are, from the first, parts of a larger configuration and in the course of their development must adapt to this as well as to each other. Actually, such cases of the internal origin and development of trait complexes are rare. Most complexes owe their presence in the culture configurations in which we find them to diffusion. This means that, as far as the particular configuration is concerned, form precedes the other qualities and has a continuous influence on their development. It is actually dependent upon a different set of factors which are largely historical. In other words, the trait complex is presented to the society as a definite entity which is incorporated into the configuration by the attachment to it of use, meaning, and function. Although its form may be progressively modified during the process of incorporation, the initial form has a strong influence on the initial ascriptions of use, meaning, and function and through these on all subsequent ascriptions.

Actual studies of diffused complexes show that form may persist with only slight modifications in the face of wide differences in the other qualities. Thus the Sun Dance, which occurred in the cultures of a whole series of Plains tribes, varied much more in meaning, use, and function than it did in its form. Although there were marked similarities of procedure wherever the dance occurred, it might be given for quite different purposes. Thus in some tribes the dance was pledged as a thank-offering for recovery from illness, in others to ensure revenge for a slain relative, while among the Comanche it was given as a test of the powers of a new medicine man who took this means of announcing himself. Each of these differences was correlated with only slight adaptive changes in form, and it is clear that the general form derived, in every case, from historic factors.

This brings us at once to the problem of whether cultures may include elements which lack meaning, use, and function. Conclusions with regard to this depend primarily upon which category of culture elements we consider. It seems safe to say that all trait complexes possess at least meaning and function, although use cannot always be ascribed to them under our definition. However, many trait complexes include elements which do not contribute toward use. Except in the rare cases where a society studies and analyzes its techniques, as in our own "scientific management," there is no particular stimulus toward the elimination of such elements. Individuals learn the techniques as wholes and are not conscious that any part of the whole does not contribute toward efficiency. A good example of this would be the Betsileo formula for making indigo dye, which prescribes the addition of ashes from a whole series of plants, some of them difficult to obtain, although ashes of any sort would serve the purpose. Of course if an element actively interferes with efficiency it is likely to be gradually eliminated, but elements whose effects are neutral may survive indefinitely.

The presence of such useless elements may be due to mere accidents of inclusion in the course of the complex's development, but they are more commonly due to accidents of diffusion. We have already seen that elements of culture can be transmitted only through their overt expressions and that a receiving society is only cognizant of that part of an element which can readily be expressed. In other words, what it receives is primarily *form*, with the qualities of use, meaning, and function largely stripped away. In the process of integration the new society attaches these qualities to the borrowed element, but the *form* may very well include features which are in no way related to these. The accepting group assumes such features as an integral part of the new element, and the associations built up about this element are as intimately linked with them as with the other features. To put it in colloquial terms, a tool or applaince will not "look right" if it does not include these features, and a technique abbreviated to the elements actually necessary for successful performance will not "seem right." Such an abbreviation will interfere with established muscular habits and will thus be almost as unfamiliar as a new technique.

When we turn to the question of whether there are meaningless or functionless elements in culture, an answer becomes more difficult. There are no simple objective tests of the sort which can be applied to prove lack of utility. In one sense, every element can be said to have a function. It is the sharing of a common culture by a society's component members which makes it possible for them to exist as a society. Simply *because it is shared,* every element of culture therefore has the function of contributing to social solidarity. However, such universal ascription of function is the *reductio ad absurdum* of the whole idea. If function is to have any meaning for the study of culture, the concept must be made more specific. Elements which are without utility may still have function and meaning if, in themselves, they provide responses to particular needs of the individual or group. Thus the inclusion of magical rituals in many occupational complexes does not contribute directly to the success of the work but does contribute toward the assurance and peace of mind of the worker. However, there seem to be numerous instances in which elements within a complex have no meaning or function aside from that of the complex as a whole, and it seems justifiable to class such elements as meaningless and functionless.

If the influence of initial form is strong enough to ensure the survival within a complex of elements which are useless, meaningless, and functionless, we should expect it to exert a very strong influence on the development of all these qualities. These influences are most obvious in the case of use. Those expressions of culture which have material form, for example, tools, utensils, and ornaments, possess certain physical qualities which have a limiting effect upon the uses which can be assigned to them. Such physical qualities are always multiple and may be made to contribute toward use either singly or in combination. Thus a bow has such qualities as length, weight, hardness, and elasticity which may be utilized differentially in the various trait complexes into which this object is incorporated. The qualities just listed make possible the use of the bow not only for propelling arrows, but also as a club. This usage is mentioned in many Comanche stories. The same qualities, plus the addition of a sharp point, make possible the bow's use as a lance. The quality of elasticity is utilized when the bow is incorporated into a drilling complex, the tension of the bowstring serving to hold and rotate the drill shaft about which it is wrapped. Again, an ordinary tin can has physical qualities which make possible a variety of uses. To cite only a few of these, it can be employed for the preservation of sterilized foods or as a darning-ball. With one end removed it can be used as a drinking cup, a flower-pot, a circular cookie-cutter, or an instrument for scaling fish.

Even culture traits which are not expressed directly in material form may have qualities which limit and direct their use. Thus an act or series of coördinated acts which expresses a particular culture pattern may be incorporated into several different trait complexes and contribute to the production of a different result in each case. In Northwest Coast culture the same twining technique underlies the manufacture of objects as diverse as baskets, hats, blankets, and slat armor. This technique apparently reflects a particular set of motor habits. When such a pattern of motor habits has once become established, it is easier for individuals to follow it than to develop a new set of motor habits, and the technique associated with this pattern is consequently applied to a variety of uses. The pattern's potentialities for use are constant, while the actual uses depend upon the association of the pattern with other traits to form particular trait complexes.

The inherent qualities of a trait thus set broad limits to its potentialities for use but do not account for actual usage. Such usage always involves a selection of certain potentialities and a neglect of others. Thus to revert to the bow, this object has potentialities for use as a musical instrument which were ignored by the Indians but exploited by the Bushmen, while conversely its potentialities as an aid to drilling were exploited by the Indians but ignored by the Bushmen. The actual usage of any culture element or complex seems to be controlled as much by the associations established with regard to it, i.e. the meaning or meanings assigned to it by the particular culture, as by its potentialities. This factor of meaning is often strong enough to inhibit certain usages completely. There is nothing in the physical qualities of a tin can which would make its use as a flower-pot less effective in the parlor than in the kitchen, or its use as a drinking cup less effective at a formal banquet than in a hobo "jungle." However, the associations which have grown up about the tin can in our own culture make us feel that it is out of place in parlors and at banquets. In some other culture the associations may be quite different. Thus to most Malagasy a cup made from a tin can is a treasured rarity displayed with pride and offered only to honored guests.

Because of its subjective nature, *meaning* is much less susceptible to diffusion than either form or use. In the great majority of cases a receiving culture attaches new meanings to the borrowed elements or complexes, and these may have little relation to the meanings which the same elements carried in their original setting. Thus a ceremony which carries a high emotional context for one society may be copied by another society simply as a form of amusement. Note the imitations of Indian dances by some of our own fraternal organizations and the transfer of the rigidly formalized, semi-sacred Hawaiian *hula* to our vaudeville stage. Actually, the ascriptions of particular meanings to newly borrowed culture elements seem to depend upon a highly complex series of factors such as the auspices under which the trait was introduced, partial understanding of its meaning in the parent configuration, and accidents occurring in the course of its acceptance. Nevertheless, when a meaning has once become established it has a strong influence on all subsequent developments in the field of use. To cite a current example, the meaning already attached to tin cans has created a certain opposition to their use as beer containers. This is increased, in at least some individuals, by the shape of some of the new cans, which is painfully reminiscent of those used for insect exterminators. Even if canned beer were actually better, it would take some time to overcome this resistance and a still longer time to establish it in favor for convivial occasions. It is safe to say that it will come into general use in cheap saloons long before it will be considered appropriate for banquets or birthday gifts.

Any culture element's potentialities for meaning are almost unlimited. In the case of techniques and appliances the factor of use may impose some strictures, but, as we have seen, the relation between use and meaning is always reciprocal and the range of possible variation correspondingly wide. There are many aspects of culture in which the ascription of meaning seems to depend upon free association. Thus to Americans black carries a meaning of mourning and a bow of black crape immediately suggests a funeral. To a Chinaman white is the color of mourning and a bow of crape has only personal associations if any.

Again, in our culture the number three carries a mystical meaning. If one of our own stories begins, "A man had three sons," we are at once prepared for the fabulous and our enjoyment of the tale is not lessened by any elements of improbability. Conversely, when called upon to invent a fairy story for a small relative we will be almost certain to use three as the number of brothers or sisters, for the wishes the fairy grants, or for the obstacles the hero has to overcome. To the Indian, much the same associations attach to the number four.

The relation between form, use, and meaning is thus a rather tenuous one. Use and meaning are probably more closely related to each other than either one is to form, but even so their mutual adaptations are loose enough to permit of a wide range of variation. When we try to ascertain the relation of these three elements to function, the situation becomes vastly more complex. Function seems to derive least from form, somewhat more from use, but most from meaning. Any attempt to analyze these relationships in a particular case reveals still another disturbing factor. Many elements of culture have multiple uses, but nearly all of them have multiple meanings. We are not referring, of course, to individual associations based upon accidents of experience but to the associations which are a regular part of the culture configurations and which are transmitted and shared like any of its other elements. Perhaps we can illustrate this point best by analyzing the meanings of a particular trait complex in our own culture, say the sending of flowers. Incidentally, interest in flowers and appreciation of their beauty are, in themselves, results of cultural conditioning. Members of most Indian tribes think that our reaction to flowers is mildly ridiculous.

Our society considers the sending of flowers appropriate to a number of different situations. It is the proper thing to do at funerals and also when a friend is sick. It is suitable at weddings, at birthdays, after staying with a family as a visitor, as an accompaniment to courting, and as a form of congratulation for a successful performance of some sort, say an opera début or graduation. In death or sickness this pattern carries a meaning of sympathy. In connection with birthdays and weddings this connotation is entirely lacking. In fact if this were the only meaning attached to the pattern its employment on such occasions would be highly ironic and would produce anything but the desired response in the recipient. So precise are the meanings given to the pattern relative to particular situations that even the type of flowers is indicated. It would be considered bad taste, with an undercurrent of unfavorable meaning, to send a wreath of immortelles to a wedding. When sent to a family after a stay with them, flowers are an expression of gratitude for favors received. When used in courting they are more in the nature of a bribe, sent in hope of favors to come. Lastly, when used in congratulation, they express the sender's pleasure at the recipient's success and his general good wishes.

If we take all these meanings together, the only element which appears to be constant is that of a feeling of good-will on the part of the person who sends the flowers. However, to say that good-will is the meaning of the flower-sending pattern and that the function of this element of our culture is to express good-will is certainly an oversimplification. Within the broad frame of this general meaning and function the element has a number of specific meanings and functions, each of which is related to a particular suitation. A moment's introspection will convince the average reader that these specific meanings are the only ones of which he is conscious and that these, rather than the general meaning of good-will, provide the motivations for his behavior. After all, good-will can be expressed in many ways beside sending flowers. What our culture prescribes is that, in certain situations, it should be expressed in this way. It will also be clear that in this case the functions of the pattern derive exclusively from its meanings. Any other pattern, say the public recital of a prayer in honor of the individual, could perform all the functions which the flower-giving pattern has in our own culture if corresponding meanings were attached to it.

Hitherto we have focused our attention on the trait complex and its qualities, but there is another possible approach to the problems of function. Culture as a whole consists of the sum total of a society's patterned responses to its needs. The function of any particular element of culture might therefore be defined as the contribution which it makes toward the satisfaction of a particular need or needs. Before trying to establish the relationship between needs and trait complexes it may be well to review briefly the needs of society and their general relation to culture.

Every society has as its foundation an aggregate of individuals. It is one of the primary functions of culture to transform this aggregate into a society by organizing the attitudes and behavior of the aggregate's members. It does this by providing patterns for these attitudes and behavior and techniques for training individuals to the habitual exercise of these patterns. Culture must further ensure the continuity of social life by providing techniques for inhibiting individual tendencies which might interfere with coöperation and for the suppression or elimination of individuals whose conduct is anti-social. It must also contribute to this continuity by providing techniques for the satisfaction of the physical needs of the society's members; i.e., it must include patterns for exploiting the natural environment and for protection against enemies. Lastly, it must provide the individual with techniques for escaping from reality and with a series of compensations for the discomforts and thwartings which his submergence in the corporate existence of the group inevitably impose upon him.

The psychological needs of individuals have been largely ignored by certain investigators, yet they are important and hold the key to the understanding of the functions of many culture elements. Social life entails the rigid repression of many of the individual's desires and imposes upon him forms of behavior which he may find unpleasant or even injurious. Thanks to the adaptability of the average individual, social regimentation can be carried to surprising lengths, but every one has his breaking point. The individual submits, but, since he still has a mind of his own, he is conscious at times that the regulations thwart him. He may not attempt to analyze the causes of his discomfort, but, if it becomes acute enough or still more if it is too long continued, he will be driven to action of some sort. Every individual is thus a potential disruptive force as far as his society is concerned.

The delicate adjustments in attitude and behavior on which the existence of society depends are constantly threatened from within as well as from without.

If society is to survive, culture must not only provide techniques for training and repressing the individual, it must also provide him with compensations and outlets. If it thwarts and suppresses him in certain directions, it must help him to expand in others. It is well enough for a society on occasion to immolate a member for the good of the group, but the sacrifices which it demands of all its members in the mere routine of daily living must be made up to them in some way. Socially desirable behavior must be rewarded, if only by the respect and approbation of other members of the society. *Dulce et decorum est pro patria mori* expresses the social point of view. The individual who has to do the dying may acquiesce in its propriety, but it can hardly seem sweet to him. The act must be sweetened by the admiration of his fellows, the favors of the women, expectation of enduring fame or a fine funeral, or anticipation of a glorious reward in the next world. Society must not only train the individual to the behavior which it desires but ensure also that such behavior is not too irksome.

Culture must also provide the individual with harmless outlets for his socially repressed desires. In certain societies this need is met, in part, by recognized periods of license. The Roman Saturnalia or the medieval All Fools' Day would be cases in point. During such periods a part of the ordinary regulations for social life are suspended. The individual can get along fairly well between such periods of release, since he has something agreeable to remember and also to look forward to. However, such periods are likely to have undesirable aftermaths. The more usual method of affording release seems to be for the culture to stimulate and direct the individual's imagination, providing him with satisfactions in the realm of make-believe. Esthetic activities, games with their triumph of the player over self-imposed obstacles, literature with its identifications and vicarious enjoyment of experience, and the dreams of posthumous delights offered by certain religions all work toward this end. After such experiences the individual returns to the real world refreshed and better able to endure the discomforts and drabness of everyday life. Without occasional vacations of this sort for its members, society could hardly endure.

While human needs, in the abstract, are probably constant, the forms in which they present themselves to the members of societies are rarely twice the same. Even if we leave out of account the factor of differing environments and their influence in shaping man's biological needs, cultural factors cannot be ignored. The average individual desires not simply food, but the type of food to which he has become accustomed. In many cases he will endure considerable discomfort before he will take food of another sort. The same thing applies to needs of all other categories. The need is associated in the individual's mind with a particular response or limited series of responses. Because of this, unfamiliar responses which are adequate enough in themselves and which serve to meet the needs of the members of one society may quite fail to meet the same needs for another society. This will be brought home to the reader if he remembers some occasion on which he had to play Authors instead of his accustomed Bridge. This edifying game met the amusement needs of two or three generations of educated Americans, but it is highly probable that the reader was not amused. Here, as in so many other cases connected with culture, we are dealing not with a clear-cut sequence of cause and effect, but with an interaction in which each of the interacting elements affects the other. The need shapes the cultural response, but this response, in turn, shapes the need.

In spite of this interaction and the specific forms which needs derive from culture, the whole complex of needs is susceptible of at least a general analysis. Culture also can be analyzed into its trait complexes. The next step would seem to be that of establishing the relationships existing between particular trait complexes and particular needs. However, as soon as we try to do this it becomes evident that clear-cut, one-to-one relationships between needs and complexes are extremely rare. In nearly all cases it is evident that a particular complex contributes toward the meeting of several needs, while each need is met, at least in part, by several different complexes. Reduction of both the complex and need to a series of smaller components reveals no closer or more constant relationships. The situation may be made clearer by an analysis of the functions of the clothing complex in our own culture.

In the region in which we live the use of clothing is the protection of the body from low temperatures. Clothing may therefore be said to function in response to one of the biological needs of the individual. However, this need is seasonal. Clothing is a biological necessity in winter, but it is unnecessary and even uncomfortable in our sub-tropical summers. In spite of this we wear clothing all year round, subject only to changes in weight and material of our garments. This is because the clothing complex has assumed a number of functions which are in no way connected with the basic biological need and which consequently are not affected by seasonal changes in temperature.

The clothing complex has been incorporated, in our culture, into what might be termed the sex activity. Thus it has been made the basis for the major part of our ideas on modesty, playing an important rôle in the inhibition of sexual desires. Conversely, it is used to excite the interest of the opposite sex and to stimulate sexual desires. It has various functions in connection with both chastity and courting. These functions depend much less on the inherent qualities of clothing than they do on the associations which have been developed about it, i.e., the meanings which our culture has given it. These meanings are very numerous, with all sorts of delicate shadings. Thus while remaining well within the bounds of strict propriety a woman can indicate by her costume whether she is favorable to male advances or not and whether her interests are commercial or matrimonial. As Dorothy Parker has said, "Men rarely make passes at girls who wear glasses." Conversely, a man who is anxious for female company considers dressing well as the first requirement, although male attire lacks the delicate and specific meanings of female. This may be due to the fact that in our culture the male's interest in females is likely to be more generalized.

Clothing also contributes toward meeting the need for social identification by serving to indicate the wearer's social status. This function is rapidly losing its importance in our culture due to the rise of cheap mass production and techniques of high-pressure salesmanship. However, garments still serve to indicate the sex and to a lesser degree the age of the wearer, although they have ceased to tell much about his or her social position. As recently as a hundred years ago this function was still important. The peasant dressed in one way, the *bourgeois* in another, and gentlefolk in still another. In spite of this breakdown in the old distinctions we still hear comments that So-and-so dresses like a farmer, a gangster, or a missionary. By indicating social status, clothing does much to facilitate the relations between individuals. It makes it possible for a stranger to determine at once the social category to which the wearer belongs and thus avoid acts or attitudes toward him which would be social errors.

Lastly, clothing affords an outlet for the esthetic desires of the individual and helps him to satisfy his longing for the admiration of his fellows. Most of us have felt the satisfaction which comes from a new and becoming costume. Even the business of selecting such a costume, with its handling of colors and materials, its anticipation of effects, and the vicarious enjoyment of garments which one cannot afford, offers a pleasant and stimulating escape from reality. Many women have discovered that few things are more soothing to a battered ego than an afternoon's shopping even when no purchases are made.

Clothing, then, provides responses to a long series of needs. Every one of these needs may also be satisfied through the medium of other trait complexes within our culture. Thus protection from low temperatures is also afforded by houses, steam heat, and closed cars. Sexual behavior is directed and controlled by a long series of customs and formal institutions. The social categories to which individuals belong are indicated by their habits and speech as well as by their costumes. The individual's need for esthetic expression or for other escapes from reality can be met in a great variety of ways. Even if he is not a creative artist or musician he can go to exhibitions or concerts, decorate his home, or buy a victrola. Lastly, the universal desire for response and the admiration of one's fellows can be satisfied by anything from regular church attendance to making a good showing in a hog-calling contest.

The author has been unable to discover a single case in which a particular need is met completely and exclusively by a particular trait complex. Such situations are possible but certainly very rare. The effect of such an exclusive one-to-one relationship between need and complex might be immediately beneficial, making possible a complete adjustment of complex to need, but it could hardly fail to be deleterious in the long run. Culture must function not only with relation to the individual and society but also with relation to an environment which is never completely static. The participation of a number of complexes in the meeting of a particular need makes it much easier for the society to adapt to changes in the external situation. Thus if the need for food were met exclusively by a single complex, say rice culture, a prolonged drought or blight on the crop might well mean the extinction of the group.

Under normal conditions the load of meeting any need is distributed over so many trait complexes that when one of these is rendered inoperative the rest can take over completely, thus ensuring the society's survival. Thus in our own pioneer settlements the need for food was met mainly by hunting and fishing. There was an agricultural complex in the culture configuration, but it was functionally in abeyance. During the same period the need for manufactured articles was met almost entirely by home industries. Firearms, ammunition, and a few iron tools were the only significant imports. As the supply of game decreased, the agricultural complex increased in functional importance. Home manufactures became less and less important, and the functions which they had performed were indirectly transferred to agriculture and trade. It was easier to grow and export surplus food in exchange for needed articles than it was to make them. Lastly, the population in certain regions became so dense that it could no longer be supported by agriculture. Such populations turned to manufacturing, exporting goods to and importing food from areas of sparser population. Thus in many parts of the Mississippi Valley we find that the need for food has been met successively by the hunting activity, the agricultural activity, and a combination of the trading and manufacturing activities. All three of these activities were present throughout the entire history of the region, and the shifting of the main burden of meeting the food need from one to another was a gradual process correlated with changes in the total situation.

If we observe the multiple functions of any trait complex at a given point in its history, we are almost certain to find that these functions are of differing importance. The main contributions of the complex toward meeting the needs of the society will be along one or two lines, with incidental contributions along other lines. Such minor functions are usually associated with needs which are adequately met by some other complex or complexes. Thus most of our fraternal orders exercise some control over the behavior of their members, but this is one of their minor functions, the need for control being adequately met by other agencies. Again, advertising is one of the minor functions of moving pictures, while it is a main function of newspapers and the radio. These minor functions of trait complexes might be said to constitute the society's accident insurance. They are held in abeyance under ordinary circumstances but can be brought into play whenever the need arises. Thus if advertising should suddenly be barred from the daily paper and radio, it could still find an outlet in moving pictures and would be provided from the outset with developed techniques.

It is not unusual for trait complexes to change their functional emphasis in the course of their history. Thus in the Mississippi Valley the hunting and fishing complexes originally had food-getting as their main function. They also had the minor function of providing amusement, but they were serious business to the average pioneer. As the food-getting function was increasingly taken over by other complexes the sport function increased in importance until to-day we have hunt clubs breeding and preserving game at great expense simply for the pleasure of killing it. Similarly, the once serious business of agriculture has become a sport in certain sections of our society. A man who really gets his food by selling bonds will take delight in having a garden and boast of his early peas, ignoring the fact that they cost him several dollars a peck.

Trait complexes may even, with the passage of time, lose certain functions entirely and acquire other and quite different ones. Thus fencing was originally a necessary training for self-defense. Any man in the upper classes who was not familiar with it was a poor life insurance risk. At the present time it has become purely a sport. Even the modern army officer usually leaves his sword behind when he goes "over the top." Again, in its inception the main function of astronomy was in connection with divination and the science had made important advances, including the determination of the length of the solar year and the forecasting of eclipses, before it was realized that there was no connection between the movements of the heavenly bodies and human affairs. The loss of the divination function did not bring astronomical work to an end. The science had other and originally minor functions in connection with the calendar and with navigation, and, as astrology declined, these rose to primary importance. Only within the last few years the complex has acquired a new function, that of satisfying our curiosity as to the nature and possible origins of the universe and as to the behavior of matter under conditions which we cannot produce on earth.

Whether we approach the problems of function from the direction of the trait complexes or from that of the needs, certain facts are evident. The first of these is the strong tendency for form to persist with only minor changes in the face of much more marked changes in meaning and function. The second is that function derives more completely and directly from meaning than from any other of the complex's qualities. We have already seen that, although meaning is influenced by the other qualities, it seems to owe even more to accidents of association that it does to them. In short, the two most important elements in the trait-function-need configuration are controlled primarily by historic accidents. While it is quite possible to describe this configuration as it exists at a particular moment in time, it can hardly be explained without reference to these historic factors.

The foregoing discussion is not intended to belittle the importance of the functional approach. The writer has merely attempted to clarify certain concepts and to point out the existence, even within the functionalist's chosen field, of certain conditions which require further study. Clearly, the value of functional studies can be increased by taking these additional factors into consideration and especially by a refinement of techniques which will make it possible to deal with them adequately. The most important contribution of functionalism to the science of anthropology to date has been that of drawing attention to the need for much more complete descriptions of culture, descriptions which will give not merely the form of culture elements but also their interrelations. However, even these descriptions can throw little light on the dynamics of culture as long as they are confined to a single point in the culture continuum. Comparison of a series of such studies makes it possible to go a step further and to arrive at certain descriptive generalizations. Whether these can legitimately be referred to as laws remains a question of definition. The author, who has included a good many of them in the present book, does not feel that they can. In any case, the instant that the investigator tries to deal with the dynamics of culture or to establish laws in the more commonly accepted usage of the term, he finds himself dealing with factors which operate in the field of time.

There can be no doubt that the functionalists have given a much-needed stimulus to anthropological study. At the same time, the existence of a distinct school of functional anthropology merely means that the science is still young. All sciences have passed through a period of conflicting schools each of which made extravagant claims, but this condition is always an indication of immaturity. Different sets of basic concepts as to the nature and relative importance of the materials with which a science deals can exist only as long as knowledge of these materials is incomplete enough to allow room for guesswork. As soon as the science has established itself on a firm basis of proven facts, the conflicting schools disappear, leaving a residue of techniques for investigation which are applied by all workers when they appear to be pertinent to the particular research in hand.

CHAPTER XXIV

INTERESTS

The most complex and least explored field of cultural phenomena is that of *interests*. A culture interest may be defined as anything which has meaning for two or more of a society's component members. It differs in certain respects from a *value* as that term is commonly used. Thus while it falls within the broadest definition of a value as "anything of any interest," it at once limits the field to things interest in which is shared. No matter how numerous or how intense any individual's associations with a particular thing are, this does not make the thing an interest as long as these associations are exclusively his own. Interest also differs from value in that it carries no implication of any relation to good. Although such implications do not necessarily attach to *value* under the broad definition cited above, they have come to attach to it even in philosophic usage. Thus no one would say that murder was a value to any society, although it must be considered an interest of all societies. Lastly, it must be understood that the *thing* of our definition of interest is not necessarily an object or natural phenomenon. It may quite as well be an occupation, such as carpentry or hunting, or an abstraction such as chastity, generosity, or cowardice.

It must be assumed that every interest begins its development with the direction of attention to the thing which subsequently becomes the interest. Without this the thing could not acquire associations, i.e., meaning, and therefore would not come within the scope of our definition. However, the field of possible cultural interests is at once limited by the fact that, with very few exceptions, nothing can become an interest unless it has qualities of persistence or at least frequent recurrence in time. Thus it would be extremely unlikely that a particular sunset would become a culture interest. Its brilliant colors might attract a high degree of attention and it might be remembered and talked about for a short time afterward, but, since it would never recur, its associations would never be reinforced by repetition of the original stimulus and the whole matter would soon be forgotten. On the other hand, sunsets in general might very well become a culture interest. They actually are so to our society, although the intensity of this interest is not great. The only conditions under which non-recurrent episodes have become culture interests have been those in which the society has established an association between the episode and something else which was persistent or at least recurrent. Thus the signing of the Declaration of Independence was an episode. It remains an interest of our society because of the associations which link it to a persistent phenomenon, the United States of America.

Even with this limitation upon the possible field of any society's interests the range of things available remains enormous. No culture ever extends its interests to include all of them, and the problem of why a particular society has a particular set of interests resolves itself into one of why the society has made a particular selection. Here we return at once to the factor of direction of attention, but it seems certain that the causes determining this are extremely diverse and, at least in part, subject to chance. Anything which directly affects the well-being of a society can hardly fail to attract the attention of its members and thus to become an interest. It makes no difference whether the effects of the thing are beneficial or otherwise. Thus a group which obtains its food by raising yams and lives in a region where there are tigers will be certain to number both yams and tigers among its interests. However, all groups extend their interests to include things which are intrinsically of no importance to them. The selection of certain of these from among the enormous number always available seems to be purely a result of accident. Our own interest in flowers would be a case in point.

In its inception our society's interest in flowers must have been completely divorced from utility, nor can it be accounted for on the basis of psychological factors common to the whole of mankind. It is true that the beauty and pleasant odor of flowers would be likely to attract attention, but these qualities seem to have had no effect on the members of many other societies. The complete indifference of many American Indians to flowers has already been mentioned. It is probable that all children are attracted now and then by flowers and feel some interest in them, if only as something to pull apart, but adults whose interests have been shaped by a culture which ignores flowers will rarely notice them. Our own society has developed this sporadic and non-cultural attention to flowers into an interest, has attached a wealth of meanings to them and incorporated their use into many of our culture's behavior patterns. Some sections of our society have even gone further and assigned this interest and the behavior patterns associated with it to particular categories of individuals within the social system. Thus in many rural neighborhoods interest in and care of flowers has been placed in the woman's sector of culture. It is the wife or daughter of the family who plants, tends, and appreciates them, and a bachelor who did so would feel rather shamefaced about it and would probably be subjected to some good-natured ridicule.

Things which are of no intrinsic importance to a society may nevertheless become strong foci of interest, gathering about themselves a wealth of meanings and emotional responses and having a strong influence upon the society's behavior patterns. When the group's attention has once been directed to them, associations may spring up with amazing speed. The way in which attention was first attracted or the qualities of the thing itself seem to have very little bearing upon the outcome. An interesting example of this came under the author's observation during the World War. The American 42nd Division was given the name "Rainbow Division" by the high command. It is said to have received this name because its units were drawn from many States and their regimental flags were of many colors. In the course of only a little more than a year the Division developed an elaborate complex of beliefs and behavior centering upon the rainbow, which had thus accidentally been made a focus of the members' interest. The first step in this development was the use of the name as a term of address between Division members who were not personally acquainted and on the part of outsiders. Hand in hand with this went the use of the name as a form of personal identification. A stranger's question, "Who are you?" always brought the reply, "I'm a rainbow." It is suggested that those interested in the curious workings of the primitive mind compare this with the way in which an Australian tells the ethnologist, "I'm an emu" or "I'm a kangaroo." This eponymous use of the group's symbol was soon followed by its use for combined identification and decoration. Representations of the rainbow were painted on Division property and later worn as shoulder insignia. With these usages there grew up an increasing interest in the natural phenomenon itself. The Division began to pay attention to rainbows, and within eight or nine months of the time the name was assumed it had become an article of faith that there was always a rainbow in the sky when the Division went into action. On one occasion the appearance of a rainbow over the enemy's lines at the moment of attack was immediately taken as an omen of victory and greeted with wild enthusiasm. Other divisions seem to have developed similar complexes about their own insignia.

In such cases, of course, the interest derives primarily not from the qualities of the thing itself but from the fact that it has become a symbol of something which is of intrinsic importance to the society. The development of such symbols is a widespread, although by no means universal, phenomenon of culture. In Western civilization the national flag, the cross, and, in modern Germany, the swastika are good examples of such symbolism. Although the tendency to attach symbolic meaning to animals, objects, or natural phenomena may derive from certain universal psychological factors, the use of such symbols is in itself a culture pattern and subject, like other patterns, to diffusion. When we find such symbols in uncivilized societies we usually call them totems. Here, as among ourselves, the things which the society transforms into symbols are often without intrinsic importance. Also, patterns of totemism may be diffused from unit to unit within a society much as the patterns of symbolism connected with such organizations as college fraternities are diffused. A social unit which has no totem, when other units have, feels itself in an inferior position and hastens to acquire one. One of the most curious examples of this is in Southeastern Madagascar where certain clans which trace their descent from Mohammedan immigrants have taken over the local totemic patterns completely, even to the standard type of origin myth. In doing so they have assumed as their totems animals unclean under the Islamic code. One clan has the wild pig, another the tame pig, and another the eel. The fact that these animals were taboo as food focused attention upon them and provided a link between the old and new patterns.

It will be plain from the foregoing that every society has numerous interests which cannot be explained on the basis of their intrinsic qualities. We can only say that they owe their presence to historic accidents, which means that in most cases they can never be accounted for. However, the importance of interests to the student of culture lies less in their origins than in their effects upon culture configurations. The first step toward understanding these effects is to observe how societies themselves introduce order into the great aggregates of interests which they always hold and avoid conflicts in the expression of these interests.

As we have seen in our previous discussions of culture phenomena, the behavior patterns are the only elements within a culture configuration which have to be mutually consistent and in a state of mutual adjustment. The interests of a society are elements of a different order. If we consider them as so many discreet entities, a great number of inconsistencies and apparent conflicts are always discernible. Thus our own society includes among its interests such mutually incompatible things as thrift and generosity, the saving of human life and war, competition and coöperation. All these, with the possible exception of war, are rated as desirable, yet it is obvious that all of them cannot find expression simultaneously. This difficulty is disposed of by all societies through the association of particular interests with particular situations. Each interest is allowed expression only under certain conditions. Thus our own society has ruthlessness as one of its interests and approves its expression in business situations, but definitely disapproves of its expression in personal relationships. The same shrewdness and callousness which win admiration in a business deal are considered reprehensible in dealings with members of one's own family. Similarly, we expect individuals to give precedence to thrift when they are poor and to generosity as soon as they become rich.

This patterned expression of particular interests under particular circumstances suffices to prevent conflicts and to save the individual from the necessity of constantly making choices. However, it is a relatively minor aspect of our problem. The total interests within any culture configuration constitute a system, and their individual influence upon the configuration derives more from their relations to each other than from their qualities as discrete units. Thus the influence of such an interest as thrift will depend primarily upon the importance which the society attaches to it relative to some other interest, such as generosity. Every society is interested in a great many things, but it is always more interested in some things than in others. These varying degrees of interest give the interests within any culture configuration what we may call their *ratings*. The *rating* of any particular interest is an expression of the importance which the society attaches to it relative to other interests. Such *ratings* are reflected in the extent to which a society gives expression to its various interests in its cultural patterns for behavior and in the precedence which it gives certain interests over others in conflict situations for which no patterns have been developed. Determination of these ratings is quite as important to the understanding of culture as that of the interests themselves. Thus magic is an interest of nearly all societies, but this fact is meaningless unless we also know how much interest various societies take in it.

The factors which determine the rating of interests in any society appear to be as variable as those which determine the presence of interests. There is no discernible correlation between the intrinsic importance of any interest to a society and the rating which that society assigns to it. A few examples may help to make this clear.

The Comanche had two domestic animals, the horse and the dog. Horses were of extreme economic importance to the tribe. Nearly all of its hunting techniques were dependent on them, as was its whole pattern of nomadic life. The only possible utility of dogs, on the other hand, was that they might give warning of a night attack, and even this was never mentioned in Comanche stories. The ancient Comanche dogs were small animals and were never used for tracking, transport, or even food. They were kept merely as pets and were so dependent on their masters that they were often carried on the horses when a band moved camp. In spite of this, horses seem to have been regarded somewhat as we regard machines. They had no names, aside from purely descriptive ones based on color, and their owners seem to have felt little affection for them or interest in them. No stories were told about particular horses, and the most that any Comanche will say about those he has owned is that such and such a horse was a good race horse or hunting horse. More striking still, horses seem to have had no place in the ceremonial life of the tribe. They might be given away at a dance or used to pay a medicine man, but on these occasions they merely represented intrinsic value. Horses never appeared in visions or significant dreams except as incidental details, and they were one of the very few animals known to the Comanche which never gave supernatural power.

Dogs, on the other hand, had individual names and what we may term social personalities. Their individual idiosyncrasies were known to every one in the band, and they were treated almost like children. One old man told stories of a black bitch which had, he said, been like a second mother to him in his early childhood, and any man would talk by the hour about the dogs he had known. The gift of a pet dog was on a quite different emotional plane from the gift of a horse, indicating the existence of a close personal, rather than a professional or ceremonial, relationship. One given by a deceased friend or relative was considered especially precious. This attitude was reflected in the custom of demanding such an animal as part of the indemnity paid to an injured husband by his wife's paramour. In such situations the husband sought revenge rather than profit, and loss of his dog would grieve a man more than the loss of several horses. To kill any dog, even a strange one, is still considered unlucky and likely to result in the death of the killer's children. Lastly, dogs appeared as the central figures in dreams, although they do not seem to have given power.

It can be seen that although the horse far outranked the dog in economic importance, the dog far outranked the horse in interest rating. The Comanche made more use of the horse and he was vastly more necessary to their survival, yet they ascribed more meaning to the dog. It may be urged that the comparison of interest in a work animal with interest in a pet is not a fair one, since the pet is really a member of society. The group regards it as belonging, so to speak, on the human side of the fence. However, this only brings us to the problem of why the Comanche did not make pets of their horses, as many other societies did. The answer is that they were not sufficiently interested in them. Thus we can close another of those circles into which culture elements arrange themselves whenever we study a culture continuum at a single point in its length.

Before we leave this question of the relation of economic importance to rating of interest, one more example may be cited. In ancient times the basis of Tanala economy was the cultivation of dry rice. They derived at least 90 per cent of their food from this crop, and its complete failure for even one season would have brought the tribe to the verge of extinction. Although the Tanala displayed interest in rice when it was ready for the harvest and from that point on, they seem to have had little interest in the process of growing it. In this they differed sharply from the Imerina, whose interest in rice culture for its own sake will be discussed later. This lack of interest was reflected in their indifference to the tools employed, which were of the crudest sort, and in the complete absence of rites connected with the planting or growth of the crop. The only ritual connected with rice was a small family feast held when the fields were ripe for the harvest, and there were no charms to ensure success in rice culture.

The Tanala also had cattle, but these were of so little economic importance to them that the destruction of all their herds would not have caused the loss of a single meal or the elimination from the culture of any commonly used article. There was no employment of cattle for transport or in agriculture. Milk was hardly used at all, being taken only when it was plain that the cow had more than her calf needed. Hide was sometimes used for caps and sandals, but was of so little importance in native economy that animals were usually cut up and cooked with the skin on, like pigs. Beef was used as food only at the time of funerals or other ceremonies involving sacrifices. Even the dung of the animals, which was of considerable value to tribes who raised irrigated rice, was never utilized in any way. In fact the only purely economic significance of cattle was that they provided an interest-bearing investment for surplus capital.

In spite of this the Tanala were vastly more interested in their cattle than in their rice. Families never tried to raise more rice than they needed to carry them over to the next harvest. A surplus might be a matter of some pride, but it did not improve the family's standing in the community. This standing was judged by the number of cattle, and every family worked steadily to increase its herd. Cattle were the main spoil in war and cattle-stealing was a proper activity for a young man of spirit. When direct methods failed, calves were purchased. Adult cattle were rarely sold, since this would mean a diminution of the herd. There were different names for all the possible combinations of color in cattle, for different shapes of horn, and so on, and every man could describe every animal he owned accurately. There were more charms to ensure the increase of cattle than for anything else except the general prevention of sickness and misfortune, which was governed by one general charm. Lastly, cattle were the only important ritual animals. In some clans an ox was killed as nearly as possible at the instant of a person's death so that its soul might go with him and give him company. Sacrifices of oxen were a necessary part of funerals and of all ceremonies in which the ancestors were invoked in a body. On such occasions the souls of the cattle went to swell the ancestor's herds in the spirit land, while the meat, aside from a little offered to the ghosts, was thriftily eaten. Cattle were also distinguished as the only animals which had souls.

The Tanala attitudes toward cattle were much like those of the neighboring tribes, to some of whom cattle were of great economic importance. It is possible that the Tanala originally took over cattle from these tribes and assumed the attitudes and ceremonial usages connected with them more completely than they did the techniques of utilization, but this is pure conjecture. Tanala traditions never mention a time when there were no cattle or when either their uses or the attitudes toward them were different from the historic ones. Whatever the cause, rice culture has remained a minor Tanala interest while cattle are a major interest.

Examples of such lack of correlation between economic importance and rating could be multiplied indefinitely. The reasons for it are no doubt diverse, but there is one factor which seems to contribute in a great many cases. Unusual or unpredictable phenomena are more likely to attract attention than usual or predictable ones, thus increasing the probability of their becoming foci of interest. In cases where unpredictability combines with a high degree of economic importance, the rating given to the particular interest is almost certain to be high. Thus a group who live by hunting in a region of sparse and uncertain game supply nearly always give this interest precedence over most of their other interests and build up a considerable body of ritual about it. It may even be suggested that the Tanala lack of interest in rice culture may have been due, at least in part, to the fact that it was a routine occupation which gave unfailing results. The work of cutting and burning the jungle was fairly heavy and mildly dangerous, but the monsoons arrived with perfect regularity, freshly cleared land always yielded a good crop, and there are no legends of blights or famines. A greater degree of uncertainty might well have resulted in a heightening of interest.

Of course interest ratings are influenced by many other factors beside those of economic importance and uncertainty. Things which are pleasurable are likely to be given fairly high ratings even when they are not of great intrinsic importance. The child feels a much keener interest in his birthday cake than in his regular dinner and a society frequently attaches a higher degree of interest to something which provides a brief period of pleasure, say a particular wild fruit which has a short season, than to something of much greater economic importance. When such pleasurable associations are combined with uncertainty, the probability of a high rating is correspondingly increased.

This matter of the quality of the associations attached to things brings us at once to one of the most vital aspects of interest rating. All societies grade their interests not only on the basis of intensity but also on that of desirability. They recognize that certain things are good and others bad, with an infinite series of degrees of relative goodness and badness. Although such evaluations have a strong influence upon the absolute ratings given to various interests by a society, the two systems of grading are by no means identical. The things in which the members of a particular society take a strong interest are not necessarily those which are most beneficial. Although every evil can be philosophically presented as the opposite of some good, the evil, as a focus of a society's interest, may have a very positive effect upon culture patterns. Thus societies may be obsessed with fears of disease or witchcraft. To consider the fear of disease as merely a negative aspect of the society's interest in health is, in such cases, to obscure the real situation. Health, as a normal condition, attracts little attention, and rationalizations of it, or even behavior patterns consciously directed toward maintaining it, are exceptional. Disease, on the other hand, is a strong focus of interest, its high rating being reflected in elaborate healing ceremonies, rationalizations of illness in terms of broken taboos or offended ghosts, and personifications of disease.

The reality of these interests in things which the society considers bad is reflected in many culture patterns. It is especially evident in folklore, where, since romance requires no compromise with reality, the interests and ratings of any society are always given their fullest expression. In such literature the conduct of the hero normally reflects the society's good interests in the fullest measure while that of the villain reflects its bad interests with equal completeness. If the auditors are to be satisfied, his blackness must be something much more definite and active than a mere absence of white. In other words, wickedness is as genuinely a culture interest as goodness.

The expression of this interest in things which the society considers evil is by no means limited to folklore. It is reflected in the presence in all cultures of patterns for misconduct. It is as though the society said, "Do not do this, but if you do it, go about it in this fashion." The lore of all peoples includes a number of horrible examples. Thus the story of a particularly ingenious and terrible revenge may be handed down for generations. The south European folklore motif of the husband who tricks his wife into eating her lover's heart would be a case in point. By repeating such a wicked act in all its details the individual can draw public attention to himself in the largest measure and gain full satisfaction for his ego. To turn to less extreme cases, no society approves murder, yet it is an interest of rather high rating in all societies, and most cultures include techniques for its commission. Under normal circumstances these patterns find only verbal expression, yet the individual turns to them for guidance when he is about to commit the socially disapproved act. The police of our own large cities recognize that the members of different foreign groups are likely to follow characteristic murder methods. Although such technical improvements as the submachine gun are rapidly obliterating these differences in professional circles, they still hold for amateurs. The inexperienced Italian or Spaniard commonly uses a knife, the Britisher a gun, while some southeastern European nationalities have a strong preference for strangling. Such patterns are constant enough to provide considerable aid in detection.

A society's condemnation of certain things thus does not prevent the attachment to them of interest ratings or the development of patterns for expressing them. Conversely, the society's approval of a particular thing does not mean that this interest will be given constant or universal expression in the behavior of the society's members. The patterns which correspond to good interests are, like any others, associated with particular situations. Moreover, individuals frequently act contrary to them. It should be noted that they can do this while remaining in agreement with the society's evaluations. Thus many ladies of easy virtue never question the conventional interest in and attitudes toward chastity in the abstract and may even try to prevent other women from becoming unchaste. No individual is really denying his society's evaluation of good interests as long as conduct not in agreement with them gives him a feeling of sin. He may even contribute by his bad acts to the reinforcement of the good interests for other members of his society. The old American institution of the village drunkard probably did more to maintain the high rating of his society's interest in sobriety than the village pastor.

Every interest which is included in any society's system has what might be termed an *effective rating*. This is an expression of its potentialities for influencing both the culture configuration and the behavior of individuals. The effective rating of any interest derives from a combination of its rating on the scale of absolute interest and its rating on the scale of good. It must be insisted that things which the society considers evil can still have a high effective rating, the society's interest in them being reflected by the presence in its culture of numerous attitudes and behavior patterns directly related to them. The important difference between the evil things which have a high effective rating and the good ones is that in the first case the patterns which derive from the interest are directed mainly toward averting or nullifying the thing, while in the second case they are directed mainly toward promoting it. The good interests set the goals toward which both the society and the individual work.

The average individual in all societies is unconscious of his group's interests and ratings under ordinary conditions. He merely follows the established behavior patterns of his culture without trying to analyze these or to grasp their deeper significance. Ratings and interests are brought to his attention only in conflict situations to which no regular culture patterns correspond. However, individuals find themselves in such situations with fair frequency. Most of us, for example, have had to choose at one time or another between the interest in truth and that in kindness. Societies find themselves in such situations less frequently, although conflicts of this sort are a constant accompaniment of culture change. Thus a conflict situation arose when women began to smoke in public. On one side were the interests of personal freedom and pleasure, on the other many of the interests which our society had grouped together to form its concept of a lady. In this case a state of adjustment was finally reached and it is now felt that women can smoke in public without being unladylike.

This brings us at once to another aspect of our problem. Even when individuals within a society are conscious of certain of its interests, they rarely if ever consider them as so many discrete entities. Instead they think of a particular system of interests and ratings as a unit. All societies recognize such systems, although their members may have great difficulty in verbalizing them, and express them in concepts such as our own concept of what constitutes "a lady" or "a gentleman" or "the good life." These systems are of more importance to both the individual and the society than the discrete elements of which they are composed, since the systems operate as wholes. Thus to take our own concept of the gentleman, such an individual is supposed to be brave, modest, honorable, truthful, and considerate of others. Each of these qualities represents a particular interest in our society, but the behavior patterns appropriate to the gentleman always reflect these interests in combination. Thus the gentleman's behavior toward women should express modesty and kindness in measures delicately adjusted to each other, too much of either being considered inappropriate. Bravery should always be tempered with modesty and should not be carried too far, lest it become foolhardiness. Truth and consideration of others must be exercised in constant relation to each other, and so on through the whole series of interests.

Every one in our society feels that he knows what constitutes a gentleman, but any one will find that he has considerable difficulty in putting the concept into words. A moment's introspection will convince any reader that his picture of what a gentleman *does* with respect to a whole series of situations is very much clearer than his picture of the interests and ratings which motivate this conduct. Nevertheless, the concept of the gentleman is an effective element in our culture. It cannot be dismissed as a mere abstraction which the observer derives from his observation of behavior patterns. Vague and poorly verbalized as it is, it provides a code which has a profound influence on the lives of many individuals. It gives added emotional significance to certain of our culture's patterns of behavior, thus ensuring their expression, and guides the individual in situations for which no patterns exist. Thus a man may keep a promise which he has made in a careless moment simply because he has made it and the code of the gentleman requires that promises be kept. To him the concept itself is an interest of high rating, emotionally more important than the trouble or actual loss which the keeping of promises will involve. That such conduct may bring him the respect of his fellows is, at least in theory, incidental, since the code also requires that no one shall advertise his adherence to it. A gentleman is supposed to guide his life by the code without regard for public opinion and without expectation of reward other than the maintenance of his own self-respect.

All societies have concepts of the ideal man which correspond in their emotional context and relation to behavior patterns to our own concept of the gentleman. However, such concepts may differ profoundly from our own, both in the interests which they express and in the relative importance assigned to these interests. Thus in one culture the concept may emphasize physical courage to such an extent that it overshadows everything else. Another culture may emphasize generosity and picture the ideal man as one who carries it to fantastic lengths, giving his wife or his only garment to the first one who asks. Another culture may have as its ideal the clever thief and liar of the Odysseus type. In every case the concept reflects the presence in the culture of a particular and usually unique system of interests and ratings.

At the present time we actually know less about interests and ratings than we do about any other aspect of culture. The current neglect of this field seems to be due less to an underestimation of its importance than to the extreme difficulty of approaching it through any of the usual anthropological techniques. Like meanings, to which they are closely related, interests and ratings are subjective phenomena and therefore hard to determine and still harder to express in exact terms. The average member of any society takes them so much for granted that he is hardly conscious of their existence, and even when they are brought to his attention he has great difficulty in verbalizing them. Direct approach to the problem by the ordinary methods of question and answer is thus almost useless. Moreover, it is impossible for any individual not actually reared in a society to participate in these aspects of its culture and afterward interpret them in the light of intimate knowledge and experience. A good investigator can learn to participate to a considerable extent in the intellectual life of an alien community. When his knowledge of the culture becomes complete enough he can recognize the premises from which the average member of the society reasons and by thinking logically from these arrive at culturally acceptable conclusions. The process is somewhat similar to that by which a linguist with a thorough knowledge of word roots and construction can develop new words which those who speak the language will recognize and understand. The investigator can also learn rather readily to imitate the society's patterns of behavior, and in time some of these may become habitual to him. However, he can never learn to share genuinely in the interests and attitudes of an alien society. The emotional associations which give these aspects of culture vitality and meaning are established in childhood and can never be consciously assumed. The outsider's very detachment from the culture may enable him to perceive some of its interests and ratings more clearly than the participants can, but he can never grasp their full context of meaning and emotion and, as a consequence, can never understand their full effects upon culture patterns.

Because of all this, the interests and ratings of an alien culture are, from the point of view of the investigator, pure abstractions which he can arrive at only by subjective methods. However, to the individuals who share the culture they are no more abstractions than is an Œdipus complex to the individual who has one without knowing that he has it. They have an effective reality which, while it may not be apparent under normal conditions, at once becomes so in unusual ones, especially those connected with conflict or cultural change. The interests and ratings of a society transform its members' generalized needs to specific desires, control the direction of its culture's growth, and are mainly responsible for the meanings and uses and through these for the functions ascribed to new culture elements. The influence which they exert upon cultural change is in itself enough to make them of preponderant importance to the understanding of culture. Faulty as our methods of approach admittedly are, interests and ratings are of such significance in all culture configurations that anything we can discover with regard to them will be worth the effort.

It is scarcely too much to say that interests and ratings are ultimately responsible for everything which distinguishes cultures as they exist from the minimal cultures which would suffice to ensure the physical survival of societies. It is almost impossible for us to conceive of the nature of such a minimal culture. Nothing even remotely approaching it exists. All that any society actually requires for survival is techniques for getting enough food to keep the group alive and for providing enough shelter to prevent death from exposure, enough social control to keep members of the group from habitually killing each other, and patterns for coöperation in the infrequent situations when the existence of the entire group is threatened. A horde of baboons has almost as much, and men who lived on such a cultural level would be nearer to the beasts than to any existing society.

Perhaps the importance of interests to culture can be made clearer if we take a single relatively simple culture element and try to interpret it from this point of view. The spade which the Imerina of Madagascar use to cultivate their rice fields will serve our purpose. There are fairly clear indications that this tool was developed from a digging stick. It is easy to say that the transformation of digging stick into spade through the addition of an iron blade was a natural result of the society's desire to save labor and increase efficiency. However, labor-saving and efficiency are in themselves interests which owe their effectiveness to their rating relative to other interests and to their association with particular situations. In many cases they are so completely overshadowed by other interests that they become ineffective. Thus many cultures have retained the flint knife for certain purposes long after they had more efficient metal ones because these purposes themselves were important interests which the society wished to preserve intact. However, let us return to the Imerina spade as we find it to-day.

Rice culture is, in itself, one of the dominant interests of Imerina life. Even the educated clerk or minor official feels that there is something lacking if he has no rice field, and he does not consider it beneath his dignity to work in the field himself. Although this interest must have derived in the first place from the economic importance of rice to the tribe, it has survived in spite of changing economic conditions. Men seem to take a genuine pleasure in such work, although manual labor in general is unpopular, and men of the older generation usually take leave without pay to care for their fields at the time of planting and harvest. In many cases this entails a net financial loss. The spade, as the principal instrument for rice culture, shares in this interest. It has acquired numerous meanings so that it has become almost as much a symbol as a tool. Because of this, it is always made with far more care than utility requires. Its blade is forged with delicate, exact curves and ground smooth throughout and its handle is made of some fine cabinet wood such as *palisandre* or spotted ebony. There is a proverb that a good farmer can be told by his spade, and an impoverished cultivator will expend three or four weeks' income to purchase a fine tool when he could get an equally serviceable one for a third the price. Possession of such a superior implement helps to satisfy the owner's esthetic needs and his desire for admiration, but it can only do this because of the interest which his society feels in the spade and the meanings which it has attached to it. These meanings, in turn, derive from the society's strong interest in rice culture and the spade's association with this interest. In a society such as our own exactly the same implement would be meaningless. Uses might be found for it, but it could have no functions until our society in turn had made it an interest.

Whenever the satisfaction of any need becomes one of the outstanding interest of a society there is a strong tendency to superimpose a series of non-utilitarian patterns upon those which, in themselves, would suffice to meet the need. Thus food is a moderately important, although by no means the most important, interest of our society. The only patterns directly necessary to the satisfaction of the need for food are those for getting it and for rendering edible substances which are inedible in their original state. However, our society has superimposed upon these utilitarian patterns a mass of others which make no direct contribution toward satisfying the need for nourishment. Cooking is directed not simply toward making food edible but toward giving it an appeal to taste and sight as well. With these latter ends in view an enormous number of recipes have been invented. A recently published cook-book intended for brides and similar amateurs lists 2,500. The bulk of these methods of preparation do not increase the value of the food as nourishment. In fact many of them sacrifice digestibility to pleasant taste or attractive appearance. A piece of fried dough is harder for the stomach to take care of than the same piece of dough baked, but it is pleasanter to taste and smell.

Our society's interest in food is further reflected in the elaborate ritual which we have developed in connection with its consumption. Direct attack with teeth and fingers has been replaced by a leisurely approach with knife and fork. Even the handling of these implements is governed by rigid rules, and the eater should feign a certain indifference to food, always leaving a little on his plate. Food should never be eaten directly from the utensil in which it was cooked, unless this happens to be a dish of a certain sort. In any case, it should be placed on a table, preferably in a different room from the one in which the cooking was done. The table, in turn, should be covered with a cloth.

have the implements for eating laid out upon it in regular order and, at least on formal occasions, should be decorated in some way. Food will sustain the individual equally well whether it is pulled from the pot, torn to pieces with teeth and fingers, and devoured on the spot or served by a uniformed maid at a properly appointed table. The difference between these two procedures is a reflection of the interest we take in food and provides some measure of its rating with relation to other interests.

Most of the content of all cultures consists of such embroideries, elements which, although they possess use and function, cannot be regarded as direct responses to the basic needs of the society. Their form and meaning reflect interest rather than utility and hence may vary widely even in cases where the basic need is the same. Thus nearly all societies have developed some ritual in connection with the consumption of food, but no two societies have developed exactly the same ritual. In some cultures the conventions require that each person eat alone and in private and to do otherwise is considered immodest. Again, an Arab friend of the author's considered European eating habits disgusting because we did not wash our hands immediately before and after eating and because we used forks and spoons instead of fingers. He said there was no way of telling whether forks and spoons were really clean, while a man could always be sure about his own hands. Interests and the non-utilitarian patterns which express them are the things which make human life more than a mere struggle for survival. They have given man's existence meaning and richness, directed his energies, and stimulated his mind. They lie at the very foundation of everything which distinguishes his way of life from that of the beasts.

In the matter of interests and ratings, as in that of any other category of culture elements, the participation of individuals is never complete. We can distinguish Alternatives, which seem to be mainly symptomatic of culture changes under way, and Specialties. That different categories of individuals within our own society may have special interests and ratings will be plain to any one who remembers what men usually talk about among themselves and women among themselves. The same phenomenon of Special interests is recognizable in all societies. However, every society has a central system of interests and ratings in which all its members participate. We have already seen in Chapter XVI how the Universals within any culture configuration give the whole form and coherence, providing it with a well-integrated, stable core. The Universal interests and ratings appear to dominate this core and, through it, the whole configuration. To use a rather faulty physical analogy, the other Universal elements within the culture seem to be organized with relation to these interests in somewhat the same way that a system of crystals is organized with relation to the focal point or points about which the process of crystallization began. In other words, the Universal interests and ratings of a culture give all the other stable and mutually adjusted elements within the configuration their orientations. One is tempted to believe that in the culture, just as in the crystal system, these orientations reflect actual processes of growth, but the analogy cannot be carried too far. Interests and ratings change in the course of any society's history just as do any other elements of its culture. However, at any point in the culture continuum Universal interests and ratings and orientations of the other elements with regard to them will be apparent. These orientations of cultures will be discussed in the next chapter.

CHAPTER XXV

ORIENTATIONS OF CULTURE

In the previous chapter we discussed the interests of societies and concluded that those interests which are shared by all a society's members, together with the relative importance attached to them, give any culture configuration its orientations. In the present chapter we will try to make this clearer by analyzing two cultures from this point of view. The author admits at once that the interests and ratings about which each of these cultures appears to be oriented have been determined by a process of abstraction. The conclusions presented are based upon his own subjective judgments, which are based in turn upon observations of the behavior of the societies' members, their folklore and anecdotes, and conversations with them. In neither case would any member of the society have been able to state the interests and ratings of his culture in exact terms. The conclusions, therefore, are not susceptible of proof. They represent merely an interpretation of observed phenomena and do not preclude the possibility of other interpretations which might be equally valid. At the risk of occasional repetitions, the Comanche and Tanala cultures have been selected for analysis. Any other cultures would have done as well if the author had been equally familiar with them.

Every culture always has several interests which are of primary importance and which together constitute an integrated system. To select even two or three of these as the focal points for the whole culture configuration probably involves a distortion of the actual condition, but such distortion is requisite to any comprehensible descriptive account. It corresponds to the type of distortion employed in drawings where three-dimensional objects are presented in two dimensions. Actually, all cultures appear to include a number of focal points of interest each of which provides orientation for a certain group of culture elements. However, most of these focal points themselves tend to show orientation with respect to a small number of major interests which thus dominate the whole configuration.

Most of the activities and interests of Comanche society revolved about the men of fighting age, who took precedence over all the other groupings. Boyhood was a mere preliminary to warrior status, and old age a not-too-welcome aftermath. Women of the warriors' age group dominated the other feminine age groupings in somewhat the same way, but even they derived their importance primarily from the interest which the warriors took in them. Attitudes toward the boy as a potential warrior influenced his entire training, and especially the attitudes of father toward son. The father constantly honored his son and worked for the boy's interests in preference to his own. The Comanche explained this on a double basis. The father expected his son to be killed during early manhood and lived in constant anticipation of the grief that this would cause him. In particular, he did not wish to be tormented with regrets for things which he might have done for him. Second, if the son did survive by a sort of miracle, the father would have to look to him for care and protection in his old age. His gratitude for such potential favors should therefore be expressed at once. It is an interesting commentary on the way in which the society's interest was focused on the warriors that the old regarded any help which they might receive from sons of fighting age as a favor and not a right. The father felt a deep responsibility toward his son, the son very little toward his father.

In the attempt to make the son a good warrior and to endow him with a certain initial prestige, the father did all he could not only to train him but also to honor him publicly. Any gifts made to a man's son were always met by much greater return gifts, and any specific requests which accompanied them could scarcely be refused. Thus a young man who wished to marry a particular girl would make a gift to her brother, often a child, and the father would be almost compelled to give her to him. The strength of this desire to honor the son is shown by the fact that this was practically the only case in which a father imposed his will upon his daughter in marriage. Most matches were made by the young people themselves. As soon as the boy passed puberty he was given a separate tipi where he slept, entertained his friends, and was often visited, after dark, by young women. This arrangement was not simply for the boy's convenience. Its underlying purpose seems to have been to remove him from the daily life of the household and make him more accessible to supernatural power. In particular, it kept him from coming in contact with grease and cooking, which were injurious to many forms of power. The same idea underlay the medicine men's custom of having a separate lodge in which they kept their paraphernalia and received clients.

It was considered of the utmost importance that the boy should begin to acquire supernatural power during this period, although its acquisition might continue throughout life. Fathers and elder brothers might impart power which they had to him without losing the power themselves. They would also encourage him to try to get power for himself. Since many powers were dangerous to their owners and all of them entailed the keeping of certain taboos, the boy might be reluctant. In one case an elder brother transferred his power to his younger brother without telling him he was doing so, then urged the boy to try the power to convince himself that he had it. All this was in preparation for the stern competition which awaited the boy as soon as he assumed the warrior status.

Between the full-fledged warriors there was constant competition for prestige. The only individuals in this group who did not compete were brothers and brothers-in-arms. The interest which the society took in this competition was certainly a reflection of their general attitude toward the warriors. There was little competition between individuals in the other social categories, and even that little was deprecated. Women, children, and old men were not supposed to compete with each other, but the warriors competed openly and constantly, the rest of the tribe forming an admiring audience. All the warriors in a band were ranked on a prestige basis, but their positions were constantly shifting. A man who stood at the top of the scale might drop far down as a result of a single incident such as leading an unsuccessful war party or displaying cowardice. Conversely, a man who stood low in the scale might rise to the highest place almost overnight. Because of this every warrior was constantly alert for anything which might affect his prestige and was jealous of his dignity.

The Comanche seem to have conceived of this prestige competition as a battle royal in which the rest of the society kept hands off. Every warrior was supposed to be a free agent who protected his own interests as best he could. It is difficult to get the average Comanche to see that the competition was governed by any rules or conventions, although a study of actual cases shows fairly definite patterns for the settlement of disputes of different sorts. Thus most informants were unable or unwilling to make any general statement as to what was done in cases of wife-stealing, the commonest offense between men of warrior age. They did not think of wife-stealing as a type of offense, but rather of the various instances of wife-stealing as so many distinct and unrelated episodes which derived their significance primarily from the relative prestige of the parties involved. In this as in all other conflicts between warriors the man of high prestige could behave as he wished toward men of lower prestige without interference by the society.

The relation of women to these dominant interests in the warrior and in prestige offer a good example of the way in which such primary interests may give orientation to a whole series of culture patterns. Women were not considered very important, but the young women, in whom the warriors took the most interest, were given precedence over the rest. Their first duty was to satisfy the desires of the warriors not merely in sexual matters but by providing them with companionship and relaxation. The tribe's attitudes with respect to this were linked with the idea, already mentioned, that the warrior would die young and therefore should be treated with the utmost indulgence. The night before the departure of a war party was always devoted to merrymaking. Unmarried women and even the young married ones were largely released from household duties on this account. A mother would often take over all the domestic duties of a married daughter or daughter-in-law so that the girl would be free to satisfy her husband's whims.

There was no premium on chastity before marriage, it being taken for granted that girls would yield to the warriors' wishes. Even after marriage there was little regard for chastity in the abstract. Brothers regularly loaned their wives to each other, and brothers-in-arms occasionally did. However, for a wife to leave her husband or to take a lover without his permission was a quite different matter. This was a direct challenge to the husband's prestige, and his reaction seems to have been to this rather than to the fact of adultery. In such cases the society as a whole remained neutral. Even the wife's family kept hands off. It would receive her and might try to bring about a reconciliation with the husband, but it would not formally take sides with either the husband or the lover. Each of these would call in his friends to help him in what often developed into a pitched battle, but it is significant that friends, especially the brother-in-arms, were usually called upon before relatives and that the only relatives who were mentioned as sometimes giving aid were brothers. If a man had a high prestige rating himself or was connected by ties of friendship to an individual of high prestige, he would not be likely to lose his wife, but if he had little prestige he was very likely to lose her. Actually, wife-seduction seems to have been primarily an aspect of the prestige contest. A successful lover would often abandon the woman after he had taken her away from her husband and settled his account with him, and past successes in love were one of the things which old men boasted about among themselves. This factor of prestige also led to the development of a rather curious method by which a woman could dissolve her marriage. If she tired of her husband or fell in love with a man whose prestige rating was far below his, she would join a war party, putting herself under the protection of its leader. He could not refuse to take her without serious loss of prestige, although the purpose of the arrangement was perfectly understood and he usually made no objection to her leaving him as soon as the war party returned. Leaders of war parties were usually men of high prestige, while, for the duration of the party, their followers were pledged to support them in everything. The injured husband could rarely muster a strong enough force to bring the woman back before the party was out of reach, and by the time it returned he would usually have accepted the situation. The war party leader gained rather than lost in prestige by giving the woman her freedom as soon as the party returned, since this was an indication that he had acted from disinterested motives.

Direct clashes between warriors might serve to reaffirm their prestige ratings but did little to alter them. No man could gain real prestige by quarreling with his fellows even if he systematically bested them. In particular, no warrior would gain prestige by overcoming another warrior through magic. The attitude toward an individual who attempted such a thing would be very much like our own toward an athlete who tried to get his closest rival disqualified before the contest. Under the code, all disputes were settled by open violence if they could not be compounded through the efforts of mutual friends. Each of the contestants might receive voluntary assistance from other warriors, but the number of backers he could muster was itself an indication of his prestige.

For the warrior group, prestige derived primarily from success in war and secondarily from the possession of supernatural power. These two interests were constantly interwoven, yet one feels that success in war was the primary one and this success tended to be rationalized in terms of supernatural power rather than the reverse. Thus the average man would not attempt to increase his store of supernatural power as long as he was successful in war. There was even one successful warrior, still living at the time of my visit, who had given up his powers completely early in his career and was openly skeptical as to the reality of such powers. This man was unique, and his skepticism was regarded with a certain degree of awe by the other members of the tribe, thus increasing rather than diminishing his prestige. I was told repeatedly that the thing which gave either a warrior or medicine man success was innate and that without it no amount of purposeful acquisition of power could make him great. The tribe never acquiesced in the skeptic's doubts. It merely took his success as an indication that his indwelling power was of a particularly vigorous sort.

Throughout most of their history the wars of the Comanche were mainly offensive ones, and there can be no question that they were waged primarily to enable warriors to gain prestige. Although loot, especially horses, played a fairly important part in the tribe's economy, the most stories cluster about their wars with the Utes, the tribe which was poorest for looting. The Comanche graded their enemies on two distinct scales, those of possible material gains and those of prestige gains. Expeditions into Mexico, where the looting was richest but the fighting poorest, were regarded somewhat in the light of commercial transactions. I was told that on these expeditions the Comanche rarely killed sheep-herders or even isolated poor families, since it was considered unsportsmanlike. With regard to the tribes to the north of their territory the Comanche maintain a discreet silence which suggests that they often got the worst of it. Their favorite enemies were the Pawnee, who were somewhat more than a match for them, and the Utes, with whom they felt themselves to be evenly matched. With this latter tribe they even fought battles by appointment, one side or the other sending word that its forces would be at a particular place on a particular day in case there was any one in the other tribe who would like to win a few war honors. Even when expeditions did yield loot, the warriors of greatest prestige were supposed to feel indifference to it. The leader owned all loot in theory, but he was expected to distribute it with an open hand. The rationalization of this custom in terms of supernatural power has been mentioned in an earlier chapter.

It is also significant that prestige gained through war was the only sort reflected in differences of costume or equipment. In at least one band medicine men wore a distinctive headdress when they went on war expeditions, but aside from this they had no special costume even when practising. Warriors, on the other hand, had various insignia. These included certain types of weapons which carried no-retreat obligations and the war bonnet.

The Comanche were still in process of assuming the full coup-counting and war insignia complexes of the typical Plains tribes, and their practices differed considerably from band to band. However, the general practice seems to have been not for the group of warriors to confer insignia but for the individual to assume them and then validate his claim to the associated prestige by his behavior in battle. Thus although certain of the northern bands might confer the right to the war bonnet at a formal ceremony, a man who felt that he was entitled to wear one might also make one, take it along on his next war party and put it on immediately before the battle. If he behaved creditably, his right to wear it would not be questioned afterward. The wearer of a war bonnet had a no-retreat obligation, he could save his life only by taking off the bonnet and leaving it on the field of battle. By doing this he forfeited not only the right to wear it but all his previous war honors. Another man who rode up and carried it off in the face of the enemy thereby gained not only the right to wear it but also the accumulated prestige of the man who had abandoned it. The same patterns were connected with the weapons carrying no-retreat obligations. The system indicates the preponderance of the prestige motive in Comanche warfare.

Supernatural power, which was certainly one of the main interests of the tribe, might be acquired in a variety of ways, which need not be discussed here. Only women of child-bearing age were debarred from acquiring it. Old women might gain it by any of the usual methods, and it was a rather common practice for middle-aged men who had healing powers to instruct their wives in their use, imparting the actual power to them after the menopause. In this way they gave them an additional economic resource for old age. All men of warrior age normally had power of one sort or another, and most of them occasionally doctored by special request, but very few great warriors were also great as healers. The prestige which a young man could gain by success along this line was rated much below that which could be acquired in war.

When a man passed warrior age two courses were open to

him. He could give up his powers, there being regular rituals for the purpose, or he could concentrate upon their use and attempt to increase them. The first of these courses seems to have been somewhat more approved. The man who did this made an honorable exit from the prestige battle-field and from this time on devoted his energies to compounding disputes between those who were still competing, giving sage advice and working for the best interests of the band as a whole. The so-called "band chiefs," who decided when camp should be moved, announced the day's activities, and exercised other routine functions, were nearly always men of this group. The Comanche always gave as the prime requisites for this position that the man should be old and wise and should be good to the women and children. In most cases he was a mild man who had never been a great warrior. It is also significant that this post was not considered a competitive one. It was accorded to any old man "who liked that sort of thing," i.e., was ready to assume the responsibilities. The attitude of the dominant warrior group toward these old men was one of slightly contemptuous good humor. The favorite pastime of the old men seems to have been to assemble on an evening, pass the pipe, and boast of their youthful adventures. Men of warrior age rarely attended such a session, although they were welcome to do so if they wished, and they were not above playing practical jokes on their elders. In one case a young warrior threw a live skunk into the old men's tipi and in another two young men put ordure, under a thin layer of dust, at the place where they knew the leader would rub his hands in the course of his ceremonial lighting of the pipe. In both cases the jokers were men of warrior age, not boys.

The old men who retained and tried to increase their powers were regarded quite differently. Such individuals refused to withdraw from the competition for prestige and contested with each other in magic much as the young men did in war. Many of the outstanding medicine men in the tribe belonged to this group, but they were feared rather than respected. All of them were at least potentially jealous of the young men and might employ their powers against them out of spite. A handsome young man who was a favorite with the women was felt to be in especial danger. The situation offered potentialities for blackmail, but this was kept in check by the tribal pattern of settling disputes by violence. As long as the old men used their powers against each other, the rest of the band merely watched the contest, but an attack on a younger person brought prompt action. The friends and relatives of the victim would call on the suspect and invite him to cure the illness. If he refused to take the case or failed to make a cure, he was very likely to be killed.

It remains to mention a few of the things which the Comanche did not make focal points of interest, although many other societies did. In spite of their firm belief in power and in the possibility of malevolent magic, sorcery did not loom large in their culture. Their folklore contains a fair number of references to it, but there are no stories of an injured individual employing a medicine man to work magic against an enemy, and very few persons believed that they themselves had been victims of sorcery. This situation was no doubt correlated with the deep-seated tribal patterns of self-reliance and open violence in disputes. Hates were not allowed to fester beneath the surface. Life after death was another aspect of the supernatural in which interest was lacking. Although there was a general belief in ghosts and in the possibility of obtaining power from dead medicine men, ideas as to the fate of the soul were extremely vague. The ghosts of slain enemies were not feared at all. One old warrior told me that if you were strong enough to kill a man his ghost certainly could not hurt you. The ghosts of relatives had no place in native beliefs. They rarely appeared, and the idea that they watched over their living relatives, rewarding or punishing them, was considered fantastic. In spite of their constant lip-service to the supernatural, one has the impression that most members of the tribe had a strong vein of practicality and an ability to view situations realistically.

This practicality may be related to their almost complete indifference to the remote past. Although there is historical evidence that they did not reach their present territory much before 1700, they have no migration stories. Conversely, they have no idea of having been created on the spot. In fact the only creation myth collected is probably of Christian origin. Even recent historical events seem to be forgotten as soon as the last individual who participated in them dies.

A few other rather striking lacks of interest should be mentioned. Family ties seem to have been of little functional importance. There was no conception of families as continuums and no tracing of remote relationships. Clan or joint family organization was completely lacking, and even the conjugal group was none too stable. Partners separated frequently, and children went with whichever parent they preferred. Wealth also was regarded with indifference, at least in theory. It brought no formal social recognition and little prestige. In fact there seems to have been a pattern of slight hostility toward the rich, since accumulation of property was a sign that the individual was not as generous as he should be. Lastly, there was a marked lack of interest in art. Although most Comanche artifacts were well made, decoration was of a rudimentary sort. Medicine objects such as shields were painted with significant designs, but garments and objects of utility were rarely ornamented and design symbolism was almost lacking. The only example of it was the design painted on the robe of a warrior's chief wife, which indicated by certain variations how many enemies he had killed.

We may summarize the orientations of Comanche culture by saying that it was organized about the warrior and was so arranged as to give full play to his individualistic and competitive tendencies. The Comanche was a fighting aristocrat, comparable in many ways to the European chivalry of the middle ages. The Tanala, to whom we will now turn, oriented their culture about a quite different set of interests. The following discussion refers to their culture as it existed prior to the introduction of irrigated rice cultivation and as it still exists in a few of the more conservative northern clans.

The focal point of Tanala interest was the joint family, already discussed in an earlier chapter. Membership in this group was determined by descent in the male line. Since marriages within the village were the rule, even daughters, who of necessity married out of the joint family group, remained in close touch with it throughout life. The family was conceived of as a continuum with a definite, historic beginning but no end. This concept was no doubt linked with the keen interest which the Tanala took in past events. Every family kept genealogies of its heads from the time of the founding and had a wealth of traditions which appear to be fairly authentic. In these traditions there is a striking lack of supernaturalistic elements. They refer to ordinary human beings who behaved in ordinary ways.

As a continuum, the family was divided into the living and the dead, both groups being equally real to the native mind. The dead division had its village, where its members lived exactly as they did when alive, even marrying and bearing children. Death was regarded as little more than a change of residence, and the most important feature of the funeral ceremony was the introduction of the newly dead individual to his ancestors, with a request that they would receive him and treat him well. Conversely, the dead man was informed of his new status and advised that he now belonged with the ancestors and should behave accordingly. The ties with another family which the individual had contracted through marriage in this world were terminated by a formal divorce pronounced by the living partner in exactly the same terms as an ordinary divorce. There was even a specific statement that the dead person was now free to remarry. If this rite was neglected, the ghost would be likely to return and cohabit with the living partner and to be jealous of his or her remarriage.

Although the living and the dead division of the family each had its regular residence, there was a good deal of what might be termed visiting back and forth. The dead were formally invited to be present at all ceremonies given by the living. They received their share of the feasts given at such times and were asked to take home a portion for any of the ancestors who had been prevented from attending by illness or pressing business. Individual ancestors might visit the living at any time, appearing to them in dreams if they had something they wished to communicate, or simply observing their activities. Conversely, the souls of the living might visit the ancestral village, where they were sure of a welcome. If the soul remained away too long, the person sickened and died. It was of the utmost importance that the wandering soul be recalled before it had become established in the village of the dead. If it stayed there long enough to plant rice, its desire to harvest its crop would be so strong that nothing could bring it back.

The souls of the dead were regarded as both helpful and dangerous. They aided members of their own families in all dealings with outsiders, but they also expressed disapproval of their conduct by causing illness. However, they confined their activities strictly to family members. No ghost would cause illness in another family, and the only ones who would help persons outside the family were those who declared their intention of answering prayers before their deaths. A few individuals volunteered to be of assistance to any one who asked and who made the proper sacrifices, promising to give aid in particular activities, say cattle-stealing, in return for offerings of a particular type. Such persons might, after death, become the center of minor cults, but they were rarely persons who were of importance while alive. I learned of no case in which either family heads or medicine men had assumed this rôle.

This focusing of interest upon the family was reflected in an unusually complete submergence of the individual in the group. The ideal member of Tanala society, whether man or woman, was a rather timid, retiring person keenly susceptible to public opinion and quick to espouse the side of the majority. Young people were expected to be respectful to all their elders and completely obedient to their fathers and the family head. A son could not sit in his father's presence without special permission or even sleep in a bed as long as his father lived, although in some clans he might purchase the right to use a bed at the time of his marriage. Children began to work for the family at an early age and, until marriage, were expected to turn over all their earnings to it. The boy's only consolation lay in the knowledge that, in due course of time, he could demand similar service and obedience from his own sons. Apparently the abstract justice of this arrangement was never questioned and any failure was punished by the anger of the ancestral spirits.

Such a system suggests that the society was dominated by the old men, but this was not the case. Actually, there was no one category of the population which stood out from the rest as the warriors did among the Comanche. The nearest approach to it were the heads of families, but these men might be of any age, and no one was conscious of them as forming a distinct class. Whatever social importance they possessed they derived not from their individual qualities but from the size and wealth of the families which they represented. They were symbols rather than persons. At public ceremonies the attention of the group was centered upon them and the whole family contributed toward helping them make a good showing. They were richly dressed even if the rest of the family went in rags, and they had to maintain their dignity at all costs. Within the family, the position of the head was mainly an executive one. Although his authority was absolute in theory, he never tried to exercise it unless he had founded the family himself. A hereditary family head would be extremely cautious about taking any step without consulting the other male members and making sure that he had the solid backing of the group.

The fierce competition and open violence which characterized Comanche society were utterly foreign to the Tanala. Open quarrels of any sort were frowned upon, and violence within the group was so rare that most informants had never seen a fight between adults. Families, as units, openly competed with each other in a mild way, each family trying to make as good a showing as possible at weddings, funerals, and other ceremonies, but there was little display of wealth and no ostentatious waste. Competition between individuals was so thoroughly discouraged that there were no recognized patterns for it; in fact the configuration of the culture made it extremely difficult. In his dealings with outsiders the individual was little more than a representative of his family, while the family organization offered him little opportunity to rise by his own efforts. The only outstanding position, that of family head, was strictly hereditary, this rule being reinforced by its close association with the ancestor cult. No family head could be deposed or replaced no matter how much he was disliked. The only escape for the discontented individual was to found a new family, and this required wealth. Jealousy of the family head was thus sublimated, in part, into economic activity. Even this was not directly competitive, since it did not entail taking anything from any one else within the family or village. In the absence of large-scale trade or manufacturing, the ordinary individual could become rich only by extreme frugality, hard work in the exploitation of communally owned natural resources, and occasional cattle raids on neighboring villages.

Even war offered the individual little opportunity for the acquirement of prestige. The Tanala were brave fighters, but they never fought for honor. Their offensive wars were waged either to obtain needed land for the whole village or to gain loot in slaves and cattle. There were no trophies and no war honors, and the main ambition of every warrior seems to have been to get as much as he could with as little risk as possible.

On the surface, existence in a Tanala village appeared to be completely peaceful and friendly. Actually, every village and family was a cauldron of hatreds and thwarted desires. The various joint families were jealous of each other, and every village was split into factions and riddled with intrigues. Since there were no important differences in policy between these factions and no tangible prizes of office or privilege for the victors, the struggle must have been motivated by sheer lust for power. Joint families acted as wholes in factional disputes and presented a united front to outsiders, but even within them there were numerous conflicts. The family head was jealous of any member who was rich enough to found a new family or on the way to becoming so and would intrigue against him. There were also many stresses within the conjugal family units. Marriages were often arranged by the elders, with little attention to the wishes of the parties involved, and in any case the spouses felt that their main loyalty was to their own families, not to each other. Factional disputes were thus often carried over into domestic life. Lastly, there was no love lost between fathers and sons. At present many young men go to work at a distance in order to escape their fathers' control, but in the old days this was impossible so that there was plenty of frustration and hatred.

The patterns of Tanala culture precluded both open competition and open violence, so these conflicts had to be resolved in other and less direct ways. Controversies between individuals were taken care of in part by regular legal procedure. By this means some disputes were brought into the open, and the long and noisy trials gave an opportunity for mutual vituperation and a vent for accumulated pressure. However, the real escape of the individual from intolerable repression was through magic. This was one of the main interests of the tribe. Although the Tanala lacked the hysterical fear of sorcery characteristic of some other Madagascar tribes, practically every individual believed that he had been a victim of it at one time or another, and most of them had employed it.

To understand the rôle of magic in Tanala society it is necessary to know their basic concepts regarding the supernatural. They believed that the lives of men were ruled by two distinct although not necessarily opposed sets of powers. On one side were the ancestral spirits and on the other unpersonified and rather vaguely defined forces which were regarded much as we regard the forces of nature. These were the forces which were employed in magic. There was an extreme interest in divination. The future was regarded as a working-out of the effects of present causes. The purpose of divination was to forecast the results of present trends and to evaluate the strength of these trends. If they were not too strong, the future could be changed by producing changes in the present situation. Such changes could be brought about either through the intervention of the ancestral spirits or through the skilful manipulation of impersonal forces.

The ancestors were thoroughly human in their attributes and constantly exercised volition. Their worship was almost completely socialized. In time of great stress a man might appeal to a particular ancestor, usually his father or grandfather, but this was unusual. Normally, appeals to the ancestors were made through the medium of the priest, who was usually the family head, and were phrased as from the whole of the living family to the whole of the dead family. The ancestral spirits stood for the approved mores of the group. They worked to ensure peace, coöperation, and the repression of the individual, punishing any failure in the performance of social duties. They would not even aid family members, as individuals, against other persons in the same village, since the whole village normally traced its descent from a single remote family line.

The impersonal forces were completely amoral. They possessed no volition and were mechanical in their operation. The native approach to magic was, therefore, almost completely mechanistic. Although one class of *ombiasy* (magicians) were supposed to owe their powers to spirit control, these controls merely directed them in the manipulation of the impersonal forces. Given the necessary knowledge, the same manipulations could be carried on without controls. It is significant that such individual controls were rarely if ever the spirits of the *ombiasy*'s own ancestors and might even be spirits of individuals from another tribe. The *ombiasy* might appeal to a spirit for direction in manipulating the forces, but he did not ask it to manipulate them for him.

The distinction between magic and the ancestor cult was perfectly clear in the native mind, and no individual could be both an ancestral priest and an *ombiasy*. The priest was an instrument of the family group, working toward the ends desired by that group and the society in general. The *ombiasy*, on the other hand, was an individual who worked for his own ends and for a fee placed his services at the disposal of other individuals. Something of the impersonal and amoral quality of the forces which he controlled attached to himself and his activities. His stock in trade always included formulæ for both benevolent and malevolent charms, and he stood ready to sell either to his clients. In cases of sorcery it was the man who used the charm, not the *ombiasy* who made it, who was held responsible.

The occupation of *ombiasy* was not hereditary and did not require any individual mystical experience. It was regarded as a profession which could be entered after proper training. To become an *ombiasy* it was only necessary to learn certain things, beginning with various systems of divination and the calendar of lucky and unlucky days. The good *ombiasy* was constantly on the look-out for new charms, which he obtained from other *ombiasy* either by direct purchase or in exchange for some of his own knowledge. Such exchange of information meant no more loss to the donor than would the publication of a new technique for scientific experiment among ourselves. The profession was open to all, even women, the only prerequisite being enough means to pay the necessary instruction fees.

To become an *ombiasy* was thus the main way in which a clever and ambitious individual could gain prestige and personal advancement. It brought wealth and also an escape from family domination, since *ombiasy* were the one group in Tanala society who could travel freely from village to village and settle where they liked. At the same time, success in the profession required a great deal of shrewdness and more than a little luck, and these requirements kept the numbers of *ombiasy* within bounds.

Magic provided an escape not only for its practitioners but also for the population in general. For a proper fee the *ombiasy* would provide a charm which would bring bad luck or death to a personal enemy, with full directions for its use. Conversely, he could provide charms which would fortify the individual against malevolent magic and could nullify the effects of any which had already been used against him. He was always called in in cases of serious illness and began his diagnosis by determining whether the sickness was due to an irate ancestral spirit or to magic. If the former, it became a matter for the family priest and sacrifices. If the latter, he concocted a healing charm. Although *ombiasy* worked against each other in this indirect fashion, nullifying the results of each other's charms, they did not compete openly. There were no such contests of magic as went on between the old men among the Comanche. It was even unusual to have more than one *ombiasy* resident in a village, and a young man learning the profession would usually study away from home and settle in some other place. It seems that villages preferred to have as their *ombiasy* individuals who were not closely related to any of the local joint families. Such individuals were neutrals in the local disputes, making their services available to all, while a family member would necessarily be a partisan.

Although magic provided some relief for repression, it was not enough to solve the problem completely. It was rarely used in intra-family disputes, since it was strongly disapproved of by the ancestral spirits and might lead to the death of the aggressor. The last and perhaps the most effective escape for the repressed individual was that of spirit possession. The Tanala were highly susceptible to seizures of hysteria which were patterned by the culture and interpreted in these terms. The possessing spirits were vaguely defined but seem to have rarely been family ancestors. They inspired the "possessed" with a great desire to dance and also spoke through his mouth. The possessed individual became, for a time, the center of attention for the entire village. His orders were obeyed, and every one took turns in dancing with him while his family provided food and an orchestra. I was told that the individuals who were most frequently possessed were those of little importance in everyday life and that family heads were rarely subject to such seizures. *Ombiasy* also were very rarely subject to them. The family resented the financial outlay which such seizures involved, but their fear of the possessing spirit rendered them helpless.

Just as in the case of the Comanche, extreme interest in certain things was correlated with an equally marked lack of interest in others. To one familiar with American Indian culture patterns the most striking of these was the complete indifference to individual supernatural experiences. There was no element of mysticism in either Tanala religion or Tanala magic. Even dealings with the ancestors were regarded somewhat in the light of a commercial transaction in which help was purchased by a sacrifice, and encounters with the ancestral spirits did not produce the religious thrill. I asked one man who had described an interview with his grandfather in a dream how he felt at the time; he answered that he felt sad and unhappy, since he knew that he would have to sacrifice an ox to the old man. Even the *ombiasy* who had personal controls seem to have felt little emotion toward these spirits, while those subject to possession could give no coherent account of their subjective experiences.

Another interest which was notably lacking among the Tanala was that in sex. In a repressed society one might expect sexual activities to become one road of escape, but this does not seem to have been the case. The young people were allowed to do much as they pleased before marriage and even had a house of their own in each joint family establishment, but there was little licentiousness. Girls were not expected to be virgins at the time of marriage, but numerous affairs were frowned upon. It was believed that women who were promiscuous were likely to be sterile, a serious handicap in later life. At the same time, formation of strong attachments between the unmarried was discouraged, since this would make the partners less content in the marriages which their families might arrange for them. After marriage faithfulness was expected, but single infractions were rarely a cause of divorce. In general the attitude toward sex seems to have been that it was a suitable amusement for the young but something that adults paid little attention to after they had married and settled down to the serious business of making a living. There was also a striking lack of interest in esthetics and in amusement for adults, both being regarded as a needless waste of energy.

We may summarize the orientations of Tanala culture by saying that it was organized about the joint family and that its primary purpose was to keep this unit intact. Wealth, which was the interest of second importance, derived its significance primarily from the fact that its accumulation was necesary to the founding of a new joint family. Magic owed its importance to the fact that it provided the individual with his only escape from repression and family domination. The degree of interest in it provided some measure of the extent to which the members of this society remained individuals in spite of training to the formal patterns of the culture. There is no close parallel in our own society to the Tanala conditions, but the nearest approach would be some of our own rigidly sectarian rural communities, with their belief that life is real and earnest, their outward peace and conformity, and their submerged gossip and feuds.

In spite of the profound differences between Comanche and Tanala culture, the average individual in both societies contrived to live with a fair degree of contentment and both cultures functioned adequately in meeting the needs of the individual and the group. That they could do so is only another proof of the extreme plasticity of man. Why one society fixed its attention upon a particular series of interests and the other upon another is an unanswerable question. Superficially it might appear that the roving life of a Plains Indian tribe and the frequent contacts with other groups which this entailed would be likely to focus interest on war, but it need not have done so if the Plains Indians in general had not been warlike. After all, there was enough food and other natural resources in the Plains to take care of a much larger population than the area supported, and these tribes were not driven into war by economic needs. Certainly utility did not make war the master interest of Comanche society. Conversely, the advantages of coöperation under the Tanala system of rice cultivation, while they may have provided the original impetus toward the centering of interest on the preservation of the joint family group, can hardly explain its extreme development.

In each of these cases there was a fixation of interest, but the causes of this fixation must have been highly complex and in large measure accidental. At the same time, these interests were of overwhelming importance to the culture configuration, molding the other elements within it to serve the ends which they indicated as desirable. Such interests remain an unexplained and unresolved element in all culture equations, and their presence foredooms to failure any purely mechanistic approach to the problems of culture and society.

CHAPTER XXVI

CULTURE AND PERSONALITY

The first requirement for a discussion of the relation between culture and personality is to find a satisfactory definition for the latter. In the present book *personality* has been used to designate the whole of the individual's mental qualities, i.e., the sum total of his rational faculties, perceptions, ideas, habits, and conditioned emotional responses. Although some investigators may protest that such a definition is too inclusive, these qualities together form a single configuration all of whose parts function in constant relation to each other. To exclude some of them from consideration may appear to simplify the study of personality, but it simultaneously diminishes the value of the results of such study.

That there is a close relation between this personality configuration and the culture of the society to which the individual belongs cannot be doubted. Culture, in so far as it is anything more than an abstraction made by the investigator, exists only in the minds of the individuals who compose a society. It derives all its qualities from their personalities and the interaction of these personalities. Conversely, the personality of every individual within the society develops and functions in constant association with its culture. Personalities affect culture and culture affects personality. The influence which particular personalities may exert on the development of culture has already been touched upon in our discussion of the dynamics of culture change, and in the present chapter we will confine ourselves to the other side of the picture, the possible influence of culture upon personality.

At the very outset of such a discussion it is necessary to point out that every personality presents two aspects, its content and

464

its organization. The content consists of the personality's component elements; its organization, of the way in which these elements are related to each other and oriented both with respect to each other and to the total configuration. The organization of personalities is extremely difficult to ascertain, and this aspect of psychological study is still a highly controversial one. However, there would appear to be two levels of personality organization. There is the superficial organization, dependent, like the orientations of cultures, upon the presence of certain dominant interests or specific conscious goals which the individual sets for himself, and the central organization, which gives the whole personality a distinctive character. Similarities in this central organization may be present in spite of wide differences in content and superficial organization. Thus we have certain individuals who are fundamentally alike in having their interest turned inward upon themselves, although they differ profoundly in their ideas and habits and the goals which they are striving to attain. The presence of recurrent similarities of central organization in various personalities is responsible for what the psychologists call psychological types. The study of these types has barely begun, and there is still a complete lack of exact, objective techniques for determining them. However, it seems certain that they exist and that we can distinguish a few main ones such as introvert and extrovert, megalomaniac, and paranoid.

There can be no question that culture is responsible for the bulk of any personality's content and also, through its emphasis on particular interests or goals, for much of the superficial organization of personalities. The crux of the problem of the relation of culture to personality is the question of the degree to which culture may be responsible for the central organization of personalities, i.e., psychological types. In other words, can cultural influences reach and modify the core of the personality? It is impossible to settle this question at present, but an analysis of the factors which influence the development of personality and of the relation of certain of these to culture may throw some light on the problem.

The individual has no personality at birth, merely the capacity for developing one and a few of the elements which will be integrated into the final configuration. He appears upon the scene with certain physiologically determined qualities. The presence of a brain and nervous system provides him with potentialities for thought, for the reception of external stimuli, and for the formation of habits and associations. These potentialities appear to vary somewhat from individual to individual. Thus some people appear to be constitutionally more intelligent than others, to have keener perceptions, to form habits more easily and rapidly, or to be more nervous and excitable. Although it has not been proved, these differences are probably a result of physiological ones. Thus differences in intelligence may be correlated with differences in blood supply to the brain or in metabolism, or even with structural differences in the brain and nervous system. Such constitutional differences belong to an order of phenomena completely apart from culture and can never be explained in terms of it.

The process of personality formation seems to be primarily one of integrating the individual's experience with his constitutional qualities to form a mutually adjusted, functional whole. This process continues throughout life but seems to be most active during the earlier years. Experience derives from the individual's contacts with his environment, but it is a result of the interaction of this environment with his constitutional qualities. Thus, to cite an extreme case, an identical environment will yield different experience to a blind person and to one who can see. Again, the same environment may result in widely different experience for the intelligent individual and the dull one. It is obvious that the same school will exert a different influence upon the boy who gets his lessons with ease and is always at the head of his class and the dunce who stays at the foot no matter how hard he works. Even a particular incident which constitues an important experience for a nervous, high-strung child may be only a minor experience for a stolid, apathetic one. In our own society there are a small number of persons who have an abnormal fear of cats. In most cases this fear can be traced to some early childhood incident, usually forgotten by the person in question. Such individuals are not numerous, and in view of the frequency of cats in our environment we must conclude that similar incidents have occurred during the early lives of many other persons without producing similar results.

In spite of its constant interaction with constitutional qualities, environment dominates experience. The term *environment* is here used in its widest sense to include the whole of the individual's surroundings; the personalities as well as the objects and natural phenomena with which he is in contact. It is through its effects upon the environment that culture is able to influence experience and through this the personality. Although the individual's environment is not entirely a product of the culture of his group, it is influenced by it at many points. Even the natural environment provided by a particular geographic area impinges upon the individual only after it has been filtered through the screen which culture interposes between man and nature. Thus a Wisconsin winter will result in vastly different experience for the child who lives in a steam-heated house and goes to school in a closed car and the one who has to spend the winter months in a smoky, draughty mat wickiup. Again, life in a particular region may mean perennial hunger for a society of hunters and abundant food for a society of herders.

The immediate physical surroundings of the individual always consist very largely of the things which his society makes and uses. Thus the average American is accustomed from infancy to the presence of chairs, tables, beds, pictures, and bric-a-brac. He lives in a house of a particular, culturally determined type, wears clothes of a certain sort, and does his traveling in trains and automobiles. Even his food is placed before him at certain culturally determined times of day, with different sorts and quantities of food at different times. Roasts and vegetables appear at 6:30 P.M., bacon and eggs at 8 A.M. His contacts with these things result in experiences which are quite different from those which come to a Polynesian or Eskimo. These experiences, in turn, result in the development of distinctive muscular habits and characteristic responses. He becomes so accustomed to sitting on chairs that he cannot sit on the floor without considerable discomfort, and so accustomed to sleeping in a bed that he cannot rest comfortably anywhere else. He is so used to eating at the culturally determined times of day that mounting pangs of hunger tell him when they are approaching and he is commonly hungrier at night than in the morning. Lastly, his habituation to the presence of many objects and particular sorts of objects results in the development of certain emotional attitudes toward them. A house without pictures impresses him as being somehow incomplete, and he is uncomfortable in it.

We have already said that the individual's environment includes not only objects and natural phenomena but also other persons. In determining the qualities of these and the nature of the individual's interactions with them cultural factors are again of tremendous importance. All the other persons with whom he normally comes in contact are like himself participants in the culture of his particular society. Through them he is brought into contact with its accumulated knowledge, its attitudes toward the things to which it attaches symbolic value, and its emotional reactions to particular acts or situations. Although the individual's contact with these elements of culture is through the medium of the other individuals who share them, the very fact that they are shared gives them an impersonal quality. They are as real and effective parts of his environment as trees and chairs. Common contacts with them give the members of any society a fund of common experience varied only in so far as it has been influenced by their constitutional qualities as individuals.

At least the more formal aspects of the individual's relations with other members of his society are also controlled by culture. Every society has its patterns for behavior between individuals occupying particular statuses such as the old and the young, husband and wife, and employer and employee. However, the influence of culture upon personal relationships does not end with these. Thus culture delimits the size and nature of the group of persons with whom the individual is brought into close contact. The degree to which children or women or old people are segregated by the society will have an important effect both upon the contacts of individuals belonging to these categories and upon the

opportunities which individuals of other categories have for contact with them and the types of experience resulting from it.
Contrast the young woman's opportuinties for contacts with
young men in an orthodox Mohammedan society and in our own.
Even the type of family which is standard for any society has
important effects upon the range and nature of its members'
contacts quite apart from the society's conscious patterns of behavior. Thus where interest centers on the conjugal unit, the
individual finds himself in extremely close relations with a small
number of other persons. His childhood feelings of dependence
and resentment of authority are focused upon one or two individuals. He will be in constant contact with these and will be unable
to escape from them even if he dislikes them. In societies where
interest centers in the consanguine unit, the child finds himself a
member of a much larger in-group. There may be a hundred or
more persons with respect to whom he has family status of one
sort or another. This means that he does not feel too dependent
upon any one of them and has much greater facilities for avoid-
ing persons whom he dislikes. When the whole consanguine group
lives together, as is frequently the case, this condition must result
in a diffuseness of personal attachments with a consequent weakening of their emotional intensity. It would be humanly impossible to feel the same depth of affection for twenty or thirty
classificatory brothers and sisters as for two or three real ones,
or to dislike half a dozen classificatory fathers, among whom
authority was distributed, as heartily as one real father in whom
the repressive functions were concentrated.

All these general environmental influences are continuous in
their operation and result in similar experiences either for all the
members of a society or for all those who belong to one of its
recognized categories. One other source of individual experience
should be mentioned at this time. This is the atypical and more
or less accidental incidents which may befall the individual.
Being caught in a burning house or stepping on a snake would
be cases in point. However, the potentialities of such experiences
for affecting the personality are probably determined quite as
much by the attitudes of other individuals toward the incident

as by any intrinsic qualities of the incident itself. Since these attitudes are primarily determined by culture, even this type of experience is culturally influenced. An amusing example of the way in which such incidents derive their potentialities for affecting the personality from the attitudes of other persons came under the author's observation. Some years ago his wife found it necessary to entertain a group of Camp Fire Girls on a rainy afternoon. There was in the house a collection of broken human skulls the pieces of which had become mixed in shipment, and the girls were put to work sorting these out and fitting them together. They seemed to enjoy the work thoroughly and begged to be allowed to come back the next afternoon to finish it. However, none of them came. The horror of their parents when they learned what the children had been doing produced a similar attitude in them. If these girls remember the episode at all after the passage of years, they probably regard it as a disgusting or terrifying one, although they certainly felt no such emotions at the time.

Whether culture shapes the experience of the individual through the medium of his physical environment or through the medium of other individuals and the patterns which it establishes for their behavior toward him is not of paramount importance to the present discussion. Suffice it to say that it does influence this experience so profoundly that it may be said to dominate most of it. However, culture does not affect all individuals within a given society in the same ways. From this point of view culture influences may be divided into two groups, the general and the specific. The general influences are those which culture exerts upon the developing personalities of all members of the society which bears it. The specific influences are those which it exerts upon persons belonging to particular, socially recognized groups or categories of individuals within the society. Thus among ourselves boys and girls are subject to the same general influences deriving from life in houses of the same sort, going to the same schools, eating meals at the same hours, and receiving instruction in the same ethical ideas. However, each of these groups is further subject to a series of specific influences which are no less derivatives of our culture. Thus boys and girls are dressed differently almost from infancy, are taught to perform different tasks, and are encouraged to behave in different ways in many of the same situations.

From the point of view of the person who is influenced there is no particular difference between these general and specific factors. Both of them affect his experience, and through this his personality, in much the same way. The intensity of these influences derives not from whether they are general or specific but from the degree to which the particular element of culture is participated in by the rest of the society and the intensity of its emotional connotations. Thus many of the specific influences to which girls are subjected in any society derive from elements which, in spite of their limited application, are Universals in our classification of culture content. While only girls are expected to act in certain ways, every one in the group will believe that they should act in these ways, and the influence deriving from this pattern will be exerted upon them through the medium of men and boys as well as other women and girls. The real importance for our study of this differentiation between general and specific influences is that the presence of specific influences does much to increase the diversity of experience among individuals reared within the frame of a single culture and society. It means that the environment which a given culture provides is actually different for males and females, for members of different social classes, and even for members of different families. Any attempt to establish valid correlations between culture and personality type must take this fact into account.

Although the general influences provide the members of any society with a fund of common experience, it goes without saying that such influences will differ profoundly from one society to another. Every culture is responsible for a different set of them. Man has come so far from his animal beginnings that practically everything he does is shaped by culture. Even such elementary and vitally necessary activities as the nursing and care of infants are controlled by culture patterns, not by instinct. Proof of this is afforded by the wide variations with regard to these which we find in different societies. Thus in some, infants are given the breast whenever they cry for it. In others they are fed on a regular schedule. In some they will be nursed by any woman who happens to be at hand, in others only by their mothers. In some the process of nursing is a leisurely one, accompanied by many caresses and a maximum of sensuous enjoyment for both mother and child. In others it is hurried and perfunctory, the mother regarding it as an interruption of her regular activities and urging the child to finish as rapidly as possible. Some groups wean infants at a very early age; other continue nursing for years.

In the techniques of caring for infants there is an even greater cultural range. One society may make the baby the center of attention for the entire family, various adults constantly carrying it about, playing with it, and giving it anything it wants. Another society may regard infants as a nuisance and pay little attention to them outside the satisfaction of their physical needs. In some societies the child is in almost constant bodily contact with its mother during the first two years. Madagascar mothers keep their infants in the backs of their dresses, leaving them there even when working in the fields. In other societies this constant bodily contact is lacking, but the child is handled frequently. In still others it is rarely touched except at feeding time. In some societies the child is allowed to tumble about without interference. In others it spends its first eighteen months bound to a board, even its arms sometimes being confined. I was told that among the Comanche children were kept wrapped even at night. The mother took her infant to bed with her to keep it warm, but put it in a cylinder of rawhide to prevent it from being overlaid in her sleep. For days at a time the child might be released from its bonds only twice in twenty-four hours, when it was unwrapped and cleaned. It also had to spend long hours in solitude, the cradle board being hung up near where the mother was working. The infants seem to have accepted this treatment philosophically, but it was said that they always kicked and cried when they were being wrapped.

Even the infant's exercise of its natural functions is patterned by its society. The only offense for which I ever saw a Malagasy child receive corporal punishment was that of fouling its mother when on her back. Infants only a few months old were spanked for this and learned to control themselves far earlier than European children.

The foregoing shows how different can be the influences which culture exerts upon the individual even during his first few months. Psychologists have written a good deal about the presumed effects of infantile experience upon the adult personality. It would seem that a study of individuals from societies with markedly different patterns of infant care could provide proof or disproof of many current theories, but this work has barely been begun.

As the child grows older, the general influences which his culture exerts upon him become increasingly numerous and complex. We have already spoken of the possible effects of various patterns of family organization on the individual's personal-social relations. The spacing of births which is characteristic of many societies would also affect these. Thus in a society where children were born at fairly regular eighteen-month intervals, the child would be in contact with at least two others near his own age. In societies where children were normally born at intervals of anywhere from three to six years, age differences between brothers and sisters would be marked and would affect general experience. Such intentional spacing of births is much commoner than is generally supposed. Turning to the more direct effects of culture patterns upon the developing individual, we have an almost infinite range of variations in the degree to which he is consciously trained, discipline or lack of it, and responsibilities imposed upon him. Society may take the child in hand almost from infancy and deliberately train him for his adult status, or it may permit him to run wild until the age of puberty. He may receive corporal punishment for even the smallest offenses or never be punished at all. As a child he may have a claim upon the time and attention of all adults with whom he comes in contact or, conversely, all adults may have a claim upon his services. He may be put to work and treated as a responsible contributing member of the family group almost from the moment that he is able to walk and have it constantly impressed upon him that life is real and earnest. Thus in some Madagascar tribes children not only begin to work at an incredibly early age but also enjoy full property rights. I frequently bargained with a child of six for some object which I needed for my collections; although its parents might advise, they would not interfere. On the other hand, the children in a Marquesan village do no work and accept no responsibility. They form a distinct and closely integrated social unit which has few dealings with adults. The boys and girls below the age of puberty are constantly together and often do not go home even to eat or sleep. They go off on all-day expeditions, for which no parental permission is required, catch fish and raid plantations for food, and spend the night in any house they happen to be near at sunset.

Examples of such cultural differences in the treatment of children could be multiplied indefinitely. The important point is that every culture exerts a series of general influences upon the individuals who grow up under it. These influences differ from one culture to another, but they provide a common denominator of experience for all persons belonging to any given society. This common experience provides the background against which the specific influences of the culture operate. These vary not only from culture to culture but also within each culture. The individual's exposure to certain of them and not to others is determined primarily by the social units or categories of persons to which he belongs. Thus, to begin with the smallest recognized social unit, every family has certain distinctive habits. Since these are shared by its members, they must be considered a part of culture. In our own society one family may spend most of its evenings at home while another sees every new moving-picture film. Each of these habits constitutes a specific influence to which children reared in that particular family are exposed. Again, the way in which the family makes its living will have an effect upon its members' environment. The son of a farmer will be brought into contact with the objects and techniques used in farming at a very early age. He will have a long series of experiences which the son of a doctor will never have. Conversely, the doctor's son will be reared in an atmosphere of medical shop-talk totally foreign to the farmer's household.

Differences in economic status and in social class are also a fertile source of specific influences. Even in our own theoretically equalitarian society there are profound differences in the environment of the child reared in a family which can afford an automobile or a servant and the one reared in a family which cannot. These environmental differences deriving from economic status extend far beyond mere matters of food, clothing, and housing. The members of different economic levels in a society usually have distinctive habits and attitudes. Due to the fluidity of our population these differences are less marked in our own society than in most. In groups which are frankly class-organized the differences between the classes are often so pronounced that it is not unjust to say that these classes have distinct sub-cultures. Thus in the middle ages there was a greater difference between the habits of the knight and serf within a single people than between those of knights in different peoples.

All societies are quite unconscious of the general influences which their culture exerts upon their members. They are somewhat more conscious of the specific influences, especially of those associated with differences in sex or social position, since the contrasts serve to bring them to attention. Thus any one can see that the environment which our culture provides for boys and for girls is different in each case and can even list offhand several of the ways in which it differs.

One other category of specific influences remains to be mentioned: those which derive from the society's more or less conscious attempts to train the individual to occupy a particular place in its system. This training always looms large in the minds of the society's members. Our own naïve belief in universal education as a panacea is a case in point. However, this conscious training receives its high rating mainly because it is the only aspect of cultural conditioning of which the society is conscious. The general influences and the other categories of specific ones are taken so much for granted that their possible effects are

ignored or at least greatly underestimated. The conscious training of the individual undoubtedly influences the content of his
personality, making for the establishment of particular habits
and attitudes. It also influences the more superficial aspects of
personality organization by setting certain concrete goals for the
individual's attainment and directing his energies toward these.
However, its influence is too intermittent and forms too small a
part of the total influences to which the individual is subjected for
it to have much effect on the deeper organization of personality.
To put it concretely, conscious training can develop almost any
one into a fairly successful business man or craftsman, but it
cannot make him an extrovert.

Of course societies do not think of the training process in
psychological terms. All they attempt to do is to fit the individual for the occupation of certain ascribed statuses, i.e., those
positions in the social structure which he will, in the normal
course of events, come to occupy. In our earlier discussion of
status we pointed out that the occupation of any status enjoins
upon its holder not simply certain duties but also certain emotional attitudes. The latter provide the individual with his main
incentive for the constant and conscientious performance of his
rôles. Their presence makes it possible for the entire system to
function without the exercise of direct social compulsion. Thus
in our own society the husband's affection for his wife and children is a guarantee that he will support them. In fact we take it
for granted that this affection has disappeared if the law has to
be called in to assure their support.

It is thus vitally necessary to the functioning of a society that
the personalities of its members be at least superficially adapted
to their statuses. Each society approves and rewards certain combinations of qualities when they appear in individuals occupying
particular statuses. Furthermore, it tries to develop these qualities in all the individuals for whom the particular statuses can
be forecast. In other words, each society has a series of ideal
personalities which correspond to the various statuses which it
recognizes. Such status personalities are not to be confused with
psychological types. In their delimitation societies do not go far

below the surface. The status personality does not correspond to the total personality but simply to certain aspects of the content and more superficial orientations of the latter, i.e., to those elements of the total personality which are immediately concerned with the successful performance of the individual's rôles. The status personality is a social phenomenon, the psychological type an individual phenomenon. There can be no doubt that certain psychological types are better adapted to particular status personalities than others, but individuals of more than one psychological type can usually assume the same status personality and perform the rôles associated with the status at least adequately.

Perhaps an example may make this distinction between status personality and psychological type more comprehensible. We have a fairly well-defined status personality for the business man. This calls for such qualities as energy, shrewdness, competitiveness, and ease in establishing social contacts and manipulating other individuals. It also assumes that the individual will feel a deep interest in the accumulation of wealth and will bend all his activities toward making as much money as possible. This particular status personality is especially congenial to individuals of the extrovert psychological type, and, other things being equal, such persons are likely to be more successful business men than introverts. At the same time, there are a good many individuals who actually belong to the introvert type who find themselves in this status. Perhaps they inherit a business from their fathers and have to carry it on for financial reasons. Most of these individuals contrive to assume the necessary status personality and to perform the rôles associated with the status at least passably well. At the same time, their assumption of the status personality leaves their psychological type relatively unaffected and they still behave like introverts out of business hours. Where the extrovert spends his spare time in meeting more people and enjoys the crowds and noise of night clubs, the introvert prefers to go home after business and to spend his time reading or working at some hobby.

Since every social system includes numerous statuses, the status personalities toward which any society tries to shape its

members are numerous and varied. Moreover, the qualities which
it considers appropriate to one of these status personalities may
be strongly disapproved for another. To realize this we need only
contrast the ideal status personalities for men and women in
nineteenth century England as these are revealed in the romantic
literature of the period. The ideal man was athletic, adventurous,
full of initiative, and always ready to enter into competition,
especially for the hand of some fair one. The ideal woman was
unathletic to the point of chronic ill health, non-competitive
except in a very limited and clearly defined field, timid, docile,
and above all eager to lean upon and form an admiring audience
for some dominant male. Either of these personalities was completely out of place when it happened to appear in persons occupying the opposite status, and any signs of the development of
feminine characteristics in boys or of masculine ones in girls
were met by prompt measures. The dreamy, timid boy was subjected to a "hardening" process, often of considerable brutality,
while the tomboy was punished and warned that if she persisted
in her unladylike behavior she would never get a husband.

In general, the ideal personalities for individuals in complementary statuses are mutually adjusted. Otherwise the reciprocal relationships which are the essence of the whole system of
statuses and rôles could hardly be maintained. If the Victorian
patterns for men and for women had called for initiative and
aggression in both, there would have been few successful marriages. However, many societies reveal a curious lack of correlation in their ideal personalities for statuses which the same
individual may be expected to occupy at different periods in his
life. We have already seen how, among the Comanche, there was
a genuine antithesis between the ideal personalities for the warrior and for the old man. The actual personality which would
make one of these statuses congenial to the individual would make
the other quite uncongenial, and few men who had been outstanding successes as warriors became band chiefs in their old age.

To come closer home, the ideal status personality for boys in
our own society of fifty years ago was antithetical in certain
respects to the ideal for men. Children were to be "seen and not

heard," and the approved boy was a quiet, docile individual, obedient, lacking in initiative, and always ready to defer to his elders. The ideal man's personality of the same period was strongly competitive, ruthless, with superabundant initiative and all the other qualities which went to the production of the "self made man." One might expect, *a priori,* that a psychological type which would find one of these statuses congenial would find the other uncongenial, and this seems to have been the case. The boy who was highly successful in that status and the pride of his parents usually enjoyed few triumphs after Sunday-school age and was likely to end tending counter for some one who had been the "bad boy" of his neighborhood.

In our earlier discussion of status we pointed out that every social system includes achieved statuses as well as ascribed ones. The former are usually of little importance as regards the society's conscious efforts to form personality, but they are of great importance as regards the social adjustment and utilization of individuals. Achieved statuses are those which are not forecast for particular categories of individuals. For the most part, the rôles associated with these statuses are of such a nature that their successful performance cannot be assured by training alone. Thus, as many nations have learned to their cost, a military education will not in itself produce an able general. By leaving such statuses open to individuals who reveal the necessary qualities, the society is able to utilize the special abilities of some of its members. It also provides a place for individuals whose characteristics are incompatible with the ideal personalities for its ascribed statuses, turning them into a social asset instead of a liability.

Achieved statuses are often of great functional importance to a society, and those who come to occupy them may be liberally rewarded. However, the qualities, especially the psychological type, which will make a man a success in one of them are very frequently of a sort which militate against his success in ordinary life. The achieved status is thus desired by the individual both because of the rewards which it brings and because it offers him an alternative to the ascribed status which he finds uncongenial.

It seems that from this point of view achieved statuses could be arranged in a graded series ranging from those which are highly desirable in themselves to those which could be considered desirable only as an alternative to failure in the individual's ascribed status.

One of the best examples of a status which was desirable only as an alternative to failure is to be found among our own Plains tribes. In nearly all of these tribes the ideal status personality for men of fighting age was that which we have already described for the Comanche. Men whose actual personalities were completely uncongenial to the warrior rôle assumed a special status, that of *berdache*. They wore women's costumes and carried on women's activities. At the same time they occupied a distinct status not exactly equivalent to that of women. They continued to hunt, and a little of the general pattern of male superiority still attached to them. Thus they were expected to be somewhat better than women even at women's tasks. The highest compliment which could be paid to a woman was to tell her that her beadwork was as fine or her lodge as well kept as that of a *berdache*. Some of the *berdaches* were homosexual, but the majority apparently were not. In either case the society's attitude toward them was entirely neutral. Even when they married other men there was only mild disapproval, and this fell upon the "husband," not the *berdache*. He was condemned for trying to get a partner who would not only keep his house but also hunt for him. All things considered, the social position of the *berdache* was certainly better than that of a man who was a continual failure as a warrior. He was never jeered at, and, through the excellence of his craftsmanship, he could even attain some measure of respect and prestige.

Even when achieved statuses are highly desirable in themselves, there is usually some of this alternative element in the situation. The position of *ombiasy* among the Tanala would be a case in point. This status was functionally important to the society, and those who were successful in it were liberally rewarded with both wealth and prestige. At the same time, success in this status called for qualities of initiative and self-reliance which were not only lacking in the average Tanala man but which would have been a decided handicap to him in the corporate life of a joint family. *Ombiasy* were therefore recruited from the ranks of those who were misfits in their ascribed family status. It has already been said that hereditary heads of families rarely assumed this status, since they would already have an outlet for the qualities which it required. Even in our own society a study of case histories seems to indicate a quite similar mingling of the factors of desirability and escape in providing the individual's motivation for seeking to achieve certain statuses. We are prone to phrase such statuses entirely in terms of desirability, but the other factor is certainly present. Many a man begins his climb toward what we consider the heights mainly because he is acutely uncomfortable where he is.

The special qualities or psychological types which various societies approve and reward in connection with their achieved statuses are highly diverse. Some societies even provide in this way for persons whom we would consider pathological. Thus some groups not only tolerate individuals who suffer from epilepsy, hallucinations, or hysterical seizures, but encourage these abnormalities and give those who manifest them an honored position. In pre-Islamic Arabian literature the greatest heroes are nearly always represented as epileptics. They usually throw a fit before going into action simply by way of warming up. The condition was so much respected that it was later ascribed to the Prophet himself. In a very large number of societies hallucinations and hysterical seizures are taken as signs of the individual's close contact with the supernatural. Since easy access to this is felt to be necessary to the society's well-being, persons who suffer from such conditions are assigned a special status as intermediaries between it and the Beings who are powerful to help or harm. It is felt that such individuals' vagaries of conduct are more than compensated for by their usefulness, and they are often accorded a high measure of prestige and power. Many an individual who is at present an inmate of one of our asylums would be not only free but "sitting on top of the world" if he had happened to be born into some other society.

This brings us at once to the problem of individual maladjustment, which must not be confused with that of incomplete or faulty personality organization. Even among the insane there are many personalities which are thoroughly organized and well integrated. The same holds for a large proportion of even acutely maladjusted individuals. In fact a too complete and thorough integration of the personality may in itself be a source of maladjustment, since it interferes with the individual's easy assumption of the required status personality. The discomfort of a young man who has been strictly brought up and given a strong negative reaction to smoking and drinking when he finds himself in a group where these habits are taken for granted would be a case in point. The maladjusted individual is simply one who has difficulty in assuming the status personality which his society requires, irrespective of what the causes of this difficulty may be. The condition represents a lack of adjustment to environment and cannot be satisfactorily studied except in relation to environment.

In its ascribed and achieved statuses every society provides congenial settings for a particular series of psychological types, but the range of these statuses is never extensive enough to provide for all possible types. Moreover, any individual in any society is automatically debarred from certain of even its achieved statuses. For example, some of these are open only to men, others only to women. We therefore have maladjusted individuals in all societies. Some of these are debarred from statuses which would be congenial to their actual personalities, although such statuses are present in the system, while the system provides no statuses which would be congenial to the actual personalities of others. Since status personalities differ from one society to another, it is obvious that the individual who is badly maladjusted in one group might be fairly well adjusted in another.

It seems probable that there is some status in some society which would be completely congenial to any given psychological type. However, it is very rarely that status personality and actual personality happen to coincide exactly for any individual. In spite of the psychologist's delimitation of types, individual personalities are infinitely varied, and the theoretical types represent at most greater frequencies of occurrence at certain points in the total range of variation. The average individual in all societies is able to reach a working adjustment between his actual personality and his status personality. Maladjustment is, after all, a matter of degree. The person who has been unable to make any adjustment is never encountered. Society eliminates him before he reaches that point. The individual who is perfectly adjusted does not appear once in a million times. Among the innumerable penitents and ecstatics of medieval Europe there was only one Francis of Assisi and among thousands of knights only one Bayard. The person who, by a happy combination of circumstances, finds himself with a status personality and an actual personality which fit like hand and glove is so much the exception to the ordinary condition that when he does appear he becomes the saint or hero of his society, a personification of its ideal and a proof to lesser men that that ideal is attainable.

Actually, all societies consist largely of mildly maladjusted individuals. The maladjustments may be somewhat more numerous and more varied in our own than in most, due perhaps to the rapid changes which our culture is now undergoing. The individual whose training fitted him fairly well for the occupation of a particular status in 1900 may find that it has not fitted him for the equivalent status of 1936. It must be remembered that maladjustment is not simply a lack of correspondence between the individual's psychological type and the status personality which the society indicates for him. It results when his actual personality and status personality fail to coincide with respect to any trait present in the latter. However, maladjustments and what are, for the particular society, atypical personalities are also to be found in groups whose cultures are almost static. This fact seems, to the author, to be of great importance to the whole problem of the factors responsible for personality formation.

If culture were completely dominant in personality formation, the result would presumably be a standard product differing from society to society but identical as far as the occupants of any ascribed status in any one society were concerned. Such individuals would all have been subject to the same series of general and special influences, including the same sort of purposive training. They might all be maladjusted to the status personality which their society ascribed to them, but they would all be maladjusted in the same way and to the same degree. Even allowing for the possible influence of individual accidents of experience in producing differences in the content of their personalities we should expect to find a basic uniformity in personality organization, i.e., psychological type, in all individuals holding the same ascribed statuses.

Actually, this condition is never found. It is unfortunate that we have no exact, objective techniques for identifying psychological types, but general observations lead to the conclusion that the total range of these types is much the same in all societies. Due to the superficial adjustments which individuals make to status personalities and to the great extent to which the content of personality is controlled by culture, an investigator's initial impression of the members of an alien society is that all those in any particular status are much alike in personality. This is quite on a par with his other initial impression that they all look very much alike. As soon as he comes to know Indians or Polynesians or Malagasy as individuals, he becomes conscious not only of marked differences in the basic organization of their personalities but also of striking similarities between these personalities and those of individuals with whom he is familiar in his own society. In other words, as soon as he penetrates the screen of cultural difference he finds that these people are fundamentally like ourselves. At the same time, different societies seem to show differences in the relative frequency of occurrence of the various psychological types. There can be little doubt that some of them show a higher proportion of introverts or megalomaniacs or paranoids than others.

The fact that the same psychological types seem to appear, at least sporadically, in all societies, is a fairly clear indication that some factors other than cultural ones are at work in their production. It further indicates that these factors must be of such a sort that they recur in all societies. The first and most obvious explanation of the observed conditions would be that psychological type is determined by physiological qualities. We have already spoken of the individual variations with respect to these and of their constant influence upon experience. On purely biological grounds we would expect all the possible variations to appear at one time or another in every human group, leading to the eventual repetition in all of them of all known psychological types. This theory might even explain the varying frequencies of these types in different societies. The average tribal society is composed of closely related individuals. If the physiological factors responsible for various types follow the ordinary Mendelian laws of dominance and recession, the majority of the members of such an inbred group might very well have a hereditary predisposition to a particular psychological type, resulting in a greater frequency for the type.

This physiological theory is certainly attractive and is made more so by the fact that it is exactly in line with the folk beliefs of our society. Like the members of all societies, we are unconscious of most of the influences which our culture exerts upon the individual and therefore prone to explain differences in personality organization on the basis of innate qualities. In our folk literature the high descent of the missing heir is constantly being revealed by the fact that, in spite of his peasant upbringing, he manifests the personality characteristics of a prince. Although this *motif* is now mainly confined to romances, due to the difficulty of equating it with our democratic ideas, it has not entirely disappeared from our thinking. Moreover, the belief in the physiological basis of the observed differences in men's and women's personalities in our society is still strongly intrenched. Even many psychologists when they find a "masculine" personality appearing in a woman will seek the explanation first of all in some abnormality of hormone balance.

Merely because it is so attractive the physiological theory of personality determination should be handled with caution. At the present time its validity can be neither proved nor disproved. Moreover, in view of the dominant influence which experience certainly exerts upon the content of personality and upon the superficial aspects of its organization, it is hard to believe that this influence does not extend to the deeper levels as well. Actually there are a series of what we may term sub-cultural experiences which recur in all societies, although with varying frequencies in different ones, and which might thus account for the observed conditions. Although all societies have formal, culturally determined patterns governing the interrelations of persons in particular statuses, the actual relations always include a factor which is not culturally determined. The interactions take place not between abstract statuses but between the individuals who occupy those statuses, and they derive much of their quality from the personalities involved. This is especially true as regards the relations of the child with his parents or other persons who are in close and continuous contact with him. Thus in one household the father may be an irritable tyrant exercising all the prerogatives with respect to his children which the pattern for the relationship allows him and keeping them in a constant state of fear and uncertainty. In another he may be good-natured and easy-going, exercising his prerogatives only in public. In one family the mother may be a docile, sweet-tempered individual and in another a shrew. In one the child may be dominated and bullied by an older one, in another he may be helped and cared for by his older brothers and sisters and develop a strong feeling of dependence upon them. Each of these situations will result in a different basal experience for the child.

Moreover, the same sort of personal-social relationships, as Dr. Kimball Young calls them, recur in practically all societies in spite of the differences in formal culture patterns. It makes very little difference whether masculine authority over the growing boy is exercised by his father, as among ourselves, or by his mother's brother, as in many other societies. In either case the boy may find himself dominated by a tyrant or in an easy, friendly relation with an adviser and helper. The personal aspects of the situation will far outweigh the cultural ones. Again, in all societies there are certain individuals who, through lack of physical strength or intelligence, are dominated by other children and more or less abused by them. Such situations repeat themselves in spite of culture and, because of the strong emotional elements involved, might be expected to influence the development of particular psychological types as profoundly as any sort of experience could.

It seems fairly certain that the observed conditions with regard to psychological types cannot be explained entirely on the basis of cultural influence. They can be almost completely explained on the basis of this influence working in combination with either the constitutional qualities of the individual or his personal-social relations. However, it seems most probable that psychological types are really a result of the interaction of factors of all three sorts and that the relative importance of at least the last two may vary with the individual. Thus the personal-social factors might be dominant in forming the personality of an individual who had no outstanding constitutional qualities, or strong and atypical qualities might dominate the process of personality formation in an individual who possessed them. Personalities, like cultures, derive their qualities from the interaction of numerous and varied factors, and it is unsafe to assume that any one of these factors exerts a dominant influence under all conditions.

CONCLUSION

Those who have read thus far are probably disappointed that they have learned so little about the nature of society and culture and their processes. We have made a few generalizations but have failed to present any neatly formulated laws. In nearly every chapter we have raised more questions than we have been able to answer. This situation does not require an apology, but it does deserve an explanation. All sciences have passed through a similar period in their youth, and anthropology is still one of the youngest. The first attempts to apply scientific techniques to the study of culture and society were made little more than a century ago, and the foundations of the science as it now exists have been largely laid within the memory of men still living. Anthropology has not even succeeded as yet in bringing the material with which it deals into systematic order or in developing really effective techniques for studying it. Its early attempts to apply to culture and society the approaches which had already been developed in the natural sciences have proved largely abortive, due to the fact that the phenomena with which it deals are of a quite different order. If it can borrow at all, it will probably have to turn to psychology, but this science is also in its infancy. It seems probable that anthropology will have to develop its own techniques and that these, in their final form, will be markedly different from any now extant. In particular, they will have to be adapted to the handling of configuration situations, i.e., those in which series of phenomena are mutually interdependent and interacting. The necessity for such techniques is being increasingly felt in all sciences, but none of them has so far been able to solve the problem.

Coupled with the difficulties which are an inevitable accompaniment of the youth of any science there are other and even more important ones arising from the nature of the phenomena with which the anthropologist has to deal. The task which he has set himself is the most ambitious so far attempted by man. Most of us stand appalled before the complexity of the atom as it is revealed to us in modern studies. We fail to realize that the phenomena with which the physicist deals are the simplest and most predictable with which any science has to deal. The complexity increases step by step as we advance from atoms to molecules to organic compounds to living individuals. When we take the next step from the physical to the psychological level it is increased a hundredfold, yet the anthropologist must go even beyond this and study men living in groups, with all the complexities of their relations with each other and with their environment. The surprising thing is not that we know so little but that we already know as much as we do.

In spite of these difficulties, no one can doubt that the end which the anthropologist has set for himself is worth any amount of labor and disappointment. It is, briefly, the understanding of the nature of man and the forces which are operative in society. With this understanding will come the possibility of control, and mankind will be able for the first time in its million years of existence to shape its future deliberately and intelligently. Without it no sound and enduring reconstruction of society will be possible. Those who are trying to plan society at present are in very much the position of architects trying to draw plans for a house in complete ignorance of the materials which will be used in the structure.

The conquest of society will be the greatest triumph of man's career. Even the conquest of interplanetary space sinks into insignificance beside it. There can be little doubt that it will sometime be achieved, but there is little likelihood that it will be achieved by our civilization. In ancient Greece the human mind was, for a few centuries, set free. Men could investigate and discuss without fear of Church or State, seeking for truth wherever it seemed to lie. For perhaps the first time in history the potentialities of the mind became apparent. The Greeks learned how to discipline thought with logic and use it as a tool to probe the world about them. In Alexandria, toward the close of the period, they took the first steps toward the understanding and control of the forces of nature. Then freedom waned and the imprisoned mind turned its energies to matters which were safe because they were trivial. When, after almost 2,000 years, the mind was freed again, civilization once more went forward. The Greeks were gone, but they had left a heritage of developed techniques for thinking and of problems which they had discerned without being able to solve them. Our civilization was able to begin again only a little behind the point where they had left off. It has studied the forces of nature, and with knowledge has come control so that, in 200 years, we have altered the outward aspects of human life more profoundly than they had been changed in the previous 6,000.

To-day our workers in the social sciences stand very much where the Alexandrian Greeks stood in their studies of nature. We have come to a door beyond which lies a store of knowledge that promises to give man a better life than any he has known, but there seems little chance that we will be allowed to pass through. The signs are plain that this era of freedom is also drawing to a close, and there can be little doubt that the study of culture and society will be the first victim of the new order. The totalitarian state has no place for it. In fact, for men to take an interest in such matters is in itself a criticism of the existing order, an indication that they doubt its perfection. Unless all history is at fault, the social scientist will go the way of the Greek philosopher. However, he also will leave a heritage of technique for investigation and of discerned but unsolved problems; a new frontier from which free minds will sometime press forward again into the unknown. When this time comes, perhaps after centuries of darkness and stagnation, men will look back to us as we look back to the Greeks. It is for this reason that I have dedicated this book to the next civilization.

BIBLIOGRAPHY

Physical Anthropology

Armitage, F. P., *Diet and Race* (London, 1922).

Boas, F., *Changes in Bodily Form of Descendants of Immigrants* (Washington, D. C., 1912).

Buxton, L. H. D., *The Peoples of Asia* (New York, 1925).

Darwin, C., *The Descent of Man* (1871).

Dixon, R. B., *The Racial History of Mankind* (New York, 1922).

Duckworth, W. H. L., *Morphology and Anthropology* (Cambridge, 1915).

Fleure, H. J., *The Peoples of Europe* (London, 1922).

Gates, R. R., *Heredity in Man* (1929).

Haddon, A. C., *The Races of Man and Their Distribution* (New York, 1925).

Herskovits, M. J., *The American Negro* (New York, 1928).

Hooton, E. A., *Up from the Ape* (New York, 1932).

Hurst, C. C., *Heredity and the Ascent of Man* (New York, 1935).

Keith, Sir A., *Man, a History of the Human Body* (Home University Library, New York, 1913).

——————, *The Antiquity of Man* (London, 1925).

——————, *New Discoveries Relating to the Antiquity of Man* (London, 1931).

MacCurdy, G. G., *Human Origins* (New York, 1924).

Marett, J. R. de La H., *Race, Sex and Environment, a Study of Mineral Deficiency in Human Evolution* (1935).

Martin, R., *Lehrbuch der Anthropologie* (Jena, 1914).

Smith, G. E., *The Evolution of Man* (Oxford, 1924).

Sollas, W. J., *Ancient Hunters and Their Modern Representatives* (New York, 1924).

Sonntag, C. F., *The Morphology and Evolution of the Apes and Man* (London, 1924).

Topinard, P., *Anthropology* (Philadelphia, 1878).

Wilder, H. H., *The Pedigree of the Human Race* (New York, 1926).

Wood-Jones, F., *Arboreal Man* (London, 1916).

Ethnology

Barton, R. F., *Ifugao Law* (University of California Publications in American Archæology and Ethnology, No. 15, 1919).

Beckwith, M. W., *The Hawaiian Romance of Laieikawai* (Bureau of American Ethnology, 1919).

Bell, Sir Charles, *The People of Thibet* (1928).

Best, E., *The Maori as He Was* (Wellington, N. Z., 1924).

Blackwood, B., *Both Sides of Buka Passage* (Oxford, 1935).

Codrington, Robert H., *The Melanesians* (Oxford, 1891).

Cole, Fay-Cooper, *The Tinguian* (Field Museum of Natural History, 1922).

Crooke, W., *Natives of Northern India* (1907).

——————, *The Religion and Folk Lore of Northern India* (1926).

Culwick, A. T. and G. M., *Ubena of the River* (1935).

Driberg, J. H., "The Status of Women among the Nilotics and Nilo-Hamitics," *Africa*, Vol. V, 1932.

Ellis, W., *Polynesian Researches* (London, 1832–1834).

Firth, R., *Primitive Economics of the New Zealand Maori* (1929).

Fortune, R. F., *Sorcers of Dobu* (1932).

Furness, W. H., *The Island of Stone Money* (Philadelphia, 1910).

Goddard, P. E., *Indians of the Southwest* (New York, 1913).

——————, *Indians of the Northwest Coast* (New York, 1924).

Grinnel, G. B., *The Cheyenne* (New York, 1923).

Herskovitz, M., "Culture Areas in Africa," *American Anthropologist*, 1924.

Hewitt, E. L., *Ancient Life in the American Southwest* (1930).

Hodge, F. W., *Handbook of American Indians* (Bureau of American Ethnology, Bull. 30, 1907–1910).

Junod, H. A., *The Life of a South African Tribe* (Neuchatel, 1912).

Kidd, D., *The Essential Kaffir* (London, 1904).

——————, *The Bull of the Kraal* (London, 1907).

Kidder, A. V., *Introduction to Southwestern Archæology* (1924).

Kingsley, M., *West African Studies* (1899).

Kroeber, A. L., *Handbook of the Indians of California* (Bureau of American Ethnology, Washington, 1925, B78).

Lewis, A. B., *Ethnology of Melanesia* (Field Museum of Natural History, Guides, 5, Chicago, 1932).

Lin Yutang, *My Country and My People* (New York, 1935).

Ling-Roth, H., *The Tasmanians* (1899).

Linton R., *The Tanala, a Hill Tribe of Madagascar* (Field Museum of Natural History, Vol. XXII, 1933).

Lowie, R. H., *The Crow* (New York, 1935).

Malinowski, B., *Argonauts of the Western Pacific* (London, 1922).

Mason, O. T., *Aboriginal American Basketry* (Washington, D. C., 1902).

Meek, C. K., *Tribal Studies in Northern Nigeria* (1931).

Minns, E. H., *Scythians and Greeks* (1931).

Montelius, O., *The Civilization of Sweden in Heathen Times* (1888).

Morgan, L. H., *The League of the Iroquois* (1851).

Murdock, G. P., *Our Primitive Contemporaries* (New York, 1934).

Nyabongo, A. K., *Economic Life of Uganda* (1936).

Parsons, E. C., *American Indian Life* (New York, 1921).

Powdermaker, H., *Life in Lesu; the Study of a Melanesian Society in New Ireland* (1933).

Quennell, M. and C. H. B., *Every Day Life in the New Stone, Bronze and Early Iron Ages* (New York, 1923).

——————, *Everyday Life in the Old Stone Age* (New York, 1924).

Radcliffe-Brown, A. R., *The Andaman Islanders* (Cambridge, 1922).

Radin, P., *The Autobiography of a Winnebago Indian* (New York, 1926).

Rasmussen, K., *The People of the Polar North* (London, 1908).

Ratray, R. S., *Ashanti* (1923).

——————, *Religion and Art in Ashanti* (1927).

——————, *Ashanti Law and Constitution* (1929).

Richards, A., *Hunger and Work in a Savage Tribe* (1932).

Rivers, W. H. R., *The Todas* (London, 1906).

——————, *History of Melanesian Society* (Cambridge, 1914).

Routledge, W. S. and K., *With a Prehistoric People; the Akikuyu of British East Africa* (London, 1910).

Seligman, C. G., *The Melanesians of British New Guinea* (Cambridge, 1909).

——————, *The Peoples of Africa* (1930).

——————, *Pagan Tribes of the Nilotic Sudan* (1932).

Seligman, C. G. and B. Z., *The Veddas* (1911).

——————, *The Kababish, a Sudan Arab Tribe* (Harvard African Studies, II, 105–184, 1918).

Speck, F. G., *Naskapi* (University of Oklahoma Press, 1935).

Spencer, B., and Gillin, F. J., *The Arunta* (London, 1927).

Spier, L., *Yuman Tribes of the Gila River* (Chicago, 1933).

Stayt, H. A., *The Bavenda* (1931).

Talbot, P. A., *The Peoples of Southern Nigeria* (London, 1926).

Thompson, J. E., *The Civilization of the Mayas* (Chicago, 1927).

Tregear, E., *The Maori* (London, 1908).

Williams, F. E., *Orokaiva Magic* (Oxford, 1928).

——————, *Orokaiva Society* (1930).

——————, *Papuans of the Trans-Fly* (1935).

Wilson, G. L., *Agriculture of the Hidatsa Indians; an Indian Interpretation* (University of Minnesota Studies in the Social Sciences, No. 9, Minneapolis, 1917).

Wilson, G. L., *The Horse and the Dog in Hidatsa Culture* (American Museum of Natural History Anthropological Papers, XV, 125–311, 1924).

Wissler, C., *The American Indian* (New York, 1921).

Theory

Balfour, H., *The Evolution of Decorative Art* (London, 1893).

Bartlett, F. C., *Psychology and Primitive Culture* (Boston, 1924).

Benedict, R. F., *The Concept of the Guardian Spirit in North America* (Memoirs, American Anthropological Association, No. 29, 1923).

——————, *Patterns of Culture* (New York, 1935).

Blackmar, F. W., and Gillin, J. L., *Outlines of Sociology* (New York, 1930).

Blackwood, B. M., *A Study of Mental Testing in Relation to Anthropology* (Mental Measurement Monographs, Serial 4, December, 1927).

Bloomfield, L., *Language* (New York, 1933).

Boas, F., "The Methods of Ethnology," *American Anthropologist,* XXII, 1920.

——————, *The Mind of Primitive Man* (New York, 1911).

——————, *Primitive Art* (Oslo, 1927).

——————, *Anthropology and Modern Life* (New York, 1928).

Buxton, L. H. D., *Primitive Labor* (London, 1924).

Chapin, F. S., *Social Evolution* (New York, 1919).

De Angelo, J., "The Background of the Religious Feeling in a Primitive Tribe," *American Anthropologist,* Vol. XXVIII, 1926.

Dewey, J., *Human Nature and Conduct* (New York, 1922).

Dixon, R. B., *The Building of Cultures* (1928).

Dorsey, G. A., *Why We Behave Like Human Beings* (New York, 1925).

Durckheim, E., *Elementary Forms of the Religious Life* (London, 1914).

Encyclopedia of the Social Sciences, edited by E. R. A. Seligman and A. Johnson (New York, 1930–1934).

Eubank, E. E., *The Concepts of Sociology* (New York, 1932).

Folsom, J. K., *The Family* (New York, 1934).

Frazer, J. G., *Totemism and Exogamy* (New York, 1910).

——————, *The Golden Bough* (London, 1911).

Freud, S., *Totem and Taboo* (1912).

Galton, F., *Inquiries into the Human Faculty* (London, 1890).

Gennep, A. v., *Les rites des passages* (Paris, 1909).

Goldenweiser, A., *Early Civilization* (New York, 1922).

——————, *History, Psychology and Culture* (New York, 1933).

Goodsell, W., *A History of Marriage and the Family* (New York, 1934).

Graebner, F., *Methode der Ethnologie* (Heidelberg, 1911).

Gras, N. S. B., *A History of Agriculture* (New York, 1925).

Grierson, A. H., *The Silent Trade* (London, 1907).

Haddon, A. C., *Evolution in Art* (London, 1895).

Hall, G. S., *Morale the Supreme Standard of Life and Conduct* (New York, 1920).

Hartland, E. S., *Primitive Paternity* (1909).

—————, *Primitive Law* (1924).

Hobhouse, L. T., *Morals in Evolution* (London, 1915).

Hobhouse, L. T., Wheeler, and Ginsberg, *The Material Culture and Social Institutions of Primitive Peoples* (University of London Publications, 1914).

Hubert, H., and Mauss, M., *Esquisse d'une theorie générale de la magic*, L'Année Sociologique, VII.

—————, *Melanges d'histoire des religions* (1909).

Huntington, E., *Civilization and Climate* (New Haven, 1915).

—————, *The Human Habitat* (1928).

James, W., *The Varieties of Religious Experience* (New York, 1902).

Judd, C. H., *Psychology of Social Institutions* (New York, 1926).

Jung, C. J., *Collected Papers on Psychoanalysis* (1916).

Kohler, W., *The Mentality of Apes* (1927).

—————, *Gestalt Psychology* (1930).

Kroeber, A. L., *Anthropology* (New York, 1923).

—————, *The Superorganic* (Sociological Press, 1927).

Kropotkin, P., *Mutual Aid, a Factor in Evolution* (1902).

—————, *Ethics, Origin and Development* (New York, 1924).

Kuo, Zing Yang, "Genesis of Cat's Responses to Rats," *Journal of Comparative Psychology*, Vol. XI, 1931.

Lang, A., *The Making of Religion* (1898).

—————, *The Secret of the Totem* (1905).

Leuba, J. H., *Psychological Origin and Nature of Religion* (Chicago, 1909).

Lévy-Bruhl, L., *Primitive Mentality* (New York, 1923).

—————, *The Soul of the Primitive* (1928).

Lowie, R. H., *Primitive Society* (New York, 1920).

—————, *Primitive Religion* (New York, 1924).

—————, *The Origin of the State* (New York, 1927).

Lynd, R. S. and H. M., *Middletown* (New York, 1929).

MacIver, R. M., *Society, Its Structure and Changes* (New York, 1931).

Maine, H., *Ancient Law* (London, 1861).

Malinowski, B., *The Family among Australian Aborigines* (London, 1913).

Malinowski, B., *Crime and Custom in Savage Society* (London, 1926).

—————, *Sex and Repression in Savage Society* (1926).

—————, *The Sexual Life of Savages* (New York, 1929).

Marett, R. R., *Faith, Hope and Charity in Primitive Religion* (1932).

—————, *Sacraments of Simple Folk* (1933).

—————, *Head, Heart and Hands in Human Evolution* (1935).

Mason, O. T., *The Origins of Invention* (London, 1895).

—————, *Woman's Share in Primitive Culture* (1895).

McDougall, W., *The Group Mind* (1920).

McLennan, J. F., *Studies in Ancient History* (1876).

Mead, M., *Coming of Age in Samoa* (New York, 1930).

—————, *Growing Up in New Guinea* (New York, 1933).

—————, *Sex and Temperament* (New York, 1935).

Morgan, L. H., *Ancient Society* (New York, 1877).

Myers, J. L., *Position of Woman in Primitive Society* (New York, 1926).

Ogburn, W. F., *Social Change* (New York, 1922).

—————, *Recent Social Trends* (New York, 1933).

Parsons, E. C., *The Old Fashioned Woman* (New York, 1926).

Pitt-Rivers, A. F., *The Evolution of Culture* (Oxford, 1906).

Radcliffe-Brown, A. R., *The Present Position of Anthropological Studies* (Report of the British Association for the Advancement of Science, 1931).

Radin, P., *Primitive Man as a Philosopher* (New York, 1927).

—————, *Method and Theory of Ethnology* (1933).

Randall, J. H., *The Making of the Modern Mind* (New York, 1926).

Ratzel, F., *History of Mankind* (London, 1908).

Rice, S. A., *Methods in Social Science* (Chicago, 1931).

Rivers, W. H. R., *Kinship and Social Organization* (London, 1914).

—————, *Medicine, Magic and Religion* (London, 1924).

—————, *Psychology and Ethnology* (1926).

Roheim, G., *Australian Totemism* (1925).

Ross, E. A., *Principles of Sociology*, 1st revision (New York, 1930).

Sapir, E., *Time Perspective in Aboriginal American Culture* (Canadian Department of Mines, Ottawa, 1914).

—————, *Social Organization of the West Coast Tribes* (Transactions, Royal Society of Canada, 3d series, 1915).

—————, *Language* (New York, 1921).

—————, "Culture, Genuine and Spurious," *American Journal of Sociology*, January, 1924.

—————, "Speech as a Personality Trait," *American Journal of Sociology*, May, 1927.

Sayce, R. U., *Primitive Arts and Crafts, an Introduction to the Study of Material Culture* (1933).

Schmidt, W., *The Origin and Growth of Religion* (London, 1931).

Semple, E., *The Influence of Geographical Environment* (London, 1911).

Smith, G. E., *The Migrations of Culture* (Manchester, 1917).

Sorokin, P., *Contemporary Sociological Theories* (1928).

Speck, F. G., *Family Hunting Territories* (Memoirs, Canada Geological Survey 70, Ottawa, 1915).

——————, "The Family Hunting Band as the Basis of Algonkian Social Organization," *American Anthropologist*, Vol. XVII, 1915.

Spencer, H., *Principles of Sociology* (New York, 1900).

Spier, L., *The Distribution of Kinship Systems in North America* (University of Washington Publications in Anthropology, 1925).

Sumner, W. G., *Folkways* (Boston, 1906).

Thomas, W. I., *Source Book for Social Origins* (Boston, 1909).

——————, *Sex and Society* (Boston, 1922).

Thomas, W. I., and Znaniecki, F., *The Polish Peasant in Europe and America* (New York, 1927).

Tozzer, A. M., *Social Origins and Social Continuities* (New York, 1925).

Tylor, E. B., "On a Method of Investigating the Development of Institutions; Applied to Laws of Marriage and Descent," *Journal of the Royal Anthropological Institute*, Vol. XVIII, 1889.

——————, *Primitive Culture* (London, 1913).

The Unconscious, a Symposium (Alfred A. Knopf, New York, 1927).

Veblen, T. B., *The Theory of the Leisure Class* (New York, 1912).

Wallis, W. D., "Mental Patterns in Relation to Culture," *Journal of Abnormal Psychology and Social Psychology*, Vol. XIX, 1924.

——————, *An Introduction to Anthropology* (New York, 1926).

Webb, C. C. J., *Group Theories of Religion* (1916).

Webster, H., *Primitive Secret Societies* (New York, 1908).

Westermarck, E., *Origin and Development of the Moral Ideas* (1906).

——————, *The History of Human Marriage* (1921).

——————, *Ritual and Belief in Morocco* (1926).

Williams, J. M., *The Expansion of Rural Life* (New York, 1926).

Wissler, C., *Man and Culture* (New York, 1923).

Wundt, W., *Elemente der Völkerpsychologie* (1912).

Yerkes, R. M. and A. W., *The Great Apes, a Study of Anthropoid Life* (New Haven, 1929).

Young, K., *Social Psychology* (New York, 1930).

——————, *An Introductory Sociology* (New York, 1934).

INDEX